Lonesome Roads and Streets of Dreams

Lonesome Roads and Streets of Dreams

Place, Mobility, and Race in Jazz of the 1930s and '40s

ANDREW S. BERISH

The University of Chicago Press   Chicago and London

Andrew Berish is assistant professor in the humanities and cultural studies at the University of South Florida.

The University of Chicago Press, Chicago 60637
The University of Chicago Press, Ltd., London
© 2012 by The University of Chicago
All rights reserved. Published 2012.
Printed in the United States of America

21 20 19 18 17 16 15 14 13 12   1 2 3 4 5

ISBN-13: 978-0-226-04494-1 (cloth)
ISBN-10: 0-226-04494-7 (cloth)
ISBN-13: 978-0-226-04495-8 (paper)
ISBN-10: 0-226-04495-5 (paper)

The AMS 75 PAYS Endowment of the American Musicological Society, funded in part by the National Endowment for the Humanities and the Andrew W. Mellon Foundation.

Chapter 1 previously appeared as "I Dream of Her and Avalon: 1930s Sweet Jazz, Race, and Nostalgia at the Casino Ballroom," *Journal of the Society for American Music* 2, no. 4 (2008): 531–67.

Library of Congress Cataloging-in-Publication Data
Berish, Andrew S.
   Lonesome roads and streets of dreams: place, mobility, and race in jazz of the 1930s and '40s / Andrew S. Berish.
      p. cm.
   Includes bibliographical references and index.
   ISBN-13: 978-0-226-04494-1 (cloth: alkaline paper)
   ISBN-10: 0-226-04494-7 (cloth: alkaline paper)
   ISBN-13: 978-0-226-04495-8 (paperback: alkaline paper)
   ISBN-10: 0-226-04495-5 (paperback: alkaline paper)   1. Jazz musicians—Homes and haunts—United States.   2. Music and race—United States—History—20th century.   3. Big band music—Social aspects.   4. Garber, Jan.   5. Barnet, Charlie.   6. Ellington, Duke, 1899–1974.   7. Christian, Charlie, 1916–1942.   I. Title.
   ML3508.B47 2012
   781.650973'09043—dc23   2011035817

♾ This paper meets the requirements of ANSI/NISO Z39.48-1992 (Permanence of Paper).

Contents

Acknowledgments

This book started life as a dissertation in support of my doctoral musicology degree at the University of California, Los Angeles. There I was lucky to be surrounded by a brilliant and supportive group of professors and students. I first met Robert Walser and Susan McClary during a visit to the UCLA campus while researching graduate programs. Over fish tacos at the student center (the first of many, many fish tacos), they patiently listened to my ideas about music and encouraged my still-vague ideas for research projects. From that first meeting, up through the dissertation defense, their support for my work has never wavered. I am deeply indebted to their vast knowledge, careful advice, and unflagging support. Their influence on my thinking about music, society, and history is profound and reflected on every page.

As my dissertation adviser, Robert Walser helped guide my initial, inchoate thoughts into a coherent research project. His thoughtful advice and criticism, along with his keen musical ear, were essential to the success of the dissertation and its revision into a book. I continue to rely on him for his support, advice, and sharp, critical eye. I also thank the members of my dissertation committee—professors Robert Fink, Mitchell Morris, Susan McClary, and Christopher Waterman. Each brought his or her impressive intellect to bear on my writing, and I am indebted to them for taking so much time to read and think about my ideas. Though they did not work with me directly on this project, the rest of the musicology faculty—professors

Raymond Knapp, Elisabeth Le Guin, Tamara Levitz, and the late Philip Brett—contributed profoundly to the ways I research, write, and think about music. I also need to mention an inspirational graduate seminar I took with visiting scholar Christopher Small. His ideas about music and musicking remain central to my own thinking about the nature of music and its relationship to social life.

My time with the faculty, though, was necessarily small compared to the many hours I spent with my fellow graduate students inside and outside the classroom. Working and socializing with them opened my mind and ears to entirely new ways of looking at music and the world. Although I met many students at UCLA, I became especially close to a cohort of students who began just before and after I arrived: Kate Bartel, Steve Baur, Dale Chapman, Lester Feder, Charles Garrett, Daniel Goldmark, Jonathan Greenberg, Gordon Haramaki, Loren Kajikawa, James Kennaway, Erik Leidal, Olivia Mather, Barbara Moroncini, Louis Niebur, Caroline O'Meara, Glenn Pillsbury, Erica Scheinberg, Cecilia Sun, Stephanie Vander Wel, Jacqueline Warwick, and Larry Wayte. Many of them read parts of the current project, and all offered helpful and constructive critiques. Although he had already finished his degree when I arrived there, David Ake has been a helpful sounding board for many of the ideas that found their way into the book.

The majority of the work editing and revising the manuscript happened at my institutional home, the University of South Florida. My current and former department colleagues—Dan Belgrad, the late Priscilla Brewer, Annette Cozzi, Jim D'Emilio, Sil Gaggi, Scott Ferguson, Niki Kantzios, Adriana Novoa, Amy Rust, and Elaine Smith—have been unstintingly supportive, offering unique interdisciplinary perspectives on the project. Although I can't recognize all of them, I also want to thank the many undergraduate and graduate students who have, over the years, patiently listened to me explain my book project. Their responses and questions helped me refine and reformulate many of my ideas. USF also provided more tangible support in the form of a New Researcher Grant and a Humanities Institute Summer Grant. These provided money to travel to several key archival sources and time to spend time carefully rewriting and revising the manuscript.

Three archival libraries were especially important to this project. I wish to thank Jeannine Pedersen and the rest of the staff at the Catalina Island Museum and Archives Center. Ms. Pedersen patiently helped me sort through the archive's many papers and photographs documenting the island and its great dance hall. They generously let me reproduce many essential photographs from their collection. While in Southern California, I also spent an extremely productive day at the Los Angeles Jazz Institute on the campus of California State University, Long Beach. Ken Poston and Eric Frankhauser were extraordinary guides through the library's amazing collection of jazz periodicals, recordings, and ephemera. While working at the Institute for Jazz Studies on the campus of Rutgers University, Newark, I was fortunate to have the help of head librarian Anne Kuebler and her wonderful library staff. They amiably helped me track down all sorts of obscure materials. I thank the staff at the National Museum of American History Archives Center in Washington, D.C., who patiently guided me through their vast collections. I spent many valuable hours in the Duke Ellington archives and the Sam DeVincent Sheet Music collection. A special thanks goes to Kay Peterson, who helped me obtain copies of many very useful images and archival documents. Finally, I want to thank Chris Werndly, president of the Cedar Grove Historical Society, who provided me with a historical overview of the Meadowbrook Inn, and Philip Jaeger, author of the Arcadia Publishing Images of America book on Cedar Grove, New Jersey, who graciously provided me with some rare images of that venue.

An earlier version of the first chapter appeared in the *Journal of the Society for American Music*. Editor Ellie Hisama and assistant editor Ben Piekut made many helpful suggestions that greatly improved the final version of that essay. At the University of Chicago Press, editor Elizabeth Branch Dyson first saw potential in the project, and she has enthusiastically and carefully shepherded it through the review and editorial process. I am very grateful for her support and tireless work on behalf of it. The careful and thoughtful anonymous reviewers provided essential feedback that greatly improved the final text. I wish to also thank editorial assistants Anne Summers Goldberg and Russell Damian, who helped me navigate through some key administrative obstacles in the preparation of the manuscript. Alice Bennett provided a detailed copyediting of the manuscript that besides catching mistakes greatly helped to streamline and clarify my prose. I also wish to express my gratitude to the terrific book team of Erin DeWitt, Andrea Guinn, Joan Davies, and Rob Hunt.

Finally, I offer a special thanks to my family. First, to my parents, Robert and Ilene, and my sisters, Jennifer and Bethanne: your unconditional love and support means everything to me. And to my Maria—I could not have asked for a partner more compassionate, intelligent, patient, and full of love. Through the many ups and downs of this long, long process, you steadied me, inspired me, and helped me to the finish line. During the final stages of preparing the manuscript, Maria and I welcomed Anthony into the world. You have changed our lives in the best ways possible, and we love you dearly.

During the 1930s and '40s, dance band jazz held a special position in American cultural life. Although it was not the only popular musical style of the era—"hillbilly" artist Roy Acuff, singing cowboy Gene Autry, and vocal groups such as the Ink Spots and the Mills Brothers all scored hit records—dance band jazz cut across racial, class, and gender divisions in especially powerful ways.[1] The music provided the soundtrack to daily life, and it accompanied work and leisure, filling home and work spaces alike. Inevitably for such an enormously popular music, listeners found very different personal meanings in these sounds. The music, though, also registered *social* feelings and experiences that went beyond the idiosyncratic and personal. Scholars in history and American studies have interpreted the mainstream jazz of the era, after 1935 generally referred to as "swing" or "big band," as an expression of the New Deal, as the voice of an emergent youth culture, and as an aesthetic embrace and transformation of technology and modernity.[2] These studies have greatly deepened our understanding of swing's larger societal meanings. Several of these authors—Stowe, Erenberg, and Dinerstein in particular—have written convincingly of the ways the music and the culture of swing embodied the utopian social possibilities of democracy and racial equality.[3] For all their insights, these studies spend little time on the specificity of musical sound. Although writers at the time categorized Guy Lombardo and Jan Garber as "sweet" swing bands, in practice their music differed in important ways. Each band developed its own favored songs, tempos, and phrasings within the larger stylistic category they occupied. The same was true for the many "hot" jazz dance bands that played a more up-tempo, harder-driving, improvisational style.

The musical details that constituted these differences were as important to musicians and audiences as any "extramusical" qualities a band exemplified (such as appearance or onstage demeanor), and they provided listeners with ways to discriminate and evaluate bands in a very competitive marketplace. Most scholars focus broadly on "swing," the hot, arranged jazz of large reed and horn bands. Although it is true that after 1935 many more American dance bands began incorporating musical features that were once exclusively the province of black orchestras—things such as improvisation and a smoother, driving 4/4 rhythm—we need to be careful not to ignore the rich diversity of music making that came under the discursive category "swing."[4] Furthermore, what was called swing by fans and critics changed over time. The dance band jazz of Fletcher Henderson and the Casa Loma Orchestra of the early 1930s sounded very different from that of the Count Basie and Benny Goodman bands of the middle of the decade. And both of these bands would seem only distantly related to the dense, complex, and "modern" swing sounds of the Dizzy Gillespie and Claude Thornhill orchestras of the mid-1940s. For all these reasons it is more accurate to describe the entire era spanning the late 1920s through the mid-1940s as a time dominated by dance bands, all of which to some degree or another incorporated elements of black vernacular music making. In the case of certain sweet bands—for instance, the orchestras of Jan Garber, Guy Lombardo, and Kay Kyser—the presence of these musical traits was extremely faint. But other sweet bands—for example, Russ Morgan's Orchestra—featured many elements of black vernacular musical practice such as blues notes and "dirty timbres." "Swing," then, is best reserved as a term that describes a cultural moment, roughly 1935 to 1946, a subset of a larger era of American popular commercial music dominated by large jazz-inflected dance orchestras.[5]

Yet in spite of all the variety of music these dance bands created, all were still part of the same general cultural formation. The dance bands shared a basic set of musical assumptions regarding form, instrumentation, and arranging, and each was part of the same national, and increasingly centralized, commercial music industry that put similar artistic and economic pressures on musicians regardless of musical style and aesthetic (though differing with regard to race). The many manifestations of dance band music all engaged with a similar set of historical issues.

What can attention to the musical specificities of 1930s and '40s dance band music tells us about these larger cultural concerns? Over the course of this book, I argue that this music offered listeners new ways to make sense of the changing spaces and places of American life. The geographical changes of the era, such as large-scale migrations and new patterns of urbanization, not only changed where Americans lived, worked, and socialized, they also raised fundamental questions about national identity. And because segregation and discrimination were concerned above all with the spatial arrangement of different peoples—who could live near whom—experiences of space and place were also, inevitably, about race. The art of the era engaged with these questions both directly (as in the novel, and then film, *The Grapes of Wrath*) and more obliquely (as in Stuart Davis's abstract paintings of city life). Music, too, registered these changes, and musicians created "virtual" sonic places—what cultural historian Josh Kun calls "audiotopias."[6] These musical spaces offered new ways to understand the places of daily life. In this way, the popular music of the era played an important role in a larger cultural conversation regarding the radical demographic and geographic changes caused by economic depression and global war. As the title of two popular Tin Pan Alley tunes of the era put it, Americans were caught between "The Lonesome Road" and the "Street of Dreams."[7] In an era of crisis, dance band music provided Americans not only with entertainment, but also with models of personal and national self-understanding.

During the 1930s and '40s the notion of American identity—a perennially unstable concept—was challenged in new ways by the complex centrifugal and centripetal forces of modernization. Demographic changes and rapid developments in communication and transportation technology—epitomized by the radio and the automobile—were tying Americans together into an increasingly complex transcontinental network. At the same time, these forces enabled much greater mobility, pushing Americans farther and farther out across the nation's great expanse. In their second visit to Middletown (Muncie, Indiana) in 1935, sociologists Robert and Helen Lynd find that radio has dramatically altered the nature of the city's social and cultural life in contradictory ways:

The presence in Middletown of [a] local broadcasting station with membership in a national chain operates in two directions. Like the movies and the national press services in the local newspapers, it carries people away from localism and gives them direct access to the more popular stereotypes in the national life. . . . In the other direction, the local station operates to bind together an increasingly large and diversified city.

Even in this "average" midwestern city, life was being reshaped by the contradictory push and pull of the new, national cultural industries.[8]

Dance band jazz embodied both of these forces: it unified Americans around a cohesive national musical style even as it transported sounds and experiences of distant places. Adopting a "hermeneutics of place," my study uses the music of four key musicians of the era—Jan Garber, Duke Ellington, Charlie Christian, and Charlie Barnet—to explore how music represented the era's crisis of place and identity. Each chapter is guided by several interrelated questions: How were spatial experiences embedded in big band or swing-style jazz? What kinds of mobility did the music offer listeners? And how did these musical-spatial experiences connect to Americans' lived experience of place?

Defining Space, Place, and Geography

The words "space," "place," and "geography," despite their ubiquity in everyday language, are surprisingly difficult to define, and they have generated an extensive academic literature.[9] Despite their semantic complexity, I use these words in specific ways. Space, like time, is an axiom of existence; to be, we must be somewhere. It is not, however, a priori—space is socially produced and constantly in flux.[10] In contrast to this multifaceted abstraction, "place" is concrete. We use the word in day-to-day life to describe the meaningful locales in our lives that we have imbued with individual and social meanings. Places, though, are always in danger of dissolving, of losing to time their stable meaning and identity.[11] Making and sustaining places, then, requires reiterative social practice and a certain degree of ideological and material control. "Place," as geographer Tim Cresswell writes, "is space invested with meaning in the context of power."[12]

Throughout this book I will use both "space" and "place," the first for the more theoretical or abstract parts of my discussion, the latter when writing about particular real-world locations. Both concepts, though, are always "grounded" in material reality. Abstract spaces and imaginary places are always in dialogue with the actual stuff of material life—bodies interacting with the physical environment.[13] When I discuss the Duke Ellington Orchestra's construction of a particular musical place like the "American South," I am not simply writing metaphorically: there are material places involved. That is not, however, to say that the band magically transforms one physical space into another, turning a Chicago concert hall into a Mississippi town. Rather, live musical performance is part of a real, bodily experienced geography—the musicians are performing, listeners are listening, and dancers are dancing in specific places: a dance hall, an apartment bedroom, a concert stage. Physical experiences and artistic cognition, including memory and imagination, are inextricably bound to one another. The connections might not be immediately clear, but they are always present. To capture this complex relationship, I use the word "geography." It is a shorthand way of referring to the human–space interaction that produced any particular section of the earth's surface. The "geography" of the United States in the 1930s and '40s refers not just to the roads, cities, and towns, but also to the people who lived there.[14]

Space, place, and geography, then, are not just things, but *processes*. They are ways of seeing the world, and they provide a hermeneutic orientation to history and culture.[15] Looking at jazz in terms of geography—of general, abstract spaces and specific, meaningful places—reveals new cultural meanings. This representation of spatial experience in jazz is both discursive—something registered in the writings and recollections of musicians and listeners—*and* musical. It is manifested in the arrangement of pitches, rhythms, and harmonies and in the interactions of musicians with one another. Musicians, sometimes consciously, other times not, harnessed music's ability to create a sense of space to construct "virtual" places that reinforced, enhanced, and sometimes challenged the character and definition of the places they lived and worked in. The music of Duke Ellington, Charlie Christian, Jan Garber, and Charlie Barnet provided listeners a way to "place" themselves in a time of economic and social uncertainty. In some cases their music articulated new American places that were more egalitarian and multiethnic than was true in reality. Although characteristic of all the music I consider, the "concretization" of place through performance is a practice that has specific roots in African American culture traceable back to the transformational ritual dance of the ring shout and the rhetorical flights of preachers. Amid the harsh conditions of slavery and then Jim Crow, black vernacular culture developed a performance aesthetic designed to materialize a better world—a future world—in the here and now.[16]

Place has been one of the "central motifs in the history and mythology of jazz."[17] Its history is often told through geography: New Orleans to Chicago to Kansas City and, finally, to New York City.[18] At each stage in its development, listeners and critics have understood the music as "organically rooted in some place or authentic locale."[19] Popular representations of the music tie it closely to particular locales: the streets and brothels of turn-of-the-century New Orleans, underground Chicago speakeasies, bustling Harlem dance halls, and smoky 1950s New York City nightclubs. Many jazz musicians have struggled publicly to sever these associations—a difficult task given how culturally ingrained some of these idea were (and continue to be).[20] From its beginning, jazz has been virtually synonymous with the city—the music's speed and energy understood as an analogue to the hectic, crazy dance of people, cars, and trains moving between giant skyscrapers. Writing in the mid-1930s, jazz critic Otis Ferguson described the live music of the Benny Goodman Orchestra as "more than audible, rising and coming forward from the stand in banks of colors and shifting masses—not only the clangor in the ears but a visual picture of the intricate fitted spans, the breathless height and spring of a steel bridge." Ferguson concludes with an effusive, lyrical fusion of music, city, and movement: "And if you leave at the end, before the 'Good-Bye' signature you will seem to hear this great rattling march of the hobos through the taxis, lights and people, ringing under the low sky over Manhattan as if it were a strange high thing after all (which it is) and as if it came from the American ground under these buildings, roads and motor cars (which it did)."[21]

More recent commentators identify the music with something much larger than the city—jazz stands for the entire nation. In the companion book to Ken Burns's documentary series *Jazz*, Geoffrey Ward writes: "It is America's music—born out of a million American negotiations. . . . It is an improvisational art, making itself up as it goes along—just like the country that gave it birth."[22] Rhetorically powerful, *Jazz*'s grandiose summation is also an obfuscation of historical fact. Tied as it was to the birth of modern American mass-mediated culture, since its beginning jazz has been about the tension between the voice of the local and the expression of the nation.[23] Beginning in New Orleans, the music traveled with musicians to other parts of the country. But it was the rise of records and radio that made it truly national (and then international). Despite some competition, jazz of the 1930s and '40s achieved a national, cross-cultural level of popularity that it would never hold again in the twentieth century.[24] While jazz had many regional and stylistic variants, the music was part of the rapidly growing, increasingly centralized music industry. Jazz was particularly successful at straddling the line between the local and the national. In an era of massive demographic change and social upheaval, listeners found in the music a way to locate themselves in a dislocated world.

Music synthesized in sound experiences that seemed impossible to manage or reconcile in real life. In its ability to manifest both real material locations and metaphorical, virtual ones, jazz of the era allowed the melding of "heterogeneous national, cultural, and historical styles and traditions across space and within place."[25] The big dance bands were both national entities—traveling the country, broadcasting from remote locations—and collectivities of individuals with their own personal geographies. Through performing, listening, and dancing, jazz musicians and listeners could at least temporarily locate themselves in time and space. They could find "fixity," stability in place, as well as "flow"—freedom of movement. Music, because it is both intangible (sound waves) and material (recordings, live performers), is especially good at capturing this dialectic.[26]

American Experiences of Place and Mobility in Depression and War

The 1930s and early 1940s were turbulent years in the United States. Economic collapse and global war uprooted millions of Americans from their homes and communities in search of work and better economic and social opportunities. America's entrance into the Second World War triggered enormous demographic shifts, especially for white and black southerners who left their homes in massive numbers to work in defense factories, particularly those on the West Coast. Millions of Americans who served in the armed forces also traveled to fight in Europe, Africa, or Asia. Even those who did not—or could not—move felt profound anxiety in such an unstable world. Mobility was often forced on citizens for economic or political reasons, and it shattered local communities, unraveling the fabric of familiar places. Yet mobility was also embraced and celebrated by writers, politicians, and ordinary Americans.[27] We were historically an intensely mobile population, and it was widely believed that a bright, productive, and peaceful future rested on such movement. So what bound Americans to one another? What culture did we all share, and where could it be found? What held the nation together as an idea and a geographical reality? These decades overflowed with public debates on these issues. Intellectuals and politicians sought unity in a range of ideas: regionalism, the New Deal, the Popular Front. For most Americans, though, the era's dislocations were registered most directly and immediately through popular culture.

Geographer Michael Steiner sees the nation's history as embodying a series of related dialectical relationships centering on attachments to place and a restless need for mobility, and encompassing "the interplay between security and freedom, the conflict between the familiarity of home and the lure of the open road, and the tug-of-war between nostalgia and progress."[28] The nation's sense of itself as a nation has historically been tied to general conceptions of its characteristic geography. Is this a rural or an urban nation? Are we a nation of fixed borders, a contained experiment of democracy, or are we defined by our expanding frontiers? Our history is in part the story of changing investments in the nature of America as a place or a network of places.[29]

The massive movements of people during the Great Depression and the war years seriously challenged existing conceptualizations of cities, towns, and states as well as the nation itself. During the 1930s, the country seemed, paradoxically, to be spreading out to ever farther corners of the continent, even while "shrinking" through the use of cars and the ubiquity of radio and film. Important technological changes were quickly eroding the "friction of distance" between Americans spread out across a continent.[30] Through increasingly nationalized corporate structures, centralized mass media—particularly radio and film—and transportation improvements (new roads, cars, buses, and trucks), Americans experienced what David Harvey terms "time-space compression," a new, often jarring, change in "the objective qualities of social space and time."[31] Although still spread across a vast continent, Americans were now much "closer" to each other than they ever had been. At the same time, industrialization was dramatically urbanizing and concentrating a once dispersed, largely agricultural population. For Americans across the social landscape—politicians, businessmen, teachers, artists, factory workers, domestic laborers—the geographic instability of the era was a central experience, one that focused a complex set of concerns regarding American national identity.[32]

A deep anxiety about national unity among politicians and intellectuals, not a new concern in American political and social life, was intensified by the economic collapse. "Thus," historian Warren Susman writes, "the American people entered an era of depression and war somehow aware of a culture in crisis, already at the outset in search of a satisfactory American Way of Life, fascinated by the idea of culture itself, and with a sense of some need for a kind of commitment in a world somehow between eras."[33] One manifestation of this cultural crisis was the "search for the primal spatial structures of the country, or for what was perceived to be the true, underlying fault lines of American culture."[34] How could a nation so geographically diffuse and so multiethnic survive the turbulence of economic collapse and global war? What centripetal force could counteract the centrifugal ones that were spinning Americans out across the landscape, away from communities that sustained a sense of belonging, a sense of unity?[35]

Vigorous debates between politicians, academics, artists, and intellectuals about the character of community and American national identity permeated the era. Regionalist activists, administrators of the New Deal, artists, and intellectuals all spoke and wrote frequently about these issues, but their attitudes were often distant from people's day-to-day life.[36] Most Americans knew from their own experiences about instability and uncertainty—about needing to leave the farm for the city, or moving across the country in search of work. Michael Steiner, borrowing the words of poet Gary Snyder, writes that "during the Great Depression, many Americans seemed deeply concerned with knowing the where of who they were." And while "most Americans were not visited by the tribulations of Job during the Great Depression . . . many persons were afflicted by a prolonged, insidious fear of rootlessness and the imminence of disaster." A desire for "closeness to the land and persistent affirmation of place were the vernacular counterparts to the regional theorizing of the 1930s."[37] Susman similarly suggests that the widespread fear and insecurity of the era were the result of a feeling of geographical instability. According to Susman, "The mobility provided to an increasing number of Americans by the machine age helped heighten the lack of security. Such mobility, long characteristic of civilization in the United States, became even more part of the way of life in the 1930s." For Susman nothing summed up both the anxiety and the possibility of this mobility better than the "ironic idea contained in the new concept of 'mobile homes.'"[38]

With the outbreak of war and the massive mobilization for United States participation, these dreams of mobility were suddenly and dramatically realized. Wartime work pulled Americans onto the roads in extraordinary numbers. Historian John Jeffries writes that "some sixteen million Americans joined the armed forces during World War II, and another fifteen million moved across county lines, eight million of them across state lines. In all, one in every five Americans made a significant geographic move during the war."[39] The migrations of the era, such as the massive movement of Americans in the South and Midwest out toward the enormous defense plants on the West Coast and the renewed flow of African Americans out of the rural South and into the industrialized cities of the North, Midwest, and West, fundamentally altered the nation's demographic, political, and cultural map.[40] The abstract, intellectual concern for community, for national identity and unity, expressed by writers of the 1930s gave way to a dynamic, living experiment in close quarters pluralism. Now Americans were facing head-on the paradoxical forces driving American life. If the 1930s were about the possibilities of mobility, the 1940s were about its difficult and painful realization.

The war years created all kinds of new, dynamic American places that were strikingly multiethnic and culturally heterogeneous.[41] These demographic and geographic changes often generated violent social confrontations between Americans now face-to-face in the streets and in the factories. Some of the most explosive and devastating of these were between whites and blacks. Racially motivated conflict and violence surged in the early 1940s: 1942 race riots over public housing in Detroit; "hate strikes" in 1943 in Mobile, Baltimore, and Gary by white workers who refused to work alongside blacks; a bitter transit strike in Philadelphia where white employees walked off the job to protest promotion of blacks. In 1943 off-duty white servicemen in Los Angeles attacked Chicano, Filipino, and African American "zoot-suiters." The conflict in Los Angeles soon spread to other cities around the nation: race riots broke out in San Diego, Philadelphia, Chicago, Evansville, Detroit, and Harlem.[42]

African American artists and intellectuals of the 1930s and '40s created many works that resonated with the travel and place experiences of black life in this era of migration. In the mid-1930s, novelist Zora Neale Hurston—herself a migrant from the South—working for the WPA, produced *Mules and Men* (1935), an account of black folk life that she compiled from her field trips back South, particularly to her home state of Florida.[43] Her stylized collection of oral traditions (as well as her regionally oriented fiction) spoke to a desire to trace and recapture oral traditions lost in the migration north. Hurston's retelling of folk stories not only helped connect the contemporary experiences of northern and southern blacks but provided a means to bridge past and present and resolve a sense of historical discontinuity between the radically different space-time of the rural South and the urban North. What Hurston did for the South, black writers Claude McKay and Roi Ottley did for the North. McKay's *Harlem: Negro Metropolis* (1940) and Ottley's *"New World a-Coming"* (1943) both offered descriptions and commentary on the current state of life in the black ghettos of the North. In their landmark study *Black Metropolis* (1945), St. Clair Drake and Horace R. Cayton provided a comprehensive, scholarly examination of Chicago's black residents.[44] A fellow Chicagoan, novelist Richard Wright, offered harrowing and complicated accounts of the same experiences. His novel *Native Son* (1940) and his autobiographies *Black Boy* (1945) and *American Hunger* (written at the same time as *Black Boy* but not published until 1977) were unprecedented in their complex, often brutal, depiction of African American life, particularly the damaging psychological effects of segregation, discrimination, and racism in both the South *and* the North.[45] Offering less nihilistic visions, writers such as poet Gwendolyn Brooks (*A Street in Bronzeville*, 1946) and novelist Ann Petry (*The Street*, 1946) surveyed the richness of urban life, especially as it affected women, showing its dynamism and excitement as well as its daily tragedies.[46]

By the end of the 1940s, the notion that white Protestants were at the center of American life and culture had dramatically eroded. The idea of "cultural pluralism" articulated by Horace Kallen and others in the Progressive Era was gaining traction as a viable conceptualization of the nation. The profound ideological aspect of the Second World War had put the issue of the nation's cultural diversity permanently on the table. The debate over American identity—what made Americans American—of course would not end, but its contours were now dramatically different. A reconfigured, more abstract ideological notion of American identity had transformed Jews, Italians, and other "white" ethnic minorities into "real" Americans. African Americans and other racial "minorities" would, over the course of the coming decades, begin to challenge this revised but still highly racialized vision of American identity.[47] A. Philip Randolph's threatened March on Washington in 1941 to protest discrimination in the hiring practices of war-related industries, although averted by Roosevelt, was the sign of a new, more radicalized civil rights movement willing to embrace more direct action tactics along with legal battles.[48]

The war years generated a cultural ferment in the popular and "elite" arts, but these movements would not manifest themselves until well into the postwar era. For instance, abstract expressionism arose in the 1940s but did not became mainstream until the early 1950s.[49] Similarly, in the "elite" music world, the retreat from the accessible populism of the Depression and war years into high modernist techniques such as serialism did not become dogma until after the war ended.[50] More directly relevant here were the developments in popular music incubated during the war years. The stripped down, amped-up "jump" and rhythm-and-blues styles did not produce its cultural revolution until rock 'n' roll swept the country in the mid-1950s. In the same way, modern jazz—bebop—while posing a challenge to the swing jazz style during the 1940s, would not completely transform and displace that style until early in the next decade. Dance band–style jazz—whether hot or sweet, big band or small group—dominated the American popular music scene from the late 1920s through the end of the Second World War.

During these decades, this mainstream popular musical culture provided a powerful unifying force for a nation split by class, regional, and racial affiliations. By the 1920s Americans were increasingly listening to the same music, watching the same films, reading the same books, playing the same games, and buying the same nationally advertised consumer goods. "Sound," in film and in radio, "helped mold uniform national responses; it helped create or reinforce uniform national values and beliefs in a way that no previous medium had ever before been able to do."[51] But this national culture was never monolithic, and even as it united Americans, shows like Amos 'n' Andy, with their presentation of regional and ethnic specificity, fought against cultural homogeneity. The programs were recognitions of a fundamentally pluralistic nation that could not that easily be made uniform. Thus, regional accents could convey a sense of rebellion against the homogenizing influence of mass media.[52] Radio, along with film and music, existed between the local, regional, and national—the technology that could bring cultural difference to others was also the engine for its erasure.[53]

For historian Morris Dickstein, the whole era was suffused with a "dream of mobility": images of travel and unhindered movement were vividly manifested in American popular culture. According to Dickstein, "the real dream of the expressive culture of the 1930s was not money and success, not even elegance and sophistication, but mobility, with its thrust toward the future."[54] The massively popular films of the era were permeated with dreams of motion. The Fred Astaire–Ginger Rogers films, the Busby Berkeley musical spectaculars, the "crackle and speed" of the era's screwball comedies, were all "circle and swirl, all movement and flow."[55] These representations in film, radio, literature, and visual art let Americans believe that security and stability were "out there," available to those who could move and travel. At the same time, these cultural texts, in transforming and resolving immediate anxieties, provided a sense of stability in the now, a sense that we did indeed have a place in the modern flux of day-to-day life.[56]

Music, Race, and Place

The cultural representations of place and mobility in American art and popular culture were intimately shaped by America's distinctive racial ideology. Racial difference in the United States was realized and experienced *spatially*. Places were designated for specific racial identities— either directly through segregation laws or more obliquely through structural inequalities. This racialized "spatial mediation" of modern life was a way for Americans to create order amid the fragmentation triggered by modernization and migration. By "attaching identities to physical moorings, from bodies to buildings to larger geographies like region and nation," America's political and economic leaders could counter the space-compressing effects of new technologies such as trains and automobiles and new national media such as radio and film.[57] "In effect," writes Grace Elizabeth Hale, Americans "translated the specific and individualized linkages between identity, place, and power that had reigned in an earlier, smaller world into connections between categories of people and imagined spaces that moved far beyond local boundaries."[58] In an increasingly interconnected nation, race became a primary way of ordering American geography. Popular culture registered this racial ordering of American space.

In the United States at this time, Americans heard music, including jazz, through a racial ideology designed to differentiate black from white.[59] Although individuals might have disagreed in specific cases, the written records of these years—oral histories, journalism, and academic writing—clearly show that most Americans had available a general cognitive framework for identifying certain sounds as "black" or "African" and others as "not-black" (thus, implicitly "white").[60] There were, in sociologist Barry Shank's words, audible "musical signatures of racial identity" that musically "encoded" blackness.[61] This is an underlying premise for my study: by employing certain musical procedures socially coded as "black," white bands could perform a kind of "blackness" for certain audiences in certain times and places. Conversely, black bands could play "white." The racial identity of a musical performance was created through an articulation—a joining together—of racial thinking and musical sound.[62] And because this connection was not "natural" but historically determined, it was inherently unstable. The voices of cultural authority such as writers, intellectuals, and teachers had to actively promote these articulations, to reiterate them again and again. Music and racial identity become mutually constitutive and part of a circular social argument: music is proof of racial difference, and racial difference "naturally" produces different music.[63] Oftentimes Americans reiterated this articulation of race and music in oblique language: during the 1930s, jazz was frequently categorized as either "hot" or "sweet." As chapter 1 will explain in some detail, these two terms had strong racial connotations. Describing a band as "hot" was another way of saying that the music was played in, or at least approximated, a black style. Sometimes, however, the connections between racial identity and musical sounds were deliberately made explicit.

In the mid-1930s the Casa Loma Orchestra—one of the most successful of the early white jazz dance bands—recorded and released "Black Jazz" and "White Jazz." Each song represented a set of musical characteristics (tempo, form, timbre, harmony, rhythmic groove) widely understood as representative of one side or the other of the segregated commercial jazz world. "Black Jazz" is a twelve-bar blues form that features bluesy, muted trumpets, sharply defined melodic "riffs," and a driving 4/4 rhythm. "White Jazz," by contrast, has a much "stiffer" two-beat feel that evokes the Charleston rhythm of the 1920s and the "jazz age." The track features less of the timbral variations of "Black Jazz," instead favoring open horns employing a cleaner sound. These Casa Loma records were undoubtedly meant in good humor, but for the joke to work listeners had to understand that the performances represented generalized types.[64] Many in the band, especially guitarist and arranger Gene Gifford, were very knowledgeable musicians aware of the diversity in black and white dance band styles. In fact, the Casa Loma band was central in bringing the hot style of certain black bands to a wider white audience.[65] The very fact that the band members could play "black" or "white" shows, on one interpretation, how they were undermining the categories they were illustrating. On another view, though, the deliberate pairing of the two songs (they were actually released on separate discs) reinforced the racial binary. Musicians such as Gifford may have been sensitive to racial stereotypes and sincere in their appreciation for black musical practices, but their records, once released, became a seamless part of a racially defined commercial music industry, reinforcing existing ideas and prejudices.

Thus, through particular musical choices musicians could perform race. They did not, though, do this in the same ways. Take, for example, 1940s rhythm and blues musician Johnny Otis. Considering himself "black by persuasion," the drummer, vibraphonist, and bandleader adopted the speech, dress, and behavior of the Los Angeles blacks he knew, and he was accepted as black by many in the community. When the Casa Loma band, or any band of the time, played in a black style, they were performing race in a much more limited way. What matters most for my study is not whether a band such as the Casa Loma Orchestra played black music authentically (a questionable notion) but what social uses their musical evocation of "blackness" was put to.[66] How did the players understand their musical choices in the context of African American life and history? Did they situate themselves inside a particular notion of African American cultural tradition and continuity?[67] As we will see, sweet bands such as Jan Garber's, although occasionally playing in a recognizably "black" style, did not, generally speaking, understand their performances as part of a black community. Charlie Barnet, on the other hand, made it central to his music making. His identification with African Americans was complicated and contradictory, but his musical evocation of "blackness" was an attempt at positioning the music of a predominantly white band in the larger continuum of African American music making of the time.

The musical evocation of blackness was not about presenting a kind of static "sign" that a listener decoded. Music, Christopher Small reminds us, is an *activity* and not a thing.[68] Playing "black" or "hot" happened during a performance and over time in dialogue with larger cultural ideas about race. As Patrick Burke writes, "Ideas of racial authenticity . . . influenced musical practice even as they were formed by it."[69] Presenting blackness to a listener involved all aspects of the performance from the formal arrangement of the music to the interactions between musicians. Once race is performed in this way, it is given a voice—a presence—that raises it to the direct apprehension of listeners. With its musical evocation, racial identity could be put discursively into play. It is then open to a "renegotiation of the meaning."[70] Simply bringing race to this kind of audible presence was not inherently positive or negative, but by making it more audible, more plainly apparent, the structure of racial thinking—and by extension a society structured by it—was open to a kind of direct engagement not always available in other aspects of daily life.

This did not mean the category of black music was (or is) an empirical fact with an essential, definable core. Scholars have long debated the ontology of African American music: Is it a single historical entity that scholars can clearly describe? In a series of well-known articles, musicologist Olly Wilson argued that "there is indeed a distinct set of musical qualities which are an expression of the collective cultural values of peoples of African descent." These musical qualities share

"core conceptual approaches": an emphasis on rhythmic and metri-
cal contrast, percussive capabilities of the voice and other instruments,
call-and-response structures, high density of musical events in a short
time frame, a heterogeneous sound ideal, and bodily engagement.[71]
Working along these lines, musicologist Samuel Floyd developed a similar analysis but centered on a different conceptual-cultural framework,
that of the ring shout.[72]

More recent scholarship has challenged these earlier approaches,
criticizing them for essentialism. In *Lying Up a Nation*, ethnomusicologist Ronald Radano argues that uncritically upholding "the myth of
black music as a stable form or even as a 'changing same' . . . forestalls
consideration of the interracial background from which ideologies of
black music developed in the first place." In place of this, Radano has
argued vigorously for a more discursive understanding that sees "black
music's very constitution as part and parcel of the broader emergence
of race in American public history and culture."[73]

The "truth" of black music, then, lies between the discursive and the
sonic fact. Although we can trace the national and transnational roots
of certain African American musical practices such as the "blues scale"
or a conceptual principle such as "heterogeneous sound ideal," these
facts are mediated by discursive practices specific to time and place.
Cultural practices and their local meanings are fluid. According to musicologist Guthrie Ramsey, European Americans and African Americans
"have continually (re)articulated, questioned, abandoned, played with,
and reinforced their ethnic identities."[74] In the black community music
has been especially central in fashioning and refashioning notions of
"blackness." At the same time, many of the cultural markers of race in
American life have been very stable over decades—arguably centuries—
and historical actors work within and against these ideas. At the day-
to-day, level "blackness" was very real to those Americans with dark
pigmentation. The same ideas about racial identity that led to racist
actions also provided a center around which communities organized
to help each other, comforted each other, and protested larger societal
injustices. Music in particular has been central in the affirmation of
an African American identity. As a "participatory group activity," the
production and reception of black music have helped reinscribe and
validate a cultural continuity of tradition.[75]

My book is not concerned with the empirical truth of black music
now or during the 1930s and '40s. I do not engage the ongoing scholarly debates about African cultural continuity and memory in the New
World.[76] What I focus on is the music's social life in the American cul-

ture of the era—the way it was used to register larger historical concerns. This does not mean looking exclusively at the "talk" about music from the era—the ways jazz was written about in print, talked about on radio, or depicted in newsreels or feature films. Musical sounds themselves have a kind of semantic content. That content is much more indeterminate and flexible than spoken and written language, but it is nonetheless real and identifiable. To delineate this interaction between sound and discourse means correlating music analysis with a sensitive accounting of how people understood these sounds.

Jazz historian Krin Gabbard writes, "Jazz is the music that large groups of people have called jazz at particular moments in history."[77] This is only partially true. Americans attached the label "jazz" to specific sounds they *believed* defined the genre. Americans were arguing over musical details, even if they could not always label them with the correct terminology. Listeners identified the racial character of the era's jazz based on the rhythms, melodies, forms, harmonies, and timbres they heard. A great deal of the analysis in the chapters that follow explores these specific musical materials in detail.

The "blackness" that the music manifested had tremendous social significance during the era because musicians (and their music) were so mobile. Jazz orchestras traveled relentlessly and to surprisingly remote corners of the nation. Similarly, local and national radio broadcasts gave listeners access to the same sounds across vast distances. The music's mobility made it part of the larger social and political articulation of race with spatial ordering. Because musical performances of "blackness" or "whiteness" were always located somewhere, jazz of the era was an integral part of a national conversation on the connections between racial identity and American places.

Toward a New Understanding of Depression and Wartime Dance Band Music

Popular big band dance music offered reassurance and understanding, a sense of belonging to an America larger than one's immediate surroundings. As Joel Dinerstein argues, the music helped Americans assimilate the technologies of the machine to their minds and bodies. The energy, force, and movement of the machines of the machine age were resized to a human scale. Historian Gena Caponi-Tabery develops this idea, narrowing the scope of Dinerstein's analysis to the cultural trope of the "jump": "Jazz music, dance, and basketball were three cultural practices through which African Americans challenged those in power, and the jump was a key ingredient of that challenge. Through the powerful, assertive, and identifiably black jump, men, women, and adolescents reclaimed a central gesture of African American culture, defying the Jim Crow stereotype by reclaiming Jim Crow's jump. Jump tunes, the athletic jitterbug, and the jump shot helped to form a new black image: not self-deprecating or shuffling but self-assertive and literally uplifted."[78]

Dinerstein and Caponi-Tabery both usefully situate jazz-inflected music of the 1930s and 1940s as a central interpretative node in a society coming to terms with new technologies and dramatic social change. Both authors frequently describe the music of the era as embodying movement, energy, and force. Building off these ideas, I want to both narrow and expand their insights: narrow them by focusing closely and specifically on the reality of the musical sounds and practices of the era, and expand them by situating the music in a larger historical discussion about the nature of American spatial life. At its most progressive, dance band music constructed musical places that suggested a nation that was fundamentally multiethnic, fluid, and dynamic.

But as I mentioned earlier, the term jazz covered a very large cultural terrain and represented a wide range of concerns. Most Americans had a very broad understanding of what fell into the genre, and it included a diverse array of musical practices: sweet milquetoast dance bands that played syrupy arrangements of pop tunes; novelty orchestras that specialized in musical skits and humorous songs; sturdy, workaday dance bands that had at least a toe in the world of hot jazz; and the top-tier hot bands that featured dynamic arrangements and a good deal of solo improvisation.[79] This spectrum of musical styles, from sweet to hot, was often mapped onto race—the hotter the band the "blacker" it was often perceived to be, whether its members were African American or Caucasian. Yet, in spite of these differences, just about every dance band shared many of the same experiences, and they made music in very similar ways. Hot or sweet, white or black, the bands almost always featured a male or, more commonly, female singer. Some bands carried two or three vocalists. Many bands also traveled with dancers and comedians, making them a traveling show that could be adapted to dance halls or theaters. Above all, whatever their personal musical tastes, the vast majority of white and black professional bands were pragmatic—they played what audiences and record companies wanted to hear. Bands were artistic, but they were also business enterprises, and regardless of race, they all negotiated a similar set of artistic-commercial issues.

Considering the scope of the music in question—reader polls in jazz magazines consistently listed about three hundred "name" jazz bands—my focus in this book is necessarily narrow.[80] Partly this is to provide depth rather than scope, since close attention to music and cultural context requires space to develop connections that might at first seem obscure. My choices, though, are not arbitrary. Each musician I look at was immensely popular and influential across the United States (and in some cases internationally): they were all, in other words, *national* figures. In addition, these musicians had significant connections to one another that demonstrate that, despite their great variety, commercial dance bands shared many of the same experiences regardless of their musical orientation or racial makeup. The band world was big, but it did allow for significant interactions and overlaps. These interactions were widespread, often were interracial, and demonstrated that these bands lived and shared in a particular stratum of American life with its own set of concerns. For example, white bandleader Charlie Barnet used discarded arrangements by Jan Garber as the book for his first band. Garber had abandoned those arrangements to play sweet dance band music, a style that secured him his greatest fame. But Barnet was also good friends with Duke Ellington, and he bought and recorded many of Ellington's arrangements. Hot and sweet, white and black—what Stanley Dance called the "world of swing" was replete with connections, affiliations, and unexpected relationships between musicians and bands.[81]

Music as Spatial Experience

My analytical approach in this book—using the music of swing-era musicians to illuminate American conceptions and experiences of place and mobility—is a decidedly new take on the jazz of the era. The extant histories, biographies, and musicological studies on swing have largely divorced musical discussion from historical and cultural analysis. In musicology, scholarship on swing and big band jazz has focused overwhelmingly on the analysis of arranging techniques, innovative soloists, and biographical accounts of musicians and their individual musical development. There are many studies of the life and music of bandleaders such as Duke Ellington, Fletcher Henderson, and Benny Goodman and of soloists such as Lester Young, Ben Webster, and Billie

Holiday.[82] Recently more specialized music histories have focused on particular aspects of the swing era. Sherrie Tucker's *Swing Shift* is the first comprehensive and critical study of all-girl dance bands of the 1940s.[83] In *Come In and Hear the Truth: Jazz and Race on 52nd Street*, Patrick Burke examines the complex intersections of musical practice and racial ideology in the nightclubs that lined New York City's famous Fifty-Second Street. Finally, many scholars have published comprehensive histories of the era's music, most impressively Gunther Schuller with his mammoth 1989 survey *The Swing Era*.[84]

These books are all important contributions, and they have provided detailed biographical and historical information as well as close musical study of composing and performing styles. They have not, though, offered systematic explanations for the cultural significance of this massively popular American musical style. This burden has largely been taken up by historians and American studies scholars. Books by David Stowe, Lewis Erenberg, Kenneth Bindas, and Joel Dinerstein all look at swing culture as a development closely related to broader social currents such as the resurgence of youth culture, the ideology and practice of the New Deal, and the American experience of Depression and wartime modernity. Unfortunately, in these excellent interdisciplinary studies, the music itself is treated vaguely, with little attention to specific formal issues of musical organization and construction. By combining an analysis of specific music with a broader interdisciplinary perspective, this book bridges the two dominant scholarly approaches to the music and offers a comprehensive new understanding of the social and emotional power of the era's musical sounds.

Over the past thirty years, musicologists and ethnomusicologists have also explored the social meanings produced by music. Scholars have produced important work explaining how music constructs personal and community identities in terms of race, class, and gender. Fewer scholars, though, have looked at music as a communicator and shaper of more general categories of social experience such as time and space. The issue of human spatiality—how music partakes in our spatial existence, how it constructs our sense of social space, and what it contributes to our general "sense of place"—has been especially neglected, perhaps owing to a long-standing celebration of music as the temporal art par excellence.[85] But space and place permeate musical discourse and are an integral part of the musical experience in terms of both production and reception. Music is an experience of time *and* place. It is probably most accurate to write about the "space-time" or "place-time" of musical experience.

Calendars, for example, spatialize time by giving it a material form with measurable dimensions (the box on the paper that marks off January 1, 2011).[86] Conversely, in the domain of the arts, we experience space—a Broadway theater, a Gothic cathedral, an art installation— through time. (Notice, too, how often we use metaphors of space to talk about time!) However, throughout this book I bracket the temporal. This necessarily distorts the reality of musical experience, but for argumentative and practical reasons it is analytically useful. My narrow focus on space and place is a heuristic—an analytical model that is deliberately narrowed to promote new perspectives and insights.

Music's intimate connection with the human body and its movements is perhaps the most basic spatial component of musical experience. The relation between music and dance is historically deep, extending back millennia, likely even longer. It is easy to see the strength of the intimate connection between the body and music: watch people with their iPods bobbing their heads, tapping their feet, and shaking their hips. When listening we hear the movements of the performers' bodies. On stage (or on television) we can see them move in specific ways to generate and accompany the sounds they make. Even when we can't see them, we can still hear and feel traces of a performer's movement: music encodes the force of bodily motion.[87] When Duke Ellington plays one of his off-kilter, syncopated, and dissonant piano chords, we hear the physical force necessary to make the sound. We hear, and feel, traces of Ellington's physical movement.

Not surprisingly, this fundamental relation between space, movement, and music is part of a long historical discourse on music. Music is routinely and very consistently described in explicitly spatial terms—it moves and transports us, it can take us on a journey, it can generate a profound "sense of place." The association between music and motion (an implicitly spatial concept) goes back at least to the ancient Greeks, where musical harmony was part of a larger universal harmony of heavenly bodies in motion.[88] Nearly five hundred years later, at the turn of the twentieth century, Arnold Schoenberg explained his twelve-tone system as a spatial reconfiguration of musical composition and experience.[89] Exactly how the space of music is conceptualized is determined by culture, and certain musical features with specific spatial associations in the West have different or no spatial associations in other parts of the world. For musicians in Bali, pitches are small or large. In the Amazon, the Suya correlate pitch with human age.[90]

Spatial metaphors continue to be a defining feature of how we talk about and describe music today. The titles of recent books suggest that music itself is a journey.[91] Spatial metaphors also saturate the language of music, television, and concert reviews and are central to our personal understandings of music.[92] In her essay "The Sensuous Production of Place," Sara Cohen provides an ethnographic account of Jack, an elderly resident of Liverpool, England, and his important relationship with music. Describing his experiences during the 1920s listening to jazz on the radio, Jack speaks about music's ability to let him "travel in an imaginary sense to different times and places." According to Jack, "It doesn't matter if it's dance music or what, it's there in my radio, and you're in another world. It takes you to a new world."[93]

Academics who study music have not completely ignored spatiality in music, though the number of works dealing with the topic is at odds with its ubiquity in historical and contemporary discourse. Perhaps one reason for this resides in the difficulty of defining the notion of musical space. Music, as sociologist Ray Pratt writes, "evokes a 'sense of space' . . . different from that evoked, say, by sight or touch, both of which can be avoided through averting the eyes or withdrawing from reach."[94] Musical space, and "auditory space" more generally, is pervasive, all-encompassing yet invisible, untouchable, and ephemeral:

Auditory space has no point of favored focus. It's a sphere without fixed boundaries, space made by the thing itself, not space containing the thing. It is not pictorial space, boxed in, but dynamic, always in flux, creating its own dimensions moment by moment. It has no fixed boundaries; it is indifferent to background. The eye focuses, pinpoints, abstracts, locating each object in physical space, against a background; the ear however, favours sound from any direction. We hear equally well from right or left, front or back, above or below. If we lie down, it makes no difference, whereas in visual space the entire spectacle is altered. We can shut out the visual field by simply closing our eyes, but we are always triggered to respond to sound.[95]

Music (and sound) not only fills the space around us, commanding our attention (we cannot shut off our ears), it *alters* that space, in effect creating something new. This transformative ability is central to my argument: all music creates a sense of space that has a *specific and definable relation* to lived spatial experiences. Music shapes and is shaped by our understanding of the specific places of our lives. Most of the extant scholarship on musical space, though, has largely separated out discussion of music's spatiality from general physical and historical experience. With a few key exceptions, most scholars who have considered the relation between space and music have studied it either as a metaphorical construct tied to the formal manipulation of specific musical materials or as something external to the formal aspects of the music—a discursive category like identity, race, class, or gender that provides a new perspective for understanding the social meanings and uses of popular music.[96] In these two approaches the spatiality of music, the experience of musical elements moving in relation to each other, is separated from the lived experience of space.[97]

In contrast to these two trends—the dominant ones in musicology, ethnomusicology, and music theory—a small body of work has suggested that musical space is neither completely virtual and metaphorical nor entirely discursive. Susan McClary, Steven Feld, Charles Hiroshi Garrett, and Vijay Iyer have all sought to connect the specificities of musical sound and experience with the larger physical and social experience of space. For these writers musical space shapes and is shaped by the experience of historically and culturally situated bodies.[98] Other recent work in musicology and music theory has incorporated findings in cognitive psychology to offer new ways of looking at musical space and its relation to "nonmusical" experience. Phenomenological approaches, for example, treat perceptual experience as empirical reality, and thus the "virtual space" of music as an actual space.[99]

Following this line of thought, I will argue that music itself is a *spatial practice*; it creates places that are stable and familiar, at least for the length of the performance. At the level of musical detail—form, melody, harmony, and rhythm—listeners follow specific trajectories, cognitively exploring the song's various tonal locations or melodic topographies. But musical experience comprises more than abstract formal events, and music, whether live or recorded, evokes people. The sounds we hear are attached to the people making them, and in a sense we are with them for the length of the performance. Musical performances present the attentive, receptive listener with auditory spaces phenomenologically full; these spaces have an "overwhelming presence" that "fills space and penetrates . . . awareness."[100] The music inhabits the listener, affecting body and environment. This musicospatial experience overlays ordinary experience and provides a counterpoint to it.

If hearing is a major component of our sense of emplacement in the world, then music, a particular, culturally determined manifestation of sound, must also contribute to a sense of place, a feeling in a listener of being meaningfully located. The physical production (or electronic reproduction) of musical sounds can invest the spaces of our lives with deep, long-standing affective meanings.[101] In these ways, music "sensuously produces place," imparting meaning to the geographical locations we inhabit.[102] The places created by musical activity—either through production or through listening—are not necessarily true reflections of an actual relationship with the places of real experience. As many scholars have demonstrated, in the realm of commercially recorded music the imperatives of global capitalism force the producers and marketers of music to "delocate" it in order to create products that will be bought by consumers separated by vast cultural and geographical distances. This can be a negative attribute—erasing local experience and contributing to the hegemony of global capitalism and its attendant values.[103] But music's ability to register social relationships and different experiences also travels. This information might be obscured or mistranslated, but it is still present and offers the possibility for genuine cross-cultural interaction, understanding, and even political action.[104]

French philosopher Henri Lefebvre has developed a useful theoretical structure for coordinating the various dimensions of human spatial experience. His sociological and historical orientation provides the tools for an analysis of music that keeps the abstract, formal elements of music and our perception of them in an active relationship with individual and social experience. Arguing against the a priori understanding inherited from the Enlightenment, Lefebvre asserts that space is socially produced, the result of the combination of our mundane day-to-day movements, the routes and paths laid down by planners, architects, and governments, and the imaginative transformations we, as individuals and communities, make of this spatial order. For Lefebvre, socially produced space is composed of three interrelated components: (1) perceived space, the result of *spatial practices* (our day-to-day movements); (2) conceived space, the result of *representations of space* (routes and paths laid down by others such as city planners); and (3) lived space, realized in *representational spaces* (imaginative transformation of the previous two categories).

In this schema, music is both a *spatial practice*—musicians, listeners, and dancers occupy and modify the spaces they inhabit—and a *representational space*—a cultural text that interprets the varying levels of spatial experience. In his discussions of art (including, briefly, music) Lefebvre puts special emphasis on his third category. *Representational spaces*, he argues, are created from the lived experiences of place, and they meaningfully interpret our *spatial practices* and the *representations of space* that guide those practices. In his "trialectic" schema the *representational spaces* of lived space are key: "*Representational spaces*: space as directly lived through its associated images and symbols, and hence the space of 'inhabitants' and 'users.'" For Lefebvre, it is also "domi-nated—hence passively experienced—space which the imagination seeks to change and appropriate. It overlays physical space, making symbolic use of its objects," creating a "more or less coherent systems of non-verbal symbols and signs."[105] Representational spaces connect spatial practices and planned spatial structures with the artistic and mental representations and understandings of these experiences. Art, through its manipulation of cultural materials into new, symbolic forms, is a representational space par excellence.[106] Thus music is an-other representational space: it orders sounds and transforms them into meaningful, socially experienced structures that symbolically make sense of life's perceived and conceived spaces.[107]

Although there is a danger here of reifying musical practice into static musical texts, Lefebvre allows us to convincingly link a variety of spatial components of music (the physical arrangement of musi-cians, the physical space filled by sound waves of various frequencies, the more metaphorical space enacted in formal musical structures) to the real spaces of our lives, and by extension to the other nonspatial forms of social life. Musical activity is an arena where the perceived and conceived spaces not only can be represented but can also be ana-lyzed, restructured, and even reconfigured. As Rob Shields argues, this representational space has a revolutionary potential to resolve the con-tradictions of our historically conditioned spatial experience and free us from forms of dominations, helping us reach our potential as "total" beings in the world.[108] Music's own spatiality can, in certain circum-stances, challenge imposed conceptual spatial orders and even refine our very idea of spatial limits and freedoms.[109] Lefebvre's theoretical framework provides a new, more satisfying way to examine the con-nections between the experience of abstract, musical space and actual lived space. To hear space and place in music, the analyst cannot nar-row the focus to any specific dimension of musical experience, whether that be the formal, discursive, perceptual, cognitive, or social. We must keep all the dimensions of human spatial experience in dialogue with one another.

Hearing place in music means first attending to the spatial practices of the people involved in making music. These include the day-to-day movements through the environment, the roads traveled and the cities and towns visited, as well as the activities of musicians and audiences inside and outside the locales for musical performance and listening. Second, we need to examine the "representations of space" that created the specific routes and paths that the musicians and listeners occupied. Traveling dance bands were enabled (and also constrained) in their movements by the transportation infrastructure available to them. Cars and buses provided the most flexibility, allowing access to both very small and very large audiences. However, regional laws and customs regarding spatial behavior—racial segregation, for instance—circumscribed the movement of black or integrated bands. Finally, we need to consider the "representational spaces" created by the musicians themselves. This is primarily the music "itself"—the melodic, rhythmic, and harmonic structures, but also the discursive material attached to the music, including such things as titles, programs, live or recorded introductions, journalism, and music criticism. Specific musical sounds, in an American context, create certain perceptual and cognitive experiences of space.

But music does not only engage existing spatial arrangements; it allows the creative expression of new ones. Through the act of "musicking," performers can juxtapose emotions and ideas and instantiate relationships that would be impossible in real life.[110] They can create "audiotopias" where real-world social problems can be transformed and re-presented, providing other sensitive musicians and listeners with an emotionally charged, sensorily rich parallel reality.[111] As Josh Kun writes, "Music functions like a possible utopia for the listener," where we experience sound not just as audio signals "but as a space that we can enter into, encounter, move around in, inhabit, be safe in, learn from."[112] Musicians help create this space, and describing how they occupy it, and what this might mean historically, is at the heart of this book.[113]

———

In the rest of the book I offer four instructive examples of how jazz made and remade American places of the 1930s and '40s. Chapter 1 begins with white bandleader Jan Garber—a wildly popular purveyor of sweet jazz through the 1930s and '40s. Garber was a midwesterner whose sweet big band style came to embody the experience of Catalina Island, a small Southern California tourist resort just off the coast of metropolitan Los Angeles. Performing summer after summer at the island's grand Casino Ballroom, the immensely popular Garber band broadcast its dance sets all across the nation via radio remotes. The melodic, saxophone-heavy sound and light dance beat transmitted a sonic representation of the Catalina resort experience that was contemporary but also deeply nostalgic for a white-dominated social order under increasing pressure from the reforms of the New Deal. The sweet music of Garber and his band was part of a larger cultural effort to defend the boundaries of American places against the fracturing and democratizing impact of modernization.

Chapter 2 examines a very different, and also commercially successful, dance band leader, Charlie Barnet, who developed for his orchestra an explicitly black musical style. Starting out as a "hotel"-style sweet orchestra, in the late 1930s Barnet dramatically transformed his band into one of the nation's most successful purveyors of hot jazz. This journey from sweet to hot was also a social journey across the color line. I then turn to two Barnet songs—1940's "Pompton Turnpike" (named after the highway that led to a well-known dance hall in suburban New Jersey) and 1944's "Drop Me Off in Harlem" (a cover of Duke Ellington's 1933 homage to the black neighborhood)—that embody the move from sweet to hot, segregation to integration. Significantly, both songs do so through the language of travel, specifically the road.

Chapter 3 turns to the Duke Ellington Orchestra, a band that was, by the mid-1930s, nearly completely nomadic and "placeless." The 1930s and '40s Ellington book of original and cover tunes was a musical atlas filled with songs that explicitly or implicitly referenced specific places and more general place experiences. Night after night in their relentless travel, on theater stages and dance hall podiums, the orchestra members created and re-created all kinds of familiar and unfamiliar places. In this chapter I will focus on two performances from an important 1946 concert at Chicago's Civic Opera House: "Air-Conditioned Jungle," a dynamic and multivalent evocation of the urban experience, and the four-part *Deep South Suite*, a work that imagined and performed a complex, multivoiced, and contradictory American South. The band's unique social dynamic—virtuosic, highly individualized voices working to create a coherent ensemble sound—suggested to audiences not just that other places and experience were possible, but that all places were open to reconstruction.

In chapter 4 I look at electric guitarist Charlie Christian, a key swing-era jazz soloist who was also deeply influential to a generation of musicians. Christian forged a guitar style that was an idiosyncratic mixture of regionally specific musical influences—country blues, western swing, hillbilly, and Kansas City big band jazz—and a new jazz modernism that, after incubating in the after-hours nightclubs of Harlem, would emerge in the mid-1940s as bebop. The development of Christian's musical style was the result of a real physical journey from the Southwest to the nation. His playing was marked by a dynamic mixture of musical gestures rooted in the southwestern music scene and modernistic long, linear melodies that unfolded in unpredictable ways. These two modes of playing—of traversing musical space—created strong contrasts in his playing between stability and movement, place and mobility, rootedness in location and freedom of movement. Christian's approach to jazz soloing fused the fragmented geography of his life into something new—a musical locale that was racially integrated, intensely mobile, and national in scope.

The book concludes with a brief coda that looks at an emerging spatial experience: flight. The development of air travel had fascinated Americans during the 1920s, and writers of the decade coined the term "airmindedness" to capture the mood of the new "aerial age."[114] The notion of flight was (and remains) an important trope in African American culture generally and jazz in particular. In the Jimmie Lunceford band's recording of "Stratosphere" (1934) we discover an interesting connection between the era's "airmindedness" and African American experience. Literally referencing the sky, and implicitly flight, the song is a paradigmatic example of the band's distinctive, cohesive sound and defining approach to rhythm. "Stratosphere" is a sonic enactment of uplift—a musical sense of flight that resonated with the integrationist goals of the era's black civil rights movement and Lunceford's middle-class background. The expression of flight in a distinctive African American cultural form suggested that new kinds of movement could break down the social barriers of the day.

Arguing that jazz of this era was about place and mobility is not to say that the music was *only* about these issues, just that these ideas provide new and productive ways of studying the larger social meanings underlying this important cultural activity. Adopting a particular analytical angle always means focusing on one set of meanings at the expense of others. My study is intended not to supersede existing work on jazz of the 1930s and '40s, but to complement it. Meaning in music, as Lawrence Kramer points out, is not a "recoverable substance" residing in a particular musical work. It is, rather, "an activity or disposition within a cultural field." The goal of my project is not to forever define the meaning of this body of recorded music, but to "to say something consistent with what could have been said, whether or not it actually was, and in so doing to suggest how the work may have operated in, with, on, and against the life of its culture."[115]

As I will show, focusing on these sets of issues is not an arbitrary choice but one grounded in the historical reality of the Depression and war years. Throughout the book, I offer a careful accounting of the concerns, hopes, and dreams of the era and their representation in a wide variety of texts. Looking at issues of geography and race helps us situate the music in a larger conversation that was happening across the cultural field, in "elite" and "popular" cultures, and across a variety of media—film, print, visual art, and design. Jazz of the era, because it was so mobile, was an especially sensitive instrument for registering these concerns.

The two songs that make up the title of my book, "The Lonesome Road" and "Street of Dreams," are significant in ways much deeper than their literal references to place and travel. Although credited to two white men, Nathaniel Shilkret (music) and Gene Austin (lyrics), "The Lonesome Road" was actually a "revised and dressed up" black spiritual.[116] The "new" song was first recorded by cowriter and singer Austin for Victor Records in 1927. It was a hit, and many cover versions followed. The producers of the 1929 film version of *Showboat* added the ersatz spiritual to the movie version of the Kern and Hammerstein book (in the film, sung by black opera singer Jules Bledsoe dubbing Stepin Fetchit).[117] Other versions of the Shilkret and Austin song from the 1930s and early 1940s included recordings by Ted Lewis (1930), Louis Armstrong (1931), Mildred Bailey (1938), Fats Waller with Adelaide Hall (1938), Jimmie Lunceford (1939), Tommy Dorsey (1939), Will Bradley (1940), Lucky Millinder (1941), and Peggy Lee (1946). It is an impressive list—white bands and black bands, singers and instrumentalists, sweet and swing all found the song compelling as well as commercially viable. The journey of "The Lonesome Road" is a familiar one in American popular music: a black vernacular song adopted by white musicians and transformed into an ersatz popular "folk" tune that in turn becomes reappropriated by black artists for the commercial market. Besides being another example of the racial complexities that shaped the development of American popular music, the history and success of "The Lonesome Road" illustrate the era's preoccupation with place and mobility. The lyrics of the song—about the inevitability of travel and of leave-taking—reverberated with musicians and listeners alike. Using the same basic musical materials, musicians of the era found different ways of framing some of the same underlying concerns.

Published in 1932, with music by Victor Young and lyrics by Sam M. Lewis, "Street of Dreams" was an instant hit, and it became one of the twentieth century's most recorded songs. Initially popularized on recordings by crooners Bing Crosby and then Russ Columbo (both

1932), the song was similar to many other popular ballads of the early 1930s. Its impressionistic lyrics capture the dreamy, wistful mood of those early, brutal years of the economic collapse. In this magical place, "dreams broken in two / can be made like new" and "no one is poor." But it is also where "all you can hold is in the moonbeams." We are never quite sure if we could ever find such a place. Like the lyrics, the core melodic motive—a short rising chromatic gesture that repeats again and again—is an incantation willing this dream world to reality.

Tommy Dorsey (with Frank Sinatra on vocals) revived the song in 1942 during the anxious and uncertain early years of the war. Other versions by Boyd Raeburn (1944), Ray Eberle (1945), and Johnny Bothwell (1945) soon followed. Like "The Lonesome Road," the raw material of the song lent itself to a wide variety of interpretations by very different kinds of singers and orchestras. The popularity of the song also demonstrates how the swing era was never exclusively dominated by hot, up-tempo dance music. The popularity of sweet jazz ebbed and flowed, but it was always present; nearly every band had tunes like "Street of Dreams" in its active repertoire. The Dorsey recording in particular, featuring Sinatra's warm, emotive voice and lush, romantic strings, arguably outsweets the sweet Columbo recording from eleven years earlier.

Even though the two songs represent stylistic poles of the dance band era, they also show the many complex musical and social interconnections that defined this cultural period. Whether swing or sweet, white or black, the dance bands of the 1930s and '40s were working from similar raw musical materials in a broadly shared commercial and aesthetic milieu. And though not all this music explicitly referenced particular places or spaces, the pieces that did—and there were many— confirm that this preoccupation was also broadly shared in this musical culture.

Jazz, and popular music more generally, is both an "artistic form and [a] social location."[118] In the formal workings of these collectively made sounds, we can discern actual and desired values and social relationships. Jazz musicians created musical spaces—at once real and imagined—that represented the geographic and demographic dynamism of the nation, the growing pluralism of America's cities and towns, and the fluid movement and flows of its people. From a widely represented view of the United States as a set of fixed places—ideally small towns, anchored in the local or regional and stratified according to race—a great deal of jazz music of the 1930s and '40s articulated an alternative ideal that celebrated the nation as a modern, fluid, and developing collection of dynamic, racially integrated cities tied more and more into a national, culturally pluralistic network. Although these hopes, embodied in sound, would prove difficult to realize in the post-war decades, the music of the 1930s and '40s still provides a taste of the era's optimism.

I Dream of Her and Avalon: 1930s Sweet Jazz, Race, and Nostalgia at the Casino Ballroom

The immense Casino Ballroom sits at one end of the city of Avalon, on Catalina Island, about twenty miles from metropolitan Los Angeles. In the institutional memory of this small Southern California island community, and in the surviving documentation and recollections of those who visited, the Casino Ballroom was a central location—in both a physical and a symbolic sense—for the era's big dance bands.[1] Jazz historian and writer Floyd Levin recalls tuning in to the broadcasts from Catalina to hear his idol, saxophonist Eddie Miller: "I can still hear the saccharine-voiced announcer purr his introduction to the [Bob] Crosby broadcasts 'from the beautiful Casino Ballroom at romantic Catalina Island overlooking the harbor lights of Avalon Bay and the Blue Pacific.' I listened attentively to my bedside radio anxiously awaiting the Bob Cats." Yet despite its historical importance for Southern Californians, most jazz writing scarcely mentions the ballroom at all.[2]

Part of the reason for the scholarly inattention has to do with the nature of the jazz that was played on Catalina. The ballroom rarely featured the hot jazz of groups led by Bob Crosby, Benny Goodman, and Duke Ellington. In the 1930s and early '40s a visitor or radio listener would most likely hear the sedate dance music of Jan Garber, Ben Bernie, and Kay Kyser. Contrary to the current-day television and film images of the era, the Casino Ballroom was not the scene of ecstatic jitterbugs dancing to driving, up-tempo jazz. Instead, the modernistic dance hall featured almost exclusively white dance bands playing sweet jazz, a style that avoided the most obvious musical signifiers of its hot sibling. In rediscovering this lost venue, we learn a great deal about how people used jazz to create a very specific sense of place in an era of social and geographical instability. For the owners of the Casino, jazz was to be the sound of modernity suffused with nostalgia for a threatened social order. Not only were no African American bands hired to play the ballroom—even black bands that played sweet—the managers listened carefully to the sounds of the white bands they hired. The story of Catalina's Casino Ballroom provides new perspectives on how popular music represented American experiences of place.

Since the actual sounds of the ballroom from its heyday have not survived on recordings, the best way to hear them is to study commercial recordings of bands favored there.[3] I will examine several versions of "Avalon," a tribute to the island city of Catalina written by Al Jolson, B. G. DeSylva, and Vincent Rose. Although the song predates the construction of the ballroom, management appropriated it as an integral part of the island experience. Visitors would hear the song many times during their visit, as bands played it for incoming and outgoing ferries and to introduce their stage shows.[4] Through a comparison of three commercial recordings of "Avalon" that span the hot-to-sweet spectrum, I will show how the music of sweet jazz bands popular at the ballroom differed from the hotter styles of bands that never appeared there.

Unlike the hotter sounds of the Jimmie Lunceford and Casa Loma orchestras, the sweet "Avalon" of Jan Garber's band established musical relationships and values that were easily fused to the ideology of the island's promoters—the music created a sonic place that could be brought smoothly in line with the physical place. Garber was extremely popular at the Casino, returning summer after summer to large crowds.[5] The owners of the venue, the Wrigley family and its corporate voice, the Santa Catalina Island Company, sought very specific musical sounds as part of a larger project to create on Catalina Island what Michael Kammen calls "nostalgic modernism"—an American place that embraced the new while struggling to inject past traditions and social ideals into an unsettled contemporary life. In their embrace of this difficult position, the owners and managers of the island resort sought to resist the democratizing implications of rapid technological and social change.[6]

In examining the history of the Casino Ballroom, we rediscover the lost sounds of these sweet bands, a massively popular segment of the American musical landscape. One goal of this chapter is to provide an analysis of sweet jazz as a musical genre with its own particular musical priorities different from hot jazz, but intimately related to it. Studying this particular dance hall, though, accomplishes much more. It illuminates a powerful contradictory impulse that ran through a large segment of American popular music of the 1920s, 1930s, and early 1940s: the entire ballroom experience was designed as a technologically and culturally modern event, even though it was saturated with nostalgia and a rejection of the social changes inherent in modernization. Big band music of the 1930s resonated with the strong belief, held by many people, in the rightness of the new and a steady, though seriously challenged, faith in the power of modern, reformed capitalism to lift society out of economic crisis and into a more egalitarian and prosperous future.[7] At the same time, large parts of the American populace feared the social implications of such modernization. Writing of the 1920s, historian Lawrence Levine has aptly described this impulse as "the desire to have things both ways—to accept the fruits of progress without relinquishing the fundamentals of the old order."[8] As automobiles, new roads, New Deal federal programs, and mass culture brought the nation closer together, Avalon remained rigorously segregated, set off from the rapidly intensifying urban nature of American life. Yet the island's growth as a tourist destination was predicated on 1930s technological and economic modernization.[9]

The dance band music of the era—even in its sweet guise—was a thoroughly hybrid music, the product of a complex fusion of African American and European American musical practices. The quest to absolutely match sound and place was impossible, and the music at the ballroom, with its audible crosscurrents of influences, testified to a multicultural reality. This truth heard in the music helps to explain, in part, why the Casino owners sought white sweet bands when African American bands could easily have accommodated the preferred musical style. In these choices, the administrators of the ballroom were not just hiring particular musicians but were making an argument—a spatial-social argument—about the desirable relation of music, social structure, and place. Black sweet bands would challenge the illusion of the particular social order being created and reveal the inherent contradictions behind the Catalina Island project—a white fantasy California where racial others were confined to servicing the basic infrastructure of the island. There were to be no black bodies onstage and a minimum of black sounds echoing in the venue.

The Avalon Experience

Although not nearly as popular as it was in the first half of the twentieth century, Avalon remains a tourist destination today, and on weekends day-trippers fill the streets of the small town. Island historians credit the birth of a tourist industry to George R. Shatto, who purchased Catalina in 1887 and, rather than mining the island for precious metals or other natural resources, decided the real gold was in tourism.[10] Allegedly at the suggestion of Shatto's wife, the new town was christened Avalon, after a passage from Tennyson's *Idylls of the King*.[11] Development accelerated when a local shipping tycoon, Captain William Banning, acquired the island in 1892.[12] Over the next twenty-seven years, however, the financial costs of maintaining and developing the resort proved too much, and in 1919 the Bannings sold Catalina to the chewing gum magnate William Wrigley Jr.[13] Wrigley sank millions into improving the island's water supply, housing, and roads and was committed to making Catalina an affordable getaway: "There is to be nothing of Coney Island flavor about Santa Catalina. It would be unthinkable to mar the beauty of such a spot with roller coasters and the like." For Wrigley, "Catalina was developed to put within reach of the rank and file of the United States—the people to whom I owe my prosperity—a playground where they can enjoy themselves to the utmost, at such a reasonable figure of expense that all can participate."[14]

Wrigley's aversion to Coney Island and its roller coasters was not an antitechnological position but a social and aesthetic critique. Catalina was not going to be mobbed by massive working-class crowds enjoying cheap, lowbrow entertainment such as freak shows and thrill rides.[15] The island was to retain its natural beauty while not compromising on modern amenities. By the time of Wrigley's death in 1932, Catalina had been transformed into a popular middle-class vacation spot. The island had affluent visitors and upscale accommodations to cater to them, but Wrigley, through various promotional plans, was committed to middle-class affordability.[16] Besides fishing and water sports, he developed an array of attractions to take advantage of the island's natural resources: a bird park, a horse farm, and glass-bottom boat tours. Wrigley also made Catalina the spring training home for his Chicago Cubs.

Under his guidance, the island became a tourist destination that provided modern comfort, entertainment, and natural experiences that showcased the island's beauty.[17]

William Wrigley's son Philip inherited the island at the nadir of the Great Depression. Philip not only managed the island through the economic crisis but expanded on his father's vision, adding his own distinctive nostalgic touches. Along with an array of cosmetic enhancements such as importing palm trees and sand to replace the island's natural pebble beach, he hired troupes of performers to dress as early Anglo and Spanish "settlers" and wander the downtown streets greeting visitors and singing to them in a sanitized performance of California history.[18] For Philip K. Wrigley, "The historical background of Catalina Island, the last Spanish grant, its natural beauty and romance lend themselves admirably to the preservation of the atmosphere of old California. . . . Gradually we may be able to make all of Catalina Island a monument to the early beginnings of California."[19] This nostalgic presentation of early California was in sharp contrast to its reputation for modern Hollywood glamour, the result of vacationing movie stars and frequent film productions on and around the island. Used as a military base during World War II, Catalina Island reverted to tourism after the wartime mobilization, though it never fully recovered its earlier glamour and popularity.[20] From the end of the war through the 1960s, the island lost many of its large hotels, including the grand Hotel St. Catherine. In 1975 Wrigley, through the Santa Catalina Island Company, deeded nearly 86 percent of the island to the recently created Santa Catalina Island Conservancy, effectively stopping most commercial development and ending the Wrigley family's great Catalina project.[21]

One of the centerpieces of that development program, of course, was the giant Casino Ballroom, pictured in figure 1.1 ("casino" was used in an older sense describing any place of entertainment; there was never gambling). Built between 1928 and 1929, the massive theater and ballroom complex was constructed on the small Sugarloaf Point that straddles Avalon harbor and neighboring Descanso Bay. The circular edifice, with its orange-tiled roof and whitewashed walls, rises twelve stories and is nearly 180 feet in diameter—it was (and remains) one of the first sights of Avalon visible from the ferry.[22]

A grand theater occupies the first floor, and two sets of six ramps lead up to the second-floor ballroom, an enormous space that, at its 1929 opening, allegedly had twenty thousand square feet of dancing space (with subsequent remodeling and modifications the dance area is

Figure 1.1 The Casino Ballroom, Avalon, Catalina Island. From *Catalina Island* (Charleston, SC: Arcadia Publishing, 2004), 86, by Jeannine L. Pedersen, curator of the Catalina Island Museum. Photographer and date unknown (ca. 1932). Photograph courtesy of the collection of the Catalina Island Museum.

now ten thousand square feet).[23] The building's chief designers, architects Walter Webber and Sumner A. Spaulding, created a cantilevered structure capable of holding up both theater and ballroom ceilings with no supporting columns.[24] Figure 1.2 shows a large crowd of dancers filling the especially broad dance floor. Buttresses reach out from midway up the building's outside walls to support a balcony that circles the upstairs ballroom, offering impressive views of land and ocean. The Casino was designed, in both form and function, as a scientific, state-of-the-art building. Wrigley built a radio broadcast room "equipped with all the latest sound devices" adjacent to the ballroom, allowing for transmission of its musical entertainment to listeners on the island (the ability to broadcast nationally would come several years later).[25] The first-floor movie theater was built in consultation with engineers specifically to handle the new "talkie" films.[26]

The modernistic art deco decoration—specifically the many murals on the inside and outside of the building—wrap all this modern technology in a fantastical ambience that emphasizes what the island

Figure 1.2 Dancers on the floor of the Casino Ballroom, 1932. Jeannine L. Pedersen, *Catalina Island*, Images of America Series (Charleston, SC: Arcadia, 2004), 85. Photographer unknown. Photograph courtesy of the collection of the Catalina Island Museum.

promoters called the "romance and adventure which is the essence of Catalina."[27] The giant tile mural outside the main ticket booth features an underwater scene presided over by a lithe, naked mermaid. Inside, the movie theater walls depict highly stylized historical and mythological figures—hooded Spanish friars, Native Americans on horseback, and Venus and Neptune surrounded by abstract patterns evocative of the sea.[28] Publicity material created by Wrigley's office for its opening in 1929 celebrates this mixture of fantasy and modernism: "Nothing has been omitted that ingenuity, imagination, experience, skill, with unlimited means, could devise to make the Casino one of the world's outstanding pleasure palaces. . . . [T]he Casino is alone worth a trip to the Magic Isle."[29]

The grand opening of the building on May 29, 1929, featured a fashion revue, marching bands, dancing, and speeches. The proceedings were highlighted by the amphibious arrival of "King Neptune" and his six pirate "lassies," who carried a "pleasure chest" containing the "golden key" that symbolically opened the building.[30] Figure 1.3 reproduces a photograph of the festivities, staged just outside the building's grand entranceway with its sea-themed murals. We see Neptune, trident in hand, holding forth before a faux treasure chest, surrounded by women in elaborate costumes. David M. Renton, the general manager of the Santa Catalina Island Company, is holding the giant golden key with which he will officially open the new building, the island's real-life "pleasure chest."

A close look shows two adolescent African Americans dressed in uniforms flanking the main scene.[31] The names of the black teens are unknown (along with the names of many of the women), though Catalina historian Patricia Moore has identified several other figures in this scene.[32] The young men are clearly subservient to the main action; they are decorative touches to this theatrical opening. In their uniforms and peripheral position, they embody long-standing ideas about African Americans as the servants of white fantasy. They are also evi-

Figure 1.3 "Neptune" presenting the key to Catalina Island's new "Pleasure Chest," the Casino Ballroom. Date and photographer unknown. Photograph courtesy of the collection of the Catalina Island Museum.

dence that African Americans were involved in the island's functioning at various times, though as laborers rather than vacationers. Published histories of the island do not discuss any permanent or part-time African American residents of Catalina or its main city.[33] A survey of the island's only newspaper, the *Catalina Islander*, from the mid-1930s through 1941, also reveals no presence of any African American community.[34] Photographs like the one reproduced in figure 1.3 seem to be the only archival materials that document an African American presence on Catalina. On display at the Catalina Island Museum (located in the Casino Ballroom building) is another telling image, an undated photograph titled "Porters, Stevedores, and Concessionaires of the S.S. Catalina." The photograph shows a large group of uniformed African Americans, twenty-four men and one woman, arrayed before the ship. It is another brief acknowledgment of the role African Americans had in the operation of the resort island. This island "pleasure chest" was for whites only.

At this time such segregation was the norm in most places across the United States, but the exclusionary racial policy of the owners of the island extended even to the entertainers who could play the ballroom—no African American bands played there during the 1930s and early 1940s.[35] This is especially unusual considering that even in the most racially segregated parts of the country black bands often played for all-white audiences.[36] Photographs of the bands that appeared at the ballroom, especially from the 1930s and '40s, are almost all the same: instrumentalists and singers are dressed in neatly tailored and freshly pressed light-colored clothes (suits for men, dresses for women) and spread in a semicircle, often in front of the Casino.[37] Figure 1.4 shows four of these band portraits.[38] Striking in these photographs is the absence not only of any African American bands, but also of many of the most famous white bands of the era.

Indeed, a surprisingly large number of the best-known bandleaders, both white and black, never played the Casino: Louis Armstrong, Charlie Barnet, Count Basie, Cab Calloway, Tommy Dorsey, Duke Ellington, Jimmie Lunceford, Glenn Miller, Harry James, and Artie Shaw. These bands, though primarily known as hot outfits, could easily have accommodated the sweet style favored at the venue. In addition, there is no evidence that Mexican or Chicano bands played there—which would have been plausible given the island's small but long-standing Mexican American community. Other large ethnic groups in the Los Angeles area are also absent from the ballroom's musical stage.[39] Con-

Figure 1.4 Formal photos of bands in front of the Casino Ballroom. Clockwise from the top left, the bands led by Kay Kyser (1939), Dick Jurgens (1939), Freddy Martin (1939), and Jan Garber (1937). Patricia Ann Moore, *The Casino: Catalina's "Two Million Dollar Palace of Pleasure,"* rev. ed. (Avalon, CA: Catalina Island Museum Society, 2002), 88, 90, 91. Photographers unknown. Photographs courtesy of the collection of the Catalina Island Museum.

trolling the presence of these racial others went hand in hand with the development of the island into a particular kind of whites-only Southern California resort that combined modern amenities with the nostalgic ambience of "early" California.

The Casino Ballroom: White and Sweet

Starting with the very first band to play in the new building, Maurice Menge and his El Patio–Catalina Orchestra, the ballroom became a major venue for the increasingly popular jazz-inflected big band dance music. In summer, bands would draw nearly three thousand people during the week and more than five thousand on the weekends.[40] From its first days, though, the venue featured only sweet bands that played in the mold of Paul Whiteman and Guy Lombardo. But hotter jazz, with its intimations of racial difference, was never far away, bubbling beneath the sweet, placid surface. On the last night of their initial run,

Menge's band let loose and abandoned "their season's restrained repertoire of waltzes and fox trots and jazzed it up," playing hot tunes such
as "Twelfth Street Rag" to an appreciative crowd.[41] As the island developed under the Wrigleys' guidance, these outbursts of hotness became
scarce as the dance hall was molded into a premier venue for sweet
dance band music.

The use of the terms "hot" and "sweet" to describe various manifestations of jazz music was common in the literature and reporting from
the 1920s through the 1940s. Today we might hear profound musical
differences between these two styles, but historically speaking, the
situation was far from clear. Similar to the post-1935 explosion of hot
swing, sweet jazz had moments of commercial dominance. Historians
of American popular music often cite the early 1930s and then the
years of World War II as moments where sweet dance music trumped
swing among listeners. As Lewis Erenberg notes, these surges in the
popularity of sweet music happened during the worst years of the Depression and the darkest years of the war—moments of profound uncertainty and pessimism for many Americans. Swing, on the other hand,
reflected the renewed optimism of the New Deal, and, later, the Allies
success on the battlefield.[42]

In its broadest outlines, this story is basically true—the king of sweet
music, Guy Lombardo, was most successful in the years immediately
after 1929, when his band was booked into New York's Hotel Roosevelt
and reached a national audience over the hotel's radio hookup. But
sweet music never lost its appeal in the 1930s (Lombardo continued to
be one of the era's most successful artists), and just a quick survey of the
recordings made by the hundreds of national dance bands from 1930
through 1946 will show that nearly all bands featured sweet-style music, with its emphasis on slower tempos and straightforward, romantic
interpretations of melodies. In his history of swing, Erenberg attempts
to make a distinction between post-1935 swing bands playing sweet
versus the earlier sweet orchestras of Lombardo, Abe Lyman, and Jan
Garber: "When a good swing band focused its hot sound on love songs,
it intensified the personal meanings of ballads." In contrast to the music of Lombardo and his ilk, "swing fused love songs to a jazz style
that gave ballads a lift and heightened their emotional power. Each
band's use of individualized arrangements and versatile instrumentation helped make love songs seem more personal."[43] After listening to
the many recorded ballads of the swing years, I find it hard to justify
this assessment on musical grounds (Erenberg focuses almost entirely

on lyrics). Bands with impeccable swing credentials, such as those led by Charlie Barnet and Tommy Dorsey, played ballads that featured all the prominent characteristics of sweet jazz purveyed by Lombardo and Garber.[44] The distinction between sweet and hot was more a discursive practice than a musical fact.

Most jazz critics of the 1930s and '40s made a distinction between "jazz" (the loose, small-group improvised music made famous in 1920s Chicago largely by expatriated New Orleans musicians) and "swing" or "orchestral jazz"—the large-ensemble dance music of the big bands.[45] Other critics insisted less on clarifying the jazz/swing boundary than on making distinctions within the large and growing world of commercial dance bands—by the early 1930s the dominant organizational form of this American popular music.[46] For these writers, making the distinction between jazz and "not jazz" or between hot and sweet rested on identifying certain key musical parameters—especially improvisation and rhythm—as well as the influence or presence of African American musical culture.[47] As defined by the writers in the major music publications such as *Down Beat* and *Metronome* (many of whom were opinionated devotees of "authentic" hot jazz), sweet jazz, also labeled "commercial" jazz, was a diluted version of hot, improvised "Negro" jazz. Featuring little or no improvisation and prominent, easily accessible melodies, sweet jazz was often based on stock arrangements of popular Tin Pan Alley tunes.[48] Rhythms were staid and lacked the hard-driving, forward push of hot swing rhythms. Hot jazz, of course, was the opposite of this: full of rhythmic excitement, improvisation, unusual timbres, and "Negro" influence.

In an article written for *Down Beat* magazine in 1936, Paul Eduard Miller offered a definition that neatly ties together all these concerns. Ostensibly designed to help the magazine's readers distinguish good jazz from bad, Miller's descriptions are useful summaries of widely understood distinctions between sweet and hot popular music. Note also his use of the word "jazz" rather than "swing"—further evidence that there was no consensus, at least among knowledgeable critics, regarding the differences or similarities between jazz and swing as musical styles or genres:

Sweet jazz is popular music in 4/4 tempo; it is music utterly lacking in musical intelligence and genuine emotion; it is crass music, manufactured on request by the songsmiths of Tin Pan Alley, one end of which is in New York and the other of which is in Hollywood. The popular song, comprising the huge bulk of what goes by the name of jazz, is the choice of the musically untutored. It belongs part and parcel to the bands led by Guy Lombardo, Wayne King, Johnny Green, Eddie Duchin, and Fred Waring.

Hot jazz is also music in 4/4 tempo, but it is genuine music as well. That is to say, the point in which it differs from sweet jazz is not in its form but in its musical quality. . . . Compositions such as Variety Stomp, Alligator Crawl, Dallas Doings, Radio Rhythm, and Mad Moments are representative examples of the finest hot jazz. Even when badly executed, these works possess a remarkable and undeniable quality rich in Negro tradition and unique in background. Hot jazz thus differs from the other . . . in that it is a sincere expression of an emotional feeling and is founded on something more than mere sophistication.[49]

As a prominent journalist and one of the most vociferous supporters of the New Orleans–Chicago style of "hot" jazz (a style waning in popularity), Miller represents an extreme of opinion.[50] Yet the relation he articulates between "hot" sounds and blackness (music "rich in the Negro tradition") was widely held, if not always so clearly stated. In a similar way, sweet music, or jazz drained of its "color," is implicitly "white" music. Miller's distinction between hot and sweet also involves commerce. For many 1930s and '40s jazz writers, a great deal of big band jazz was musically empty, a product that corporations foisted on an ignorant public that didn't know any better.[51] Some jazz musicians shared these views.[52] In contrast, hot black jazz was less commercial—even anticommercial—than the watered-down sweet jazz so popular on national radio programs in the early and mid-1930s.[53]

These categories of hot and sweet, though, were gross simplifications that never could encompass the fluid world of jazz-inflected dance band music: very swinging rhythms were often applied to stock arrangements in performances that featured little improvisation. Conversely, original "jazz" compositions often featured little improvisation and gentle rhythms. Some music, such as Benny Goodman's big band arrangements of "Stompin' at the Savoy" and "Sing, Sing, Sing," seem to obviously belong to the hot world of jazz or swing—they are up-tempo, intensely syncopated, and rhythmically driving, riff-based recordings. But how do we categorize a Goodman performance like "Stardust on the Moon," broadcast October 20, 1937, from the Madhattan Room in the Hotel Pennsylvania in New York City?[54] This medium tempo Tin Pan Alley pop tune, with its muted rhythm section, vibrato-laden saxophone passages, and relaxed, sentimental vocal by Martha Tilton, is clearly related to "Stompin' at the Savoy," though it represents something different—and very common—during the era. Female lead singers were de rigueur for dance bands well before swing became mainstream. Contrary to the impression given in most historical writing on swing, it is impossible to escape the fact that the repertoire of even the most respected and "hottest" swing bands (in the post-1935 sense of the term) included a huge variety of music, much of it like "Stardust on the Moon" and distinctly closer in style and spirit to the arrangements of such alleged enemies of jazz and swing as bandleaders Guy Lombardo and Abe Lyman. Evidence from the era, such as articles and fan polls in *Down Beat* and *Metronome*, further suggests that audiences (at least male audiences), musicians, and many writers did not make such hard-and-fast distinctions. Pop tunes, ballads and up-tempo "killer dillers" were all part of jazz and, after 1935, of swing.

A June 1940 poll in *Metronome* magazine offers an interesting and ecumenical viewpoint that sharply differs from Miller's ideas quoted above. The poll asks readers to vote for their favorite dance bands in three categories: "swing," "sweet," and "overall." For the swing division, the editors asked that readers "imagine . . . going out for an evening of really, solid swing—either listening or dancing, whichever you prefer. What band would you take for the full evening? Okay, put it down for first." But what if you want "some pretty music, remembering of course, all the time that you're a musician," music that "you could take your best girl to and really get into a mellow mood by listening to stuff that would satisfy you musically too"? This would be your choice for a "sweet" band. The final category, "favorite of all," let readers put down their "three favorite bands, whether they play mostly swing or mostly sweet, or whether they play some of each."[55] The writing is strongly gendered and conveys a strong sense that "sweet" music is effeminate and, maybe, feminizing. (It is good, high-quality music that a man could take his "best girl" to.) Nonetheless, it is significant that a major national music publication treats "swing" and "sweet" as part of a larger dance band experience. Regardless of how a band played, *Metronome* is asking its readers to help determine what musicians were playing "the finest dance music existing today." In fact, bands such as the Glenn Miller Orchestra and the Casa Loma Orchestra consistently polled high in *both* hot and sweet categories.[56]

After achieving fame in 1927, Guy Lombardo and His Royal Canadians became perhaps the embodiment of "sweet dance" music. Their sedate, saxophone-heavy arrangements of pop tunes featured virtually no solo improvisation, riffs, or driving swing rhythms. But "sweet" was also relative: next to a society dance band that played quadrilles and waltzes, Lombardo's group was distinctly jazz-inflected. The Royal

Canadians might not sound much like jazz or swing to us today, but their music was undeniably modern and part of a larger popular music landscape that had been profoundly influenced by black musical practices, especially 1920s-era jazz. In reality, most bands featured a mix of "sweet" and "hot." In the 1920s Paul Whiteman's jazz orchestra famously featured one of the best "hot" improvisers of the day, white cornetist Bix Beiderbecke. Black bandleader Andy Kirk, remembering his band's heyday in the 1930s, spoke fondly of the waltzes and ballads his band played so well. In fact, it was a sweet ballad, "Until the Real Thing Comes Along," featuring the smooth vocals and falsetto of Pha Terrell, that became the band's signature tune when it broke into the mainstream dance band world.[57] Much jazz historical writing and criticism does not fully address the ambiguous usages of sweet and hot to describe the music of black and white bands of these years.[58] Although these terms were powerful discursive formulations that shaped musical understandings, they did not necessarily reflect the actual musical diversity of the era.

This pervasive mixture of musical, racial, and commercial concerns in the reception of jazz is key to understanding the predilection of the Casino Ballroom owners for particular bands. They could easily have hired black bands to play sweetly—many black bands were highly versatile and able to accommodate the needs of any audience. If patrons wanted waltzes or polkas, professional bands would provide them.[59] As Elijah Wald has noted, commercial pressures and rigid racial expectations often made it difficult for black musicians to record sweet arrangements they were proud of.[60] Furthermore, there is evidence that many black listeners of the time greatly enjoyed the sounds of bands such as Guy Lombardo and Paul Whiteman that played familiar Tin Pan Alley melodies to sedate rhythms.[61]

Despite this complexity, the discursive connections between race and hotness were strong because the roots of this formulation extended deep into nineteenth-century United States history. In the final chapter of *Lying Up a Nation*, Ronald Radano traces the creation of the idea of hot black rhythm to nineteenth-century accounts of British travelers in Africa. Radano explains how American writers of the nineteenth and early twentieth centuries fixated on intense and dynamic rhythm as the central characteristic of black music in the United States. Hotness was rhythm, and rhythm was blackness. This association would, in the interwar years, serve both the celebrants and the critics of jazz dance band music.[62] Radano's discussion usefully suggests that even if no hot bands played at the Casino Ballroom (black or white), their music was still "present" as the necessary other: "Claims of black essence presume white ones too." The discursive creation of black music was inextricably part of the "broader emergence of race in American public history and culture."[63] Hiring appropriate music for the Casino Ballroom was part of an ongoing process of separating white musical sounds from black ones.[64]

The Santa Catalina Island Company (SCIC), as operator of the ballroom, was explicitly concerned not only with who came to the ballroom, but with what they heard there. Their need to control the sounds of the Casino Ballroom was in part a response to a larger social and economic trend: the rapid growth of new dance venues across the country that were more inclusive and, in some cases, racially integrated. The growing popularity of "hotter" jazz meant that many whites, especially in large urban centers, sought out black bands and predominantly black venues. This created genuine opportunities for cross-racial interaction and the breaking of taboos, particularly interracial dancing.[65] As historian David Stowe writes, "The conventions of ballrooms and dance halls themselves changed in important ways during the swing years. With the repeal of Prohibition in 1933, nightclubs began to lose the covert, illicit quality that had characterized them during the 1920s and became acceptable and popular in regions and small cities that earlier would have resisted them." As a result, these old and new venues "became more inclusive, more open to a range of class backgrounds, and, perhaps most significant, more racially integrated, at least in certain large cities."[66]

In a letter dated July 5, 1932, David M. Renton, William Wrigley's confidant and general manager of the SCIC, wrote to J. C. Houck, father of bandleader Curt Houck, who had recently performed at the ballroom.[67] The elder Houck was a Los Angeles businessman and an acquaintance of William Wrigley, and Renton's tone is casual. The letter details the great success of Curt's band—Renton claims that in the past two days 16,400 people danced to the band's music—and suggests that the ballroom engagement could lead to bigger things, a chance to "get his name before the public, as a real Catalina dance orchestra."[68] Renton specifically mentions the band's sound: "The music is just what I have been trying to get for the past few years; it does not have the blare that a great many bands do, and goes well with the acoustics of the Casino." Renton's use of "blare" strongly suggests that the Houck band played a more tempered dance music, toning down the raucous timbres of hotter bands. It was these hot timbres—the growling sounds of trumpets played with plunger mutes, the sharp, syncopated, staccato attack of ensemble horn passages—that intimately tied big band jazz to its roots in African American musical practices.[69] By 1932, jazz had indisputably entered American popular music, infusing other styles of popular music with its characteristics. But it was still an edgy music that had to be tamed before it achieved widespread acceptance into the white middle and upper classes.[70]

Renton's comment that Houck's music "goes well with the acoustics" suggests further that for the management of the ballroom there was a particular kind of music that fit the building. Although bands of eleven to fifteen musicians could be very loud, in an era of cruder electrical amplification (the ballroom was initially built with microphones installed) it is hard to imagine that the ballroom would have been unable to handle the volume of certain dance bands.[71] Acoustical appropriateness seems to stand in for more general requirements of musical aesthetics, social propriety, and morality.

The suggestion of an appropriate music for the space was clearly put into practice during the 1930s. The groups hired all conformed to Renton's dislike of "blare." After 1934, when Philip Wrigley installed the remote radio transmission wire, the ballroom began booking national name bands rather than local musicians.[72] Wrigley became friendly with the bandleaders who played the ballroom—another indication of the close ear the Catalina Island owners and management kept on the music of their cultural centerpiece.[73] With the exception of Benny Goodman in 1940 and Bob Crosby in both 1940 and 1941, all the bands that played the ballroom from 1934 until the Casino was closed during World War II were known primarily as sweet bands or resided well on the sweet end of the hot-to-sweet spectrum.[74] Table 1.1 lists the bands featured in the ballroom through World War II.[75]

But the issue of appropriateness extended beyond just the sounds allowed, to the management of the people in the ballroom themselves. Even after the repeal of Prohibition, the Casino did not offer alcoholic drinks until 1948. According to Patricia Moore, under William Sr. and his son, the Casino was operated with "utmost propriety": a strict dress code prevailed, requiring jackets and ties for men and skirts or dresses for women. A special law enforcement officer was stationed at the Casino to deal with any drunken or rowdy behavior.

A floor manager also policed the ballroom to make sure dancers kept "proper" distance from their partners. It was a practice that explicitly sought to contain any potential eruptions of public sexual behavior unleashed by the music.[76] With a growing number of youth adopting black vernacular dance styles such as the Lindy Hop, such close

Table 1.1 Bands at the Casino Ballroom, 1929–41

1929	Frank Hobbs and the Hotel Saint Catherine Orchestra
	Maurice Menge and the El Patio-Catalina Orchestra
1930	Frank Hobbs and the Catalina Concert Orchestra
1931	Frank Hobbs and the Catalina Concert Orchestra
1932	Curt Houck and His Orchestra
1933	Hal Rees and His Orchestra
1934	Irving Aaronson and His Commanders
	Jan Garber and His Orchestra
	Hal Grayson and His Orchestra
1935	Ben Bernie and His Orchestra
	Jan Garber and His Orchestra
	Buddy Rogers and His Orchestra
	Frank Sortino Orchestra*
	Capolungo Orchestra
1936	Little Jack Little and His Orchestra
	Jan Garber and His Orchestra
1937	Dick Jurgens and His Orchestra
	Jan Garber and His Orchestra
	Herbie Kay and His Orchestra
1938	Roger Pryor and His Orchestra
	Dick Jurgens and His Orchestra
	Ted Weems and His Orchestra
1939	Kay Kyser and His Orchestra
	Ted Weems and His Orchestra
	Freddy Martin and His Orchestra
1940	Kay Kyser and His Orchestra
	Benny Goodman and His Orchestra
	Dick Jurgens and His Orchestra
	Bob Crosby and the Bob Cats
1941	Ray Noble and His Orchestra
	Dick Jurgens and His Orchestra
	Hal Grayson and His Orchestra
	Bob Crosby and the Bob Cats

*Both Frank Sortino and the Capolungo orchestras played, from 1935 through the beginning of World War II, at yearly benefits sponsored by President Roosevelt for the fight against infantile paralysis. Moore, *Casino*, 92.
Source: Information compiled from Patricia Ann Moore, *The Casino: Catalina Island's "Two Million Dollar Palace of Pleasure,"* rev. ed. (Catalina Island: Catalina Island Museum Society, 2002), 29–36, 85–114.

surveillance was also closely tied to anxieties over racial identity and mixing.[77] Lew Oesterle was the official responsible for this through the middle to late 1930s. The *Catalina Islander* describes him as stern in enforcing "dance routine regulations" but generally liked for his geniality and "suave manner" in fulfilling his duties.[78] Oesterle himself described the atmosphere of his dance floor:

When you dance at the Casino, you will be impressed by the atmosphere of refinement, for the good manners on the part of the dancers constitute part of the enjoyable time had by each guest. The policy of the Casino Management stresses courtesy for all and this is why visitors to Santa Catalina Island, both young and old alike, find at the Casino an atmosphere that insures the pleasantest of enjoyable evenings as well as Sunday afternoons from 2 until 4 o'clock.[79]

Control over the ballroom experience—visual, sonic, and corporeal—was never total. As in the photo documenting the opening of the Casino Ballroom, racial others do appear at the margins.

A 1936 gossip column called "Doings at the Casino" contains a striking throwaway description of two "Harlem Boys" tucked between statements about bandleader Jan Garber's fashion sense and descriptions of celebrity visitors: "Known as 'Dutch,' the Bachelor's Club's houseboy, and 'Nathan,' Jan Garber's personal valet, [the two 'Harlem Boys'] did their stuff last Saturday night with a 'Trucking' contest held on the stage at the Ballroom. Jan says they both won."[80]

Like the young African Americans photographed at the 1929 opening, the episode recounted is another reminder that blacks were present on the island. Although black entertainers were not engaged at the ballroom, two young workers could briefly claim the spotlight. The tightly controlled experience—Oesterle's prudish remarks and strict rules, the alcohol policy, the physical exclusion of racial others—has a parallel in the actual music played there. Which sounds were welcomed, and how did they differ from those that were not? What was it about the sounds and technical workings of certain white sweet bands that made them attractive to the owners and management of the ballroom? To answer these questions we must explore in some detail how sweet dance music worked in relation to the hotter sounds it was so often compared with.

Avalon as Sound

Though the song "Avalon" (1920) preceded the Casino Ballroom's construction, the Santa Catalina Island Company adopted it as an unofficial anthem for the island. The song became an integral part of a tourist's experience. Songwriter Vincent Rose composed the music for "Avalon," with B. G. DeSylva and singer Al Jolson collaborating on the lyrics. First introduced in Jolson's 1918 Broadway show *Sinbad*, a version was recorded by the singer for Columbia Records in 1920.[81] There is little information on the circumstances surrounding the song's genesis and its relation to the actual city of Avalon, though a brief 1936 article by Hollywood music writer Hal Holley suggests that Jolson bought the song for $5,000 after hearing Rose sing it while the two were playing golf at the Midwick Country Club.[82] Holley writes, "Jolson is said to have received $50,000 from the Wrigley interests alone for introducing that song."[83]

Jolson's first recording of the song sold very well and was among the most popular songs of 1920; other singers and bands soon recorded their own versions, including a successful version by Paul Whiteman and His Orchestra.[84] The tune remained popular throughout the decade and into the big band era; recordings were made by Helen Morgan, Teddy Wilson, Django Reinhardt, Kenny Baker, Harry James, Harry Reser, the Cliquot Eskimos, Benny Goodman, Jimmie Lunceford, and the Casa Loma Orchestra. The song is still often performed and recorded, though it does have a very "old" sound, out of tune with the more sophisticated melodic and harmonic developments of both later Tin Pan Alley and modern (bebop and post-bop) jazz.[85] Like many early Tin Pan Alley songs, it has verses that frame a thirty-two-bar AA[1]BC chorus, and recordings commonly dispense with the verses entirely.

Example 1.1 is a typical lead sheet featuring just the chords and melody to the chorus. Consisting almost exclusively of half notes on the strong beats (one and three), the chorus melody is straightforward rhythmically and harmonically: it is strongly diatonic, and each eight-bar phrase of the AA[1]BC structure begins with an upbeat on beat three of the previous measure. With the exception of the bridge, the melody's initial leap is followed by a stepwise scale ascent in half notes for two measures and a brief descent by quarter notes in the third measure. Melodically, the bridge follows the same profile (leap up and stepwise scale ascent and descent). And while the chorus bridge does provide a brief modulation to ii (Gm7), it feels much more like a preparation for the dominant chord (C7) in measure 24 than a real presentation of contrasting musical materials. The last eight measures provide some variation, avoiding that melodic leap in favor of a step down and tonic arpeggio up, but the general melodic outline sounds very similar to what came before.

The sameness of the melody throughout the chorus combined with the static, largely diatonic harmonic progression imparts a strong sense of uniformity over the entire thirty-two bars. There are few troublesome spots for an improviser to negotiate—no significant key changes, complex rhythms, or dramatic melodic shifts. Perhaps because of this very effective simplicity, the song has led a long life both as a popular vehicle for swing era big bands with their cutting-edge arrangements and New Orleans–style small jazz ensembles that favor simultaneous

Avalon

Example 1.1 Lead sheet for "Avalon." Words by Al Jolson and B. G. DeSylva, music by Vincent Rose 1920. (Renewed) Warner Bros., Inc. All rights outside the U.S. controlled by WB Music Corp. and Redwood Music Ltd. All Rights Reserved. Used by Permission of Alfred Publishing Co., Inc.

improvisation over a two-beat feel.[86] Its malleability meant "Avalon" lent itself to all sorts of reworkings by dance bands of the 1930s and '40s, and it could easily be made sweet or hot.

Below I will survey three commercially recorded versions of "Avalon," by Jimmie Lunceford and His Orchestra, the Casa Loma Orchestra, and Jan Garber and His Orchestra. The songs document a move from hot to sweet, in the language of the era. But close study reveals a more complex reality that the sweet and hot labels cannot completely encompass. Although all three bands spoke the distinctly modern language of big band dance music to a mass audience through the newest technologies of radio and recording, they presented different musical places with their own set of social relationships. Each of these "Avalons" presented a particular "momentary acoustic community"—a set of musical practices that enacted certain social relationships.[87] These musical relationships intersected with the larger cultural discourses on race and identity. In the case of Garber, his "Avalon" would prove an excellent match to the ideology of the real Avalon.

Jimmie Lunceford and Casa Loma's Hot "Avalon"

Many jazz historians and critics consider the Jimmie Lunceford band one of the most polished and hottest of all the African American bands of the era (George Simon called it "the most exciting big band of all time").[88] A strong leader who had little tolerance for mistakes, Lunceford set a high standard for extremely tight, error-free performances.[89] This musical polish was combined with a keen sense of showmanship; the brass section pioneered the use of derby hats as plunger substitutes, a stage technique that was quickly adopted by other bands such as Glenn Miller's Orchestra.[90] Though the group enjoyed its greatest success from about 1938 through 1941, the band continued playing, weathering many personnel changes, until Lunceford's premature death in 1947 from a heart attack.[91]

The Lunceford band's "Avalon" is a striking arrangement for its 1935 recording date, in part because of its adventurous digressions from the conventional Tin Pan Alley form.[92] As was typical of the group, the performance emphasizes impressive ensemble work over individual solos. Column 1 of table 1.2 summarizes the most important elements of the recording. Just a quick glance at the chart shows just how many interruptions arranger (and guitarist on the recording) Eddie Durham has inserted into the expected cycles of the AA[1]BC form. In the first chorus, a four-measure connecting passage overlaps with preceding material creating an odd number of measures (see chorus 1, C, table 1.2). A little later Durham writes another four-bar intrusion that connects the third and fourth choruses while also changing the rhythmic feel. Perhaps most dizzying of all, the final chorus is abruptly short-circuited and transformed into an elaborate tag that brings the tune to a blazing conclusion. The record also features the band's trademark rhythmic feel of two strong beats to a measure: "the Lunceford two-beat."[93] As the tune develops, the two-feel gives way to a more driving four beats to the measure. The gradual replacement of the two-feel is part of the overall dramatic arc of the arrangement—as the ensemble passages become more virtuosic and the pace of the musical activity quickens, the shift to a driving 4/4 rhythm greatly enhances the drama.

The recording is a constant interplay of part and whole, individual and collective, section and ensemble. The introduction sets up the aesthetic priorities: from the opening notes, the recording establishes a dramatic contrast of instrumental colors and players. The very first sound we hear is the high "ping" of the pianist striking F octaves (F5 and F6), followed almost immediately by horns and reeds entering with the rising, harmonized melody. Just as quickly, the horns drop out, leaving an unusual solo spot for the electric guitar. Responding to the guitar's chordal solo, the horns and reeds reenter with their melody, and Durham responds with another chordal statement. Over the next four measures the back and forth between guitar and horns moves faster—from two bars to one bar apiece—and the conversation spills over the bar lines.

It is a striking and dizzying opening with its barrage of shifting instrumental voices played with heavy syncopation against a strong underlying pulse. As an opening it synoptically introduces the Lunceford band's approach to the tune and its particular musical priorities: texture, rhythmic flexibility, call-and-response, and precision. Surprisingly, the melody is interpreted in a very straightforward way—the arrangement sticks close to the original sheet music's unsyncopated half notes (though they do rhythmically compress the written phrase endings). However, from the pickup to the bridge until the end of the chorus, Durham's arrangement departs more and more from the written music. The increasing use of syncopation is combined with shorter rhythmic values to create a small climax in the last A section. The remainder of the performance is an expansion of that first minute—a vigorous dialogue between section and soloist, rhythm instruments and melody instruments, two-feel and four-feel.

Table 1.2 Comparison of three recorded performances of "Avalon"

Lunceford	Casa Loma	Garber
Recorded Sept. 30, 1935 Total time—3:01 Bpm—224	Recorded Aug. 16, 1934 Total time—2:53 Bpm—237	Recorded Sept. 16, 1937 Total time—2:53 Bpm—132
12 mm. intro: 2 ensemble/ 2 guitar; 2 ensemble/ 2 guitar; 1 ensemble/ 1 guitar/ 1 ensemble/ 1 guitar	Chorus 1: Melody statement A: two-beat feel for entire chorus	4 mm. intro
Chorus 1: Melody statement A; two-beat feel, muted trumpets state melody	A¹: same	Chorus 1: Melody statement A: harmonized saxes and piano obbligato
A¹	B: same	A¹
B	C: last two measures of section ensemble break, and begin solo	B: muted trumpets
C ensemble break mm. 7-8; four-bar bridge to next chorus overlaps with last A section creating three-measure addition to form	Chorus 2 A: switch to four-beat feel; trumpet solo	C: harmonized saxes
Chorus 2 A: trombones take whole chorus	A₁	Verse sixteen measures; chromatic descent leads back to chorus
A¹	B	Chorus 2: Melody statement A: Vocalist sings entire chorus
B	C: mm. 7-8 of last A feature another ensemble break but now followed by four-bar bridge section to next chorus	A¹
C: break for measures 7 and 8	Chorus 3 A: tenor saxophone solo for entire chorus	B
Chorus 3 A: alto sax solo	A¹	C
A¹	B	C repeated for tag; ritardando for end
B: plunger-muted trumpet	C	
C: tenor sax solo; end of eight-measure section is elided with . . .	Chorus 4 A: clarinet solo for entire chorus	

(continued)

Table 1.2 (*continued*)

Lunceford	Casa Loma	Garber
six-bar bridge; change to driving four-beat feel after two measures	A¹	
Chorus 4 A: melody by muted horn	B	
A¹: same	C	
B: alto sax solo	Chorus 5: Melody out A: ensemble	
C: four-measure horn "pyramid" without rhythm section that leads into extended twenty-four-measure "tag" divided into eight-, four-, five-, and seven-measure units	A¹	
	B	
	C: mm.7-8 of this section feature ensemble break, two-measure repetition	

Sources: Jimmie Lunceford and His Orchestra, "Avalon," The Original Decca Recordings, *An Anthology of Big Band Swing, 1930–1955*, Decca/GRP GRD-2–629 (2 CDs), 1993; Glen Gray and the Casa Loma Orchestra, "Avalon," *Best of the Brunswick Years, 1932–1934*, Collectibles, Sony Music Entertainment COL-CD-7574, 2004; and Jan Garber and His Orchestra, "Avalon," Jan Garber, *"The Idol of the Air Lanes" and His Orchestra: A Melody from the Sky*, Living Era CD AJA 5326, 2004.

These musical characteristics are practices that scholars such as Olly Wilson, Samuel Floyd, and others define as African American. Lunceford's "Avalon" employs nearly all the elements of Samuel Floyd's "master trope of Call-Response": a musical-rhetorical notion characterized by "calls, cries, whoops, and hollers; call-and-response, elision, pendular and blue thirds, musical expressions, vocal imitations by instruments, and parlando; multimeter, crossrhythms, and interlocking rhythms."[94] Whether this is an example of "true" black music is less important than that the characteristics Floyd uses in his definition neatly summarize the kinds of musical devices that listeners of the period used to determine the racial identity of the era's music. And while the definition of black jazz varied over time (and from place to place), the Lunceford recording clearly represented one significant pole in the spectrum of black jazz to white jazz. For a white band to feature this kind of arrangement of a Tin Pan Alley song was to align itself with a general, if always amorphous, black musical identity. The Lunceford recording is thus a helpful benchmark to help us understand what musical dimensions listeners used to identify the race of a specific performance.

For their recording made a year earlier in 1934, Glen Gray and the Casa Loma Orchestra take a slightly different approach. While selectively holding on to certain key musical practices, the Casa Loma band aims for a milder version that tones down the musical breaks and interruptions and lightens the driving rhythm and attack. Like the Lunceford band, the Casa Loma Orchestra features prominently in most histories of jazz dance bands.[95] Its "Casa Loma Stomp," recorded and released in 1930, is considered a major forerunner of swing—Gunther Schuller calls the song "the full-blown progenitor of hundreds of swing-style offspring."[96] It was the first band of its kind to appear on a commercial radio series, the *Camel Caravan*, and its mix of hotter up-tempo numbers with languid ballads proved immensely popular to a diverse American audience.[97] Many members of the group owned a share of the band, an effort at collectivity that was unusual for the industry. Whereas all dance bands needed to be flexible in terms of musical style, the Casa Loma band truly straddled the sweet-hot divide, polling consistently in both categories in magazines such as *Down Beat* and *Metronome*.[98]

From the first notes, the Casa Loma band reveals different musical priorities. The arrangement (probably by the band's primary arranger Gene Gifford) dispenses with an introduction and begins with the "Avalon" melody. Featuring just muted horns and rhythm section, the opening is rather minimalist for a group of fourteen musicians. The rhythmic feel is similar to the "Lunceford two-beat," but much of the rest of performance is very different. First, the Casa Loma performance is less fragmented—the opening statement of the melody is played entirely by the horns, with no commentary from the reeds. The sense of wholeness and ensemble unity is emphasized by the larger formal structure. With the exception of a few two-bar breaks at the end of choruses and a brief four-bar connecting passage between choruses 2 and 3, the arrangement rarely digresses from the cyclical AA^{1}BC structure of the song. Unlike the rapid back-and-forth of the Lunceford recording, the Casa Loma arrangement gives entire choruses to solo instrumental improvisations (trumpet in chorus 2, tenor sax in chorus 3, clarinet in chorus 4, all shown in table 1.2).

Listening closely to the Casa Loma interpretation of Vincent Rose's melody alongside the Lunceford version reveals some subtle but essential differences. First, the Casa Loma reading, from the opening bar to the end of the first chorus, is uniformly syncopated with shorter rhythmic values—all the half notes of the sheet music have been compressed into quarter notes and eighth notes. Despite all this rhythmic activity, this interpretation is just noticeably smoother—not legato, but the attacks are less front-heavy than those of the Lunceford band (the Casa Lomans do not lean so heavily on the beginning of the note, but spread the force throughout it).

The Casa Lomans toned down the edgier musical techniques associated with the hottest bands. Hotter sounds, as Miller explained, brought you closer to authentic black music, and to unpolished, straightforward emotional expression. As Renton might have put it, the Casa Lomans had less "blare." They also play the song with far fewer disruptions and reconfigurations. The Casa Loma version represented a tentative reaching out and recognition of a complex culture deeply implicated in the African American experience. As Lewis Erenberg writes, "In making black music the basis of swing, white musicians and bandleaders—as well as audiences who accepted the music—expanded the definition of American culture."[99] In their deliberate mixture of hot and sweet playing, they combined black-identified sounds and rhythms with the musical styles of the famous sweet white bands led by Paul Whiteman and Guy Lombardo. The Casa Loma band seems to recognize the difference between a Guy Lombardo and a Jimmie Lunceford band, but also the strong connections and cross-relationships. Song titles such as "White Jazz" and "Black Jazz" (discussed in the introduction) suggest the band's awareness of socially constructed racial differences.[100] Yet, despite the players' comfort with different dance band styles, the Casa Loma band was too hot for the Casino Ballroom.

Jan Garber's Sweet "Avalon"

Despite their tremendous popularity and commercial success during the 1930s and '40s, Jan Garber and His Orchestra have mostly vanished from chronicles of American music and jazz. With just a few exceptions, the group's recordings are out of print, and you have to look very hard—in the case of George Simon's encyclopedia *The Big Bands*, literally at the fine print—even to find the band named, let alone discussed in any detail.[101] Most of Garber's output was of the sweet variety, and in the vast majority of the band's recordings there is just a hint of the rhythmic drive, exciting arranging, or improvisational skill that we now associate with the great swing bands. The groups who made this sweet dance music—and there were many, many of them—have largely been ignored or dismissed by jazz historians. The situation is somewhat understandable: this music contains few of the musical markers of hot jazz or swing and seems to have little connection to any hot band, white or black, whether it be Benny Goodman's, Harry James's, Bob Crosby's, Duke Ellington's, or Jimmie Lunceford's. Jan Garber, though, is the exception that proves the rule—while most of his output was mid-tempo ballads that were primarily vehicles for his baritone, Lee Bennett, he could also play hotter if the occasion demanded. George Simon called Garber the "Dr. Jekyll and Mr. Hyde" of bandleaders. In fact, most sweet bands played a mixture of styles. Successful bands were those that catered to their audiences.[102]

Born at the turn of the century, Garber began his career as a classical violinist. After returning from a tour of duty during the First World War, he formed a small "jazz" band modeled after groups like the Original Dixieland Jazz Band—piano, bass, and drums, with himself on violin. When he combined forces with another bandleader, Milton Davis, the group suddenly grew to fifteen musicians and—moving away from the New Orleans approach—changed its sound to match the other popular white jazz dance bands of the time. While far from what we understand today as jazz, these groups were nonetheless clearly understood by vast numbers of Americans to be jazz bands, even if they did feature strings and played dance tunes without the driving rhythm or improvisation of their black counterparts.

About 1933 Garber met a Canadian alto sax player and bandleader struggling to shape an American career. Garber proposed a deal that would merge the groups. This new band became the foundation for the most successful incarnation of the Garber Orchestra, a band that would see significant financial success for the next several decades. Sensing that musical tastes were shifting, Garber again radically overhauled the musical direction of the group, moving away from the hot, brass-dominated numbers to a more mellow, rhythmically subdued, vocal-orientated approach modeled after Guy Lombardo's Orchestra, at the time the leader of the sweet dance bands and one of the most successful groups in the nation. While Garber also employed a series of female vocalists, his male singer, Lee Bennett, proved a consistently bankable star. The more subdued dance music of Garber's group was especially popular in the Midwest and the West, and the group achieved its greatest successes in these areas of the country. But the band clearly had a national appeal and secured high-paying and high-profile gigs at many of the country's premier dance venues: New Orleans's Roosevelt Hotel Blue Room, Memphis's Peabody Hotel Skyway, Chicago's Trianon Ballroom, and Los Angeles' Biltmore Bowl. The Trianon Ballroom, with its live radio feed, proved especially beneficial to the band, helping to spread its music across the United States. Garber at one point also held the record for appearances at Catalina's Casino Ballroom.[103] The band's great popularity led to several movie appearances and return gigs on several national radio shows like *The Burns and Allen Program*.

A savvy businessman and measurer of public taste, Garber shifted musical gears yet again after 1941 and began playing hot jazz for the swing-oriented audiences, now made up of thousands of young GIs. Now a true "swing" band, "barely discernable from the others of its ilk," Garber jettisoned the smooth male baritone and hired Liz Tilton along with a new arranger and a younger group of musicians.[104] Although he was successful during these years, Garber's star had dropped considerably—competition in the hot band market was especially stiff with so many polished outfits like Glenn Miller, the Dorsey brothers, and Benny Goodman (not to mention Cab Calloway, Duke Ellington, and Count Basie). Sensing yet again that tastes were changing, Garber returned to his Guy Lombardo style, hoping for a return to former glory. Enlarging the band and sweetening the sound, Garber again proved very successful, and while most of the hot groups disbanded or limped on into the 1950s, Garber's Orchestra survived remarkably well by returning to its loyal fan base in the Midwest and touring throughout the 1950s and '60s. From early jazz through the swing era, past bop and on into the era of rock 'n' roll, Garber's band's not only survived but made a handsome living playing a shifting variety of jazz-inflected dance band styles. Like so many other resilient American popular artists, Garber ended his music career in Las Vegas. During his time in Nevada he also developed a successful side business in horse shows. Even Garber's death in 1977 did not dampen his music's continuing popularity: Dick Wickman, a small bandleader from the Midwest, purchased the bandleader's library and successfully toured the country using the Garber name for several years and playing the band's old charts.

After his emergence to national prominence in the early 1930s, Garber ran a tight ship, demanding high levels of professionalism from his players. His nickname, "the Idol of the Air Lanes," became a brand name denoting professionalism. Despite his strictness (no drinking was allowed during working hours), Garber paid well, and his musicians stayed with him much longer than was typical. The band's finances let them travel by train when possible (for instance, between major cities), and the comfortable traveling conditions no doubt helped maintain a stable personnel. In his liner notes to an album of previously unreleased Garber radio transcriptions, Leo Walker suggests that the bandleader was one of the men who "contributed the most to elevating the dance band business to the level of big business which it attained during the '30s and '40s and maintained into the '50s."[105] The Garber band operated like a small corporation, its leader enforcing discipline, professionalism, and a strong consumer orientation. And this combination of attitudes is another reason Garber has not survived well in the literature on jazz. With its shifting musical styles and corporate bearing, the band patently defies any notion of autonomous art or music for music's sake. Garber's orchestra not only lacks many of the prized musical characteristics of jazz (or the post-1935 genre of swing), it also lacks that more amorphous aesthetic ideology that has become such a pervasive part of jazz criticism and historical writing.

After exploring the band's history, one fact is very clear: the Garber Orchestra was, at several times during the late 1920s, 1930s, and 1940s, indisputably a "jazz" band. Garber's musical flexibility not only demonstrates that he was intimately familiar with the jazz idiom as it was practiced in these decades, but further reminds us just how implicated in jazz practice all the dance bands were. If bands like Dick Jurgens, Freddy Martin, Guy Lombardo, and Jan Garber seemed (and still appear to be) far from the "real" jazz of the period, it is only because they are, in fact, much closer than detractors probably care to acknowledge. These bands looked the same on stage—nicely dressed in sharp uniforms—had the same orchestration (trombones, trumpets, horns, and rhythm section), and frequently played many of the same songs (though with very different arrangements). Seeing how the Garber band, in its Guy Lombardo way, handled the same music as Jimmie Lunceford or the Casa Loma Orchestra helps us see much more clearly what this music might have meant for the listeners and the musicians who were playing it.

"Avalon" as Sweet Groove

Jan Garber and His Orchestra recorded their version of "Avalon" for Brunswick in Los Angeles on September 16, 1937. The recording features a fairly straightforward arrangement of the song with a vocal performance by Russ Brown (along with Lee Bennett, one of Garber's featured singers). It is a relaxed rendition that emphasizes understated rhythms and breathy saxophone melodies. A brief introduction—a descending figure by trumpets with reeds over a bass pedal on C (V in the recording's key of F)—leads quickly into the song proper, a full ensemble treatment of the AA¹BC chorus. With gentle harmonizing reed support, saxophones play a vibrato-heavy version of the melody. Short bell-like piano fills of arpeggios and scale fragments complement the mellow reeds. Along with saxophones and piano, an upright bass fills the rest of the musical space with half notes. The sax playing, the waves of unobtrusive tinkling piano fills, and the bowed bass combine to create a sense of sonic fullness—not crowded, but comfortably occupied. The mid-tempo performance (quarter note = 132 bpm) feels relaxed despite all the musical activity. A full sound blankets any possible openings in the musical texture.

Unlike the Lunceford and Casa Loma recordings, where the rise and fall of the melody contrasts with the rhythm section's insistent and energetic two-feel, the Garber band articulates the rhythms very differently. For many jazz historians the transition from the small group jazz of the 1920s to the big band style of the mid-1930s was focused in large part on a transformation in the approach to rhythm—a change in the *swing* feel (not to be confused with "swing" as a name for the historical style of the era's jazz). With the gradual substitution of the string bass for the tuba beginning about 1930, bands could more smoothly articulate the underlying 4/4 pulse, placing relatively equal emphasis on each beat. This created a more driving, forward-directed rhythm than the "oompah," one-two, sound of small jazz bands of the 1920s.[106]

Generally speaking, this is basically accurate. Comparing a King Oliver recording from 1923 and a Count Basie recording from 1937 reveals distinctly different approaches to marking the underlying pulse. But if we listen more closely, these generalizations become less reliable. Both the Lunceford and the Casa Loma recordings discussed earlier feature what most historians and musicologists would identify as a "swing" rhythmic feel, notated like this ♩ ♫♩ ♫ but played more like this, ♩ ♫♩ ♫ with the eighth notes "stretched." This rhythm has a forward-directed motion and bounce to it, and it was part of jazz at least since it was recorded in the late teens and twenties. Yet, in practice, a swing rhythm could vary tremendously—there are, as jazz musicians have long recognized—many ways to swing.[107] Although all the musicians are involved in creating the global rhythmic feel, it is the rhythm section—bassist, drummer, piano or guitar or both—that is most central.

In their versions of "Avalon," the Lunceford and Casa Loma rhythm sections both play a version of the modern smoothed out "swing" rhythm that gradually began to define the jazz style of the 1930s and '40s. But *how* they each play this rhythm, how they *swing*, is strikingly different. The Lunceford band alternates dramatically between a clipped "two-beat" feel and a driving four-beat one. (See the book's conclusion for a lengthier analysis of the Lunceford "two-beat.") A clear distinction is made between the two "feels": in the first, the bass player strikes only beats one and three, but in the four-beat feel the bassist "walks," plucking notes on all four beats of the measure. Except for the statement of the melody, the Casa Lomans play a four-beat feel, and although the bass player walks, the drummer clearly accents beats two and four. What we hear is a walking bass line articulating all four beats of the measure with a drummer accenting the second and fourth "backbeats": a 4/4 rhythm we can also describe as at least partly a "two-beat" feel. Thus we shouldn't generalize too far when claiming that 1920s jazz bands played in "two" and swing bands in "four." The new dance bands that emerged in the 1930s played in two-beat and four-beat feels, but also in ways that combined the two or inflected the rhythm in idiosyncratic ways.

In jazz historical writing, the notion of "swing"—defined as jazz's characteristic approach to rhythm—is used in very different ways for very different rhetorical and analytical purposes. Many jazz writers often use "swing" as an implicit criterion for distinguishing authentic from spurious jazz.[108] To avoid bringing into the discussion the term's evaluative connotations (as well as all its other rhetorical baggage), it is helpful to employ a broader idea: *groove*. Groove is the word musicians and writers most often use to describe a band's or a performance's rhythmic feel or character. The term is usually reserved for music that exemplifies a solid, infectious rhythmic feel, that demonstrates what Charlie Keil would call "vital drive."[109] It is a positive term usually denoting something prized, and something that affects listeners in an immediate and visceral way. "Groove" music is music for dancing.

Ethnomusicologist Steven Feld, following Keil, offers a broader notion that embraces more than just rhythm or even music: "In the vernacular a 'groove' refers to an intuitive sense of style as process, a perception of a cycle in motion, a form or organizing pattern being revealed, a recurrent clustering of elements through time." Grooves are processes, and they are created in real time through "feelingful participation."[110] A groove, in its fullest experiential sense, is not notatable—it exists only in and through performance. Listeners attuned to this dimension of the musical experience find deep satisfaction in hearing and feeling the subtle differences in what might otherwise seem a very repetitive musical framework. By being receptive to this particular mode of listening—one that focuses on "timing inflections and tiny timbral nuances"—listeners participate in a groove's creation.[111] The joy and excitement of groove music is reveling in the predictable unpredictability, the "productive dissymmetry" of the rhythm's articulation and rearticulation.[112] Small changes surprise us but do not disrupt; the variations work to reaffirm the underlying solidity of the rhythmic feel.[113]

The use of the word "groove" in a specifically musical context likely originated in the African American community. Although today the word most often describes black musical styles such as funk or hip-hop, the term was around in the thirties and forties, and we can usefully apply it as a way to talk about a range of approaches to rhythmic feels by dance bands of that time.[114] Swing, as a rhythmic practice, is a type of groove. The concept might have originated as an insider's description of black musical practices, but it is a useful way to analyze all types of popular music from the era, including sweet bands that, to critics of the time (and to historians of today) did not swing—or groove—in a way we might recognize. Sweet bands such as Jan Garber's were successful in part because they created a groove that audiences responded to. This sweet swing rhythm is closer to the characteristic driving, 4/4 swing rhythmic feel than most musicologists and historians recognize. These bands often employed the signature jazz rhythmic pattern (presented above) and similarly marked the 4/4 pulse in a more even fashion than bands of the 1920s.

Given the frequent disparagement of many of these dance orchestras by historians and jazz critics over the years, it is worth pointing out that the successful sweet dance bands of the 1930s and '40s, such as those led by Guy Lombardo and Jan Garber, did what they did extremely well and were celebrated by listeners and sympathetic critics for their high level of craft. Making a sweet band "work" musically—pleasing dancers and listeners—meant careful attention to *all* the musical details, including the groove. In a brief essay from the mid-1930s, bandleader Guy Lombardo elaborates on his approach to rhythmic feel. He writes about "sticking to his guns" during the band's early years in the mid-1920s when promoters repeatedly asked him to play faster and closer in style to the hot jazz so popular at the moment. Holding his ground, Lombardo worked closely with his band to perfect its sound. And one of the keys to this was the players' approach to rhythm: "The fact is that we play a faster tempo than most realize. We do a chorus for instance, that runs a minute and half ordinarily in 55 seconds. Our tempo is really fast but there is no rhythm under it, no accented beats which imitators usually put in. *That makes the difference"* (italics in the original).[115] As purveyor of the same style of music, Lombardo's comments also describe well the groove of the Garber Orchestra.

Lombardo's assertion that there was no "rhythm under it" is not literally true, but it does suggest a particular approach to marking the pulse that, in contrast to the "hotter" styles, didn't strongly accent beats or groups of beats (such as one and three or two and four). This generally describes the Garber Orchestra's approach to rhythm, something we can hear in its recording of "Avalon." Similar to the Lunceford and Casa Loma recordings above, Garber's bassist plays in a two-feel, but the notes are much fuller than the playing on either the Lunceford or the Casa Loma recording. Even with the bassist's elongated half notes, the performance has a distinct and audible drive to it.

In an influential article titled "Motion and Feeling in Music," Charlie Keil argues that the most effective grooves result from a "discrepancy" between musicians, particularly bassists and drummers. Looking at bebop and post-bop bassists and drummers, Keil argues that the "discrepancy" between a "stringy" on top of the beat bass player and a behind the beat drummer creates the strongest groove.[116] A great deal of the Garber band's subtle rhythmic energy comes from the productive tension—the discrepancy—between the loose feeling of the bass player's long half notes that swell over and around the beat and the drummers' much sharper and more precise articulation of the four-beat pulse. Even if sweet dance band music of the thirties and forties is not conventionally understood as "groove" music, the Garber band has a distinctive and definable rhythmic feel that captivated many, many listeners. The players undeniably had their own groove.

As Lombardo mentions, the Garber groove is surprisingly fast (bpm = 132), but it *feels* slow. The groove enacts a particular sense of movement and mobility—steady, reliable, with a clear drive, but also substantial (those round, swelling bass notes) and relaxed. This is dance music, but it is not for jitterbuggers doing the Lindy Hop. It suggests body movements that are languid but precise, relaxed but with clear direction. In sum, this is the kind of movement, a sense of motion, that the managers and owners of the ballroom wanted, precisely because it aligned so well with their larger ideology. This is the sound of middle-class activity at an American resort—relaxed with focus and direction.

The Garber groove occupied one pole on the hot to sweet dance band spectrum. It was one *version* of the swing rhythm, albeit one that constructs a very different sense of motion. With Garber, most of the key musical markers of hotness have been greatly attenuated: the rhythm lacks the driving forward motion of the other two performances, the Tin Pan Alley song structure is rigidly obeyed, and the melody is played clearly with virtually no embellishments. For those contemporary listeners who were familiar with Garber's career, his band of the 1930s was a dramatic turn from his jazz groups of the 1920s—a switch from the hot sounds of New Orleans and Chicago to the sweet music of Guy Lombardo and His Royal Canadians. For those unaware of this trajectory, the music Garber made in the 1930s (until he went hot again in the early 1940s) was built on musical practices that were set up as deliberate contrasts to hot practices. Here the commonalities between dance bands play a central role: dressing a lot like the Lunceford and Casa Loma bands, the Garber band spoke the modern musical language of the day with a decidedly different accent. The band made sense only in relation to other groups, and with race and musical practice so intimately intertwined, it was deeply marked by the careful avoidance of racially freighted musical gestures.

Considered together, the Lunceford and Casa Loma bands create a musical "Avalon" that is far more open to other voices, far more willing to allow musical disruptions and digressions—to recognize in some way the complexities of American musical and racial identity. This is not to say that either band's music was a perfect sonic analogue to United States democracy or racial equality. Both bands were, in their different ways, participating in a debate that at the least employed similar frameworks. Perhaps it is not surprising that neither was welcomed at the Casino Ballroom. The music would have presented a challenge to the ideals of the venue and its developers. Garber's music was a logical fit, a sonic corollary to the modern social vision of the island. His "Avalon" is not escapist or a simple pandering to the demands of commerce, but a profound and uncomfortable disengagement with the fundamental hybridity of United States culture.

Nostalgia and Modernity

[verse] Ev'ry morn' my mem'ries stray
Across the sea where flying fishes play

And as the night is falling
I find myself recalling
That blissful all-enthralling day

[chorus, AA¹BC] I found my love in Avalon
Beside the bay
I left my love in Avalon
And sailed away
I dream of her and Avalon
From dusk till dawn
And so I think I'll travel on
To Avalon

[verse] Just before I sailed away
She said the word I longed to hear her say
I tenderly caressed her
Close to my heart I pressed her
Upon that golden yesterday

[chorus repeat]

After the statement of the melody, the Garber arrangement moves surprisingly to an instrumental version of the verse, unusual among the recordings in this discussion (and other versions from the era). The reintroduction of the verse is a deliberate gesture backward in time and a rejection of the efficient, streamlined versions of Lunceford and Casa Loma. Rather than stripping away excess musical baggage to feature more soloists or more elaborate section work, Garber adds back elements, deliberately weighing down the song with the past. The inclusion of the verse is, in part, a direct link to the famous version Jolson recorded in 1920. Furthermore, Russ Brown's singing contains just enough hints of Jolson's full, broad, and nasal voice to suggest that famous recording without re-creating it.

The presence of a singer obviously sets the Garber recording apart from both other examples, and it is the first performance that lets us hear some of the song's original words. Unabashedly sentimental, they tell of the anonymous narrator's happy memories of time spent in the resort town. Whereas the verses directly suggest the actual town of Avalon (in the first verse there is a reference to "flying fishes"—real creatures inhabiting the waters surrounding the island; the fish can glide substantial distances just above the water), the chorus tells us much of what we need to know. First, the song is a reminiscence of Avalon; it looks back in time. Second, the lyrics fuse romantic love and place, explicitly connecting the two ("I dream of her and Avalon"). Finally, the song is framed by movement, first away from the place of lost romance and then perhaps a return ("And so I think I'll travel on / To Avalon"). The song is a curious celebration of the city—rather than enumerating the island's modern offerings, the song's narrator reflects on a previous time and a moment of lost perfection. Since "every morn'" the narrator's memories stray, the song suggests that some time has passed since his island idyll, though it could be weeks, months, or even years. The ambiguous time frame of the events recounted further strengthens the song's nostalgic ambience.

The word nostalgia, as Svetlana Boym points out, is formed from two Greek roots—*nostos*, meaning "return home," and *algia*, meaning "longing." It was coined in a Swiss medical doctor's dissertation in the seventeenth century. Johannes Hofer was searching for an appropriate name for a melancholic condition that afflicted certain geographically displaced peoples he had encountered. From this medical origin the term passed into popular usage but has accumulated meanings that exceed the narrow definition first proposed: from missing a particular place, the term became more generalized to describe a yearning for another time—an era at odds with the present.[117]

Boym provides a helpful refinement of Kammen's "nostalgic modernism" and a more nuanced view of what the Catalina Island project was all about. According to Boym, "nostalgia is a rebellion against the modern idea of time" and, by extension, the modern world that invented it.[118] In fact, the very concept of nostalgia is "coeval with modernity itself." The two ideas "are like Jekyll and Hyde . . . alter egos."[119] Despite economic turmoil and global world wars, Americans of the first half of the twentieth century were at the forefront of modernization, their social practices and state policies driven by an underlying belief in rational organization and progress and characterized by industrialization and technological development.[120] Many scholars have adopted the moniker "machine age" to describe the United States of these years.[121] The nation was engaged in a large-scale debate—manifested in a wide range of cultural forms—on the benefits and drawbacks of such rapid social and economic change. For historian Lawrence Levine, "The central paradox of American history . . . has been a belief in progress coupled with a dread of change; an urge towards the inevitable future combined with a longing for the irretrievable past; a deeply ingrained belief in America's unfolding destiny and a haunting conviction that the nation was in a state of decline."[122] This paradox was particularly strong in the decades between the world wars, a period characterized by a wholesale embrace of modern life as well as a vicious backlash in the form of anti-immigration laws, racially motivated violence, anti-Semitism, and exclusionary nativist sentiment. One pervasive solution to these contradictions was an embrace of nostalgia. Americans of these years found "it easier to come to terms with the new if it could be surrounded somehow by the aura of the old."[123] The decade that produced the Empire State Building, streamlined trains, and the futuristic utopia of the 1939 World's Fair also brought to completion Colonial Williamsburg, an attempt to re-create a living colonial city.[124]

Much of the literature on dance band jazz has not dealt with the nostalgia permeating this cultural form, choosing rather to emphasize its embodiment of fast, urban machine-age culture.[125] But the conservative tendencies of the 1920s were not dropped wholesale in the face of the economic catastrophe of the Great Depression—there remained in many of the cultural productions of the time a profound ambivalence.[126] Whereas swing would explode into public consciousness in the mid-1930s, dance band jazz already had a comfortable niche in American popular music. The largely youth-driven development of swing had its origins in the emergence and growing popularity of jazz and social dancing at the turn of the century. Thus, just focusing on youth culture, or on post-1935 dance band jazz, obscures the participation of vast numbers of other Americans—many of them white and part of a growing urban middle class. It was in their responses and the responses the culture industry made to them that many of the era's most popular cultural forms took shape. Radio shows, the films of Frank Capra, the animation of Walt Disney, as well as sweet dance band jazz, all helped this segment of the United States make sense of a world in disorder.[127]

Looking just like the hippest, sleekest swing bands with their horn sections (no violins), snappy uniformed musicians, and precise, polished performances of popular tunes of the day, the Garber Orchestra was as modern as its hot compatriots. It made records, broadcast over the radio, and operated as an efficient modern business. It was unequivocally a product of what Adorno and Horkheimer famously called "the culture industry," in this case the increasingly consolidated, vertically integrated, and homogenized New York City music industry of radio, publishers, recording companies, and management agencies. Yet, dressed in the clothing of 1930s modernity, the Garber band played a music that embodied a hesitant and ambivalent embrace of the era, particularly as that involved engaging with African American life and culture.[128] In its recordings, exemplified by "Avalon," the Garber band attempted to manage some of the contradictions of American modernization, the big business of swing, and the music's "latent sense of racial experimentation."[129]

Nostalgia, though, is also about attachment to place, and the song is firmly grounded in the real Avalon on Catalina Island. Garber's orchestra was one of the most popular bands to play Catalina Island—it was a fixture of the Casino Ballroom through the 1930s. The music was a strong complement to the experience and ideology of the place, projecting an image of American modernity that was peaceful, secure, and grounded in a particular location.

In the coming years, playing just a few bars of "Avalon" would be enough to create a mood of pervasive nostalgia. In one of the most famous scenes from Michael Curtiz's 1942 film *Casablanca*, Ilsa (Ingrid Bergman) asks pianist Sam (Dooley Wilson) to play "some of the old songs." Sam complies by softly playing the chorus to "Avalon." Ilsa listens for a bit, then asks, "Where is Rick [Humphrey Bogart]?" Sam claims he doesn't know, and Ilsa answers with another request: "Play it once, Sam, for old times' sake." Sam hesitates, but Ilsa insists: "Play it, Sam. Play 'As Time Goes By.'" This is the song of Ilsa and Rick's Paris love affair, and it will return again and again as a reminder and symbol of that fleeting happiness. "Avalon" is only incidental to the film's larger narrative, but it is the first thing Sam thinks to play when Ilsa asks for an "old song." For viewers who knew the words, Sam's choice was especially apt: Ilsa really did leave her love, though in Paris, not on Catalina Island. The viewer could also interpret the song as referencing Rick's exile in Morocco. Sam's "old song" is set in the United States—a place Rick has abandoned (for reasons we never find out). And despite his protestations, we sense that Rick misses America, his home. "Avalon" appears in *Casablanca* for only a moment, but its performance is critically timed to trigger an intense, painful nostalgia in the film's characters. Audiences likely felt similar feelings of nostalgia and loss. They too were watching the war transform their lives, making the past of just a few years earlier seem impossibly distant. Throughout the 1930s and '40s, "Avalon" was an easily accessible and widely understood sign for a complex of nostalgic emotions: yearning, loss, and memory.

Of course, for bands that played the song over and over again for the Catalina audiences, "Avalon" could be painful in a very different way.

In his autobiography *Those Swinging Years*, bandleader Charlie Barnet recounts his time playing the ballroom in the 1950s. Over the years a practice developed, encouraged by the Santa Catalina Island Company, of playing "Avalon" when guests arrived and when they departed. According to Barnet, the band "had to play it on the street before the boat from the mainland arrived, as it docked, when it left," as well as when starting and finishing the ballroom show. "Like a prisoner crossing off the days he had to serve," the players "had marked on the wall backstage" how many more times they had to play the song. The situation was so unbearable that Barnet claims he did everything "short of mayhem" to try to cancel the band's contract, even telling off city officials as "a bunch of old fuddy-duddies, thirty years behind the times." Unfortunately for the players, the contract remained in place, and they had to finish serving their time in "Alcatraz."[130]

Beneath the humor of Barnet's anecdote is a deeper lesson on the relation between music and place. The establishment of a place—a delimited locale imbued with social meanings—takes a great deal of work, attentiveness, and above all reiteration. Place making is a constant and active process that is always threatened by contestation.[131] In the face of the Great Depression, the Wrigleys had to work with special diligence to transform Avalon and the ballroom and maintain them as the kind of modern-nostalgic locale they so desired for economic reward and psychological comfort. The constant need to play "Avalon" in Avalon is a demonstration of the power of music to participate in the constitution of social and spatial experience. Although the Wrigleys literally built and rebuilt the island to approximate their vision of a tourist utopia, they were also acutely aware of the power of music to support or challenge their project. By regulating the sounds of the ballroom—the cultural centerpiece of the island experience—they could work to protect one especially potent avenue of cultural infiltration.

In the end the effort was futile, because the very existence of the "white" sounds of sweet bands presupposed a "black" other. But the problem is deeper than this. As Radano reminds us, "The musical concept [of black rhythm] was profoundly and intimately connected to the idea of modernism itself: black rhythm not only reflected society but infiltrated the very texture of American social existence, giving to the social a perceptible musicality expressing 'racial' (black) influence."[132] The owners and managers of Catalina and the Casino Ballroom were attempting to create a complete and seamless resort experience, but in insisting so hard on their particular racialized view of the United

States, past and present, they failed to see the contradictions that un-
derlay their project—to be modern in America was to be both black
and white. In their attempts to marry sweet jazz to a particular place,
the owners and managers of Catalina Island sought to constitute, at
least temporarily, a modern place that could hold on to an increasingly
challenged white, middle-class social order.

TWO

From the "Make Believe Ballroom" to the Meadowbrook Inn: Charlie Barnet and the Promise of the Road

Saxophonist and bandleader Charlie Barnet was one of the best-known "characters" of the big band era. Among the many larger-than-life figures of the time—Cab Calloway, Glenn Miller, Benny Goodman—Barnet stands out for his wild, freewheeling attitude. He was notorious to fellow musicians as a hard-partying playboy who claimed he was guided by the three Bs: broads, booze, and Benzedrine.[1] He married eight times and published his music under pseudonyms to avoid paying alimony to his ex-wives.[2] Barnet admits that he was first attracted to the musical world because it was a way of life—a freedom of movement—that was the antithesis of his staid upper-class background. He "thought it was just the greatest thing to have a room of [his] own at the Chesterfield," a New York City residential hotel popular with jazz musicians.[3] For Barnet life on the road proved just as enthralling as the music. Over the years he logged thousands and thousands of miles with his band, playing North and South, small towns and big cities. Not surprisingly, he also loved cars and named a song "Blue Juice," after his beloved blue Lincoln Continental.[4]

While his bandmates all attest to his crazy pranks, boozing, and womanizing, they just as quickly swear to his seriousness about the music they were playing. Barnet loved jazz, and he especially loved the hot jazz recordings of Duke Ellington and Count Basie. Barnet used the jazz musician's life as way to seek out new experiences and pleasures, but he also channeled that same restless energy into a search for new ways to make music. Like so many other white jazz musicians of the era, Barnet dived headfirst into the African American musical world of New York City. As a teenager in the 1920s, he sought out any music he could find, and he was particularly drawn to black musicians who played either the large white-patronized downtown ballrooms such as the Roseland and the Arcadia or the uptown Harlem venues like Connie's Inn and the Savoy Ballroom.[5]

In most histories of swing, Benny Goodman stands as the primary figure embodying the interracialism of the swing era of the middle to late 1930s. For Lewis Erenberg, Goodman's January 1938 concert at Carnegie Hall "presented a portrait of American culture that was racially and ethnically mixed."[6] The Goodman Orchestra was made up of white and black musicians and represented a sampling of America's ethnic and class makeup (though the two African American musicians, Lionel Hampton and Teddy Wilson, were most often featured as a separate small-group attraction). Goodman himself was a symbol of American pluralism: raised in Chicago in a poor Jewish family, he had risen to the top of the commercial music industry. At the 1938 Carnegie Hall concert, the band played onstage with some of the best black musicians of the time: Harry Carney, Cootie Williams, and Johnny Hodges (all with the Duke Ellington Orchestra at the time) and Buck Clayton, Walter Page, and Freddie Green (all from the Basie Orchestra). And when the show ended many of the performers and patrons rushed up to Harlem to watch two of the most exciting black dance bands—led by Count Basie and by Chick Webb—battle at the Savoy Ballroom.[7]

Goodman was indeed a significant and progressive force in the dance band world, but he was not alone, and when we compare him with similarly progressive musicians such as Charlie Barnet, some clear differences in perspective and behavior emerge. Unlike Goodman, Barnet never sat atop the dance band world. He was very successful at various points in his career, and among the best-known hot white bands of the late 1930s and 1940s, but he was never in the same artistic or commercial sphere as Goodman. Because of this, Barnet proved more experimental, more willing to challenge musical and social lines in ways Goodman couldn't or wouldn't. As I will show, Barnet, even more than Goodman, is the true representative of what David Stowe calls swing's "utopian" impulse—the music's "expression of freedom, individualism, ethnic inclusiveness, democratic participation."[8] At the same time, Barnet represented some of the starkest limitations of this egalitarian promise. Even as he sought to break down racial barriers, he participated in behaviors and a larger discourse that reinforced certain aspects of American racial ideology.

A Self-Made Nomad

Charlie Barnet's life is a story of *movement*—movement in geographical space, across the nation, from white neighborhoods to black ones, but also in social space, toward new interpersonal and intercultural relationships.

Raised in a wealthy family, Charlie Barnet defied his parents by learning the saxophone (first the tenor instrument, then the alto and soprano) and, while still in grade school, skipping out to play with jazz bands in New York City. Because of his privileged upbringing Barnet was able to travel extensively as a child, both around the United States and internationally (there is a picture in his autobiography of a young Barnet in front of the Great Sphinx of Egypt).[9] His mother's divorce when Barnet was two led to a comfortable but itinerant lifestyle—the small family bounced around apartments in New York and Los Angeles. Barnet's schooling was even more unsettled—he spent some turbulent years in a variety of private boarding schools in New York City, Los Angeles, and Chicago. Yet Barnet was attracted to an even more intense life of continual movement. His early years as a professional musician involved enormous amounts of long-distance travel. Barnet worked freelance and with his own bands up and down the East Coast, frequently traveling to New Orleans and then back to New York. His early years also brought him to Texas and briefly to California. In his autobiography, he vividly describes his attraction to this life: "I found the idea of life on the road very intriguing. I wanted that experience, too, and I took a romantic view of the whole scene. And as it unfolded, it was even better than I had imagined."[10]

It was not simply the travel that attracted Barnet. Something about the lifestyle as a whole was freeing and, as he says, "intriguing." One aspect was certainly the oppositional, even deviant, element. Barnet is not shy about recounting the presence (and his partaking) of prostitution, drugs, and alcohol. The decadent elements of life on the road, though, were also rebellions against other aspects of middle- and upper-class respectability such as racial segregation. The freedom of movement was intimately wrapped up with freedom of thought and behavior. And all of this was enabled by the economic and technological changes of the era—roads, cars, trains, and radio.

In 1933 Barnet formed his own group. An admirer of Duke Ellington and other black and white hot jazz groups, Barnet sought early in his career to balance his music between hot styles that featured more syncopation and improvisation and the commercially viable sweet sounds preferred in hotel dance halls. In his survey of the swing era, historian Gunther Schuller describes Barnet's early groups from 1933 through 1938 as "hotel bands," suggesting that their overall sound and musical style was very sweet, closer to Guy Lombardo than to Duke Ellington.[11] But Schuller underemphasizes the insistent pull Barnet felt toward those hotter sounds—sounds most associated with black groups.

In his autobiography Barnet explicitly connects these hotter sounds to black musicians. Recalling his experiences at the Glen Island Casino in 1934, Barnet remembers playing in the shadow of the Casa Loma Orchestra. His comments are revealing about the connection between musical style and race: "The discipline that existed among the Casa Loma guys was not to my taste at all, and Dezutter [the club manager] wanted a lily-white approach to any jazz we played. He frowned on our black leanings, but we played out the summer."[12]

A desire to incorporate these hot sounds, in turn, would bring him into contact with the black musicians and arrangers he admired. In 1934 Barnet worked with black alto saxophonist and trumpeter Benny Carter to write arrangements for his band. Carter also sat in with the group, live onstage and in the recording studio.[13] According to Barnet, one of Carter's earliest live performances with the band went largely unnoticed because "the lighting was such that nobody could tell who was sitting back there."[14] Although no one in the audience noticed it, Barnet claims he had just presented one of the first integrated big bands, beating Benny Goodman (who hired vibraphonist Lionel Hampton and pianist Teddy Wilson in 1936) by two years. Barnet's relationship with Benny Carter led to a gig at Harlem's Apollo Theater; they were one of the first white jazz bands ever to play the venue.[15]

Despite these tastes of success and a growing sense of the kind of music he wanted to play, Barnet disbanded his group in 1935 to try an acting career in Hollywood. Although movie stardom never materialized, his playboy reputation and Hollywood connections resulted in several amorous adventures with movie celebrities, such as his widely reported affair with actress Dorothy Lamour. In the summer of 1936 he formed another group. Torn once again between what he saw as commercial compromises and "authentic" jazz, Barnet yet again overhauled his musical direction, forming a new band in 1938. It was with this group that Barnet finally achieved the kind of sustained success that had eluded him since he started leading bands back in 1933.

The group's breakthrough hit was a version of Ray Noble's "Cherokee." The tune proved popular in both white and black markets, and soon Barnet was playing not just the Apollo but the entire network of black theaters and dance halls across the country. The hiring of white trumpeter and arranger Billy May helped cement a new and identifiable sound, one far looser and far hotter than anything he had done before.

More than the product of personal idiosyncrasy, Barnet's urge for movement reflected broader cultural concerns playing out across the popular and "elite" cultural landscape—from Hollywood "road" movies (Frank Capra's *It Happened One Night*), to nonfiction documentaries (James Agee and Walker Evans's *Let Us Now Praise Famous Men*) and regionalist paintings (works by Thomas Hart Benton and Grant Wood). All combined an urge for travel and an attention to place-specificity with a concern for the changes being wrought by rapid modernization.

The idea of *mobility*—geographic, musical, and social—is a useful trope for understanding Barnet's career and its significance in the larger American culture. In this chapter I will look at two recorded performances by the Barnet band, "Pompton Turnpike" (1940) and "Drop Me Off in Harlem" (1944). The recordings represent well the band's approach to dance band music in the late 1930s and early 1940s. But they also reveal how this aesthetic was wrapped up in questions of place and mobility. The places referenced in these songs are evoked with a deliberately cross-racial musical style: a white band self-consciously adopting the hot style widely associated with the best black bands of the time. As with "Avalon," musical spaces and material places work together to generate new cultural understandings of the country.

The music of Barnet and his orchestra offered a type of freedom in a time when economic collapse either froze people in place or forced them onto the road out of desperation.[16] Barnet and his band embraced movement. Their music constructed locations—musical places—where, at least temporarily, white and black America could mingle on more equal terms. They offered listeners of the late 1930s and 1940s what Josh Kun calls "audiotopias," "almost-places of cultural encounter" that overlaid material lived experience.[17] Barnet's music was a realization of progressive social ideals, even though the musicians themselves did not always conceive of it this way. Reaching this point of cross-cultural interaction and understanding, however, did not happen overnight. It required its own journey.

Sweet Beginnings

In 1936 Charlie Barnet, his Glen Island Casino Orchestra, and the Barnet Modernaires, a singing quartet, recorded a version of Andy Razaf and Paul Denniker's "Make Believe Ballroom." Singing in close four-part harmony, the Modernaires coax the listener onto an imagined dance floor:

Let's dance
Any mansion or hall room
Is a make believe ballroom
Let's dance

Romance, at the tip of your fingers,
While the melody lingers,
Let's dance, dance, dance

Just started swaying while the band is playing
Music is worth your while
Let this station give you dancipation
Simply turn the dial

And keep on dancing
Though you've only a small room,
Make it your ballroom,
Let's dance[18]

The lyrics read like a panegyric to the "swing era"—a time when radio was king and the ballrooms were filled with jitterbuggers exuberantly dancing in the face of economic depression and war. But the lyrics are only half the story: "Make Believe Ballroom" is also music.

The performance is closer to the sweet jazz of Jan Garber and Guy Lombardo than to the hot swing of Benny Goodman or Count Basie. The song features a moderate tempo, less syncopated rhythms, toned-down solos, and a more accessible timbral palette. While the rhythm section plays a half-time feel (emphasizing two beats to the measure) and the reeds and horns exchange phrases in a conventional call-and-response pattern, the Modernaires sing a close harmony arrangement of the melody. Intended as the recording's focal point, the Modernaires employ harmonic practices common to jazz of the time, such as chord extensions and chromatic voice leading, especially in the use of dominant seventh chords.

The recording became the theme song and program name for Martin Block's popular and controversial radio show on New York's WNEW; Block was among the first disc jockeys to play commercially available records on the air, a practice the musicians' union fought vigorously.[19] The feature on Block's show was great publicity for the band and good news for Barnet's still struggling musical career. But the song's fame as a radio show theme also made it a symbol of the much larger entity of radio broadcasting.[20] In just under two decades radio had grown exponentially as a force in American life, connecting people in widely disparate parts of the country (and the globe) and allowing new kinds of social relationships. As historian Susan Douglas writes, radio had made music "one of the most significant, meaningful, sought after, and defining elements of day-to-day life, of generational identity, and of personal and public memory."[21] Now whole communities could be brought to you through the ether, re-creating different worlds right in the very space where you were listening. Your living room could be a ballroom. This new medium could be frightening—letting in unwanted sounds and voices—or it could be exhilarating—opening new and unheard sonic vistas. Just as significant, the sound entering Americans' private spaces was invisible, a serious problem for those trying to maintain the color line. In this situation black bands could pass for white (or vice versa). Lionel Hampton recounted many surprised agents and club managers who booked the vibraphonist thinking, because he formerly played with Benny Goodman, that he was white. "By rendering the performing subject invisible," David Stowe writes, "the new aural media of recordings and particularly radio facilitated the crossing of racial boundaries."[22]

What meanings might "Make Believe Ballroom" have had for listeners who heard it over the radio waves? Was this a frightening or an exhilarating example of radio's power to bring exotic sounds directly to you in your home? In the context of the era, this is indisputably safe music—the bouncy rhythm with a moderately strong backbeat is danceable but a far cry from the energy and drive of hotter black and white bands like those led by Harry James, Benny Goodman, Count Basie, or Jimmie Lunceford. The recording's particular combination of sweet and hot, of more sedate ballroom music with a hint of hot jazz's exuberant rhythms, is a musical mixture carefully constructed to allow a predominantly Euro-American audience to enjoy a very modern music—one heavily indebted to African American musical practice—without embracing too much "blackness." As a radio theme, Barnet's "Make Believe Ballroom" created a new, localized space in which to enjoy a potent but relatively safe mix of other sounds and other people. In this way, it effectively reaffirmed the decade's social and racial status quo. The radical potential of radio to transmit new sounds is held in check. In "Make Believe Ballroom," the mobility of radio—its ability to connect people across large geographic areas—is referenced in the lyrics and realized in its role as Block's theme song. But this musical expression of mobility was packaged in a musical style that, although modern and jazz-like, suppressed the markers of hotness and, by extension, blackness.

If Barnet had continued on the musical trajectory suggested by this recording, he would no doubt be remembered as a minor figure among the many popular sweet bands of the era. But throughout his career Barnet was committed to playing hotter music, in particular the music of the black bands he so admired. In the mid-1930s he struggled with managers and recording executives to shape a career that would be commercially viable and artistically satisfying. Before swing became a cultural force and a commercial bonanza, many in the industry didn't believe a white band playing "black" could be successful. When circumstances changed in the years after 1935, Barnet's aesthetic preferences coincided with a new commercial landscape, and he was able to shift his band's musical direction. He abandoned the relative safety of the "Make Believe Ballroom" for a musical identity that was far more direct in its engagement with African American music. Like most dance groups, Barnet's musicians continued to play sweet—their "book" (the band's collection of ready-to-play arrangements) always had plenty of ballads and low-key dance numbers. But they also developed a repertory of much harder-driving swing modeled on the Ellington and Basie bands. With the swing era in high gear, studios were now recording hot white bands, and the Barnet Orchestra had a string of hits—"Cherokee" (1939), "Redskin Rhumba" (1940), "Pompton Turnpike" (1940), and "Skyliner" (1944)—that solidified their new reputation as one of the edgi-est white big bands. The music of the "new" Barnet band embraced a new kind movement, a mobility that was directed out into the world, beyond the confines of the Make Believe Ballroom.

Route 23, the Newark-Pompton Turnpike

The people who first built a path between two places performed one of the great-est human achievements. No matter how often they might have gone back and forth between the two and thus connected them subjectively, so to speak, it was only in visibly impressing the path into the surface of the earth that the places were objectively connected. . . . Path building, one could say, is a specifically human achievement; the animal [on the other hand] does not accomplish the miracle of the road: freezing movement into a solid structure that commences from it and in which it terminates.[23]   GEORG SIMMEL

Pompton Turnpike
That's a very famous Jersey roadway
Full of country charm

Pompton Turnpike
Leads you to a place not far from Broadway.
Still, it's on a farm.
You dine with lights subdued

The music interlude
Puts you right in the mood
To dance and find yourself romance.

Pompton Turnpike
Ride your bike or if you like just hitchhike
Come to Pompton Turnpike.[24]   WILL OSBORNE AND DICK RODGERS

I first came across mention of the actual Pompton Turnpike inde-pendent of Barnet's swing era hit. In a used record store in Los An-geles I found a two-album set that preserves bits of sixty-four dance band theme songs. Many of the performances were taken from radio show remotes, programs broadcast live from ballrooms scattered across the United States. Most of these remotes emanated from one of three American cities: Los Angeles, Chicago, or New York. A few others came from smaller cities like Miami or San Diego. What all these places had in common was a sense of size, glamour, or exoticism—the bustle of Chicago's inner Loop, the congestion and excitement of New York City's Manhattan, or the glamour and hedonism of Los Angeles. But what does one make of a program coming from "Frank Dailey's Meadowbrook located on Route 23, the Newark Pompton Turnpike in Cedar Grove, New Jersey?"[25] What possible glamour could be waiting for someone on an exit off a New Jersey turnpike? And why were prominent and successful bands like Charlie Barnet's Orchestra playing there?

Today's comedians have made New Jersey's enormous network of highways a running joke. Its official moniker, the Garden State, strikes anyone who has traveled through densely settled northeastern New Jersey as ironic or absurd. From our perspective today it is hard to imagine anyone, let alone a national radio broadcast, wanting to draw attention to such a place, let alone tout it. The suburbs of Newark might be lovely, but how could a dance club off a New Jersey turnpike compare with even the smallest, dankest basement nightclub in New York City or Chicago? Yet during the 1930s and '40s the Newark-Pompton Turnpike really did have this aura of excitement.

In a moving passage from his book *All That Is Solid Melts into Air: The Experience of Modernity*, Marshall Berman poignantly captures a similar sense of lost excitement and possibility when he recounts the destruction wrought on his Brooklyn neighborhood by the great city builder Robert Moses. Standing above the construction site for the Cross-Bronx Expressway, Berman is angry at the destruction but also reflective. The Grand Concourse, with its "large, splendid apartment houses," had at one time replaced earlier buildings. The landscape he so loved was itself the result of modern capitalism's creative destruction. Someone else undoubtedly wept at that site of earlier destruction. Berman concludes, "So often the price of ongoing and expanding modernity is the destruction not merely of 'traditional' and 'pre-modern' institutions and environments but . . . of everything most vital and beautiful in the modern world itself. . . . The modernity of the urban boulevard was being condemned by the modernity of the interstate highway."[26]

With today's massive superhighways built over the remnants of the old local and county roads and turnpikes, we forget that these back streets, run-down commercial districts, and freeway exits were once the representatives of the newest and best that government and business could provide. During the 1930s and '40s the Pompton Turnpike symbolized the power of roads and personal automobiles to free Americans from congested cities and inflexible train routes—to free them, many believed, from the past itself. This ballroom in Cedar Grove, New Jersey, was a direct result of the new speed and flexible mobility of the country's infrastructural development. No train service needed here, just hop in the car and go.

As a reality and symbol, the road permeated popular culture of the era. In many of the successful films of the 1930s and '40s—*It Happened One Night, I Am a Fugitive from a Chain Gang, The Grapes of Wrath, Sullivan's Travels*—the road was a familiar narrative device, a symbol of the "restless nation" in search of better opportunities. For film historian Bennet Schaber, it was also a metaphor for America's search for itself, for the "people," a term of great cultural resonance at the time. According to Schaber, the character of Muley, in John Ford's screen version of Steinbeck's *Grapes of Wrath*, says it best: "One hundred folks and no place to live but on the road . . . they just threw us into the road." For the "Okies" in the film, the road meant the loss of everything that gave meaning to their lives—their homes, their kin, their farmland. But for the film's director, the road was also a symbol of hope, a way to bring Americans together in a new kind of community. The road gathers up these displaced people, "migrants, Indians, truckers, roadside workers (gas jockeys to waitresses, etc.)." Together they "assert the persistence of honest and generous life against the police, border guards and Pinkertons."[27] In their study of Preston Sturges's 1941 road film *Sullivan's Travels*, Kathleen Moran and Michael Rogin describe the road as a place "outside convention, neither the city nor the country." This liminal space "generates new myths and alliances" where "artificial barriers break down, impossible connections are made, social relations are reinvented, and new communities form."[28]

The actual roads Americans were traveling in the 1930s and '40s were undergoing rapid expansion and development. In their mordant travelogue of 1930s America, the Soviet humorists Ilya Ilf and Eugene Petrov find a nation obsessed with cars and crisscrossed by endless roads: "Oh, that road! For two months it ran to meet us—concrete, asphalt, or grained, made of gravel and permeated with heavy oil." "America," they write, "is located on a large automobile highway."[29] Despite the Great Depression, the 1930s saw the construction of many key parkways and bridges that would lay the groundwork for future developments, in particular the massive post–World War II suburbanization. New York's Triborough Bridge and Pennsylvania's new turnpike, for example, were both paradigms of civic leaders' belief that the future lay in the movement and mobility offered by new roads and new vehicles. The most famous rendering of this belief was Norman Bel Geddes's popular Futurama exhibit at the 1939 World's Fair in New York City. Visitors boarded small cars that circled above a giant diorama of a future American landscape where dense, modernist high-rise cities were connected by networks of long, curving highways.[30]

The development of the nation's intra- and interstate roads and highways was, along with radio and recording, a central component in the spread of jazz dance band music across the nation. As is characteristic of modern mass culture, all these factors were interrelated and fed each other. Extensive road coverage and affordable buses and automobiles allowed bands to tour many cities in a short time. The exposure to new audiences created new consumers for the band's records as well as new listeners for their radio appearances. But many patrons would already have heard about the band and its music from those records and radio appearances.

Roads, though, are important to the history of American popular music in ways that transcend the business of making music. In his 1994 book *A Sense of Time, a Sense of Place,* historian John Brinckerhoff Jackson eloquently pinpoints the necessity of carefully studying roads and their tremendous power to transform entire communities:

One of the least investigated aspects of our European-American culture is our ambivalent attitude toward the road and the street. In their infrequent mention of roads, historians and even many geographers tend to adopt the establishment point of view that roads are essentially for the maintenance of order and for commerce (or warfare) with neighboring states. Nevertheless, there has always been and probably always will be a widespread distrust among average men and women of all roads which come from the outside world, bringing strangers and strange ideas. Reactions to such roads vary from age to age, from one region, one class, one stage of economic or social development to another; yet underlying all those variations, there seems to be a basic human response: the road is a very powerful space; and unless it is handled very carefully and constantly watched, it can undermine and destroy the existing order.[31]

The roads that were integral to the financial success of the dance band industry were also the conduits of social change. Dance bands brought with them traces of other places. The bands themselves were composite creatures, worlds unto themselves, made up of musicians from different parts of the United States, frequently with very different ethnic and class backgrounds. The music they made, no matter where it fell on the jazz continuum between sweet and hot, was itself a modern American hybrid fusing black and white, high and low, folk and urban. And it was the road, as Jackson points out, that allowed in all this difference, these "strangers and strange ideas." To understand the radical meanings this music could have for its listeners requires understanding a little more about those "very powerful spaces" that provided major access points to these sounds. Roads brought more than music—they brought new ways of hearing and understanding America, ways that could challenge racist beliefs.

Throughout United States history, politicians and planners have been vexed by the difficulties of the country's enormous size. Road construction was imperative not only for commerce but also for military defense. However, the most immediate incentive for the physical construction of an extensive, well-maintained, and coherent road system came with the rise of the automobile in American life. Henry Ford's introduction of the Model T in 1908, and his institution of the moving assembly line, the eight-hour workday, and the five-dollar wage in 1913–14, made auto manufacturing enormously more efficient and cars far more affordable for a wide segment of Americans, including, most importantly, the very people making the cars in the factory.[32] The discovery of oil in east Texas also contributed to the affordability and financial practicability of owning an automobile. While campaigns for good roads developed earlier in the late nineteenth and early twentieth centuries, it was the demands of new car owners that intensified the pressure on states to enhance road development and improvement. The impact of the car is difficult to overstate—the statistics are staggering: in 1900 Americans had registered 8,000 motor vehicles; in 1905 about 78,000 motor vehicles were registered in the United States. By 1916 Americans registered about 2.5 million, and by 1940 there were over 32 million registered vehicles, 27 million of them passenger cars.[33] By 1910 America was already the leading automobile culture in the world, and by late 1920 over half of American families owned cars.[34] As historian John Rae emphasizes, car ownership is not the whole story: even without all the passenger cars, the huge increase in the number of trucks and buses alone would have radically reshaped American life.[35] These vehicles, working alongside existing train routes, radically expanded the distances Americans could live from another yet still be in contact for work or leisure.

During the early 1930s, the nadir of the Great Depression, even while federal and state investment in roads declined, the purchase and use of automobiles continued to climb.[36] Returning to Middletown in

1935, sociologists Helen and Robert Lynd note how, despite six years of depression, "the word 'auto' was writ large across Middletown's life." New filling stations had become "prominent physical landmarks," and downtown parking was increasingly hard to find: "Local sentiment, as heard over and over again, is that 'People give up everything in the world but their car.' "[37]

President Roosevelt and the other architects of the New Deal saw road building as an excellent way to put people back to work and contribute to the country's capital resources. A lot of this work went into fixing and restoring roads, although new construction would remain very important even if it was statistically not as impressive as it had been in the previous two decades. Stephen Goddard writes that despite the trauma of the era, "road building was the success story of the demoralized 1930s."[38] According to historian Mark Rose, "Between 1921 and 1940, government officials at all levels spent $34.6 billion for road construction and repair." In this twenty-year period, 418,000 additional miles of paved road were constructed (raising the total mileage of American roads to 3 million), and 387,000 additional miles of road were surfaced.[39]

A significant part of road building during the first four decades of the twentieth century was the construction of farm-to-market roads, a development that would prove key in the spread of dance band music. Policy makers considered agriculture central to the national economy and made the construction of roads from farm to city a top priority. Thus it was rural Americans who first experienced some of the dramatic transformations enabled by the automobile.[40] Despite the Great Depression and the fractured nature of road policy and construction, vast stretches of the nation, including large amounts of rural land, had more than passable roads. Cities might have been painfully congested, but the country as a whole was gradually being integrated into a huge network that connected rural to urban, villages to towns, and towns to cities. As we will see later, not only did roads open up access to areas around cities (places like Cedar Grove, New Jersey), the commitment to farm-to-market roads allowed easy access to geographically remote towns such as Strawberry Point, Iowa.[41] The relentless, almost absurd, traveling regimes of many dance bands were in large part shaped by this situation.

One of the greatest chapters in the history of Depression-era road building was a kind of hybrid rural-urban creation—the construction of the Pennsylvania Turnpike. A massive technical and engineering feat, the building of the Turnpike combined the pressing need for roads with new engineering innovations and a tremendous faith in a modernized future. For Stephen Goddard the Pennsylvania Turnpike was the beginning of the "age of the American superhighway."[42] On October 1, 1940, the Turnpike opened to the toll-paying public. The financial and administrative force behind the road, Turnpike commissioner Walter Adelbert Jones, called it "the cynosure of all eyes, a dreamway."[43] Initiated in 1935, the limited access toll road covered 160 miles stretching from Harrisburg to Pittsburgh, burrowing through seven mountains and going over or under 307 bridges.[44] Despite fears that a toll road would be a financial disaster, the Turnpike proved immensely popular—drivers were more than willing to part with their money to travel on the modern, high-speed road with its unusually smooth surface, long, banked curves and gradual, even grading. During its first year the Turnpike carried an average of 6,500 people a day.[45] The great success of the Turnpike saw a flood of similar programs across the country: Maine opened its own turnpike in 1947, New Hampshire followed in 1948; the New Jersey Turnpike opened to traffic in 1952.[46] All this development would culminate in the massive national interstate highway system begun in 1956 after money was finally allocated to the project.[47]

In the minds of politicians, bureaucrats, and planners, the development of roads, whether designed to connect small cities or entire states, was part of a larger vision of social improvement. Automobiles offered a kind of personal mobility and freedom very different from that offered by railroads and streetcars. Massive and coordinated road construction would relieve urban congestion and all the social ills that were believed to follow from it. All Americans would have more space, cleaner air, and an environment better suited to physical and psychological well-being. The improvement of rural areas provided new places for city residents to visit and even settle in.

The belief in roads as a social and economic panacea was outsized and hopelessly optimistic. Mass production democratized consumption and altered American society, but it did not equalize it. This is a key point, a reminder that the promises of modern development, of new social and personal freedoms, were not equally distributed or available to everyone. Access to cars and highways fell along lines of class, race, gender, and ethnicity.[48] Car culture and its dramatic geographic and social changes created new social conditions while magnifying existing societal tensions and inequities, including racial ones. Even though the vision of a road-bound utopia would never pan out in the way its most ardent champions hoped, new and improved roads still represented in physical form the faith in modernization as a force in the improvement of American life. The same roads that could connect white communities could also connect black ones and, of course, connect them to each other. In cars, black and white sharecroppers could much more easily escape the virtual peonage that trapped them. Cars also accelerated the migratory movements of the era, particularly the massive migration of southern blacks to the urban North. Roads were indeed powerful spaces.[49]

The Pompton Turnpike is a paradigm of the nation's broad commitment to roads and the power of modern industrial capitalism.[50] The turnpike has a long history stretching back to 1809, when a frustrated merchant, Israel Crane, initiated a fund-raising program to construct a better road between Newark and West Caldwell, New Jersey. As was common in the early years of the United States, the road was locally funded and charged a toll to help pay for its construction and upkeep. These turnpikes were sprouting up all over the infant country to service a growing population and new commercial demands. The 11.2-mile road with a lengthy spur running north to Pompton became one of the most important thoroughfares in New Jersey, and many towns grew up along its busy margins: Bloomfield, Montclair, Verona. As the population increased there was continual demand for improvements, and additional roads were constructed. By the 1930s the rapid rise of automobile ownership forced city planners to rethink the Turnpike, now known officially as Route 23. The road was soon expanded into a four-lane undivided highway, part of plan to create a better corridor to Route 46. Today residents in the area closer to Newark refer to it as Bloomfield Avenue, and the spur that ran to Pompton is now Route 23 (though still informally called the Newark-Pompton Turnpike).[51] The road was typical of the increasing spread of the population to areas outside the immediate boundaries of cities (in this case Newark and New York City) as well as the incipient suburbanization of the entire nation.

Of the many businesses that lined the Turnpike, the most relevant to our discussion here is, of course, the Meadowbrook Inn, the ballroom, nightclub, and restaurant in Cedar Grove, just outside Newark, New Jersey, only about ten miles from New York City. Figure 2.1 is an image of the ballroom from a postcard. Tired of constant touring, a local dance band, Frank Dailey's Syncopators, purchased an existing building, the Pavilion Royale, in 1930, and converted it to a large dance hall. Frank Dailey ultimately bought out his bandmates to become the venue's primary owner and manager. Under Dailey's savvy management the ballroom became a major venue during the height of the dance band era and hosted a musically diverse lineup of black and white bands from 1935 through to the end of the war: Glen Gray and the Casa Loma Orchestra, Glenn Miller and His Orchestra, Benny Goodman and His Orchestra, Fats Waller's Big Band, and Count Basie's Orchestra.[52] Modest by the standards of the New York hotel ballrooms, the Meadowbrook was still an inviting destination for listeners and dancers, featuring a large dance floor, one hundred feet by forty, with room for fourteen hundred or more patrons, as well outdoor seating.

But there was one feature that made it different from the many similar venues in the metropolitan New York area: a dedicated, glassed-in state-of-the-art radio remote and recording studio. This was the key to Dailey's success and made the Meadowbrook economically competitive with the big New York hotels that offered similarly long engagements with radio remotes. The network broadcasts provided dance bands with the best way to promote themselves. With national attention, they could command high fees for lucrative one-night engagements and also draw the attention of recording companies seeking artists for their labels. In his June 1941 exposé of the dance band business, Irving Kolodin describes how "twelve times a week, representatives of one or another of the major networks make the adjustments that carry music from Meadowbrook to radios all over the country. Each Saturday afternoon one of the radio chains (it is Columbia at the present time) allots a full hour of its time to a Meadowbrook broadcast." "Of course," Kolodin continues, "the band does not win such prestige as at the Pennsylvania, but the radio listener in Omaha who hears this chromium-trimmed barn described as the 'beautiful Meadowbrook Country Club' can imagine it as he pleases." To be fair, the Meadowbrook was hardly a "barn," and the broadcasts I have heard announce it as the Meadowbrook Inn, not Country Club, but Kolodin's larger point stands: the nature of radio made it possible to create an image of a ballroom that was far more glamorous, urbane, and sophisticated than it was in real life.[53]

In a 1999 article for the New Jersey *Record*, George Norberg of Cedar Grove remembers how "back then, everybody knew about Frank Dailey's Meadowbrook. When I was in the service [during World War II] you'd run into a guy from, say, Kansas, and you'd tell him you were from New Jersey. And the guy from Kansas would say, 'Hey didja ever go to the Meadowbrook?' He'd have heard the radio broadcasts. . . . The place really put Cedar Grove on the map."[54] The venue was so widely known that, in an attempt to demoralize American troops, an

Figure 2.1 Image from a postcard of Frank Dailey's Meadowbrook Inn, Cedar Grove, New Jersey, ca. 1935.

English-language Japanese propaganda radio station allegedly broadcast news that the ballroom had burned down.[55]

Despite its relatively progressive approach to band bookings—hiring a mix of black and white, hot and sweet bands—the venue was conservative in its rules for guests. Owner Dailey required men to wear ties and coats and allowed only couples inside, measures he felt cut down on vandalism and fighting. More significant, the venue was open only to white patrons.[56] In an interview with the *Newark Star-Ledger* in 2008, African American Edwin Burke—in 1945 a senior at Newark's Central High School—tells how he was unable to attend his own senior prom at the Meadowbrook Inn because it would not admit blacks. A delegation of black students protested the segregated location, but they could not get the dance moved.[57] Still, the Meadowbrook exemplifies the democratization of nightlife of the era that opened this avenue of leisure to broad segments of the nation's middle and working classes. Kolodin describes how during "a typical week-end night" a visitor can see "1,500 or 1,600 youngsters from Newark, Paterson, Montclair, and Plainfield (there is a population of three and half million within forty-five minutes' drive of Meadowbrook) shagging and bouncing on the floor." These youthful patrons rarely paid more than the two-dollar minimum, but Dailey's low overhead, along with the attendance of "more prosperous elders who come to see the fun and hear the music" could bring in as much as four thousand dollars.[58]

When the big band industry crashed in the late 1940s, owner Frank Dailey changed the venue to a dinner theater managed by his brother Cliff. When Dailey died in 1958, the building was transformed into a "theater in the round." In the 1970s a disco replaced the theater, and in 1984 it was closed altogether. A Macedonian church bought the dilapidated building and began renovating in 1994. Aside from nearly a thousand coat-check tags, a few music stands, and a small collection of programs and other ephemera, few remnants of the Dailey era have survived.[59]

Traveling the Turnpike with Charlie Barnet

In 1940 the Barnet band recorded a Billy May arrangement of "Pompton Turnpike," a song recently written by former 1920s crooner Will Osborne and bandleader Dick Rodgers. Along with "Cherokee" and "Skyliner," the instrumental version of "Pompton Turnpike" was a huge success. A June 1940 *Down Beat* column covering the music publishing industry announced the release of the new song, written "in honor of the famous road which runs alongside Frank Dailey's Meadowbrook."[60] In his autobiography Barnet described the venue as an attractive place, with outdoor seating in the summer. The mosquitoes were a problem, but far worse was the toxic "preparation" sprayed to fight them. Despite that hazard, the group had a successful run at the club, and "another hit came out of this, Billy May's *Pompton Turnpike*, on which I played soprano."[61]

So what does "Pompton Turnpike" sound like? What kind of musical space or spaces does it offer the listener? What experiences or qualities of movement does it present? Unlike the early rock 'n' roll music of 1950s, the dance band music of the 1930s and '40s has not provided us with many songs explicitly about cars or roads.[62] There are, however, many songs that reflect a feeling of increasing speed, urbanization, and interconnectedness, all aspects of American life closely related to the explosive growth of the automobile. The popular swing era tune "Flying Home," Artie Shaw's "Traffic Jam," Jimmie Lunceford's "Stratosphere," Count Basie's "9:20 Special," and Spud Murphy's "Transcontinental" are just a few examples of titles that evoke speed and movement, by road, rail, or air. Though the Barnet band recorded an all-instrumental version of Osborne and Rodgers's "Pompton Turnpike," the song is still an important conjunction of music and title, of sound and social history. The recording opens a window onto a larger cultural pattern—the widespread preoccupation with secure, directed mobility in an era of confused and turbulent movement caused by the Great Depression.

A first listen doesn't give up too much—there is no "tone painting" of car horns or traffic noise and no lyrics about cars, roads, or traveling.

Intro: four bars	Horns supported by reeds followed by piano solo with walking blues bass (scale degrees 1–3–5–6)
Chorus 1: A section	Reeds set off against piano; muted brass "wah-wahs"; growling trumpet of Billy May finishes the first eight measures
A	Same arrangement of reeds and horns; soprano saxophone solo in place of trumpet closes the section
B	Low brass pedal; trumpets state descending chromatic melody; soprano sax solo over the top; marchlike cadential figure connects bridge to final A section
A	Reeds again state the melody; trumpets answer fortissimo; reeds alone for last two measures
Chorus 2: A	Soprano sax and trumpet duet
A	Continuation of duet
B	Ensemble reprise of previous bridge section material; Barnet sax solo
A	Final ensemble A section; reeds against much more active horn sections—the climactic, most intense ensemble playing of the performance

Figure 2.2 Chart of "Pompton Turnpike." Words and music by Will Osborne and Dick Rodgers and arranged by Billy May. Recorded July 19, 1940, in New York City.

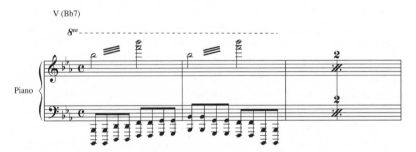

Example 2.1 Piano introduction to "Pompton Turnpike." Transcribed by the author for use in this volume.

But the song's clever structure and its rhythmic groove convey a distinct quality of motion and a sense of musical space. We hear a lot of activity, but it is relaxed and exploratory. Structurally the tune is a Tin Pan Alley, thirty-two-bar song in the standard AABA form. Figure 2.2 provides a chart mapping out its structure and significant events. Melodically the composition is strongly inflected with the blues, especially in the many solo spots taken by trumpeter Billy May and by Barnet. The first music we hear evokes the blues: following an opening blast of horns, the piano emerges playing a melodic blues cliché—a bouncy eighth-note arpeggio of scale degrees 1–3–5–6–8 (example 2.1).

Harmonically, the song is built around a handful of chords cleverly chosen to provide new contexts for the simple melody. The opening four measures alternate between tonic and supertonic (E-flat6 and F minor). A move to V in measure 6 is preceded with a chromatic passing chord (B7) that adds a momentary twist to an otherwise very static A section. The bridge features an insistent pedal on E-flat, supporting an E-flat7 chord and a slippery descending chromatic melody. We have relatively long periods of time to inhabit the song's two closely related harmonic locales—the static, alternating chords of the A sections, and the pulsing dominant sound of the bridge. And because both sections emphasize E-flat, the shift between these harmonic places is especially smooth. It is as if we are examining the same vista from a slightly different angle. Rather than an involved tonal plan with a strong teleology, "Pompton Turnpike" has a looser harmonic layout that moves with less urgency through the chord progression.

Equally important to the experience of the song is the quality of movement created by the performance's groove, a rhythmic feel anchored by drummer Cliff Leeman. Barnet and his band play the composition at a relatively unhurried eighty-eight beats per minute with a solid and relaxed rhythm of an even four beats to a measure. The tempo is a swaggering andante, and the slow quarter-note pulse is "stretched" by the drummer's heavily swung eighth notes. Playing on slightly opened hi-hats, the drummer's swing groove is very full, and the swooshing sound of the hi-hats contrasts with the shorter attack of the walking bass. During the bridge of the first chorus the rhythm section, following the syncopated, chromatically intensified descending melody, accents the first offbeat of every other measure. These accents hint at a stronger backbeat, something the drummer almost realizes as the loose swing of the A sections pushes toward a full-fledged driving "shuffle" rhythm in the bridge. The combination of the chromatic descending melody in the trumpets and the insistent pedal on the low horns and reeds further ups the rhythmic intensity—the unstable melody contradicting the stubborn honking notes of the pedal in the brass and rhythm section. The rhythmic energy of this section is rapidly dissipated by a brief marchlike, cadential figure at the end of the bridge. Throughout the short song, the steady but loose swing will rise and fall in waves of intensity, moving toward a full-fledged backbeat, then retreating.

For all its laid-back qualities, the rhythm is always insistent. It suggests a particular kind of relaxed but energized bodily movement. In the expansiveness of the groove we *literally* hear more open space between the quarter notes and eighth notes of the conventional swing rhythm. The song's particular balance between sound and silence, between the explicit statement of the pulse and the "virtual" rhythmic structure (implicitly understood by the listener), gives the groove a quality of motion very different from, for example, the Jan Garber Orchestra's precise, on-the-beat groove heard in "Avalon" (chapter 1).[63] In "Pompton Turnpike" we feel a sense of forward motion, but the looseness of the groove—the literal spaces *in* the groove—give these forward pushes less urgency.

One facet of automobile life was that it could move you in completely new directions at your own pace. With no train schedules to follow, you could dance all night and still comfortably make it home for work the next day. The kind of movement offered by the automobile is analogous to the kind of motion conveyed in "Pompton Turnpike"— intense, driving, but open and full of space and flexible movement. It is not coincidental that Barnet would choose this way of swinging as his tribute to the Turnpike and the Meadowbrook Inn, a venue away from the city but still intimately connected to it. The Meadowbrook offered the excitement of an urban venue without the crowds and traffic. It was a new kind of space—a suburban one that offered the excitement and energy of modern life at a slower, more expansive pace.

Besides this characteristic sense of movement, "Pompton Turnpike" constructs a sonic space, a "virtual room of sound," that is similarly full, but not crowded.[64] Billy May's arrangement takes full advantage of the orchestra's pitch range, featuring Barnet's high soprano saxophone, Billy May's own bright trumpet sound, and the deep, rich lows of the lower-pitched brass and reeds. Structurally, the recording moves back and forth between very spare textures (the bluesy bass and piano introduction immediately before the main melody and the sax-trumpet dialogue in the second chorus) and very dense ones (both bridge sections and the final A section in the second chorus). The most dramatic timbral and registral contrast comes during the two bridge sections, where Barnet plays high, sustained notes against a thick ensemble texture anchored by honking low reeds. This concern with texture was a central aesthetic for big band arrangers of the era, and May was particularly skilled at creating interesting, compelling arrangements within rigid formal frameworks.[65]

In addition to the basic phenomenological experience of the musical space, we also hear *people*—musicians working together to create ordered sonic structures. The performance offers the listener (and the participating musician) a model of community and social interaction. Like a lot of big band jazz of the era, the community enacted in "Pompton Turnpike" emphasizes cooperative group effort balanced with brief individual expression.[66] Sections of musicians (rhythm players, brass, reeds) play seamlessly with each other and then against each other in antiphony. "Pompton Turnpike," however, presents a very particular take on the larger individual-versus-collective theme of the big band style.

Central to the evocation of community in "Pompton Turnpike" are the layers of dialogue embedded in May's arrangement and realized by Barnet's musicians. In fact, the idea and practice of "dialogue" permeate the performance; it is one of the song's overarching organizing principles. The centerpiece of the 1940 recording is a literal conversation between Barnet's soprano saxophone and Billy May's muted trumpet during the first two A sections of the second chorus. I have transcribed the first eight measures in example 2.2. Barnet and May have a musical back-and-forth that twists and bends the melody into new formations, squeezing out of the now familiar notes and rhythms an array of timbral and rhythmic variations. The solo exchange has a particular order: during the sixteen measures, Barnet speaks first and May responds. Using mostly pitches taken from the tune's melody, Barnet plays swooping, grace-note-inflected manipulations of the melody that May answers with muted, growling responses. Their dialogue is playful, each offering a range of timbres, rhythmic displacements, and blue-note interpolations.

Even though we are listening to just two individual musicians, their playing is deeply informed by the black musicians and musical practices they both so admired. Barnet and May are talking not only to each other but also to the larger African American community, past and present. In their improvisational dialogue, they reference, sometimes directly, other times more obliquely, a tradition of players central to their musical development—Louis Armstrong, Bubber Miley, Lester Young, Coleman Hawkins, Duke Ellington, and Count Basie.

The Barnet-May duet on the second chorus, though, is only one of the many dialogues that make up "Pompton Turnpike." The entire arrangement is built around even larger structural dialogues. Following conventional dance band practice, the various sections are set off against each other, particularly reeds and trumpets (echoing the Barnet-May dialogue). Over the course of the three-minute performance, the conversation between reeds and horns builds in complexity and intensity. For the first two A sections, harmonized reeds state the melody with

Example 2.2 First eight measures of Barnet-May duet on "Pompton Turnpike." Concert pitch. Transcribed by the author for use in this volume.

low "wa-wahs" from trombones and trumpets. During the bridge the horns and reeds switch—the trumpets take the descending chromatic melody and the reeds support them with a pedal. The final A of the first chorus again features reeds with the melody, but this time the horns answer with bold exclamations, real melodic phrases rather than pianissimo nods. During the second chorus the whole ensemble reenters with the reprised bridge material, replacing Barnet and May's one-on-one conversation. Moving from individual dialogues to sectional ones, the arrangement draws our attention to the close relationship between the single instrumentalist and the collective ensemble.

In addition to these dialogues, there is yet another, more abstract one unfolding at the same time. The song's laid-back rhythm, prominent dialogue between instrumentalists, growling and muted trumpets, and extreme contrasts between section and individual all show the influence of the Duke Ellington Orchestra. In fact Barnet sought out Ellington arrangements directly from the bandleader. Ellington originals such as "Ring Dem Bells," "Rockin' in Rhythm," and "Drop Me Off in Harlem" were staples of the Barnet Orchestra's book. Historian

Gunther Schuller describes Barnet as "the first well-known jazz figure consistently to perform other major jazz composers' repertories."[67] The Barnet band is not covering an Ellington song, but they are referencing some of that band's defining features—particularly the focus on the interaction of strongly marked instrumental voices. From this view, Barnet and company are having a kind of conversation with the Ellington band. This dialogue, of course, is only half realized—the other half, the Ellington sound, is located in the jazz world at large. We have no literal references to particular Ellington works or recordings, but we do hear an engagement with their style, an individuation and transformation of the Ellington band's aesthetic priorities. Some writers at the time criticized Barnet for copying black bands, specifically Duke Ellington's Orchestra. But "Pompton Turnpike," and in fact a great deal of Barnet's repertory, was created not just as homage to other black bands, but as a creative engagement with their musical practices.

One way of making sense of this large-scale cultural conversation is to see it as something resembling what Henry Louis Gates Jr. defined as the rhetorical trope of "Signifyin(g)," a revision with difference of well known cultural styles, texts or practices. "Signifyin(g)," for Gates, is a mode of textual production and critical engagement born within, and specific to, the black vernacular.[68] Claiming Barnet as fully a part of an African American culture of the era exaggerates his role in black life. Still, Barnet's engagement with black life was more sustained and intense (if not uncomplicated) than that of many other socially progressive white bandleaders of the era. In trying to emulate the black musicians he so admired, it makes sense that Barnet would work to understand their larger artistic strategies and aesthetic preferences. Many of the band's recordings such as "Pompton Turnpike" are deliberate "riffs" on the Ellington style. These performances pay their respects to other recordings while also offering new twists and revisions.

With this recording Barnet has traveled far from the "Make Believe Ballroom." In its formal properties the song conveys the new geographic and social configurations of the era: the flexibility of modern movement—exemplified by the unhurried and shifting treatment of the simple melodic material—is combined with an explicit mixture of black and white musical forms and gestures to create a blues-inflected, Tin Pan Alley structure. The musical-spatial characteristics of "Pompton Turnpike" are closely related to Barnet's understanding of certain black musical practices and what they offered his band.

"Pompton Turnpike" is a "representational space" that enacts the new kinds of mobility offered on the nation's highways. It is a sonic integration of dance band jazz musical practices. Barnet's move toward hot jazz was a journey outward from the atomized imagined ballroom of the radio listener to the larger, conflict-ridden social world of real segregated ballrooms. With "Pompton Turnpike" the road and the automobile, two of the most powerful symbols of modern development, align with the popular dance band music of the era to create in sound a temporary sonic place embodying values at odds with a segregated American society riven by racial divisions.

The musical language and performance of "Pompton Turnpike," this tribute to Frank Dailey's great Meadowbrook Inn, is soaked in the specific practices pioneered by black American musicians. This explicit integration of black musical practices happens in a place made possible by machine age modernization. Place, movement, and race intertwine in a powerful musical statement of the social possibilities of the Depression era's faith in the possibilities of car and road.

Dance Bands on the Road

The promise of the road was, in actual experience, pretty far from what was represented in sound. Between the Barnet Orchestra's sonic representation of "Pompton Turnpike" and the day-to-day travel, there was a deep chasm; a lot of work was involved in making the radical social possibilities of the road a reality. Along with rural Americans, dance band musicians were one segment of the nation's population that most directly felt the effects of the new automobile culture and the profound social issues this development posed for American society. While most bands desired a long engagement at a prominent hotel or dance hall venue, touring could be much more lucrative—some one-night stands paid better than several days or weeks at a major urban venue. Touring was also good for record sales and general audience exposure, two things that could lead to more radio appearances and maybe even a commercial sponsor.[69] But to make touring really pay for the upkeep of a dance band, the group had to move, and move *a lot*. Historians Bill Crowther and Mike Pinfold write that "the reality of life on the road was a hard, bone-shaking, sleepless matter of consuming hundreds of miles before fulfilling the expectations of audience, and bandleader, with a performance of impeccable musicianship."[70]

Even in our very mobile early twenty-first-century world, the scale of these bands' schedules is staggering. For the most commercially successful black and white bands—Duke Ellington's, Cab Calloway's, or Benny Goodman's—train travel was possible. For the vast majority of bands without such resources the only options were crowded and uncomfortable cars and buses.[71] In his memoirs trombonist Dicky Wells recalls cramming a ten-piece band into a single Packard.[72] African American bandleader Andy Kirk estimated that from 1937 through the war years, the band did about fifty thousand miles a year.[73] In George Simon's history of the dance bands, Jimmie Lunceford estimated that the group did "a couple of hundred one-nighters a year, fifteen to twenty weeks of theaters, maybe one four-week location and two weeks of vacation." According to Lunceford, this equaled close to forty thousand miles a year.[74] Overnight trips could easily reach three or four hundred miles, sometimes even passing five hundred. In his autobiography Benny Goodman explains that for these long trips his band would travel at night when roads were clearer, and that the extra travel time was extremely useful in dealing with any crises, mechanical or human, that came up. Nighttime travel, though, did not even afford the benefit of watching the landscape or seeing the sights; as Benny Goodman remembers, "There are more towns in America that I have only seen after dark than I care to think about."[75] Many bands could claim to have seen nearly every corner of the country, including forays into Canada. By 1949, Andy Kirk says, "he had reached the farthest corners of the country—over 300 cities in nearly every state . . . and into Ontario, Manitoba, and British Columbia, Canada." The band had traveled from the far north all the way south to Key West.[76]

White bandleader Clyde McCoy describes the difficulties, inconveniences, and frustrations such intensive long-distance travel could bring. After the final day of a successful run at the Lowry Hotel in Saint Paul, Minnesota, the band packed up almost immediately for the next gig, a nighttime journey of "260 miles of ice-coated highways to Ames, Iowa":

All that night we slipped and skidded at the rate of 20 miles per hour. As morning came and the snow became deeper, we found ourselves under the command of snow plows. For miles, for hours, we followed those tractor driven plows. These incidents repeated many times before we made any headway. After twelve hours we arrived at our next stand. . . . After the dance we managed to get six hours sleep. The next day we headed for Davenport, Iowa, then more trouble began. Due to small leak in the crank case of my car, the oil leaked out, causing three rods and three bearings to burn out. Stranded on those icy highways in Iowa is an experience. Finally, after several hours I managed to persuade a motorist to tow the car to Davenport which was 65 miles away. We got in just in time to play the job—no time for food or relaxation—we were doing one-night stands.[77]

Andy Kirk relates a similar story regarding the perils of automobile travel. Driving back from a gig in Estes Park, Colorado, eighty-five miles from Denver and eight thousand feet above sea level, Kirk and a bandmate were winding their way down the narrow mountain roads. An oncoming car accidentally forced them off the road. When they recovered from the shock, they saw that they were "caught in a tree jutting out on the mountainside [with the] rear wheels hanging out in space." They crawled out of the vehicle and eventually flagged down help to tow the car back onto the road.[78]

In 1941 the American Federation of Musicians (AFM) tried to alleviate these conditions by limiting extreme distances. The union "voted a law making it illegal for any booker to book, or any band leader to accept, or any member to fulfill an engagement which necessitated traveling by auto or bus a distance in excess of 400 miles within any 24 hours."[79] Though only affecting unionized musicians, it was still an attempt to exert some control over what had become a grueling part of dance band life. Only a few years later World War II requisitioning and rationing would put further restrictions on all groups, limiting trips to about two or three hundred miles.[80]

Even these lighter travel schedules, though, were uncomfortable and sometimes outright dangerous (the AFM ban described above was in part a result of a recent surge of highway accidents). In his autobiography, Andy Kirk claims that "in all my years on the road, criss-crossing the US in cars, busses, and trains, I was only in 14 or 15 accidents, none serious."[81] Kirk, though, was lucky. The 1930s and '40s produced a long list of musicians killed in automobile accidents, including bandleader Hal Kemp and legendary saxophonist Chu Berry.[82] A 1935 bus crash killed Earl Hines's sideman Cecil Irwin.[83] In the early 1940s, music magazines like *Down Beat* featured many articles about car and bus accidents involving musicians. A July 15, 1941, issue described a terrible fiery wreck in Gary, Indiana, involving the Skinnay Ennis band. Leader Ennis, his wife (also the group's vocalist), and the band manager were not on the bus, having traveled to Chicago in a private car. Although no one died, the magazine provided a grim, detailed list of the injuries to each musician, from broken bones and internal injuries to various cuts and bruises.[84] In another accident reported four months later, the musicians involved were not so lucky—bandleader Red Sievers and five other musicians were killed when a cattle truck "sheared off the entire left side of the band bus." The group was making its five-hundred-mile trip home to Minneapolis after a one-night stand in Marshalltown, Iowa.[85] Other hazards of the road, though, could be less mortal. Shady promoters and bad business decisions could leave musicians without money to get home, stranded wherever they happened to be.[86] Compounding these risks, many hotel managers and restaurant owners saw a chance for easy profits and charged much higher prices to traveling bands, especially black ones.[87]

The mobilization for World War II added new challenges to the usual inconveniences and dangers. With the Japanese conquest of Southeast Asia, American industries could not import many key raw materials. For the music industry, the sudden shortages of gasoline and rubber had the most immediate impact (though shortages of shellac were also serious and hurt the production of new commercial recordings). These shortages—initially downplayed by a federal government hypersensitive to claims that it was not ready for war—led to rationing and then restrictions on automobile, bus, and truck travel. This ban on nonessential travel had an "immediate impact on dance orchestras," and hundreds of bands had to shift to railroads to get from gig to gig.[88] Since rail service was best in large urban centers, musical life flourished in the nation's largest cities. In fact, the wartime economic boom fed a thriving nightlife—Americans now had some extra money to spend on movies, shows, and dancing. Of course, black bands were often left out of these good times. First, the new concentration of bands in the cities made competition that much tighter for the most lucrative theater and hotel jobs. Promoters and bookers were often reluctant to take a chance on a black band when popular white bands were nearly guaranteed draws.

Second, gas and rubber rationing, followed by the bans on driving—active off and on from 1942 through 1944—put black bands in a difficult situation. Travel by rail was expensive, and many chronically underpaid black bands had trouble affording it. In the South, travel by rail was especially trying because black musicians were forced into crowded and poorly ventilated "Jim Crow" cars.[89] Throughout the 1930s and early 1940s many black bands relied on buses to move around the country. In parts of the country—especially the South—buses were the safest option. The sudden appearance in town of fifteen to twenty black men driving cars was often perceived as a threat—the arrival of dangerous interlopers. Band buses, on the other hand, presented the image of a professional organization. And buses also provided a safe, and if need be mobile, locale in an unpredictable and hostile racial environment. As Scott DeVeaux writes, "During the Swing Era, the band bus had become a symbol of life on the road for black musicians. It was their rolling home on wheels: the locus of good conversation and endless card games in the involuntary camaraderie of constant travel, and—all too often—a place to eat and sleep when no accommodations were available."[90] In fact, musicians, promoters, and managers immediately perceived the loss of bus travel as a mortal threat to the livelihood of black bands. In mid-1942 Joe Glaser and Irving Mills, both white managers of successful black bands, and Walter White, head of the NAACP, went directly to the president to explain the situation and seek some compromise that would allow at least some bus travel. An agreement was worked out allowing for five buses to be shared among the forty-five black dance bands. In exchange for the use of the buses, the bands were to play at least twice a week for military institutions in the South.[91]

Charlie Barnet's career was shaped intimately by this traveling culture, and he writes often in his autobiography about the difficulties and dangers of this lifestyle, particularly during the 1930s and '40s at the height of dance band popularity. In 1938, not long after a fire at the Palomar Ballroom destroyed all of the band's equipment and charts, the group suffered another setback when vocalist Lloyd Hundling and guitarist Bus Etri were killed in a car accident on their way home from a gig at the Casa Mañana. It was a terrible tragedy for the group, and the next night "many of the guys had tears streaming down their faces." Barnet waited years before hiring another guitar player.[92] Despite this tragedy and the usual run of touring headaches and misery, Barnet never soured on the freedom offered by the mobile lifestyle he so enthusiastically adopted.

In 1941 the Barnet band recorded "Blue Juice," the title based on a nickname the bandleader gave to one of his most treasured belongings, a light blue Lincoln Continental. Echoing the larger culture, fascination and attachment to cars was widespread. In his autobiography black bandleader Andy Kirk could recall in great detail the many automobiles he'd had: "We had been using a fleet of Dodges at first. I burned out an axle in Port Arthur, Texas, called a wrecker, and then bought a Buick. It was a dream. I had it two years then bought another, a 1940 Buick—green with white walls, and a radio, before radios were standard equipment."[93] In Bill Crow's *Jazz Anecdotes*, bassist Milt Hinton recalls how Cab Calloway, his boss at the time, would bring his big green Lincoln on the train with the group as it traveled across the country. "Everywhere Cab went he took that beautiful car with him, and when he got into town the rest of us would get taxis, but Cab would roll out that old Linc down off the train, with his coonskin coat on and a fine Homburg or derby, and drive off into town looking for action."[94]

Other bandleaders eagerly bought cars when they were financially within reach, and it was not uncommon for leaders to travel separately from the rest of the group. Musicians who saved some money might be able to buy cars themselves and climb the socioeconomic ladder. Stuff Smith, the violinist and bandleader, made some money after recording "I'se a Muggin'" and bought a car in 1936, though he managed to wreck it pulling out from the showroom lot.[95]

For black bands the automobile was a mixed blessing. On the one hand, it offered an intense experience of freedom, an escape from the cramped existence of southern Jim Crow or the de facto segregation of the urban ghetto. But car culture brought into being new structures of racial discrimination and new kinds of racialized fears, not least of which was the "uncomfortable idea of a black man at the wheel of a speeding vehicle."[96] All the difficulties that Barnet and his orchestra experienced paled in comparison with the chronic frustrations and indignities suffered by all-black bands.[97] On entering a new town, black musicians had to find the black neighborhood, the only place they would be able to secure food and accommodations or even a bathroom. Recalling his time touring Pennsylvania, Andy Kirk remembers having to make their headquarters in Pittsburgh and "fan out from there into Latrobe, Johnstown, and Youngstown, Ohio," because the state had so few accommodations for black bands.[98] In fact, Kirk helped compile a United States guidebook for the Travelguide Company (where his wife worked at the time) designed specifically for black Americans. Besides listing the many places blacks could stay and eat while traveling the country, the book would also guide travelers "out of embarrassing situations."[99]

Those bands that ventured into the most explicitly segregated parts of the country, large swaths of the American South, also had to face the possibility of real violence, including lynchings.[100] In the early 1940s Charlie Barnet was reluctant to take his integrated band, featuring singer Lena Horne, to a gig in Alabama.[101] The South, dangerous as it could be, was a complex place with its own rules. Andy Kirk's band had its greatest success in the South, and it toured the region often during the 1930s and '40s.[102] It was not uncommon there for black bands to play for white audiences, with African American patrons often allowed to watch from the balcony. The same situation applied at black dances: whites often attended but were allowed only in designated areas.[103]

The car and the road were necessities, part of the basic economic structure of the industry. For many musicians, black and white, the relentlessness of the traveling life proved just too difficult. Arranger Sy Oliver suggested that one reason Jimmie Lunceford was not able to sustain his band through the 1940s was that the talented and intelligent musicians he hired would eventually realize "there were other things in life more worthwhile than traveling all year and living in bad hotels."[104] Gene Krupa remembered wistfully looking into the lighted windows of the passing houses "yearn[ing] for the same kind of life."[105] Many bands, including reasonably wealthy ones that paid well, such as Duke Ellington's, eventually lost many members who ultimately decided the benefits of band life did not outweigh the constant instability.[106] One way around all this travel was to secure steady gigs at hotels—hard jobs to find, especially for black bands.[107]

Yet despite all this instability and danger, the road had an irresistible pull that crossed the boundaries of class and race. For every account of the misery and difficulties of road life, musicians just as often speak eloquently of its attractions. Andy Kirk praises the brutal one-night stands that made up the bulk of his performing career: "You always hear about one-nighters, how awful they were: 'Man, those one-nighters are killing me. They're a drag, man.' I want to talk about how *good* one-nighters were. If it hadn't been for one-nighters, I wouldn't have met Mrs. Mary McLeod Bethune, and Dr. George Washington Carver, and a lot of other wonderful people whose names aren't in anybody's 'Who's Who.'"[108]

Travel created unique opportunities for musicians, black and white, to encounter people and cultural practices far different from their own. Andy Kirk recalls working the ballrooms in Minnesota and hearing and playing polkas.[109] Long bus trips were educational in other ways too. They provided a kind of traveling musical conservatory with plenty of time for instruction from older, more experienced players.[110] Along with the educational opportunities, such touring created a very tight, intense community.[111] Some musicians have even suggested that traveling during the Depression was "better" for its slowness, unpredictability, and inconvenience. Count Basie's longtime drummer, "Papa" Jo Jones, speaking to Graham Colombé, makes this point explicitly:

They never saw the people, they weren't on the circuses and carnivals, they didn't hit the forty-eight states—villages and hamlets, you know. After World War II it got so they could get in an aeroplane and they never see nothing. I say, "Where are you guys going?" They say, "California." They get on a plane. "What did you see?" They didn't see nothing. "It sure was a rough trip—five hours and five minutes." That's a rough trip! It used to take us days to get to California, and from Chicago to New York with Basie's Band. We were playing one-nighters and we'd puddle-jump. They didn't have those beautiful highways then and the Clipper service didn't come in until 1939.[112]

Vibraphonist Terry Gibbs, who played with Buddy Rich's and Woody Herman's bands in the 1940 and '50s, tells a story that sums up the persistent allure of road life. After losing all their money in Reno, Nevada, Gibbs, Jackie Carman, and Frank La Pinto had one hundred dollars wired to them and drove back across the country to New York City, surviving on salami and cheese. The car finally gave out, right in the middle of the Lincoln Tunnel. When he finally arrived home, Gibbs swore he'd abandon the itinerant life for good. "It wasn't an hour later," Gibbs recalls, "that I got a call from the Woody Herman band. Would I join them in Chicago?" He immediately "dressed, showered, shaved," and jumped "on the next plane" out.[113]

If a song like "Pompton Turnpike" seems an idealization after considering the day-to-day grind of touring bands, it was nonetheless a powerful sound that evoked the profound attraction of the highway. The road, whether as symbol (as in "Pompton Turnpike") or reality, was full of possibilities for alternative identities and lifestyles. The road opened new communities, allowing in new sounds, new ideas, and new ways of being. For restless, questioning leaders like Barnet, the freedom of the road naturally intersected with issues of race. The technology that could reshape his own life could also be used to reshape larger cultural ideas regarding the nature of race in American life.

"Drop Me Off in Harlem"

While the freedom of the nation's crisscrossing roads was a continual source of inspiration and excitement for Barnet (if not always for the rest of the band), the bandleader would travel one particular route to one special destination again and again: the roads that led to New York's Harlem neighborhood. Harlem was the incubator of the Duke Ellington Orchestra's sound and the site of its first success. It was also home to the Savoy Ballroom and dynamic dance bands such as Chick Webb's, as well as Harlem's Apollo Theater, another cultural landmark that would play an important role in the Barnet Orchestra's career.

Unlike the downtown whites who toured and partied in Harlem during the neighborhood's vogue in the 1920s, Barnet sought out a more substantial relationship with the place. In an interview with Patricia Willard, Barnet claims that he came within two hundred votes of being elected honorary mayor of Harlem.[114] The band's breakthrough hits— "Cherokee," "Pompton Turnpike," and "Skyliner"—were massively popular in Harlem and in other black neighborhoods across the nation. In 1940 *Metronome* printed an exuberant article headlined "White Bands Big in Harlem: Barnet Kills Sepians in Debut at Apollo; Miller Big at Savoy; Feeling Reciprocal." Although the tone of the story undoubtedly reflects the magazine's underlying progressive attitude toward American race relations, it does provide a sense of Barnet's position as a genuine success in Harlem: "The colored folks have been vociferous in their acclamation, as for example the near riot that broke out when Charlie Barnet shattered all precedent and opening day records as he brought the first white band into the Apollo Theatre." (It is also worth pointing out that the all-white Glenn Miller band—a sweeter-sounding band than Barnet's—was similarly well received at Harlem's most famous dance hall, the Savoy Ballroom, more evidence of the cross-racial appeal of all kinds of dance band jazz.)[115]

Actually, this was not Barnet's first time at the Apollo. He played there in 1934 with an earlier version of his band. Black saxophonist Benny Carter suggested the group to the theater management as a replacement when Fletcher Henderson's group canceled.[116] Barnet himself spoke fondly of his experiences playing the famous theater: "It was quite an experience. And I still say that is the greatest audience I ever played to in my life. Boy, when that curtain came flying up and everybody—it was an exhilaration, and they used to pour it on you. We did as many as eight shows a day there. We at one time held the house record for business."[117]

During the 1930s and '40s, Barnet would travel to Harlem repeatedly: literally to play in its theaters and clubs, but also symbolically as he sought new sounds across the racial divide of the big band industry. After "Pompton Turnpike," Barnet would more and more achieve in reality the racial hybridity he performed in his music. He famously hired African American singer Lena Horne to record with his group in 1941, but she was just one among many black musicians Barnet hired: trumpeters Peanuts Holland, Al Killian, and Howard McGhee, trombonist Trummy Young, and bassist Oscar Pettiford. At the same time Barnet (somewhat reluctantly), along with Woody Herman, began incorporating into his band the edgier, decidedly black sounds of the emerging "modern jazz" or "bebop" style.[118]

In 1943 Charlie Barnet and His Orchestra recorded a version of Duke Ellington's "Drop Me Off in Harlem" (originally written and recorded by Ellington in 1933).[119] The tune had been in their book since 1934 and was one of their featured jazz pieces, a song very different from the sweet hotel-style jazz they often had to play around that time. Barnet recalls how the band angered the staid patrons and management of the New Orleans Roosevelt Hotel by "pouring it on with 'Drop Me Off in Harlem.'" Apparently, to Barnet's surprise, the hot jazz one could hear just down the street in the French Quarter was off-limits at the tony, middle-class hotel.[120] The incident is also a fascinating glimpse into the complex geography and racial politics of jazz at the time: a white New York band playing a hot jazz tune written by a nationally famous black Harlem bandleader in New Orleans, birthplace of the music. In its movement and development, jazz had taken on a host of associations that transformed a local music into the sound of black, urban, northern cosmopolitanism. Jazz was now carrying the substantial additional weight of a host of new social developments in American race relations and social life.

The Barnet Orchestra's 1944 recording of "Drop Me Off in Harlem" features the band at its hottest, and it is a high point in the band's history of cross-racial musical interactions. The recording opens with a dramatic chromatic blast of chords and begins at a speedy 295 beats per minute. Not explicitly about cars or roads, the song is still deeply suggestive, the title implicitly suggesting an uptown taxi ride. But it is the reference to Harlem that is most provocative. In their reworking, however, Barnet and company dramatically increase the intensity, ratcheting up the speed and the interplay between soloist and ensemble. In his liner notes to the Decca reissue of this track Loren Schoenberg discusses the synthetic nature of the recording, with its mixture of new and old sounds: "With Roy's [Eldridge] exuberant solo, the stark horn lines, the variation on 'Cottontail' towards the end, and the Armstrong-inspired coda (and Roy's response to it), this performance encompasses the past, present and future of jazz as it stood in 1944."[121]

Structurally the tune is a direct arc upward—the performance is one long increase in energy as if accelerating on the open road. Figure 2.3 is a schematic representation of the song. Arranger Billy May squeezes all sorts of variations out of the rhythm changes material, dividing up choruses, reharmonizing the bridge sections, contrasting solo voice with ensemble backing. Like "Pompton Turnpike," the song is primarily a feature for the band's trumpet section, featuring Roy Eldridge as a guest. Barnet and pianist Dodo Marmarosa also get some solo room (a

Intro (eight measures)	Descending chromatic chords; horns dominate
A (eight measures)	
A	"Rhythm changes" in F major; full chorus
B	piano solo
A	
Break (four measures)	Syncopated solo spot for ensemble horn and reeds
A	Ensemble
A	
B	Barnet on tenor sax
A	
A	These sixteen measures are repeated four times. Trumpet battle
A (×4)	continues through to the end of the song, accompanied by repeat of syncopated ensemble shout figure
B	Ensemble interrupts the trumpet battle to play in the final bridge section
A	Trumpet battle continues for sixteen more measures
A	
Tag (four measures)	Trumpet soloist ends on high F (F3)

Figure 2.3 Form of "Drop Me Off in Harlem," Charlie Barnet and His Orchestra, music by Duke Ellington and Nick Kenney. Recorded February 1944.

half and a full chorus, respectively). However, it is the trumpet solos, played over a repeating horn figure on the A sections, that become the focal point of the recording. From Barnet's brief half-chorus solo until the end, the tune becomes a trumpet battle, with the stakes intensifying as the notes climb higher. The final string of Louis Armstrong–inspired high Cs is one-upped with a higher F at the final bar.

"Drop Me Off in Harlem" is about as hot as the Barnet band played, a way of making music that Barnet himself understood, self-consciously, as "black." In mood it is the flip side to the laid-back groove of "Pompton Turnpike." Here all is speed and motion. "Drop Me Off in Harlem" is urgent in its insistence and embrace of change. Here musical journeys echo literal ones. In the span of only two years, Barnet had pushed his band even further into the future, musically adopting some of the sounds of an emergent bebop and racially integrating his group. From 1936's "Make Believe Ballroom" down through "Pompton Turnpike," Barnet and crew sped outward across the nation and then back to the city, toward Harlem. The full promise of the moment, its possibilities for a new, nonracist American social order, would remain unrealized, but in Barnet's music we can still hear a celebration of the era's mobility.

Barnet wasn't the only musician of the early 1940s celebrating the interracial possibilities inherent in travel. The 1940s, Lewis Erenberg points out, were "a liminal period" in American racial ideology and practice. The fight against Nazism and its racist ideology showed America's own racial practices in a harsh new light. New economic opportunities and significant demographic changes "undercut the fixed racial standards of many communities."[122] In the dance band world, the war years saw many more overt efforts to present the music as an interracial activity. So many more white bandleaders were hiring black musicians that Dan Burley, the black music critic for the *Amsterdam News*, feared the practice would completely undermine the viability of all-black outfits.[123] Los Angeles, New York, and Washington, DC, all had integrated nightclubs—"canteens"—for soldiers. Margaret Halsey, the manager of New York's Stage Door Canteen, believed that a "Negro serviceman who was good enough to die for a white girl was good enough to dance with her."[124]

Barnet's ode to Ellington and Harlem was not an isolated gesture. In 1942 the Gene Krupa band, featuring Anita O'Day on vocals and black trumpeter Roy Eldridge on trumpet, recorded the Redd Evans–Earl Bostic tune "Let Me Off Uptown"—one of Krupa's biggest hits as a bandleader. The song, as O'Day describes it, "was just bits of dialogue over vamping music followed by a chorus, more dialogue and then Roy's spine-tingling trumpet solo."[125] The bluesy riff vamp, strong 4/4 swing, and hip patter were not that unusual for the time. But the duet between the white O'Day and the black Eldridge was. For O'Day, "*Uptown* was my old Chicago neighborhood, [but] to most people it meant Harlem." In order to sing the song right, O'Day traveled up to the neighborhood to visit "Minton's and some other swinging places."[126] In the bridge of the chorus, O'Day sings of some of the special Uptown pleasures: "Rib joints / juke joints / hep joints—where could a fella' go to top it?" After the chorus, O'Day and Eldridge have this half-sung, half-spoken exchange:

Eldridge: Anita, O, Anita. Say I feel something?
O'Day: What do you feel, the heat?
Eldridge: No it must be that Uptown rhythm. I feel like blowin'
O'Day: Well, blow, Roy, blow.

The playful, "hep" dialogue (Eldridge sings "Anita" with syncopated, bluesy swagger) lends itself to an alternative, sexually charged reading, made all the more risqué by the interracialism of the speakers. Like Barnet's "Drop Me Off in Harlem," "Let Me Off Uptown" features white musicians (O'Day, Krupa, and a predominantly white band), celebrating black culture through a musical journey to Harlem.

Ironically, this musical homage to the dynamism of urban black life and the egalitarian opportunities offered by new kinds of mobility was recorded at the verge of the massive suburbanization that in the coming decades would radically depopulate the inner cities and push middle-class white life—and the center of popular American culture more generally—into the suburbs. As Paul Gilroy points out, "White flight from urban centres was not just accomplished by means of the automobile—it was premised on it."[127] The roads, cars, and movement that created such promise of change in the 1930s and '40s became in the 1950s the engine for demographic developments that would undermine city life and real interracial integration, even as the civil rights movement was getting into full gear to successfully challenge legal segregation in the South and reshape American race relations.

Barnet and Race: The Unintended Ambivalence of Good Intentions

Barnet's decision to go hot and move away from a sweet sound provided opportunities for genuine social interactions in the highly racialized and segregated American social order. Adopting a "black" style of jazz meant incorporating specific musical techniques widely understood as racially coded: "dirty" instrumental timbres, blues gestures, and a harder-driving swing groove. These musical changes operated in, and derived their meaning from, a larger discursive field. For the band to sound "black," it had to focus on musical devices that most immediately and transparently signified "blackness." In addition to specific musical alterations and additions, Charlie Barnet bought arrangements directly from his idols (particularly Count Basie and Duke Ellington), hired black arrangers and musicians, and played a national circuit of black theaters. This literal movement, abetted by the musical changes he made, brought him closer to large segments of the black community than the vast majority of his fellow bandleaders on the national scene. It is in this sense that we can understand the Barnet band as playing "black music." As scholar Barry Shank writes, "For music to be functionally black, it must bring the black audience and the musicians together into an embodied group performance of cohesion and unity."[128] The Barnet band not only was popular among blacks (many white bands were also popular) but also aimed to be part of that community.

Most of the impetus to cross these racial boundaries came from Barnet himself. In his autobiography he insists he was motivated simply by the demands of making good music:

A lot of people credit me with helping to break down the color barrier in our business. It is true that I did hire a lot of black musicians in my bands over the years, but it was not done with any thought of being a crusader. I simply hired what I thought were the best men available at the time, and I never experienced any serious trouble about having a mixed band. Some work was probably withheld because of my policies, but there was then plenty of alternative employment to offset the engagements I lost. It never occurred to me that I might be doing something revolutionary or that some folks might have been upset by what I was doing. A mixed band today is the norm and nobody thinks twice about it. The one question was, and should always be, "How well does the guy play?"[129]

His modesty on this issue is genuine; Barnet was no civil rights crusader motivated by an overriding sense of racial injustice. His orchestra's breakthrough performance, and a record that remained its calling card for decades, was a version of Ray Noble's "Cherokee"—a song with embarrassingly racist lyrics (though Barnet's recording was instrumental)—that Barnet promoted wearing a faux Indian headdress.[130] Barnet never made any public statements on the issues of African American segregation, discrimination, and lynching. Perhaps most troubling of all, the bandleader, along with some other musicians, would occasionally play inexcusably cruel jokes on the black musicians who traveled with him.[131] In his autobiography Barnet tells of a particularly terrifying prank played on the group's African American arranger Andy Gibson by a friend of Barnet's named Aphriam J. Kahn: hanging out with the band during a tour of the South, Kahn and some friends, pretending to be Klan members, sneaked up on Gibson. According to Barnet, "Andy didn't think it was so funny and even after they had wined and dined him handsomely, he was still mumbling under his breath."[132]

Despite all this, Barnet was special in the musical world of the 1930s and '40s. Not only did he embrace African American music, he disseminated it through his very successful, nationally popular band. The music of the group bridged the two halves of the segregated big band world in very public ways. Like Benny Goodman, Barnet actively sought out black musicians to play with his group, and he officially integrated the band in the early 1940s.[133] In the late 1930s Barnet hired black arranger Andy Gibson to write charts for the group.[134] Most significant, through,

Barnet and his orchestra were one of the first white dance bands to play the Apollo Theater in Harlem, and the great success of that gig opened up a regional network of black theaters in Chicago, Baltimore, Detroit, and Washington, DC, eager to hire them.[135] Barnet's public choice to play "black," along with his widespread acceptance in the African American community, worked to undermine the racial "metaphysics" of American popular music that assigned specific musical practices to a discrete "Negro" identity.[136]

Barnet's experiences with crossing the color line were fostered and inspired by the road. With all their suggestions of movement and interconnection, roads also had profound implications for race relations, particularly issues of black segregation and discrimination. Roads could separate blacks and whites, but they could also bring them together. The possibility of movement was a specific challenge to racial segregation—a social order predicated on the management of people in space. Although a lot of what Charlie Barnet and his band recorded was not explicitly about roads or cars or travel, songs such as "Pompton Turnpike" and "Drop Me Off in Harlem" would turn out to be key moments in the band's history.

These performances show how Barnet's fascination with travel was not idiosyncratic but part of a much larger cultural development. For a progressive-minded American of the era, the new mobility offered by cars and roads offered new ways to think about place in American life and, by extension, American identity. These "road" songs become, following Lawrence Kramer, "hermeneutic windows."[137] Sound, discourse, and historical context converge, allowing us to see the band as part of a larger field of cultural activities and preoccupations. In its mobility, literally as a traveling band and figuratively in its self-conscious movement toward "black" jazz, the Barnet orchestra expressed a new kind of social and geographic mobility born from the reality and promise of America's roads.

From this point of view, Barnet's bridging of the racially segregated popular music world was simply an honest recognition that the music he played, and that many, many white bands were playing (and making a lot of money at it), was in fact deeply indebted to black musicians who forged this style from a multicultural stew of musical sources. In this view, Barnet brought to public consciousness what writer Albert Murray famously called the "incontestably mulatto" character of American life.[138] Yet the situation is still more complicated. Even from the moment of jazz's emergence into national consciousness in the 1910s, the music had been adopted—some would argue co-opted—by a white music industry seeking to make money off this wildly popular new music. Over time, the "social connotations of the sounds" defining jazz changed from black to white, and swing jazz would be understood by many Americans across the country as simply their music, not one marked by "blackness."[139] This discursive process, though, was never complete—even Paul Whiteman, the self-styled "King of Jazz"— acknowledged the music's origin in "African" culture. Much of the history of twentieth-century American popular music—and especially jazz—reflects this complex process where "blackness" is recognized even while being effaced. Barnet, in challenging the segregated band world of the late 1930s, also reinscribed racial difference.

His devotion to hot music and his growing distaste for hokey, sweet bands reinforced the racial divisions of the music industry that often locked black musicians into specific "racial" music styles.[140] Jazz critics who celebrated Barnet's "authentic" jazz further reinforced racial categories and an implicit essentialism about black music and musicians. In a 1939 article for *Metronome*, jazz critic George Simon declared the Barnet Orchestra the "Blackest White Band of All." According to Simon, "The band's style is distinctly negroid," and they show the world "that white men can play Ellington music too."[141] Simon was a progressive-minded critic, deeply sympathetic and knowledgeable about black musical culture, jazz, and American music. Still, his comments inadvertently reveal the complexities of American racial thinking of the time.

The double-sided nature of Barnet's adoption and celebration of certain black vernacular musical practices—in this case hot improvisatory music—reflects larger tensions in the progressive racial politics of the era. For example, *Down Beat*, a magazine central to the post-1935 swing culture, was suffused with the progressive New Deal–Popular Front "swing ideology" that celebrated the music as an example of the best of America's liberal, pluralistic tradition. But in their articles and editorials, many of the key writers at the magazine revealed a much more ambivalent stance toward racial equality in the dance band business. In an editorial celebrating Goodman's hiring of black pianist Teddy Wilson, the magazine reserves special praise for white pianist Jess Stacy, who nobly stood aside "without the slightest trace of resentment" to let Wilson play. Further, the magazine's calls for desegregation in the music world were often hedged, stepping back from the most radical positions. Roundtable discussions in the magazine, such as "Should Negro Musicians Play in White Bands?" suggest that integration was up for debate and a question reasonable people could disagree on.[142]

Even Barnet's willingness—in fact, eagerness—to hire black musicians proved to have unintended negative consequences for black musicians. White bands that hired black musicians—a situation that happened more and more frequently by the mid-1940s—could generally offer better pay, working conditions, and public exposure than could most black bands, even the relatively successful orchestras of Duke Ellington, Cab Calloway, and Jimmie Lunceford. Ironically, the breaking of the color barrier in white bands ending up hurting many black bands, which lost out on talented musicians. Most important, integration in white bands did nothing to change the basic structure of white privilege at the heart of the music industry. Black bands still could not secure important hotel gigs in major cities such as New York, Chicago, and Los Angeles, and they remained second-class citizens in the recording and publishing side of the music business.[143]

Hybridity, as ethnomusicologists Ronald Radano and Philip Bohlman remind us, does not necessarily "signal a move away from racialized metaphysics." It can, rather, "reinforce that metaphysics."[144] The aesthetic urge to cross racial boundaries, with its progressive political implications, did not necessarily undo false and damaging notions of racial identity. Barnet's freedom of movement was an ability not shared by the vast majority of black musicians he so admired. His cross-racial gestures could not be publicly reciprocated. Even as famous and influential a black musician as Duke Ellington could not fully maneuver around the categories of the music industry or the expectations of music critics (perhaps one reason he so adamantly insisted on seeing everything "beyond category").

Road Songs

The recordings of Charlie Barnet and His Orchestra, especially key tunes such as "Drop Me Off in Harlem" and "Pompton Turnpike," were, in the end, about possibilities for social change, embodied in sound; they were not necessarily a representation of any particular lived reality. Despite Barnet's progressive ideas regarding race in American life, the band that recorded "Pompton Turnpike" was all white. In the coming years Barnet would integrate his band full time, but at this point he felt that was too risky for a group that had just achieved a measure of financial stability and public acceptance. The promise of the road was in actual experience pretty far from the place represented in sound. Much work would be involved in making the social possibilities a reality.

Barnet's tribute in "Pompton Turnpike" remains an important moment of hope for a machine age America that invested tremendous faith in technological development. The song is also an excellent example of music's power to register not only real social change but also the *possibility* of social change. In the process of going hot, of writing and commissioning edgier new material with greater syncopation, more blues notes and gestures, and more solo improvisations, Barnet was explicitly incorporating "blackness" into his music. His move to this kind of music in the years after 1936 certainly had substantial commercial benefits. Between the early 1930s and the end of World War II, many bands would attempt to capitalize on the sudden popularity of the hotter brand of jazz that exploded into mainstream public consciousness after Benny Goodman's successes of 1935. And, of course, sweet jazz was still a more than viable economic option; Guy Lombardo, for example, remained immensely popular from his first major success in 1927 through the 1950s and '60s. But just as it would be wrong to assume that Barnet's musical choices were made solely based on some abstract artistic imperative or some principle of social justice, it would also be wrong to assume that his aesthetic choices were motivated by nothing but dollar signs. In the complex flow of lived experiences, decisions about life are often made intuitively or for reasons only dimly understood at the moment. The fact is, whatever the particular mixture of reasons, the way Barnet chose to remake his musical style was effectively a political statement.

From his writings and the evidence of his recordings, it seems clear that Charlie Barnet felt a disconnect between the "Make Believe Ballroom" of his 1936 record and the reality of experience in America during the late 1930s. The escapism of "Make Believe Ballroom" was an inaccurate vision of the country that smoothed over seething social tensions with a deracinated, placeless imaginary dance hall. In his 1984 autobiography Barnet discusses his music from this pivotal time. Records such as "Make Believe Ballroom" and "Milkman's Matinee" gave the band a lot of exposure, securing them financially rewarding gigs. But this new success did not change the fact that Barnet felt his band had no distinct personality—"neither fish nor fowl"—and that it was being molded into a "middle-of-the-road commercial band" like Abe Lyman's group. Barnet believe that in their "spirit" and "wildness" his players could never be like these tepid commercial outfits.[145]

Commerce and music are closely intertwined (the industry couldn't sell a band with no "identifiable direction"), but Barnet's decision to head hotter rather than sweeter was built on deeper ideas about what his music should and could be. Using his own language, the shift in musical style was the band's "spirit" catching up with its music: trying to open that safe, neither fish nor fowl "Make Believe Ballroom" to new intercultural reality. Barnet wanted something more for his band and its music. Radio could certainly create a "ballroom in a small room," but other forces, in particular roads and automobiles, were allowing people to move out of these spaces into new communities. Why settle for the "Make Believe Ballroom" when real ones were so close? The proliferation of swing provided the opportunity to realize his dream of a band that was successful but also able to play and record the black music he admired.

In his survey of 1930s culture, historian Morris Dickstein writes that "out of the stagnation" of the Depression, the "1930s had invented the future." Norman Bel Geddes's vision of an automotive nation, although wrong in some specifics, largely came true: "The GM Futurama rightly predicted the automotive America of the 1960s, crisscrossed by ribbons of new highways." All the movement embedded in the music and art of the era was realized in a postwar life of real mobility: "The loops and curves of art deco eventually became the cloverleafs of the interstate highway system, superseding the right-angle grid of downtown traffic patterns. . . . In the postwar years, with the growth of suburbia, Americans at last achieved the mobility that had been denied to them during hard times."[146] With the realization of this dream, of the egalitarian promise of the road, came stark ironies and unexpected consequences. The Pompton Turnpike, in fact the entire local, state, and federal program to build roads *out* of the cities, would lead in the postwar years to a gradual but steady and dramatic disintegration of city life, especially for blacks and other people of color.[147] The promise of the road, of the automobile, would, like so many promises before, fall largely to country's white middle class. Rather than connect and integrate, roads would end up dividing the country even further, isolating the inner-city ghettos and moving valuable tax money into the burgeoning suburbs.[148] Further, it would lead to a diagnosis of a new American cultural malady: rootlessness. "Even before the huge migrations to the Sunbelt and California, social critics of the 1950s (such as William H. Whyte) suggested that America was becoming a much more rootless society."[149] Mobility had, in their view, undermined a sense of community and belonging. It is a criticism echoed in today's writing on Americans' sense of place and self-identity.[150] "In the end," Dickstein writes, "the dream of mobility turned into a terrible disappointment for some who succeeded and others who were left behind, and the depression era, like the wartime, would come nostalgically to seem more authentic, more genuine—a time when life seemed more real and Americans lived much closer to the bone."[151]

The promise of the road, of new kinds of freedom, turned especially sour for African Americans. Taking the large historical view, cultural historian Paul Gilroy sees the car as the "ur-commodity" of American consumer culture and its importance in black life as, on balance, a political loss in the century's freedom struggles. Buying automobiles, African Americans "discovered themselves and their agency" through consumerism rather than political citizenship.[152] Further, the privatized mobility of the car significantly damaged "the possibility of collective experience, synchronised suffering, and acting in concert." Particularly after World War II, the car became "the instrument of segregation and privatisation, not an aid to their overcoming."[153]

The reality and metaphor of the road, addressed obliquely in the jazz of the 1930s and '40s (though more directly in the blues), would become a major lyrical trope in popular music through the coming decades, carrying the weight of all types of utopian American dreams. In an article reprinted in the *Chicago Tribune* on June 23, 2004, author Dan Neil claims that this trope is dying, that road songs are in decline. Speaking specifically about rock, pop, and country songs from the 1950s on, Neil suggests, "the Road is disappearing."

Fading from popular music is the body of imagery, the poetic conventions that evoke the Mythic American Road. Where are the songs written in the cadence of white lines and the key of singing tires, like Willie Nelson's "On the Road Again"? Where are the songs about fugitive romance, like Kris Kristofferson's "Me and Bobby McGee" . . .? Even country music has grown increasingly immobile and domestic, its imagery hemmed in by suburbia. . . . Regardless of the list you consult—and there are plenty—it seems apparent that songs of the road are running on empty.[154]

If Neil is correct, then the loss of this symbol signals a new American era. The paradox of the road and the automobile, of their liberating and destructive powers, was a powerful engine of American cultural production. It was the nexus for a deep and thorough engagement with the contradictions of twentieth-century American modernity. The highways that crisscross our country, that have divided—and in many cases destroyed—entire communities, also connected us to each other and forced into American consciousness the need to recognize, come to terms with, and in some cases actively shape a new social arrangement.

For African Americans, roads and their own cars meant greater free-dom, freedom that implicitly and explicitly challenged the existing racial order. As Paul Gilroy astutely points out, the twentieth-century social movements for racial equality were "animated by people who had very good reasons to fear the constraints involved in being tied to one place. That anxiety may well have inclined them towards the pleasures of speed, autonomy, and privatised transport, quite apart from their attraction to the automobile as a provocative emblem for the wealth and status they desired but were so often denied."[155] The progressive possibilities of car ownership and greater mobility were met with strong, sometimes violent, resistance. Still, these new technolo-gies did enable some important cross-cultural interactions. As a white bandleader, Charlie Barnet realized many more of these social oppor-tunities made possible through this mobility than did his black col-leagues. The many socially progressive gestures of his career—publicly celebrating the music of black bands he admired, hiring black arrangers and musicians to play in his group—could not be reciprocated. It was an imbalance that, in hindsight, points to the severe limitations of the many cross-racial projects of the 1930s and '40s. Still, Barnet's musical journey from sweet to hot, from white to black was a powerful demon-stration of how dance band jazz of the era allowed whites to "indulge their long-standing fascination for African-American culture without protective coloration of blackface."[156] The music of Charlie Barnet and His Orchestra represented a powerful aesthetic and intellectual coming to terms with the new social relationships permitted by a rapidly mod-ernizing nation.

THREE

A Locomotive Laboratory of Place: Duke Ellington and His Orchestra

Over their long career, Duke Ellington and His Orchestra produced an impressive body of music that evoked many familiar and exotic places. Although song titles are not necessarily the most reliable indicators of meaning in jazz—especially instrumental jazz—the quantity of place-themed songs recorded by the Ellington Orchestra is unusual and striking: "Birmingham Breakdown" (1926), "East St. Louis Toodle-O" (1926), "Drop Me Off in Harlem" (1933), "Caravan" (1936), "Warm Valley" (1941), "Chelsea Bridge" (1941), "Paris Blues" (1960), *Far East Suite* (1966), and *New Orleans Suite* (1970).[1] In his writings and interviews, Ellington often cited specific places as defining influences on his music. He opens his memoir, *Music Is My Mistress*, with a brief prologue titled "The Road." Over two pages the bandleader spins out a synopsis of his life built around a single conceit: travel. For Ellington, his story is one of movement—from the front yard of his childhood home in Washington, DC, to his apartment in New York City. From there he traveled the globe, visiting "Jugoslavia, Okinawa, the Philippines, Taiwan, Hong Kong, Thailand, Malaya, Laos, Burma, Indonesia, Australia, Fiji, New Zealand, U.S.S.R." Ellington defines himself neither by the musicians in his band nor by the voluminous catalog of his recordings but by the places he has been.[2]

In a 1962 interview with Stanley Dance, Ellington insisted that his compositions were "descriptive of something. Always."[3] Place experiences were everyday sources of musical inspiration both to Ellington and to his writing partner, Billy Strayhorn. 1966's *Far East Suite*, for example, was inspired by the band's travels through Japan two years earlier.[4] Modes of travel—particularly trains—were also frequent sources of inspiration. In 1939 Billy Strayhorn, wanting to impress Ellington for their first meeting in New York City, wrote a song based on the bandleader's subway directions. The tune, "Take the A-Train," eventually became the band's theme song.[5] Ellington loved traveling by rail, and he wrote a string of songs about it: "Choo-Choo" (1924), "Daybreak Express" (1933), "Happy-Go-Lucky Local" (1946), and "Track 360" (1958). Recent musicians and critics have celebrated this preoccupation with geography and travel. In 2002 Jazz at Lincoln Center broadcast a public radio program titled "In the Spirit of Place," featuring arrangements of Ellington's place-themed works along with commentary by writer Albert Murray and musician Wynton Marsalis.

In this chapter I focus on a particular moment in the Ellington Orchestra's history of musical place making: a live 1946 performance at Chicago's Civic Opera House, an important gig in the band's career at one of the nation's elite urban music venues. It was a concert filled with place-themed works. I will focus on two performances from the concert, "Air-Conditioned Jungle," a dynamic and multivalent evocation of the urban experience, and the four-part *The Deep South Suite*, a work that performed a complex and contradictory American South. Looking at the band through a hermeneutic of place will show how the music and the "extramusical" (titles, programs, context) worked together to create new kinds of American places. This analytical lens could be focused on any number of Ellington works spanning the band's professional life, but the specific performances discussed in this chapter are paradigmatic. These works also suggest important links with other black artists of the time working in visual arts and literature who also were preoccupied with representing the black experience of travel, migration, and urbanization.

Musical Place as Social Process

In the introduction I established the basis for describing musical experience as spatial. Musical "places" are created when the formal and phenomenological spatiality of music meets the lived social experience of space. The musical performance of a place is not a thing but a dynamic process, a social interaction between people and musical sound. Thus, the places evoked in musical performances are more than metaphors; they are a kind of materialization of the places referenced and of specific social relationships. We should not hear these Ellington performances as documentaries in sound or as a kind of musical tourism. Yet there was a change, a partial transformation of the space, and it provided a glimpse of other places and other social arrangements.

The relentless travel of the Ellington band made these nightly performances of places especially urgent: it was one of the most mobile groups of Americans during the era, repeatedly crisscrossing North America. The orchestra's creation of musical places happened as part of a daily grind of actual, literal movement from place to place. As they traveled, the Ellington Orchestra created what art historian David Hickey describes as "momentary acoustic communities."[6] The band's unique social dynamic—virtuosic, highly individualized voices working to create a coherent ensemble sound—suggested to audiences not just that other places and experience were possible, but that all places were open to reconstruction. For example, the anonymous northern city with its simmering racial tensions and the Deep South with its legally segregated racial order were not permanent places but could be unmade and remade.

This urge to represent places, particularly those central to black life, such as "the South" or "Harlem," was one shared by many black artists of the 1930s and '40s working in visual arts and literature. Throughout the Depression and war years, an interest in place by African American artists was closely tied to recovering a "lost" history of black America and documenting contemporary rural and urban black life. Inspired by the residual energy of the 1920s Harlem Renaissance and given new impetus by some of the more progressive New Deal programs, artists and writers such Jacob Lawrence, Aaron Douglas, Richard Wright, and Zora Neale Hurston worked to document the full scope of the black American journey, from Africa to the New World, slavery to freedom, South to North, and country to city.[7] And even though America's entrance into the Second World War ended these New Deal programs and shifted the nation's focus toward unity and patriotism (and away from unflattering social history or documentary that emphasized inequality or cultural difference), the war years provided new political and intellectual energy to black artists seeking to document, analyze, and explain African America's "place" in the nation's life. The rapidly growing war industry opened new kinds of employment to blacks, and these opportunities created new waves of domestic migration, particularly to the West Coast.[8] The war years saw an intensification of many of the same themes of the 1930s: What was the relationship of these new migrants with the South they left behind? What kind of place was this new urban environment?[9]

In 1941 the twenty-three-year-old painter Jacob Lawrence exhibited his Migration Series at Edith Halpert's Downtown Gallery in New York City. The "Series" was a collection of sixty paintings based on the history of African American migration from the South to the North. Along with the images, Lawrence provided sixty short captions. The paintings are figurative but do not strive for a true-to-life realism; they are distinctively modern in their abstraction and transformation of real world people, objects, and events. The images do not offer a strict documentary narrative of the Great Migration, though they do loosely follow the story from past to present and South to North. Many of the panels show people in transit—walking with luggage across rural and urban landscapes, watching the passing landscape from train windows, maneuvering through crowded city streets. Others depict the specific places involved—especially the landscapes of the rural South and the urban, industrialized North.

For scholar Farah Jasmine Griffin, Lawrence's paintings are part of a larger cultural form she calls the "migration narrative." This artistic trope, manifested in visual arts, literature, and music, provided black artists with ways to explore the impact of the "massive dislocations" caused by migration from the rural South to the urban North. While differing in their specifics, works that adopted the migration narrative shared several key topics: a presentation of the reasons for migration, a representation of the initial confrontation with the urban environment, a struggle in coming to terms with the city's positive and negative effects, and a reflection on the limitations and possibilities of both the city and the country, North and South.[10] Ellington's works of the 1930s and '40s are usefully understood as manifestations of Griffin's trope. Through a rich juxtaposition of titles, program notes, in-performance talks, and musical forms and gestures, Ellington created a body of work in the mid-1940s guided by the conceptual framework of the migration narrative. His lengthy works, in particular the suites he wrote for his Carnegie Hall appearances in the 1940s, are musical kin to Lawrence's epic Migration Series, as well as the writings of many black authors of the era such as Richard Wright, Zora Neale Hurston, Ralph Ellison, and Gwendolyn Brooks.[11]

As important as Ellington was as an individual artist and guiding force for his band's musical compositions, we cannot put the entire creative burden on the bandleader himself. He created these musical geographies—these migration narratives—with partners: the overwhelming majority of Ellington's music was performed and sometimes written by musicians he employed. The initial inspiration, perhaps even the bulk of the writing, might have been Ellington's (or Strayhorn's), but the sonic, real-time performance—the aesthetic event—was the result of an entire band.

By focusing on the interaction of the players in the realization of these musical locales, I will shift the focus away from the Ellington-centric narratives that dominate scholarship on the band. Ellington was the leader of a complex group of individuals belonging to a complex social institution. The music was created through the interaction of a leader with the individual instrumentalists. It was a process open to disagreement and contention. In most scholarship on Ellington, his band and his personality are conflated: Ellington *is* his band, and the music of the band is an expression of his compositional genius. Given the justifiable push to celebrate Ellington as a great American composer, it is not surprising that the discourse around the bandleader is now nearly identical to that surrounding the great composers of Western classical music.

Literary theorist Mikhail Bakhtin famously described (and celebrated) certain single-authored novels as dialogic, as revealing the "heteroglossia," or contextual contingency, of all linguistic practice.[12] Following Bakhtin, prevailing scholarship reads Ellington's music "monologically," as embodying a single discourse and a single perspective. A hermeneutic of place helps deconstruct this prevalent bias conveyed in jazz writing that Ellington *is* his orchestra and helps reinterpret the band's music as dialogic, reflecting the basic heteroglossia of social practice where the meaning is always contextual and contingent.[13] Listening closely to the music of the Ellington Orchestra, we hear competing voices, meanings, and representations of the spatial experiences of black America.

Fragmenting the Ellington Effect

The Smithsonian Institution houses a remarkable collection of photographs of prominent jazz musicians taken between 1938 and 1948 by photographer William Gottlieb. Figure 3.1 is a photo of the Ellington band that Gottlieb took right around the time of the 1946 Chicago Opera House concert. The photo captures the band in media res—onstage during a show, but at a pause in the performance.[14] The oblique angle of the shot (looking up from a corner of the stage, maybe from a lower riser), along with its apparent candidness, emphasizes each single musician over the larger group. As Ellington leans over the piano and smiles, looking out over the crowd, the musicians rise above him in a steep curve, crowned by Sonny Greer behind his drum kit. Maybe between numbers, maybe about to start, maybe just finished, the band looks around with no single focus. Clarinetist Jimmy Hamilton, visible almost in the direct center of the image, examines his clarinet as he holds it in front of him. Just a little bit down in the reed section our eye moves rightward, catching baritone saxophonist Harry Carney glancing at the camera—at us—with a playful smile. Below Carney at the bottom right of the image is Cat Anderson, muted trumpet in mouth, pointing his finger toward the audience. Above Anderson, Carney, and Hamilton, and just behind alto saxophonist Johnny Hodges, Ellington's great trombone section is clearly visible. Valve trombonist Claude Jones (Ellington's replacement for the recently departed Juan Tizol) looks at us, the stage light reflecting off his glasses. Next to him Lawrence Brown turns toward drummer Sonny Greer, a hint of a grin on his face.

The energy of the picture comes from so many little scenes within the larger one. The presence of so many people, each occupied in a slightly different way, overwhelms the centrality of the bandleader who seems, in this one instant, an appendage far from the center of our attention. The Ellington Orchestra, it is immediately apparent, is a complex thing. Who are these people, and where did they all come from? Exactly how did this organism operate, and how were all these individuals integrated (or not) into the group?

While all the large big bands of the swing era had to deal with these problems, Ellington's group was unique in that the very success of the band, the central aesthetic appeal of the group, was constructed around unique individual voices.[15] From very early in its career, the Ellington Orchestra built its sound around a compelling blend of highly original instrumental voices (and just as often idiosyncratic and strong-willed personalities). Much Ellington scholarship shows a deep tension, even schizophrenia, when speaking about this characteristic. Writers as diverse as Gunther Schuller, John Edward Hasse, Martin Williams, and Stanley Crouch all emphasize the collaborative nature of just about

Figure 3.1 Duke Ellington and His Orchestra, ca. 1946. From Smithsonian Institution's "American Memory: Historical Collections for the National Digital Library," "William Gottlieb: Photographs form the Golden Age of Jazz." The photo can be found at http://memory.loc .gov/cgi-bin/query/D?gottlieb:24:/temp/~ammem_K1Ep; digital identification number is "gottlieb 02461."

all of Ellington's "compositions"—all these writers recognize the importance of figures such as trumpeter Bubber Miley, clarinetist Barney Bigard, and arranger and pianist Billy Strayhorn. But at the same time, the rhetoric always, almost imperceptibly, slips back into assertions of Ellington's singular compositional genius. Gunther Schuller's analyses frequently culminate in lists that begin with Ellington and end with Verdi, Wagner, Bach, Mozart, or Beethoven.[16]

Historian Martin Williams, although sensitive to the collaborative nature of Ellington's music, ultimately uses this fact to justify his assessment of Ellington's compositional genius. In a famous essay he describes songs like "Ring Dem Bells" as emblematic of the band ("some of his most effective pieces have basically been strings of solos by his musicians"). But Martin immediately falls back into talking about the music as Ellington's, effacing those individual voices.[17] Interestingly, it was not these scholars but Ellington's collaborator, Billy Strayhorn, who came up with what has been the most popular phrase to describe the unique achievement of the bandleader and composer. He called it the "Ellington Effect"—a term so evocative and vague that it is useful for proving just about anything you want it to. While originally referring to Ellington's orchestration, it easily bleeds into ideas of composition.[18]

In fact, the exact nature of Ellington's compositional practice is unclear. He undoubtedly wrote a significant amount of original material, but he also worked closely with the band to generate music. There is scattered but significant documentation of this. Since the band's inception in the mid-1920s, a great deal of the group's music was generated through a constant and informal give-and-take, with musicians often contributing the central melodies and harmonies to written arrangements.[19] While he certainly spent hours alone writing music, Ellington also was an extremely active bandleader whose busy schedule of engagements meant that music was written quickly and often at the last moment. Some instrumental parts were memorized and known only to the players themselves, and some were never even marked on the written arrangements.[20] As these informal, oral composition practices illustrate, the members of the Ellington Orchestra operated within the bureaucratic and often undemocratic nature of big band life, but they also helped shape it into something far more complex. While nominally the musical and financial head, Ellington did not—in reality could not—have the final say on his musical output. Within the tightly structured environment of big band jazz, there was far more room for individual creative freedom than is generally acknowledged in the scholarly literature.

Gottlieb's photograph echoes the fluidity of the band's social and artistic structure: the closer we look at the Ellington Orchestra, the less centered on its leader it seems to be, and the more we are aware of the multitude of competing instrumental and compositional voices. The "Ellington Effect" begins to fracture. We see a group of very different individuals held loosely together by a tenuous combination of shared artistic goals and larger economic and social circumstances. Ellington's position as one of the preeminent African American entertainers of the 1930s and '40s, and his location in the migrant magnet of New York City, allowed him to hire many of the nation's best black musicians. In this sense the band was a composite not only of personalities but of American places as well.

Table 3.1 shows the birthplaces and travels of the members of Ellington's 1946 band. Birthplaces are not the most accurate indicator of where a musician spent his childhood or adolescence, but they do

Table 3.1 Ellington personnel, November 1946

Player	Instrument	Biographical geography before joining Ellington
Duke Ellington	Piano	b. 1899, Washington, DC; d. 1974, New York
Shelton Hemphill	Trumpet	b. 1906, Birmingham, Alabama; attended Wilberforce College in Ohio; d. 1959, New York
Taft Jordan	Trumpet	b. 1915, Florence, South Carolina; lived in Virginia and Philadelphia; d. 1981, New York
Cat Anderson	Trumpet	b. 1916, Greenville, South Carolina, placed in an orphanage in Charleston; traveled extensively around the South with the Jenkins Orphan Home band; after leaving, joined Hartley Toots band in Florida; eventually settled in New York; d. 1981, Norwalk, California
Harold "Shorty" Baker	Trumpet	b. 1914, St. Louis, Missouri; d. 1966, New York
Ray Nance	Trumpet	b. 1913, Chicago; traveled extensively with pianist Earl Hines's band in the late 1930s; d. 1976, New York
Lawrence Brown	Trombone	b. 1907, Lawrence, Kansas; raised in California and began professional career on the West Coast, where he joined Ellington's band in 1932; returned to California to retire in 1974; d. Los Angeles, 1988
Claude Jones	Trombone	b. 1901, Boley, Oklahoma; d. 1962 at sea
Wilbur de Paris	Trombone	b. 1900, Crawfordsville, Indiana; performed on TOBA circuit with dad's circus band; moved to Philadelphia in 1920s and then to New York; d. 1973, New York
Russell Procope	Alto sax and clarinet	b. 1908, New York; d. 1981, New York
Johnny Hodges	Alto sax	b. 1907, Cambridge, Massachusetts; raised in Boston but traveled to New York frequently; d. 1970, New York
Jimmy Hamilton	Tenor sax and clarinet	b. 1917, Dillon, South Carolina; raised in Philadelphia, moved to New York in his late teens; d. 1994, St. Croix, Virgin Islands
Al Sears	Tenor sax	b. 1910, Macomb, Illinois; began professional career in Buffalo in the late 1920s before moving to New York; d. 1990, New York
Harry Carney	Baritone sax and clarinet	b. 1910, Boston; started career in Boston, then moved to New York in 1927; d. 1974, New York
Fred Guy	Guitar	b. 1897, Burkesville, Georgia; raised in New York; d. 1971, Chicago
Oscar Pettiford	Bass	b. 1922, Okmulgee, Oklahoma; starting playing with his Minneapolis-based family's touring band; joined Charlie Barnet and left for New York in 1943; d. 1960, Copenhagen
Sonny Greer	Drums	b. 1895, Long Branch, New Jersey; moved to Washington, DC, and met Ellington at the Howard Theater in 1919; d. 1982, New Jersey

Sources: Information compiled from the biographies by Collier, Hasse, and Lawrence as well as John Chilton's *Who's Who of Jazz: Storyville to Swing Street*, 4th ed. (New York: Da Capo Press, 1985); Stanley Dance, *The World of Duke Ellington* (New York: Charles Scribner's Sons, 1970); *Grove Music Online/ The New Grove Dictionary of Jazz*, 2nd ed. (2001), ed. L. Macy; Mark Tucker, ed. *The Duke Ellington Reader* (New York: Oxford University Press, 1993).

provide some very useful information. The birthplaces of the seventeen band members encompassed seventeen cities in eleven states and the District of Columbia: Alabama, Georgia, Illinois, Indiana, Kansas, Massachusetts, Missouri, New Jersey, New York, Oklahoma, and South Carolina. This geographic diversity is magnified when we consider the amount of traveling these musicians did before ever reaching the Duke Ellington Orchestra. Trumpeter Shelton "Scad" Hemphill was born and raised in Birmingham, Alabama. After high school he began touring as a member of Fred Longshaw's Band, the backing group for blues singer Bessie Smith. Traveling the Theater Owners' Booking Association (TOBA) circuit with Longshaw and Smith, Hemphill logged many miles around the southern and southwestern United States. In 1924 he moved to Ohio to attend Wilberforce University, where he also met Horace Henderson and joined his popular and talented band, the Collegians. And it was with that group that Hemphill made his way to New York City and the Duke Ellington Orchestra.[21] Many of the other musicians listed in table 3.1 had similarly long and involved journeys.[22]

It is clear too that the members of Ellington's band were also direct or indirect participants in the Great Migration.[23] For example, Jimmy Hamilton's family moved to Philadelphia from Dillon, South Carolina. Trombonist Wilbur de Paris moved from Birmingham, Alabama, to Ohio to attend college, and trumpeter Cat Anderson ultimately left the southern territory bands he played in for New York City.

A musician's life has traditionally been one of travel, but in the American context the movement of these African American musicians was inextricably tied to the larger migration of African Americans from the South to the North, Midwest, and West. From the nation's most rural population, African Americans became, over the first half of the twentieth century, the nation's most urbanized.[24] The musician's intensely mobile lifestyle greatly magnified the dislocations caused by such large-scale population shifts. It is arguable whether any population of Americans understood the dynamic of place and movement in American culture better than these black musicians. They were itinerants among itinerants, a subpopulation within the larger group of African Americans seeking better lives in other parts of the country.

The Ellington Orchestra, composed as it was of such different individuals drawn from across the country, necessarily did not belong to any place in particular—the band constituted its own peculiar sense of place. Often a sense of place is rooted in a material location with some sense of boundaries, of scope or limits. But as a mobile unit, virtually always on the road, the Ellington band necessarily would have developed a different sense of place and a different way to carve out temporary "permanences" from the flux of modern life.[25] Many of Ellington's musicians have spoken about the band's strange, nearly hermetic, world unto itself. In their recollections, former Ellington members often remember little else but the constant movement. Reminiscing years later, trombonist Lawrence Brown spoke about the group's first trip to Great Britain in 1933: "All I remember about that trip was work, work, work. We never got a chance to do anything else."[26] Valve trombonist Juan Tizol left the Ellington band in 1944 when an offer came from Harry James's Los Angeles-based group: "I wanted to come to California, I wanted to go home. I didn't want to keep on the road any more."[27] With such profound feelings of dislocation, the creation of some sense of place, however attenuated or unusual, would be a psychological necessity.

Although the band certainly had its own particular offstage culture to help orient itself and create community, what happened onstage was something different. There the band could create more malleable spaces—spaces that could be transformed, through musical performance, into new kinds of places. And each performance was an opportunity to renew and reaffirm these places. The musicians drew on history and on the particularities of African American culture to guide their efforts, but in the end what they performed was something quintessentially modern. While not all their music evoked the geography of Griffin's migration narrative, much of it did. Both performances I will analyze from the 1946 Chicago Civic Opera House show, "Air-Conditioned Jungle" and *The Deep South Suite*, deal directly with places central to the migration narrative of African Americans: the urban metropolis of the North and the cities and towns of the American South.

November 10, 1946: Chicago's Civic Opera House

"Few events," historian Eric Foner writes, "have transformed American life as broadly and deeply as World War II."[28] The war and its aftermath dominated the 1940s, upending virtually every aspect of American daily life. The strongly ideological nature of the conflict, along with the massive mobilization required to fight it, created profound challenges to long-standing and widely held notions of gender, class, race, and national identity. Musicians were inevitably caught up in these upheavals, and the music industry suffered, both during the conflict and in the economic reconversion that happened afterward. War rationing limited bands' travel, the draft depleted the supply of musicians, and labor disputes between the American Federation of Musicians and the recording industry led to recording bans in 1942 and 1947 that shut off the supply of new big band dance music. More ominous for the financial viability of the big bands was the shifting taste in popular music. New forms and styles were developing—rhythm and blues, singer-centered popular music (Frank Sinatra and Doris Day, for example), and bebop—that were splitting audiences away from the ensemble style of dance band jazz that had been so popular since the late 1920s and most dramatically since 1935. The year 1946, in particular, was a kind of annus horribilis for the "swing era" specifically and the larger culture of big band jazz more generally. In December 1946 eight of the most successful bands broke up (though some would later reunite): Benny Goodman's, Woody Herman's, Harry James's, Tommy Dorsey's, Les Brown's, Jack Teagarden's, Benny Carter's, and Ina Ray Hutton's.[29] In the face of the news, *Newsweek* proclaimed "the biggest depression the band business had ever known."[30]

For the Ellington band, the war and immediate postwar years were complex, turbulent, and paradoxical times. For many critics, the band started the decade at its creative peak. The group had relatively stable personnel of extraordinarily talented players, especially the newly arrived bassist Jimmy Blanton, who had an electrifying effect on his bandmates (according to Rex Stewart, "his amazing talent sparked the entire band"), and saxophonist Ben Webster, recently poached from Cab Calloway's band.[31] Clearly inspired, Ellington and the recently hired Billy Strayhorn were producing a flood of new works to feature all this talent. But the productive stability of this period, 1939–41, soon evaporated. Blanton died tragically in 1941 from tuberculosis. Clarinetist Barney Bigard left the band in 1942, singer Ivie Anderson in 1943, and trombonist Juan Tizol in 1944. The personnel upheavals would become a permanent part of the group's existence throughout the 1940s, culminating in the departure in 1950 of three key band members: longtime drummer Sonny Greer, alto saxophonist Johnny Hodges, and trombonist Lawrence Brown. Although two of them would rejoin Ellington later in the decade (Hodges in 1955 and Brown in 1960), such instability diminished the symbiotic creative partnerships that were so important to the creation of the band's distinctive music. The financial ups and downs of the decade, along with the band's relentless touring schedule, induced many band members to seek work elsewhere either for more money, more personal autonomy, or more geographical stability.

Economic limitations forced on the band by war and reconversion compounded the day-to-day stresses of band life: they could no longer travel by private Pullman car, only in overcrowded coaches.[32] Travel by car was equally difficult with wartime rationing of gasoline and tires. The draft posed a constant threat of further personnel changes. Making records—an integral part of the band's professional success—also became challenging. Over the decade, Ellington bounced between several record companies. The recording bans of the 1940s limited studio opportunities for several years, and as a result a great deal of the band's music of the era never became widely known. Complicating these difficulties, the group was caught in a larger battle by the record companies over what format—78, 33⅓, or 45 rpm—would become the industry standard, a situation that created some confusion about the nature and scope of what could be recorded (shellac 78s, for example, held just over three minutes of music a side, but the new vinyl had room for over twenty minutes a side).[33]

Yet for all this sweeping change, 1946 was in many ways typical for the Ellington Orchestra—it was a year of relentless touring with occasional studio recording dates squeezed in when time was available. Despite beginning the year in their base of operations with their annual Carnegie Hall concert (the group had first played the prestigious venue three years earlier), the players were on the road for the better part of the year. Table 3.2 is based on information in Ken Vail's remarkably detailed *Duke's Diary* and Klaus Stratemann's *Duke Ellington: Day by Day and Film by Film*.[34]

The band's concert on November 10—they played two sets at the Opera House, one at 3:00 p.m. and another at 8:30 p.m.—was another one-nighter in a very long road trip. Sandwiched between shows in Indianapolis, Indiana, and Rochester, Minnesota, the Civic Opera House concert, despite the ritzy venue, was in many ways just another gig. At the time of the concert the band had spent only about two and a half months in New York City, and of that time only the spell in October was for any serious length of time (just about the entire month). For the rest of the year the band would be "home" for just over two weeks. And being home was not exactly a vacation either—the band had an almost constant performance schedule, including perhaps the highest-profile concert of the entire year, the November Carnegie Hall show. Looking at the band in this way is astonishing. In 1946 they played

Table 3.2 Schedule of the Duke Ellington Orchestra for 1946

January 1	Academy of Music, Philadelphia
January 4	Carnegie Hall concert, New York City
January 5–7	Two one-nighters: Hampton Institute, Hampton, Virginia; USO Auditorium, Norfolk, Virginia
January 10–15	New York, recording session
January 17	Savoy Ballroom, Pittsburgh
January 19	Masonic Temple Auditorium, Detroit
January 20–21	Civic Opera House, Chicago; Millionaire's Club, Chicago
January 22	Mayo Civic Auditorium, Rochester, Minnesota
January 23	Auditorium, Minneapolis
January 25	Topeka
January 27	Municipal Auditorium, Kansas City, Missouri
January 29	Coliseum Ballroom, Oelwein, Iowa
January 30–February 12	Lookout House, Covington, Kentucky
February 15–21	Paradise Theater, Detroit
February 22–28	Regal Theater, Chicago
March 1	Ottumwa Coliseum, Ottumwa, Iowa
March 2	Hub Ballroom, Edelstein, Illinois
March 3	Memorial Auditorium, Gary, Indiana
March 4–6	Palace Theater, Columbus, Ohio
March 7	Harrisburg, Pennsylvania
March 8–14	Royal Theater, Baltimore
March 15–16	Mercantile Hall, Philadelphia
March 17	Turner's Arena, Washington, DC
March 18	New York City
March 19–20	Trenton, New Jersey
March 21–27	Adams Theater, Newark
March 28–April 4	Apollo Theater, New York City
April 5	Taft Auditorium, Cincinnati
April 6	Fort Wayne, Indiana
April 7	Kiel Auditorium, St. Louis
April 9	Rice University, Houston
April 10	Baylor University, Waco, Texas
April 11	A&M University, Prairie View, Texas
April 12–13	Breckenridge Park, San Antonio; Treasury radio broadcast
April 14	Houston
April 15	Auditorium, Fort Worth
April 16	Beaumont, Texas
April 17–18	Xavier University, New Orleans
April 19–25	Howard Theater, Washington, DC
April 26	Municipal Auditorium, Springfield, Massachusetts
April 27	Municipal Auditorium, Worcester
April 28	Armory, New Haven, Connecticut
April 29	Town Hall, Philadelphia
April 30	Troy, New York
May 1	Claremont, New Hampshire
May 2	Rhodes-on-the-Pawtuxet, Cranston, Rhode Island
May 3	Manchester, New Hampshire
May 4	Dartmouth College, Hanover, New Hampshire
May 5	Steel Pier, Atlantic City
May 7	Newburgh, New York
May 8–June 6	Paramount Theater, New York City
June 7	Sharron Beach, Annapolis, Maryland
June 8	Reading, Pennsylvania, radio broadcast

Table 3.2 (continued)

June 10	Charleston, West Virginia
June 11	Huntington, West Virginia
June 12	Columbus, Ohio
June 13–19	Oriental Theater, Chicago
June 20	Armory, Duluth, Minnesota
June 21	Port Arthur, Ontario, Canada
June 22	Amphitheater, Winnipeg, Manitoba, Canada
June 24	Saskatoon, Saskatchewan, Canada
June 25	Edmonton, Alberta, Canada
June 26	Metawa Armories, Calgary, Alberta, Canada
June 28	Civic Ice Arena, Seattle
June 29	Sweet's Ballroom, Oakland
July 1–11	Million Dollar Theater, Los Angeles; recording sessions
July 12	Guerneville, California
July 13	Sacramento
July 14	Oakland
July 15	Fresno
July 16	Los Angeles, recording sessions
July 18–19	Fresno
July 20	Vallejo, California
July 21	Oakland; death of Joe "Tricky" Sam Nanton
July 22	San Jose
July 23–29	Orpheum Theater, San Diego
July 31–August 6	Golden Gate Theater, San Francisco
Aug. 7–September 3	Shrine Auditorium, Los Angeles; Culver City, Hollywood; recording session, film production
September 13–18	Cancelled southern tour; RKO Theater, Wichita, Kansas
September 19–21	Davenport, Iowa
September 23	Louisville, Kentucky
September 24	Kiel Auditorium, St. Louis
October 3–30	Aquarium Restaurant, New York; Beggar's Opera (a.k.a. "Twilight Alley" and "Street Music")
October 31	Atlantic City
November 1	Chestnut Street Hall, Harrisburg, Pennsylvania
November 3	Memorial Auditorium, Buffalo, New York
November 4	Music Hall, Cleveland
November 5	Auditorium Gardens, Kitchener, Ontario, Canada
November 6	Mutual Arena, Toronto, Ontario, Canada
November 7	Toledo, Ohio
November 8	Cincinnati
November 9	Murat Theater, Indianapolis
November 10	Two concerts at Civic Opera House, Chicago (3:00 and 8:30 p.m.)
November 11	Mayo Civic Auditorium, Rochester, Minnesota
November 13	Minneapolis
November 14	KRNT Auditorium, Des Moines, Iowa
November 15	Turnpike Casino, Lincoln, Nebraska
November 16	Omaha
November 17	Municipal Auditorium, Kansas City, Missouri
November 19	Memorial Coliseum, Cedar Rapids, Iowa
November 21	New Haven, Connecticut; tryout for Beggar's Opera (Ellington or Orchestra present?)
November 23–25	Carnegie Hall concert, New York City; recording
November 26	Baltimore

(continued)

Table 3.2 (*continued*)

November 27	Lynchburg, Virginia
November 28	Petersburg, Virginia
November 29	Academy of Music, Philadelphia
November 30	Lincoln Auditorium, Syracuse, New York
December 1	Boston
December 2	Rhodes-on-the-Pawtuxet, Cranston, Rhode Island
December 3	Boston, Beggar's Opera (orchestra?)
December 5	New York
December 7	Masonic Temple Auditorium, Detroit
December 11–26	New York, recording sessions
December 27	Regal Theater, Chicago

Sources: Compiled from Ken Vail, *Duke's Diary: The Life of Duke Ellington, 1927–1950* (Lanham, MD: Scarecrow Press, 2002), 288–309, and Klaus Stratemann, *Duke Ellington: Day by Day and Film by Film* (Copenhagen: JazzMedia, 1992), 264–84.

seventy-two cities in twenty-one states, including seven Canadian cities in four provinces! And of course table 3.2 covers only *one* year of the band—Duke Ellington and His Orchestra had been touring like this since the early 1930s. Besides all the one-nighters and weekly stands (usually only in large cities like Los Angeles and Chicago), the band took several European tours as well, traveling twice to Europe during the 1930s. This band was constantly on the move.

As the American music scene changed after World War II, Ellington booked his band more and more into concert halls. Like any good bandleader, he tailored his musical performances to the particular venue, presenting longer, more elaborate works at concerts than at one-nighter dances.[35] Gone were many of the very popular dance tunes, replaced now with more of Ellington's solo concertos and ambitious longer arrangements such as *Black, Brown, and Beige* and the array of suites he subsequently wrote and cowrote.

The shift to theaters was partly the result of changing economic conditions, particularly the postwar decline of social dancing that economically devastated thousands of dance venues across the country. But the move to concert halls was also part of a larger change in the public and critical reception of jazz. Since the music first emerged to national awareness, a vocal minority of critics had championed jazz as an "art music" on a par with the music of the classical "masters" heard in the concert hall. But it was during the 1930s and '40s that this claim to art status took on greater critical and public acceptance. Benny Goodman's Carnegie Hall concert of 1938 was a landmark breach of the highbrow world. The interracial character of that concert further intensified its radical implications. Ellington's appearance at Carnegie Hall in 1943 was similarly hailed as a significant achievement both for African Americans and for jazz music.

The importance of these events was buttressed by a constant stream of writing by jazz and cultural critics. Many of the prolific leftist writers and intellectuals of the Popular Front, writers such as Granville Hicks, Constance Rourke, and Lewis Mumford, were committed to finding and celebrating authentic American art, what historian Michael Denning calls the "national-popular."[36] This search was part of a larger quest to redefine America in more pluralistic, egalitarian, and working-class terms. Jazz—and for some, swing—seemed to be a perfect fit: here was a music created by black Americans that had become the popular music of the "people." The growing celebration of jazz as art by figures outside the jazz world (for instance, conductor Leopold Stokowski) also helped. The shift in the cultural status of jazz—the beginnings of what Paul Lopes calls a "jazz art world"—was neither smooth nor complete. Critics often disagreed on the basic question of what sounds even constituted jazz, let alone "artistic" jazz. Nonetheless, jazz concerts at traditional venues for classical music and opera became more and more common and less and less newsworthy.[37]

Even though the Chicago concert was in part a rehearsal for the more important Carnegie Hall performance that was scheduled for just a month later, it was still an unusually important gig that reflected the cultural prestige of both Ellington and jazz. The Chicago Civic Opera House, like Carnegie Hall, was one of the nation's central institutions of "high" art. In 1925 energy mogul Samuel Insull announced that he was building a new opera house for his city. The theater, designed by the firm of Graham, Anderson, Probst and White, was part of a much larger project: a forty-two-story building housing commercial office space (the rent was supposed to sustain the Insull-formed opera company that would be housed in the theater).[38] Completed in 1929 at a cost of $30 million, the theater hosted its first concert, a performance of Verdi's *Aida*, on November 4, 1929. Although the Insull-managed opera company lasted only three years, other companies soon took over, and the theater became a central part of Chicago's musical life throughout the 1930s and '40s. The entrance was a grand brass portal flanked by Corinthian columns and enormous piers that led up to a tympanum with art deco relief sculptures of Muses leaning on the masks of comedy and tragedy. Entering through five glass doors, opera-goers emerged into a vaulted vestibule featuring three giant crystal and bronze chandeliers. The theater itself, painted in muted ambers and gold, was lushly decorated with more geometric art deco patterns and ornamentation.[39] It was an especially lavish venue, making even the grandest of dance halls—such as Catalina Island's giant Casino Ballroom (chapter 1)—seem drab and functional. As a physical manifestation of the intersection of business and "elite" art, the Civic Opera House provided an important spatial context for the Ellington Orchestra's musical place making. Whether one thought the venue ennobling or inappropriate, it was still an unavoidable component of the concert experience. As with the Garber Orchestra at Catalina, place and music combined to generate new meanings not available in other spaces.

A partial set list for the evening show (table 3.3) featured many of the band's popular songs but also several extended works, most notably the four-movement *The Deep South Suite*. Reviews in the *Chicago Defender* and *Chicago Tribune* specifically mention two songs absent on the 1994 Music Master rerelease (and also from the original recordings made by local jazz fan John Steiner): "St. Louis Blues" and "The Mooche."[40] Discographer W. E. Timner lists several more works that were on the program that night: "Overture to a Jam Session," "The Eighth Veil," "Golden Cress," and the *Beautiful Indian* suite comprising "Chaugogagog Maushaugagog Chaubunagunamaug," "Minnehaha, and "Hiawatha" (the last was recorded by Steiner), "My Little Brown Book," "You Don't Love Me No More," "Fat and Forty," "I'm Just a Lucky So-and-So," and a medley of earlier Ellington hits.[41] Django Reinhardt, on his first and only American tour, also makes an appearance, filling out a little less than a quarter of the concert. Reinhardt's participation is obviously important—this was his first and only tour in the United States and the first time Chicagoans would have heard the French gypsy guitarist live—but here I will focus only on the Ellington band.[42]

The program offered a synopsis of the band's diverse book of dance numbers and more ambitious orchestral works. As it survives on the Steiner/Music Master recordings, we hear "old" tunes (1930's "Ring Dem Bells," 1941's "Things Ain't What They Used to Be," and "Jumpin' Punkins") and new ones (*The Deep South Suite* and "Air-Conditioned Jungle") as well as an enormous variety of instrumental colors, textures, and dynamic contours. In keeping with the spatial preoccupation of its leader, the concert program contained a large number of place-themed works: "Memphis Blues" and "Beale Street Blues," part of an Ellington tribute to W. C. Handy; "Sultry Sunset," a typical Ellington "blue" mood piece featuring Johnny Hodges on alto saxophone; "Blue Skies," a Mary Lou Williams arrangement of the Irvin Berlin tune; *The Deep South Suite*; and "Air-Conditioned Jungle."

Table 3.3 Set list for Ellington's Civic Opera House show as presented on the Music Master recording

1. "Ring Dem Bells" (Ellington)
2. "Jumpin' Punkins" (Mercer Ellington)
3. "Beale Street Blues" (W. C. Handy)
4. "Memphis Blues" (George A. Norton and W. C. Handy)
5. "The Golden Feather" (Duke Ellington)
6. "The Air-Conditioned Jungle" (Duke Ellington and Jimmy Hamilton)
7. "A Very Unbooted Character" (Duke Ellington)
8. "Sultry Sunset" (Duke Ellington)
9. *The Deep South Suite* (Duke Ellington and Billy Strayhorn)
    "Magnolias Just Dripping with Molasses"
    "Hearsay"
    "There Was Nobody Looking"
    "Happy-Go-Lucky Local"
10. "Things Ain't What They Used to Be" (Mercer Ellington)
11. "Hiawatha" (Duke Ellington and Al Sears)
12. "Ride, Red, Ride"—featuring Django Reinhardt (Lucky Millinder and Irving Mills)
13. "A Blues Riff"—featuring Django Reinhardt (Duke Elllington)
14. "Improvisation #2"—featuring Django Reinhardt (Django Reinhardt)
15. "Honeysuckle Rose"—featuring Django Reinhardt (Andy Razaf and Thomas "Fats" Waller)
16. "Blues Skies" ("Trumpet No End") (Irving Berlin, arr. Mary Lou Williams)

Note: Names in parentheses are the writers credited on the published music.
Source: Liner notes to Duke Ellington, *Unreleased Masters, The Travelog Edition: The Great Chicago Concert*, two compact discs, Music Master Jazz (01612–65110-2), 1994.

Here I will focus on just "Air-Conditioned Jungle" and the four-part *Deep South Suite*. They are both explicitly place-themed, and they reveal with particular clarity the complexities of the band's musical evocation of American places.

Traveling the "Air-Conditioned Jungle"

The authorship of "Air-Conditioned Jungle" is murky. The song is credited to Ellington and clarinetist Jimmy Hamilton, but Walter Van de Leur believes it is really Billy Strayhorn's arrangement of Hamilton's thematic material.[43] Whoever ultimately wrote the music, the work is a showpiece for the clarinetist's fluid and virtuosic style. One of the few commercial songwriting successes of this era, the piece would remain an active part of the Ellington book for years. The song had its roots in a never-completed musical comedy project from the 1930s. In his biography of the bandleader—composed just a year after "Air-Conditioned Jungle" was recorded—Barry Ulanov briefly described the story for Ellington's abandoned comic opera on African American stereotypes.

The musical was to open in the living room of an African king and queen, who are lounging in fine clothes. A phone rings and the king finds out that another expedition is arriving from America searching for the roots of jazz. Annoyed, he announces that he and his wife will have to again don their leopard-skin costumes for the visitors.[44] The project was never completed.[45] However, by 1946 Ellington had created a new piece, presumably based on the earlier project. In its revised form "Air-Conditioned Jungle" became another in a long line of concerto-like vehicles for the group's soloists.

What kind of place is this "Air-Conditioned Jungle"? Before getting to the music, we must deal with the title, a typically evocative and multivalent one.[46] As Brent Hayes Edwards demonstrates, Ellington had a long-standing interest in writing, manifested in the many poems and prose works he wrote to accompany his band's music, as well as in his fascinating autobiography, *Music Is My Mistress*. This literary inclination was an integral part of his musical career. Ellington often provided lengthy oral introductions to the music of his concerts. He also, as we will see with *The Deep South Suite*, wrote explanations for them. For Edwards, this need to verbalize was an expression of Ellington's belief that music and language were both necessary for the full communication of his art and that music alone might be subject to misinterpretation—the complete truth could manifest itself only in a combination of words and music. The titles and other words appended to the Ellington Orchestra's music—whether initiated by the bandleader, Strayhorn, or an instrumentalist—are necessary parts of any interpretation. These texts provide "a literary component to the performance that is constitutive because outside or beyond (but 'parallel' to) the music itself."[47]

In its playfulness, the title "Air-Conditioned Jungle" provides an abundance of interpretative possibilities. First there is the unlikely juxtaposition of a modern, technological convenience with the natural wild, uncivilized jungle, something that was to be part of the original comic opera. But there are other possibilities. The "jungle" of the title, for instance, could also be shorthand for the "urban jungle," a well-established metaphor in the United States since at least the 1920s.[48] Here the air-conditioning is not a literal juxtaposition of a particular technology with a particular geographic locale but a figurative, rhetorical gesture suggesting the city as a modernized jungle—with more tolerable weather but still just as wild, as complicated, and perhaps as dangerous.

"Jungle," though, has other connotations that resonate with the band's early career. At the Cotton Club in the late twenties—the launching pad for the band's national fame and great commercial success—the Ellington Orchestra provided the music for stage shows that featured men and women dancing in elaborate "primitive" costumes meant to evoke the African jungle, a performance expectation inherited from minstrelsy.[49] The Ellington band's accompanying music, with its often dark, minor-key melodies and dirty, bluesy timbres, was labeled "jungle music" by writers and critics of the time. By 1946 the Cotton Club "jungle" was long gone, but that experience stayed with the band. Many tunes from that era remained in their active songbook, and recording reissues brought the music to the close attention of many enthusiastic jazz critics and fans. The "Air-Conditioned Jungle" could be a warm reminiscence of that time in the band's career—a period of great success and musical experimentation; or it could be ironic—an acid comment on the state of black music and what it has represented for many Americans. It could, of course, be both.[50] The many possible readings of the title—and there are undoubtedly more—must be made sense of alongside the music.

The "Air-Conditioned Jungle" as Musical Sound

The song lacks any clear or even conventional musical signifiers of the "jungle," in either its natural (geographical-ecological) or its figurative (urban) meaning. In the language of semiotics, we hear no iconic or indexical signs of the jungle: no imitations or recordings of animals or other "natural" sounds that either resemble or suggest through direct association what one would really hear in this environment.[51] As an "urban jungle," the song features no sounds of honking cars, howling sirens, or bustling city crowds. What we do hear is a furiously fast (nearly three hundred beats per minute), often highly dissonant, minor-key instrumental performance focused on Hamilton's clarinet.[52] The band gives us a jagged, pointillist musical texture, full of abrupt pauses and emerging and submerging instrumental voices. There is ensemble playing, but that texture is constantly disintegrating. From the opening measures, "Air-Conditioned Jungle" is fragmented and on the verge of entropy. Figure 3.2 is a diagram of the performance.

Like other Ellington pieces, "Air-Conditioned Jungle" draws on musical conventions familiar from Western classical music. The ensemble tutti, the soloist's dramatic entrance, and the elaborate cadenza at the end all reference the eighteenth- and nineteenth-century solo instrumental concerto. However, there is no doubt that we are listen-

Orchestral introduction

Brief in-tempo clarinet solo

The tune

    First sixteen measures present the melody

    Second sixteen measures (plus two measures) present a "disintegrated" version of the melody

Solo section

    D minor bass walking

    Improvised counterpoint between Hamilton's clarinet and Oscar Pettiford's bass

    Ensemble background lines return at 1 minute, 58 seconds

Outro chorus

    Following a long clarinet trill, Hamilton and the ensemble return to the sixteen measures of the work's melody (3:09)

    The second sixteen measures are made up of six measures of Greer's tom-toms followed by sixteen measures of ensemble crescendo using melodic materials from the orchestral introduction

Cadenza (solo clarinet)

Presto, triple-forte conclusion

Figure 3.2 Diagram of "Air-Conditioned Jungle," Chicago Civic Opera House concert, November 10, 1946.

ing to something distinctly *not* classical—the instrumentation, the rhythmic feel, and the plunger-muted "wah-wahs" of trombones are steeped in blues and jazz. The performance could be read as a "Signi-fyin(g)" gesture—a revision of a classical concerto but with a differ-ence that draws on racially marked musical characteristics (note espe-cially the "African" tom-tom drum part created by Sonny Greer). In this reading, the Ellington band is playing an updated 1920s "jungle music"—complete with plunger mutes and drums—in the civilized, air-conditioned Chicago Civic Opera house.[53]

Beginning with the very first sounds we hear, "Air-Conditioned Jungle" creates tremendous tension, a feeling of heightened expecta-tion. The composition begins with a dramatic blast of staccato notes by the trumpets, swooping trombone figures, and Sonny Greer's boom-ing tympani. The song rapidly crescendos to a blaring half-cadence, leaving us stranded at the point of maximum tension. Just as that dramatic opening fades away, Jimmy Hamilton enters playing a solo flourish of notes in the minor mode (the work is in D minor). Hamil-ton's excellent technique is plain, and the notes spill out of his instru-ment with brilliant speed and clarity. We also hear Hamilton's *voice*—confident, full, and not too breathy. The clarinetist's solo ends on a full four-measure trill that leads directly into the tune proper.

The main theme of "Air-Conditioned Jungle," played by Hamilton, is moody and mysterious, a feeling created by the melody's descending profile and many dissonant (chromatic) notes. Supporting this snaking melody, the ensemble provides appropriately slippery and mysterious responses that feature more dissonances (chromatic neighbor tones and colorfully altered minor seventh chords), along with uncannily human "wah-wahs" from plunger-muted trombones. The performance's underlying groove feels similarly off-kilter and tense. Despite the rhythm section's all playing together, we hear several distinct, interlocking rhythmic feels: while bassist Oscar Pettiford supports Hamilton's quarter-note, falling melody with a halting half-time line, Greer continues his driving eighth-note brushwork. The overall effect is of a dizzying sense of multiple, simultaneous pulses—half note, quarter note, and eighth note. We hear multiple rhythms played at differing rates of speed.

After the first presentation of the "Air-Conditioned Jungle" melody, the instrumental parts rapidly and unexpectedly disengage, and the musical texture quickly disintegrates. From a cohesive ensemble sound where sections of instruments play together, we now hear something very fragmented. Individual instrumentalists begin disappearing. First the upright bass drops out; Oscar Pettiford is silent for over a chorus. Then, while drummer Greer pulses along with quick brushwork, the various horns fall into a kind of disoriented and confused conversation, saxophones echoing each other with bits of a melody derived from the song's main theme. Through a series of long notes, the musicians come to an agreement—a dominant chord—and end together on a strong downbeat. Even before that chord decays, we hear Hamilton's clarinet and Pettiford's bass emerge from the wreckage. A good portion of the piece will now be a dialogue between clarinet and upright bass, with occasional asides and supports from the ensemble. This combination of clarinet with bass is unusual and striking—the tenor/alto range of the clarinet creates a very audible spatial separation between the two instruments, enhancing the sense of individualization. We very clearly hear two strong, independent voices emerge and take control.

The clarinet and bass dialogue lasts almost two minutes. Their melodic lines rise and fall, sometimes crossing each other's paths, other times pursuing their own independent journeys. Throughout the musical pas de deux, Pettiford walks, marking each beat of the 4/4 pulse, letting Hamilton wander unimpeded through the D minor key. Gradually Pettiford's bass begins to interact more and more with the clarinet, rising and falling with Hamilton's phrases, echoing bits of melodies, and oscillating between pitches in counterpoint to Hamilton's scalar runs. The voices interweave and at one moment even play together before veering off in different directions. The virtuosic speed, the rapid back-and-forth dialogue, the quick mergings and sudden separations, make for a thrilling performance, a kind of tightrope walk that, although uncommon to the sound world of swing, was the bedrock of the recently emerged bebop style.

The lengthy duet between Hamilton and Pettiford eventually ends on a signal from the clarinetist—another long trill. Sonny Greer provides punctuation with a whack on his tom-tom that brings in the rest of the band with a restatement of the original tune. But the fragmentation of the middle section and the assertive individualism of the bass and clarinet have infiltrated the rest of the orchestra, threatening to undo the previously tight section work and blended sonorities. The trombone "wah-wahs" sound even more distorted than in the beginning, and Sonny Greer breaks up his metronomic timekeeping with violent outbursts on the tom-toms. Those rolling interruptions rise in volume, swamping the ensemble and pushing Greer to forefront of the music. Soon after, the ensemble reenters, recalling the fragmented head material from before the bass and clarinet duet. This material climaxes in a massive crescendo and another dramatic half-cadence. Hamilton then launches into an elaborate cadenza. His fantasia seems almost subdued after the intensity of the duet with Pettiford, as Hamilton sweeps up and down scales, alternating fast passages with long, breathy trills. This respite ends in a truly frightening orchestral coda—the quarter-note pounding takes on an orgiastic ecstasy. The entire work concludes on a pungent, dissonant D-minor chord with a raised seventh (C-sharp)—a dramatic, unsettling, and literally unresolved end to the wild piece.

Even for a band built around idiosyncratic voices, the tension between group and individual in "Air-Conditioned Jungle" is especially pronounced. Furthermore, in this number it is very hard to tell what was written out and what was improvised—the piece inverts the usual Ellington band dynamic between soloist and ensemble: in "Air-Conditioned Jungle" it is the soloist who gets most of the playing time, the ensemble filling in the gaps and bookending the proceedings. The work brings to the fore the Ellington Orchestra's balance between individual and ensemble, composer and performer. Speaking to Stanley Dance in the late 1960s, Hamilton noted the flexibility and creativity he was allowed in the band: "I don't think there was another band where I could have done so much, where I could have brought out the kind of playing I was qualified to do. . . . When Duke writes, he just writes, and doesn't think anything about how difficult it is. We often got things from him that seemed impractical. He would put things in front of me sometimes and say, "Okay, you've got it!" And then I would lend my own character to what he had written.[54]

Although Hamilton speaks of Ellington's difficult written parts, he also suggests that it was a dialogic composition process. A musician like Hamilton would be able to "lend [his] own character." In the "Air-Conditioned Jungle" the individual musician becomes suddenly visible, and the heterogeneous texture draws the listener to contemplate the rich assortment of personal styles. The performance is a reminder that each instrumentalist has his own story, one that is not necessarily the same as the collective.

Like the title, the music too is ambiguous and polysemous. The performance is possibly ironic, playful, and reverential. The "Air-Conditioned Jungle" is a place of striking juxtapositions—soloist and ensemble, jazz and classical, black and white. The unfolding musical events provide what Ingrid Monson calls "interactional layers."[55] We hear in the performance the enactment of particular intertextual and intermusician relationships that generate structures within structures. While at one level it is a concerto—complete with a musical subject/protagonist and the expected cadenza—"Air-Conditioned Jungle" is also an unusual vehicle for several prominent instrumental voices. In particular the song features an extended improvisatory dialogue between bassist Pettiford and Hamilton, and to some extent drummer Greer. This lengthy dialogue—nearly half the performance—is fast and virtuosic, almost frantic, and it creates a space of musical paradoxes. "Air-Conditioned Jungle" is music of tremendous movement but underlying harmonic stasis. Melodies furiously climb and tumble down scales, all on top of a single, unchanging harmony. Hamilton and Pettiford explore nearly the highest and lowest pitches on their instruments, actualizing the limits of the available pitch space. Rhythmically, they generate a complex texture of rhythmic feels and metric subdivisions that creates a feeling of both independent movement and unified effort. The musicians here are the agents of construction, creating the musical space—actualizing its possibilities—then moving through it, exploring its limits.

This complex, paradoxical musical-spatial experience of fragmentation and cohesion echoes a large sociological literature on the unique nature of twentieth-century urban life. In his famous 1903 essay, "The Metropolis and Mental Life," Georg Simmel argues that the "psychological foundation upon which the metropolitan individuality is erected, is the intensification of emotional life due to the swift and continuous shift of external and internal stimuli." The modern, urbanized individual must hold off the "fluctuations and discontinuities of the external milieu" that threaten him.[56] The Chicago school of urban sociologists—scholars like Robert Park and Louis Wirth—followed Simmel in describing urban life as transformative of individual psychology and social relationships. For Park, urban life produced a new kind of person, the "marginal man," whose cosmopolitanism reflected the inner turmoil engendered by the city's multitudinous diversity.[57] More recently Lyn Lofland identified the city as a "world of strangers" where special social codes are informally instituted to help negotiate the crowded vastness of the place.[58] Coming from a different angle, urban theorist Kevin Lynch's influential book *The Image of the City* (1960) tackles the ways urban residents make sense of the city's vast complexities. Because we cannot conceive the entirety of the metropolis—it is simply too large—we compensate with fragmentary "mental images." For Lynch, certain cities are more "imageable," more legible for their inhabitants. Others are less so, opaque to our understanding and confusing to our sense of place.[59] Later critics like Frederic Jameson have expanded and developed these ideas in a much more critical and negative light: urban experience, particularly in its postmodern manifestation, is fundamentally illegible—our mental images, our "cognitive maps," are inadequate to making sense of our current spatial condition.[60]

Twentieth-century American art has dealt explicitly with the complexities of the urban experience. African American writers in particular have been especially concerned with the sociological and psychological implications of urban life.[61] Black Americans wrote, sang, and painted the promise and peril of the city in great detail. In his 1952 novel *Invisible Man* Ralph Ellison provides a vivid portrait of the dislocation of city life for migrating blacks and its impact on the nameless protagonist's sense of racial and national identity:

My entire body started to itch, as though I had just been removed from a plaster cast and was unused to the new freedom of movement. In the South everyone knew you, but coming North was a jump into the unknown. How many days could you walk the streets of the big city without encountering anyone who knew you, and how many nights? You could actually make yourself anew. The notion was frightening, for now the world seemed to flow before my eyes. All boundaries down, freedom was not only the recognition of necessity, it was the recognition of possibility. . . . It was too vast and confusing to contemplate. . . . I wanted the props put back beneath the world.[62]

The Invisible Man's experience is of "a world where all that is solid melts into air." He feels exhilaration and fear, constriction and possibility. Previously fixed aspects of life are flexible, changeable. Yet there are limits—he is in Harlem and bound by the ideology of race that designates different places, physically and socially, for different skin colors.

Invisible Man's complex reaction to American urban modernity has many structural resonances with the musical space—the sonic city—of "Air-Conditioned Jungle." However, unlike a single-author novel, the "Air-Conditioned Jungle" is a group creation. It is a *literal* representation of Bakhtin's "heteroglossia"; instead of different rhetorical styles signifying competing discourses, here different instrumentalists literally "speak" in different ways.[63] The Ellington band's urban jungle is a rich composite of voices and perspectives. As Griffin writes, African Americans viewed the nature and significance of their rural-to-urban transformation very differently depending on their social, economic, and political status.[64] The Ellington band had musicians who represented very different perspectives. Trumpeter Cat Anderson's journey from a South Carolina orphanage to the pinnacle of cosmopolitan black life in New York City sharply contrasted with Ellington's relatively comfortable one from middle-class Washington, DC. "Air-Conditioned Jungle"—and by extension, all the orchestra's performances—integrated widely varying American experiences of place. The traveling, tight-knit Ellington Orchestra was a self-contained community that presented in sound the multiplicity of the American black experience. Through its music, the band shared its multilayered, multivoiced community with listeners across the nation's race, class, and geographic boundaries.

In analytical terms, I am arguing for a homology, "a pattern found to be ordering significant particulars of different and disparate experiences," in this case between the realms of musical form and urban experience.[65] While I believe that as listeners we do this to varying degrees, the music is also apprehended sensuously through the body. The activities of the performers—especially the physical effort needed to play at this speed—are registered bodily. According to Patrick Shove and Bruno Repp, there is empirical evidence that we as listeners translate sound back into the physical forces presumed to have produced it.[66] We *feel* the speed of Hamilton's clarinet melodies because we *hear* the musician's physical effort. We move with Hamilton, Pettiford, and the other musicians through the musical landscape, weaving with them in and out of the musical texture.

"Air-Conditioned Jungle" is a musical place of intense movement and fragmentation, but it is also a place of order through communicative dialogue. The Ellington Orchestra's brand of jazz, like its urban blues cousin, was a "means of convening community" where experiences among African Americans could be shared and compared.[67] But it also was a convening of a larger American experience that cut across racial lines. "Air-Conditioned Jungle" is an example of what Werner Sollors calls "ethnic modernism."[68] The striking juxtapositions—classical concerto/jazz big band, individual/ensemble, white/black—were creative transformations of modern American city life, interpreted through the voices of a diverse group of African American musicians. The music created a space that was an analogue to contemporary American urban experience—a place of a radical new pluralism where all types of new communities were being "convened." Hearing the "Air-Conditioned Jungle" in Chicago's elite Civic Opera House, listeners heard a construction and transformation of the urban—it was an experience both unique to African Americans and relevant to all Americans. The "Air-Conditioned Jungle" was the modern American city of the war years— diverse, complex, and full of simmering conflict. But the music suggested that this chaos has order—that there can be stability amid the constant flux, at least in the "momentary acoustic community" of musical performance.

Returning to the Deep South

The longest work on the program at the Civic Opera House was *The Deep South Suite*, composed in 1946 for the band's winter appearance at Carnegie Hall (the band appeared there seven times from 1943 through 1948).[69] Other than the last movement, "Happy-Go-Lucky Local," which was recorded several times and released commercially, the music of the suite was captured on record only twice, but in both cases in its entirety: once in front of the audience at the Chicago Civic Opera House and once more at what sounds like a private V-disc recording session conducted after (or before) the main concert at Carnegie Hall on November 23, 1946. (V-discs were designed only for distribution to American troops stationed overseas.)

Despite its relative obscurity, *The Deep South Suite* has received a large amount of critical discussion by musicians, critics, and historians. The suite has even been revived by the Jazz at Lincoln Center Orchestra under the leadership of Wynton Marsalis.[70] The scholarly debate and discussion centers on its larger political or social significance—what the work was "saying" (or continues to say) about the American South, past and present. The suite's grandness, its presentation as a centerpiece of the November 1946 Carnegie Hall concert, and its appearance as another large-scale work in the mold of 1943's *Black, Brown, and Beige* (also premiered at Carnegie Hall) suggest that the work is part of what Ellington called the "social-significance thrusts" of the band's work in the 1940s. These included the groundbreaking 1941 musical *Jump for Joy* and *Black, Brown, and Beige*.[71] However, unlike *Jump for Joy*, which was a stage show with lyrics, and *Black, Brown, and Beige*, which on its premiere was accompanied by elaborate program notes, the "message" of the purely instrumental *The Deep South Suite* has proved more oblique.[72] In fact, at a party after the Carnegie Hall premiere, William Morris Jr., head of the William Morris talent agency, berated Ellington for not saying it "plainer": for not making the meaning of the work—what he believed to be its message of protest—transparent. The composer, though, brushed off the criticism: "As with *Jump for Joy*, I felt it was good theatre to say it without saying it. That is the art."[73] This statement is a little disingenuous considering the often explicit and bitterly ironic lyrics of many of the songs Ellington featured in other pieces such as *Jump for Joy*, a show he was immensely proud of. One in particular, "I've Got a Passport from Georgia (and I Am Going to the U.S.A.)," featured lyrics by Paul Webster and Sid Kuller that were especially provocative: "I've got a passport from Georgia / And I'm going up, up. . . . Where you wear no Dixie necktie, / Where the signs read, 'Out to Lunch,' not 'Out to Lynch.'" Producers removed the song from the show after cast members received death threats.[74]

The Deep South Suite was not Ellington's first "southern"-themed musical work; the band had "Dear Old Southland" (1933), "Delta Serenade" (1934), "Alabamy Home" (1937), and "At a Dixie Roadside Diner" (1940) (with the exception of "Delta Serenade," all the songs were composed by other songwriters). The orchestra toured the "Deep South" only once, in the early 1930s, playing concerts in Alabama, Georgia, and South Carolina, among other southern states, so the work, unlike later large-scale ones such as the *Far East Suite*, was not the result of specific travels.[75] While there were no detailed notes to accompany and explain *The Deep South Suite* and its inspiration (as with *Black, Brown, and Beige*), Ellington almost certainly provided a spoken introduction to the performance. Unfortunately, the Chicago recording fades in directly to the music, cutting off any opening description. However, the V-disc recording made later in the month does have an introduction, spoken by jazz writer Leonard Feather and a likely approximation of what Ellington himself used to introduce the work:

Hello everybody, this is Leonard Feather. I would like to tell you something about Duke Ellington's new four-part work *The Deep South*, which was performed and recorded recently at his fifth annual Carnegie Hall concert. The first of these four parts is what might be called the Dixie Chamber of Commerce dream picture of the South, with the southern skies, Creole gals with flashing eyes, the fried chicken and watermelon, and those good old nostalgic melodies. And then, in the second part, which is entitled "Hearsay," we hear a different conception of the South from the Dixie Chamber of Commerce picture and, in fact, it may in some respects be directly opposite. Then in the third part, which is called "When Nobody Is Looking" we hear illustrated in music the theme that people of very different extractions can get along together in peace and harmony when nobody is looking at or interfering with them. And for the fourth and last part we have the story of the "Happy-Go-Lucky Local." This is a train that runs in the South. It's not one of those big luxury trains that takes tourists down to Miami. It's just a little old train that stops at all the places you never heard of. And it has a cheerful old Negro fireman who hums and whistles and plays tunes on the train's whistle, and he seems to recognize everybody and have a cheerful hello for everyone as he passes by, that is everyone on his side of the tracks. Well, down in the South it's known as Number 42. We just call it the "Happy-Go-Lucky Local."

Feather's comments are in many parts identical to Ellington's own description in his 1973 autobiography *Music Is My Mistress* (reproduced in the appendix at the end of this chapter). Considering together Feather's comments and Ellington's substantial elaboration, we are still left with an imprecise map of how to listen. Where exactly are we to hear "the Creole gals with flashing eyes, fried chicken and watermelons, and all those good old nostalgic memories"? (Interestingly, Feather uses "melodies" for "memories.") Even if we allow our imaginations to apply these images to the music, we are still left with only vague pointers. According to Ellington, the second movement, "Hearsay," is "concerned with other things that were told about the South, things that were not at all in accordance with the Chamber of Commerce dream picture, things that were at times almost directly opposite." The implication is clear, and the Carnegie Hall audience undoubtedly would grasp some of these "other things": slavery, Jim Crow segregation, lynching. But was there more? Do these "other things" include sexual relationships between blacks and whites? Does the work refer to miscegenation?

For Ellington's son Mercer, these "other things" did indeed include interracial sexual relationships. In his memoirs he describes the suite's third movement, "There Was Nobody Looking" as "referr[ing] directly" to "the classic liaison of *white man* and *black woman*, reverse freedom as it were." The movement was, for Mercer, his father's protest against the irrational fear of black-and-white miscegenation.[76] But according to Feather's V-disc introduction, the movement was much more general in its meanings. It was about interracial friendships in defiance of Jim Crow customs: "that people of very different extractions can get along together in peace and harmony when nobody is looking at or interfering with them." Greatly complicating the situation, Ellington himself provides his take on the movement, a figurative expansion of Feather's brief comments:

It had to do, I explained, with a pretty little flower in the middle of a field and a small dog who was fascinated by the flower. As the puppy reached over to caress the flower, a light breeze blew it out of reach, and every time he tried to touch it the flower was carried off in a different direction by the breeze. There was, nevertheless, no animosity or friction between dog and breeze, for each respected the other's right to court the flower. Moreover, the puppy and the flower were both too young to be influenced away from their natural tendencies, and, most important, there was nobody looking! The responsibility for telling this little parable in music devolved upon the piano player.

Miscegenation? Interracial friendships? Puppies and flowers? Given these competing claims, historian Graham Lock is skeptical of any definitive answer. Dismissing Mercer Ellington's claim of direct reference to miscegenation for lack of evidence, Lock concludes that the movement, and by extension the suite as a whole, is part of Ellington's governing aesthetic strategy of indirection, of using music to "say it, without saying it." But in the case of "There Was Nobody Looking," "his policy of indirection was pursued so rigorously that it proved self-defeating."[77] Lock believes, though, that overall the suite is a clear critique of racial stereotyping and the American, particularly southern, hypocrisy concerning race. The cloying sweetness implied in the title "Magnolias Just Dripping with Molasses," Ellington's employment of stereotypical racist imagery (fried chicken and watermelons), his son Mercer's gloss on the work in his own memoirs, and the racially motivated murders of four African Americans in Athens, Georgia, just ten weeks before the Carnegie Hall concert, all convince Lock that Ellington's portrayal of the Deep South was meant as an ironic critique and that the composer's "tongue was firmly in his cheek."[78]

Interestingly, Lock provides only one piece of *musical* evidence to support his reading: Lawrence Brown's quotation during his lengthy trombone solo of "Dixie" and Stephen Foster's "Old Folks at Home." Example 3.1 shows the first sixteen measures of Brown's solo from the Chicago Civic Opera House concert (the solo is almost identical on the studio V-disc recording). Writer Albert Murray, interviewed for the 2004 radio broadcast of the Lincoln Center Jazz Orchestra's revival of the suite, also points to this moment as a sure sign of Ellington's intention to critique, rather than to celebrate or simply document: "So if you listen carefully you will hear little snatches of things that deal with the South, at one point you'll hear in one of the trombone solos you'll hear the guy, he's just riffing a while, [hums] so you got the Swanee River, all these Southern things in it, and jazz can do that so well, and no one can do it better than Duke." Echoing Lock's theory of Ellington's aesthetic of indirection, Murray asserts that Ellington "didn't believe in protest art, he believed in doing it, counterstating and counteracting whatever restrictions he felt"—another way of "saying it, without saying it."[79]

Trombonist Lawrence Brown's quotation is indeed a very significant moment. But it is too simplistic to cite it as any kind of evidence of compositional intention. The quotations come during a solo, and there is no clear evidence extant in the bandleader's archival materials that these were written into the charts or done at Ellington's suggestion.[80] It is probable that the song quotations were Brown's *own* improvisatory inspiration. Significantly, there are no other musical quotations or allusions in the composed-out ensemble passages—music that was written down by Ellington, Strayhorn, or one of the hired copyists.[81] Thus it is not clear how to connect the musical quotation with any compositional intention on Ellington's part. Was it just Lawrence Brown's spontaneous take on Ellington's programmatic intentions—the trombonist, in effect, concretizing Ellington's general ideas behind the suite? Or was this a carefully worked out gesture? Was it something Ellington told Brown to do during rehearsal?

The ambiguities here point to the polysemous implications of musical allusion and musical sounds more generally. In fact, when considering all the musical sounds—not just Brown's isolated musical quotations—a listener could easily interpret the suite's music in ways completely contrary to Lock, Murray, or Mercer Ellington. In his biog-

Old Folks at Home (Swanee River)

Example 3.1 First sixteen measures of trombonist Lawrence Brown's solo on "Magnolias Dripping with Molasses" as recorded at Chicago's Civic Opera House, November 10, 1946. The melodic quotations of "Dixie" and "Old Folks at Home" are in brackets. Transcribed by the author for use in this volume.

raphy of the bandleader, James Lincoln Collier does just this. While Collier generally accepts that there is some protest or critique, he also hears a "sneaking fondness" for the South, especially in the up-tempo, major key first movement.[82] For Collier, the "pretty melod[ies]" and "happy big-band" swing of the first movement suggest a complicated attitude toward the South that shows some affection. While the contextual material surrounding the music—the titles, the introductions, the African American identities of the band members—strongly points to irony and political critique, the music, with its shifts of tempo, rhythm, tonality, and instrumentation, presents a rich palette of widely varying emotional cues.

Collier's against-the-grain reading suggests the way close attention to musical sounds complicates any simple, straightforward attribution of meaning. While we must always read the suite in its complex contextual setting, we must also never short the sounds being analyzed.[83] Ellington's program notes, likely presented at the concert as a variation of Feather's V-disc remarks, provide some guidelines, but they are frustratingly imprecise when applied strictly to the music—it is often difficult to definitively map a text description onto a musical event.[84] As Brent Hayes Edwards suggests, the programs are best understood as a "parallel" to the music, supplementing and complementing. Ellington, using both text and sound, created meanings that surpassed the semantic limitations of both.[85]

From this perspective the "message" of the suite must be sought in bringing together the "parallel text" with its music. The irony Ellington employs in his *textual* materials—the primary evidence for Lock and others—is often clear, as in the description of the Dixie Chamber of Commerce's southern image of "fried chicken, watermelons, and all those good old nostalgic memories," but the perception of any musical irony is far less obvious. For Ingrid Monson, musical irony in jazz is about intertextual—more accurately "intermusical"—bouncing: one musical component recontextualizes another at a "distance." And, of course, both components must be perceived by the listener for the reversal of meaning to take place. In this sense, irony is "co-constructed by the performer and listener."[86] But irony is only one possible mode of perception and reception; "there is," Monson notes, "always the potential for disjunctions between performers' intentions and audiences' interpretations."[87] While jazz musicians might speak about their explicitly ironic intentions, this does not guarantee that an ironic meaning will be perceived or accepted by an audience.

Ellington's *Deep South Suite*, then, has the *potential* for an ironic reading. But it can also be perceived as sincere. The suite, in fact, asks both from the listener. The variety of musical materials demands—even encourages—sincere emotional involvement, but the textual material offers ironic distance: "Be warned," Ellington's title seems to say, "what you are hearing is only an illusion of the Dixie Chamber of Commerce." Thus, what we hear in the first movement, and I believe throughout the entire suite, is a far more ambiguous South, one that seeks to honor the place as the source of black life while critiquing its violent racist history. That puts *The Deep South Suite* in line with other contemporaneous views of the South by northern blacks in the mid-1940s. As part of a 1945 roundtable discussion on black migration, journalist George Schuyler wrote in *Negro Digest* that migrants "love the South (especially if they are Southern-born) for its beauty, its climate, its fecundity and its better way of life; but they hate, with a bitter corroding hatred, the color prejudice, the discrimination, the violence, the crudities, the insults and humiliations, and the racial segregation of the South, and they hate all those who keep these evils alive."[88]

Farah Jasmine Griffin traces these ambivalent feelings in the mid-century cultural texts of black musicians and writers. Billie Holiday's version of "Georgia on My Mind," Jean Toomer's modernist epic *Cane*, Richard Wright's *12 Million Black Voices*—all these reveal a deep-seated ambivalence toward the South and its legacy for northern, urban blacks. The South is at once "home," the continuing wellspring of black American life and culture, and also the source of oppression and violence. The *Deep South Suite* is best understood, then, not simply as Ellington's uncomplicated critique of southern racism and violence, but rather as a part of this midcentury constellation of cultural texts exploring the place of the South in the North.

The Deep South Suite was not Ellington's artistic voice alone. The piece was the combined product of seventeen musicians and their own personal histories. Although few of the musicians in the band were from the Deep South, it is highly likely—almost certain—that they all had personal or family connections to the region. We can indeed hear the Deep South in the suite, but it is fluid and unstable in its meaning. A significant component of this complexity is the lingering aura of irony versus sincerity that hovers over the work: the Ellington Orchestra can say in sound collectively something much more complex than its members could say individually in words or music. The real-time, multivoiced simultaneity of musical performance brings together contradictory moods and voices into a temporary synthesis: irony and sincerity, truth and falsehood, critique and celebration.

Musical Structure and Meaning in *The Deep South Suite*

At its November performance in Chicago, *The Deep South Suite* ran just over eighteen minutes: Ellington's piano solo, "There Was Nobody Looking," was the shortest movement, clocking in at just over three minutes; "Happy-Go-Lucky Local" was the longest, taking just under six. Gunther Schuller has suggested that the mixed reception of 1943's *Black, Brown, and Beige* led Ellington toward a suite style for longer works—eschewing very long and complicated forms like the massive twenty-plus minutes of the "Black" movement of *Black, Brown, and Beige*.[89] *The Deep South Suite* bears out this notion. Each movement of the suite is self-contained and has no obvious formal musical link to any other. The effect is of shifting scenes rather than explicit linear development. "Magnolias" is a major mode, medium tempo swing number that features several long solos. "Hearsay," in contrast, is a slow, dark, minor key "ballad" filled with surprising dissonances. It functions as the "slow" movement of this four-movement symphonic-like suite. "There Was Nobody Looking" lightens the mood with its major key, dotted rhythms—a mood and structural function much like a minuet/trio or scherzo in a classical symphony. The finale, "Happy-Go-Lucky Local" is a boisterous blues that attempts to re-create the journey of a noisy southern train on the "local" run.

Even though each movement is self-contained, a listener could hear a kind of narrative trajectory; there is a very loose, overarching "story." The suite moves from the ambiguous "celebration" of the South in the first movement through a dark, troubled second movement. Pausing for a breather in the lighter, brief third movement, the suite climaxes in the relaxed but energized blues-heavy finale. The two outer movements and the two inner movements are of a piece. The first and last are large-scale features for a full presentation of the band, and they feature lots of individual improvisations and solos. In contrast, the middle two movements emphasize the "voices" of Strayhorn and Ellington: the moody dissonance and learned counterpoint of Strayhorn's "Hearsay" and the eclectic stylistic juxtapositions (hints of ragtime, stride, and swing) of Ellington's solo piano in "There Was Nobody Looking."

Because "Magnolias" and "Happy-Go-Lucky Local" feature large amounts of improvisation and many instrumental voices, they exemplify the dialogic aspect—the heteroglossia—of the orchestra's music. The first movement provides the clearest example of the suite's complex, multivoiced evocation of the South; it also contains the clearest reference to the "South": Lawrence Brown's trombone quotations of the songs "Dixie" and "Old Folks at Home" ("Swanee River") and clarinetist Jimmy Hamilton's brief reference to the melody of "When the Saints Go Marching In," a spiritual popular with early jazz musicians and closely identified with the city of New Orleans. Figure 3.3 shows the fragmented structure of "Magnolias."

With its overabundance of melodic materials and abrupt breaks and interruptions, "Magnolias" doesn't quite fit into the conventional big band performance forms of either the twelve-bar blues or thirty-two-bar Tin Pan Alley form. The sprawling movement feels improvisational, and it overflows the boundaries of familiar musical structures. Along with an opaque, shifting form, "Magnolias" also has no primary theme or tune binding it together. Melodies are introduced—sometimes by individual instrumentalists, sometimes by the ensemble—only to disappear and be replaced by new ones. However, a few musical devices hold the piece together: a B-flat tonal center, a recurring dominant chord pedal, and a sixteen-bar chord cycle that strongly resembles the changes to "When the Saints Go Marching In" (example 3.2 shows the "Magnolias" progression).

Between these anchors, "Magnolias" is crosscut with soloist and en-

Introduction

> Rubato ensemble passage (four measures in the Berger transcription; the concert recording fades in)
>
> Ellington's piano begins in tempo, drums and bass follow
>
> Rhythm section plays for eight measures, modulating from D to B-flat
>
> A dominant pedal follows (on F) for twenty measures
>
> Trumpet fanfare (six measures)

Main "song"

> Eight measure melody by saxophones
>
> Six-measures of brass, an echo of the opening pedal
>
> Four-measure saxophone break
>
> Eight-measure trumpet solo with orchestral chords
>
> Eight measures (plus two-measures) of horn and reed call-and-response; a drum break

Solos (based on sixteen measure chord cycle with occasional bridge section)

> Trumpet solo (sixteen measures)
>
> Trombone solo (sixteen measures, eight-measure bridge, eight measures plus six more)

Transitional material

> Ensemble for ten measures

Return to chord cycle (functions as return to "head")

> Eight measures of ensemble
>
> Four measures (trombone solo)
>
> Eight measures of ensemble
>
> Return of the pedal material (eight measures plus two measures, the last two for clarinet break)
>
> Clarinet solo over sixteen-measure chord cycle and ensemble crescendo

Figure 3.3 *The Deep South Suite* Movement 1: "Magnolias Dripping with Molasses." I am indebted to David Berger's transcription in helping to clarify and verify certain formal aspects of the movement.

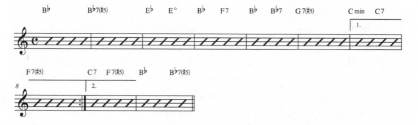

Example 3.2 Basic chord progression for first sixteen measures of "Magnolias Dripping with Molasses."

semble interruptions and digressions. For example, the long dominant pedal played by Ellington (at the piano), bassist Oscar Pettiford, and drummer Sonny Greer in the first part of the movement is interrupted about halfway through by an intrusion of reeds and brass. Later in the movement, Brown's solo is followed by a lengthy formal digression that abandons the sixteen-bar chord cycle for a section of new melodic materials passed between brass and reeds and a brief solo spot for trombone (probably not Brown this time). After twenty-two measures the band again returns to the chord progression, playing the last eight bars. And just as we realize where we are, the opening dominant pedal returns. All these interruptions and digressions make "Magnolias" exciting, even ecstatic in parts, but also unsettling and unpredictable. Our attention is constantly shifting from soloist to ensemble and back again.

These discontinuities point to a larger tension in the movement between a feeling of urgent expectancy and ecstatic release. The long dominant pedal sections create tremendous tension, premonitions of *something* to come. Trumpet fanfares and other digressions only heighten the feeling. We are relieved when we finally arrive at the delayed "head" melody. But even this moment of formal stability is quickly abandoned as the music crescendos into the first "Saints" chord cycle featuring Ray Nance's trumpet solo. After the intensity and expectation generated by the shifting textures and dominant pedals, the chord cycle feels secure and stable. It too has a sense of forward motion, but it is self-contained and powered by the familiar chord progression. But just as we settle in, there are more interruptions. The movement ends with a slow crescendo that combines the tension of the pedals with the release of the chord cycle. Here Jimmy Hamilton solos over an increasingly voluble ensemble. Are these dramatic contrasts meant to surfeit the listener with too much of a good thing? Are they meant to be over the top and ironic, an analogue to the cloying sweetness described by Ellington's title?

This is the reading that previous commentators, especially Lock and Murray, have suggested. It is a compelling interpretation, but it is too pat. Not only does it not connect with the moment-to-moment emotional narrative of the music, it falsely imputes far too much intent to Ellington as composer. The movement is decidedly upbeat and exciting—the dramatic tension and release of the pedals, the lengthy solo spots all contribute to the dynamic emotional trajectory. Irony requires a distanced perspective, one that this music strongly militates against. It is hard to imagine a cold, intellectualized response to such ecstatic music.

Whether Ellington truly intended to create a bitter, ironic statement about southern life is in my view irrelevant in the face of the movement's profoundly multivocal nature. The musical statements of "Magnolias" are the solo voices, in particular the spots for trumpeter Ray Nance, trombonist Lawrence Brown, and clarinetist Jimmy Hamilton, which become the main musical actors and inventors of melodic materials. This view now makes Lawrence Brown's quotation of "Dixie" and "Old Folks at Home" and Hamilton's oblique reference to the melody of "When the Saints Go Marching In" much more complicated. The solos move through a range of materials and moods; it is not all irony. Brown's solo, like the rest of the music, is at once sincere, ironic, playful, *and* serious. It is an idiosyncratic expression of a band member, with all the richness and diversity that entails. What we hear in "Magnolias" is a complex South, articulated by many voices.

"Happy-Go-Lucky Local"

The final movement of the suite, "Happy-Go-Lucky Local," was the only section of *The Deep South Suite* that permanently joined the Ellington songbook, and the only song to have a significant life beyond 1946. It was recorded separately as a single for the Musicraft label and again several years later for Columbia records. In a transformed version, the song became a hit, "Night Train," for saxophonist Jimmy Forrest, briefly a member of Ellington's band in the mid-1940s. Forrest's success with the tune hurt Ellington deeply, and he initiated a bitter copyright infringement lawsuit that was eventually settled.[90] Like "Magnolias," "Happy-Go-Lucky Local" is another example of the band's laboratory of musical place making. But here the music leaves behind any trace of irony for a less ambiguous embrace of the South as the taproot of African American culture.

In contrast to the preceding movements, "Happy-Go-Lucky Local" is a musical place evoked through movement—it is a song about a specific mode of transportation, the train. In *Music Is My Mistress* Ellington described the movement in some detail. "Happy-Go-Lucky Local," he writes, is a story of "a little train with an upright engine that was never fast, never on schedule, and never made stops at any place you ever heard about." It couldn't travel fast, but it was steady and reliable. A "Negro fireman" operated the train's whistle, playing all kinds of tunes, "blues, spirituals, a little 'Shortenin' Bread.'" The train itself rolled to a "suggestion of boogie-woogie rhythm." "Down in the South," Ellington concludes, "they called the train No. 42, but we just called it the 'Happy-Go-Lucky Local.'"

As I mentioned earlier, trains were frequent inspirations for Ellington. The bandleader preferred traveling by train, and the group's success made this financially feasible—many less famous bands, unable to afford such relative luxury, had to squeeze themselves into cramped buses and cars. Railroads also afforded a degree of privacy, and Ellington relished this time for writing and arranging new music. It was on one of these lengthy train rides in 1935 that Ellington began working out his longest piece up to that time, "Reminiscing in Tempo," a work that he suggested was created to help himself come to terms with his mother's recent death. The bandleader believed that the hulking machine was part of the healing process: "The past was all caught up in the rhythm and motion of the train dashing through the South."[91] Stanley Dance has even labeled this Ellington's "train period." According to Barney Bigard, "Duke would lie [in the baggage car] resting, and listening to the trains. . . . He would hear how the train clattered over the crossings, and he'd get up and listen to the engine. He'd listen as it pulled out of the station, huffing and puffing, and . . . start building from there. . . . He had the whistles down perfectly."[92]

But by 1946 trains were rapidly being pushed to the margins of American life. Despite the mobilization of rail for wartime movement of troops and matériel, the United States had for better or worse completely thrown in its lot with the automobile. The train, although still a major form of both local and transcontinental transportation for Americans, was rapidly succumbing to the automobile, a machine that was becoming increasingly affordable but also necessary in the rapidly suburbanizing postwar period. As with most technological changes, trains and automobiles overlapped, and Americans—and dance bands—lived with both as part of their daily lives. The Ellington band found itself caught in this shift from rail to road. The bandleader must have been pained when, during the mobilization for the Second World War, he and his band had to abandon trains for those detested buses and cars. The train was a complex symbol—emblematic of change and progress while also representing technological obsolescence. Despite its symbolic freight as the impetus of change in American life, the train was also tinged with a heavy dose of nostalgia. According to Joel Dinerstein, "Starting in the late 1920s, the train began to be seen as the nation's foremost *nostalgic* symbol of progress—the totemic subject of the country's experience of industrialization."[93]

Such an ambivalent symbol seems, especially in hindsight, a particularly appropriate subject for the Ellington Orchestra's always conflicted and fragmented approach to creating music and musical places. Dinerstein argues that the "most popular (and beloved) songs of the swing era were about trains." Trains, rather than cars or planes, "were the music of techno-progress itself: the rhythmic drive of technological change and the promise of social mobility."[94] Trains have played an especially prominent role in black culture. Writer Albert Murray has even asserted that all African American music is, in fact, "locomotive onomatopoeia" and that black musicians have "played the train" since the nineteenth century, incorporating and stylizing the sound of this technology into the fabric of their cultural practices.[95]

"Happy-Go-Lucky Local" imitates a train, making the machine speak with a human voice, but that does not mean there is no tension or ambivalence in the representation. Trains provided a means of escape from the segregated South, but they also uprooted people from their families and the places that made up the emotional and historical geography of their lives. Certainly "locomotive onomatopoeia" has been a central engine of African American music and cultural practice, but it is a symptom of a deeper preoccupation with place and mobility. The Ellington Orchestra's train music, and "Happy-Go-Lucky Local" in particular, is less concerned with coming to grips with technology than with exploring the ways technology shaped a more general experience of place, in this case black life in the South.

The "Happy-Go-Lucky Local," as Ellington says, is no modern train, such as the sleek, streamlined *Twentieth-Century Limited*, introduced in 1936. It is, instead, an angular, inefficient, slow coal-burning machine already made obsolete by faster and cleaner gasoline-powered ones. The Ellington Orchestra represents this mechanical beast by creating an audibly disjointed instrumental texture. The ensemble is still virtuosic and powerful, but here the heterogeneous is favored over the homogeneous. We hear a multiplicity of instrumental voices, but unlike "Magnolias," they are configured differently. Figure 3.4 diagrams the recording's key formal, melodic, and harmonic characteristics.

From the first notes of "Happy-Go-Lucky Local"—the very first attack on the instruments—we distinctly hear three separate musical voices, slightly at cross-purposes. The recording begins with Ellington's piano answered by Oscar Pettiford's bass. Sonny Greer accompanies with some quiet brush rolls on his snare drum. Ellington's pounding triplets urge the old train into movement, but Pettiford's solo interjections of triplet eighth notes slow things down. Again the piano calls, and again Pettiford responds. Greer offers his own comments between keeping the time. We hear a rhythm section working to get the "gears" aligned so that together it can propel the ensemble down the tracks.

In fact, the entire five-minute tune is a gradual, hesitant increase in momentum. After the duet between bass and piano, Pettiford begins walking, and while the rhythm section vamps on the tonic (minus Ellington's piano), the rest of the orchestra slowly starts entering, the

First chorus (twelve-bar blues: A-flat)

> Two-bar exchanges between Ellington and bassist Pettiford; strong triplet rhythmic feel; Greer with brushwork and rolls

Second chorus

> Pettiford walks; Ellington joins in with strongly syncopated comping; echoes of opening triplet figure

Pedal on I chord (fifty-six measures, nearly 3 minutes)

> Open trumpets answered by plungered trumpets followed by alto sax with countermelody; piano adds bouncing octave eighth-note rhythm; later trumpet section is featured with triple forte chords followed by a breakdown into a dialogue between trombone, trumpet, and reed sections; gradual thinning of texture and spotlight on Hodges' alto sax

Abrupt return to opening chorus (twelve-bar blues)

> Almost identical to very beginning with Ellington, Pettiford as focus

Transitional four-bar phrase (modulation)

> Ensemble section and modulation to C major

Blues chorus in C major

> Slight double-time feel; piano solo with rhythm section accompaniment

Blues chorus in C major

> Saxes (1–b3–6, blues lick; "Shortenin' Bread") answered by trumpets and trombones, short, staccato phrases

Blues chorus

> Long notes in saxes, trumpets take former sax line, swooping trumpet (Cat Anderson?)

Blues chorus with clarinet solo

> Band tutti; Hamilton solo, with ensemble passage in final two measures

Final chorus

> Alternating two-measure phrases between Ellington and orchestra; syncopated altered dominants by Ellington; walking bass; ensemble response with elaborate section call-and-response, note especially trumpet "train whistle"

Tag (overlap with final chorus, vamp on I chord)

> Eight measures and then ends on beat one of ninth measure; Ellington on a single note, a gesture to close out the entire *Deep South Suite* (an echo of the suite's opening one-note piano gesture)

Figure 3.4 "Happy-Go-Lucky Local," last movement of *The Deep South Suite*, recorded November 10, 1946, Chicago Civic Opera House

sections layering on top of each other. First the trumpets come in with a short descending figure, followed by the trombones with plungers, and then, above them all, Johnny Hodges's alto sax playing another short motive with a distinct blue note (flat third). Just before the alto sax enters, Ellington returns with a syncopated octave figure with pungent chord alterations. The entire vamp section (which continues through many short iterations) lasts just about two minutes and is the heart of the tune.

All the musical layering is constructed from short, easily remembered melodies. These "riffs" are drawn from the tonic and its related blues scale (the trumpets' descending motive is a slight variation on "Shortenin' Bread"). However, it is less the harmonic implications of the motives than their rhythmic integration that defines the vamp. Each part fits into the available open spaces. The texture is rich in ensemble togetherness while at the same time highlighting distinctive solo voices. For example, Hodges's breathy style plays against the sharp sounds of trumpets and trombones. As the vamp continues, we can hear other single voices in the spaces between the section figures. Unlike the parade of soloists in "Magnolias," the solo voices here are part of a collective, ensemble texture. But this is not the tight, blended sonority of typical big-band scoring, it is a heterogeneous sound that highlights incongruities. The "musicking" here is very different, creating very different relationships between the musicians. Drawing heavily on the melodic and gestural musical language of the blues, the Ellington Orchestra produces a coherent ensemble sound that is at the same time very loose—individual instrumentalists are given substantial leeway to embroider their melodies timbrally and rhythmically. The give-and-take between group and individual is calibrated very differently than in "Magnolias."

With the sudden return of the rhythm section's opening music—Ellington's pounding triplet figures and Pettiford's bass responses—the vamp ends. A "train whistle" blast from trumpets and trombones interrupts to announce the second half of the movement—a straight-ahead, twelve-bar blues in C (the vamp was in A-flat). After a chorus from the piano, the reeds introduce the first real "melody" of the piece, a simple, bluesy theme—also reminiscent of "Shortenin' Bread"—answered with syncopated bursts by the trumpets (this is the part of the composition that Jimmy Forrest took to build his "Night Train"). The following blues chorus builds the intensity, with the saxophones playing long notes and the trumpets taking over the blues theme. A forte ensemble transition leads into a brief clarinet solo. The final choruses alternate between piano and a noisy, unruly ensemble. If the A-flat vamp of the first half of the tune showed the train gathering steam, the blues choruses of the second half trace its gradual winding down. The accumulating layers of the vamp's first section gradually come apart in the second, and "Happy-Go-Lucky Local" fades out, the train eventually coming to an audible full stop.

The "Happy-Go-Lucky Local" is clearly in no rush. The sense of swing in the tune is very "spread out": the relatively slow tempo has a distinct triplet feel, something made explicit by Ellington's first triplet piano gesture. "Happy-Go-Lucky" bounces between downbeats. Technically speaking, the eighth-note spread is literally wider and closer to some kind of dotted quarter note or triplet feel. This rhythmic space provides room for extra voices, a situation not possible in the breathless brilliance of other much faster works like "Air-Conditioned Jungle" or even "Magnolias." The sense of *pace* is here directly connected to the sense of *place*: gone now is the "Air-Conditioned Jungle's" speed and threat of disintegration. Also gone is the uneasy exuberance of "Magnolias'" celebration of the South. Without these pressures the music— this "momentary acoustic community"—can realize itself very differently, more slowly, with a gradual layering of voices.

One reason, I believe, that this piece survived so well in the band's book was not its accurate representation of a train, but its powerful evocation of a particular spatial and temporal experience. In the sound world of "Happy-Go-Lucky Local" there is no need to hurry off to get to the next gig, no urgent need to suppress each voice to the imperatives of movement. Here movement can be savored and enjoyed bit by bit. This place lacks the edge of the earlier movements in the *Suite*, and it has a distinct nostalgic glow. The South of "Happy-Go-Lucky Local" is a place hard to reconcile with the bitter, ironic readings offered by critics over the years. Unlike "Magnolias," which walks a line between critique and ecstatic emotion, "Happy-Go-Lucky Local" is unambiguously celebratory. Ellington's words and the orchestra's music combine to create a musical place—a momentary musical South—that is blues-based, communal, and explicitly dialogic (in the Bakhtinian sense). This is the South as cultural resource, as a place that deserves to be revisited for what it can offer that the North cannot.

Looking back at the suite as a whole, what we have is a complex, contradictory portrait of a place. In this sense, the South of *The Deep South Suite* is similar to the representations of the region Griffin sees in the roughly contemporaneous African American writing by Jean Toomer, Nella Larsen, Richard Wright, and Ralph Ellison. It is a place bloodied by racial violence, but also a vital source of cultural information and spiritual renewal. While many of these writers saw little or no possibility of redemption in the region and felt no desire to reverse the northward tide of migration, the Ellington Orchestra's performance suggests a more ambivalent, open-ended view. The South is oppressive and dark, but also a source of strength and community.

The South of the suite does not exist in any simple sense—the evocation of place in the music is much more complicated than a musical quotation or allusion. It is in many respects an *absent* place. We hear an aural rendering of something that is a distant approximation of the present-day reality. "Magnolias" and "Happy-Go-Lucky Local" evoke images of the region that are soaked in myth and nostalgia as well as a difficult, often cruel reality. As a *real* place the region was undergoing tremendous economic and social change, and it is likely that another band, perhaps with more immediate experience of the region, would have produced something different. But the Ellington Orchestra's Deep South is a unique space of its own, where place is given a musical realization, a sonic concretization of multiple, contradictory conceptions. This musical Deep South is a location that has room for many voices and views, all of which can articulate a range of emotional and psychological states: joy, sadness, bitterness, fear, longing, and disgust. For all the musicians involved in its creation, the *Suite* provided a way to explore a place central to the black experience. But in a more general way, it let all listeners hear a complex dialogue on a region too often obscured by uncomplicated celebration or denigration.

The City of Jazz

Similar to the travelogue with which he opens *Music Is My Mistress*, Duke Ellington concludes his memoir with another paean to mobility. It is a typically sly passage that posits an organic and inextricable connection between music, travel, and desire. It is worth quoting at some length:

I am a minstrel, a pedestrian minstrel, a primitive pedestrian minstrel. Sometimes I imagine I paint, with water colors or oils, a crystal-clear lake in the sky reflecting the shadows of invisible trees upside-down beneath sun-kissed, cotton-candy snow. On the fringe, clouds so foamy white—tranquil on top, a raging storm inside. . . . "I'll write it," I think, before returning to that half sleep as the plane roars on to Atlanta . . . or is it Atlantis? Plans, plans, the most impossible of enormous plans, pastel or opaque. . . .

Steel on steel, thousands of miles of steel or tracks, with thousands of round, steel wheels—what a happy marriage! The rhythm of the motion, thirty-nine hours from Chicago to Los Angeles—what a marvel of masculinity, thirty-nine hours, power-stroking all the way. He gave her the high ball in the Loop, stopped in Englewood, and that's all she wrote, grinding up to ninety miles per hour, so hot the steam was bursting out everywhere. She had fine lubrication. You could hear her for miles, whistle-screaming, "Yes, daddy, I'm coming, daddy!" Don't pull that throttle out until you pull into Glendale . . . driving shaft pumping a steady beat . . . long and round, heavin' and strokin' . . . puffin' and smokin' . . . and shovelin' and stokin'. He stopped, let off a little steam. She, out of breath, panted, "Wash up, ready for that red-carpet reception." He got off, glanced over his shoulder at her as she backed out of Union station, out in the yard, with unraised eyelashes, like the dignified lady she was, she who, between departure and arrival, had given her all to a union laborer, opened her throttle wide, and allowing him his every wish. Truly, a tremendous romance. Should I write this music with the passion they pumped over the track, or should I maybe start with the wheel, the molten steel, or with those burly black arms behind the thrust that drove the spikes into the railroad ties?[96]

Here Ellington casts himself as a "pedestrian minstrel," a modern-day wandering musician. The adjective "pedestrian" suggests walking and urban life (the pedestrians of city streets and sidewalks); but it is also a playful bow of humility—the pedestrian as the "ordinary." As he "floats" in the airplane, high above the clouds, the drowsing Ellington contemplates the unreality of his destination—is it Atlanta or Atlantis? The sharpest reality is the journey itself. In the second paragraph, the bandleader contrasts the flight with an earthy, gritty, earth-bound journey on a train from Chicago to Los Angeles. The description moves from innuendo to out-and-out sexual intercourse. The metaphor, however, is fuzzy; is the train the woman and the engineer on the throttle her lover? Is Ellington the lover, "riding" the train, "letting off steam," glancing back at her on arrival? In fact, all the elements—Ellington, train, steel, pistons, throttle, and track—blur together in one erotic convergence of sound, movement, and desire.

For Ellington, all this sensuous activity becomes the stuff of his music: the molten steel wheels or the "burly black arms" that pounded the spikes into the ties become the building blocks of his music. More than just the material of inspiration, travel—the force of mobility itself—provides the energy and passion for his art. Again, inspiration for Ellington was concrete and physical. The experience of place and movement formed the core of his aesthetic. Realizing this aesthetic in the band, though, was a complicated proposition. Parts had to be negotiated, individual solos created, rhythmic grooves generated. The places constructed by the group were necessarily dialogic: many-voiced, and suffused with various, oftentimes competing meanings.

The 1946 live recording is especially valuable because it documents a band artistically and commercially in transition. In the mid-1940s the

Ellington Orchestra was in a state of flux, adapting to shifting personnel and a new popular music landscape permanently altered by the social upheavals caused by American involvement in World War II. The year 1946 also sits on the cusp of major social changes in the nation's history of race relations. African Americans, radicalized by the war, would seize the moment to demand a new place in American society. Out of the flux and flow of modern American life where, as Marshall Berman reminds us, "all that is solid melts into air," the Ellington band imagined and reimagined the geography of their, and their listeners', lives.[97]

Place, philosopher Edward Casey argues, is a word and concept with both concrete and symbolic dimensions. Among its functions, place "gathers" together everything within its boundaries: "Place gathers things in their midst. . . . Places also gather experiences and histories, even languages and thoughts." Few other concepts can hold so many various and often contradictory ideas together.[98] The musical places of the Ellington band—exemplified in the music of the 1946 Chicago Civic Opera House concert—were "gatherings" in Casey's sense of the word: an unlikely, sometimes improbable, bringing together of people and places. In his recent book, Josh Kun describes this improbable gathering in music as an "audiotopia"—a metaphorical place where unlikely sounds, traditions, and stories combine.[99] Understanding the Ellington Orchestra's music as an audiotopia helps us better understand the great success and cultural significance of the group. Each performance of the Ellington Orchestra was a laboratory for new "momentary acoustic communities," new audiotopias with their own culture, values, and social relationships. Whether the members were playing for black or white audiences, their reconstructions of America's places demonstrated the malleability of spatial and social relationships: both could be made and remade. Amid the instabilities of depression and global war, their music suggested that American society could be reconstructed on more egalitarian, nonracist lines. In its place-oriented music, the Ellington Orchestra presented America and American identity as mobile, fluid, and dynamic.

Appendix: Ellington's "Program" for *Deep South Suite*

By now, a "major" work was expected of us at every Carnegie Hall concert, and on November 23, 1946, we came up with *The Deep South Suite*.

Source: Duke Ellington, *Music Is My Mistress* (New York: Doubleday, 1973; reprint, New York: Da Capo Press, 1976), 184–85.

This was also in four parts, the first of which was entitled "Magnolias Just Dripping With Molasses." The Deep South is many things to many people, but here we were content to reproduce what might be called the Dixie Chamber of Commerce dream picture, with beautiful blue skies, Creole gals with flashing eyes, fried chicken, watermelons, and all those good old nostalgic memories. I described the mood as "Dixie flavor in a pastel (whispering) jump," and it was maintained till the last chorus, which we took out fortissimo. "Hearsay" was concerned with other things that were told about the South, things that were not at all in accordance with the Chamber of Commerce dream picture, things that were at times almost directly the opposite. "There Was Nobody Looking" illustrated the theory that, when nobody is looking, many people of different extractions are able to get along well together. It had to do, I explained, with a pretty little flower in the middle of a field and a small dog who was fascinated by the flower. As the puppy reached over to caress the flower, a light breeze blew it out of reach, and every time he tried to touch it the flower was carried off in a different direction by the breeze. There was, nevertheless, no animosity or friction between dog and breeze, for each respected the other's right to court the flower. Moreover, the puppy and the flower were both too young to be influenced away from their natural tendencies, and, most important, there was nobody looking! The responsibility for telling this little parable in music devolved upon the piano player.

The last section of *The Deep South Suite*, and the only section ever publicly available on records, was "Happy-Go-Lucky Local." This told the story of a train in the South, not one of those luxurious, streamlined trains that take tourists to Miami, but a little train with an upright engine that was never fast, never on schedule, and never made stops at any place you ever heard about. After grunting, groaning, and jerking, it finally settled down to a steady medium tempo. The train had a Negro fireman who loved to pull the string that blew the whistle, and since he seemed to know every house, and to recognize someone watching him go by in every window—in every house and every window on his side of the tracks, that is!—he was forever pulling that string. He played tunes on the whistle, too—blues, spirituals, a little "Shortenin' Bread"—calling somebody as the train rattled along with more than a suggestion of boogie-woogie rhythm. Down in the South, they called the train No. 42, but we just called it the "Happy-Go-Lucky Local."

FOUR

Travels with Charlie Christian: Between Region and Nation

Big band jazz of the 1930s and '40s was about more than tightly scripted, predetermined arrangements. Bands were flush with vocal and instrumental soloists. Nearly every dance orchestra had a singer—many bands carried two or three—and nonsinging improvisational experts, musicians who could shine in the spotlight. These soloists were featured in big band arrangements, but also in smaller offshoot groups drawn from the larger ensemble. Tommy Dorsey's "Clambake Seven," Artie Shaw's "Gramercy Five," and Benny Goodman's various trios, quartets, and sextets all featured hotter playing and more improvisation than their "parent" ensembles. And as Patrick Burke demonstrates in his study of New York City's Fifty-Second Street, some of the best-known and most highly acclaimed jazz performers of the era, players such as pianist Art Tatum, violinist Stuff Smith, and singer Maxine Sullivan, spent most of their time recording and performing with small ensembles, not big dance bands.[1]

Jazz historians have focused in particular on the new prominence of the saxophone during the era. Players such as Coleman Hawkins and Lester Young were profoundly influential and helped shift the emphasis in jazz groups away from the trumpet and toward the mellower timbres of the saxophone. Clarinetists shared a similarly high profile during the time; Benny Goodman and Artie Shaw were admired as successful bandleaders *and* as soloists. A few instruments, however, rarely took center stage. Bass players hardly ever soloed, largely because they were so essential to anchoring the rhythm and harmony of large ensembles. Guitarists weren't so tied down, but until the mid-1930s they lacked the volume to command attention through the dense musical arrangements (the banjo, a key part of the small-ensemble jazz sound of New Orleans and Chicago jazz, gradually lost out to the milder timbres of the guitar, a sonic palette better suited to the "modern" sounds of the dance bands). And although there were many highly regarded acoustic guitarists in the first half of the 1930s, such as Eddie Lang and Django Reinhardt, the widespread adoption of an amplified electric instrument led to the emergence of many new players such as Eddie Durham, Bus Etri, George Van Eps, Teddy Bunn, and Oscar Brown. Among this crop of new players and soloists, electric guitarist Charlie Christian (1916–42) stands out for the dramatic and immediate impact he had on guitarists and jazz soloists more generally. Hired by Benny Goodman in 1939, Christian played mostly in the leader's smaller offshoot groups, though he did record with the larger ensemble. Christian's recordings and radio broadcasts with Goodman definitively proved to musicians and listeners across the nation that the instrument was indeed a solo voice as compelling as any lead saxophone, clarinet, or trumpet.

For many listeners the young guitarist seemed to come out of nowhere, appearing on the "New York jazz scene full-blown, as it were, at age twenty-three, musically fully mature."[2] Teddy Hill, musician and manager of Harlem's Minton's Playhouse, famously put it this way: "When we were kids growing up here in New York, we watched Benny Carter grow from a squeaky beginner to a master musician. Or take Dizzy [Gillespie]. When he joined my band after Roy [Eldridge] left, he played just about like Roy. . . . Then Dizzy began to work out those new things with Monk and Klook [Kenny Clarke]. The point is, we could see him grow. But what about Charlie? Where did he come from?"[3] Christian appeared to have materialized from nowhere, a musician without a geography.

Christian sounded different from his fellow guitarists. His solos combined guitar-specific blues riffs with long, saxophone-like melodies. The playing was dynamic and thrilling—it had a drive that deeply impressed a generation of guitarists and musicians. As a member of one of the few racially integrated jazz bands, Christian was also thrust into a national discussion on the nature of race in America. And although Christian was mostly presented as part of Goodman's smaller groups, he was nonetheless a significant member of the Goodman organization, receiving virtually the same amount of airtime as the larger group. The presence of Christian and his black colleagues in one of the most famous national bands reminded Americans of the racial truth underlying swing: that this was a black cultural form fed by its interaction with a fascinated, if often hostile, white society.[4]

Christian is most celebrated by jazz historians for the central role he played in the development of "modern jazz"—later known as bebop—in his after-hours experimenting with like-minded musicians such as Charlie Parker, Dizzy Gillespie, and Thelonious Monk.[5] Christian's music, though, is worth studying for other reasons. His musical innovations captured on record are more than just artifacts of formal musical development; they are cultural texts that provide access to important historical experiences. They are, in Raymond Williams's words, "artistic formations and social locations."[6] In this chapter I will again apply a "hermeneutics of place" to delineate the spatial tensions and experiences embedded in Christian's approach to jazz improvisation and jazz guitar. As philosopher Henri Lefebvre reminds us, the spatiality of music—of art more generally—has a direct if complex relation to the general, lived, day-to-day experience of space. Music is a representational space that symbolically encodes actual, physical experiences of place and mobility. Christian's bluesy, fluid, and driving solo style was a performative representation and enactment of his geographical transition from "local celebrity to national superstar."[7] Christian brought a variant of the regional southwestern style of jazz "into a broader system of commercial and musical exchange" mediated by a large, national music industry.[8] This chapter will illustrate how Christian's musical style represented not just the regional and national experience of America (and the tension between the two), but also the exhilarating energy of movement that allowed such mobility. The guitarist formally incorporated into his music what Eric Lott calls the "the migratory impulse."[9]

Charlie Christian in Jazz History

Charlie Christian receives obligatory mention in virtually all histories of swing and bebop jazz. In his gloss on Christian's life, jazz writer and historian Rudi Blesh presents the guitarist's story in its most common and mythic form: "An 'impossible rube' from Oklahoma, he may have been a doomed and tragic young man but he was a supremely great artist. There are many artists from bad to good to great. But even among the great ones, the true original is rare. Charlie Christian was a true original. There was only one Charlie Christian. Yet he came from a dark and teeming multiplicity, from the flat, wide prairie, out of the crowded, black shacks. He came out of the vast, one-time anonymity of the blues—a man, a hick, an artist—the Easy Rider with his song."[10]

Other scholars, seeking to penetrate the myth, have researched Christian's life and music. Gunther Schuller and Ralph Ellison, two of the best writers on the guitarist, offer broad musical and contextual discussions of Christian's significance that attempt to locate this apparently placeless musician. In his essential study of swing, Gunther Schuller provides a fairly lengthy, detailed discussion that situates the guitarist in a larger world of southwestern American music. For Schuller, the "simple short answer" to Teddy Hill's famous question "Where did he come from?" was simple: "The Southwest is guitar country and blues country. . . . And Christian embraced all of that: a guitarist who brought the Southwestern blues into modern jazz—and more."[11] Schuller tantalizes the reader with a provocative list of likely influences: "Southwestern blues guitar, classical music . . . the highly developed diverse country music of the Texas-Oklahoma region." These southwestern regional musics were characterized by a complex mix of "troubadour-like tradition[s] of itinerant blues singers and guitarists . . . innumerable small Texas blues bands of the 1930s, the whole rich complex of earthy dance musics ranging from the Anglo-American country dances (jigs, reels, schottisches) and crude stompy polkas of the Czechs, Poles, and Germans in the region [and] the rural banjo picking tradition" all combined with an "ubiquitous fiddle tradition, both white and black."[12]

In his essay "The Charlie Christian Story," written as a record review for the *Saturday Review* in 1958, Ralph Ellison presents a different but equally compelling and influential discussion of the virtuoso guitarist, one that picks up some of Schuller's ideas.[13] For Ellison, a childhood friend who walked the same Oklahoma City streets, Christian's story with all its class, regional, and musical tensions has never been told in its true complexity. As a first step toward a more complete history, Ellison briefly describes the city's diverse musical life as he knew it growing up there, its mixture of dance hall groups, orchestras, marching bands, and hillbilly groups. There were also the newspapers and radios that brought information and sounds, some familiar, some exotic, from the big cities such as Kansas City, Chicago, and St. Louis. These sounds, Ellison emphasizes, happened in a particular place with a particular racial and class history. Christian "flowered from a background with roots not only in a tradition of music, but in a deep division in the Negro community as well."[14]

Somewhere between these competing musical and social priorities, Christian carved out his own path and created his unique musical identity. Through a mixture of talent and luck he moved from "local jazz hero" to national music star.[15] His story, though, is a reminder of how many musicians never leave the "local" and how impoverished our jazz history is for not telling their stories. These forgotten lives, Ellison insists, are signs of a larger historiographical problem with jazz writing: "When we consider the stylistic development of Charles Christian we are reminded how little we actually know of the origins of even the most recent of jazz styles, or of when and where they actually started, or of the tensions, personal, sociological or technical, out of which such an original artist achieves his stylistic identity."[16] We have narratives of certain musicians and their professional careers but not a real history that captures the intricate web of social and artistic forces that surround and shape them. With existing jazz histories "we are left with an impression of mysterious rootlessness, and the true and often annoying complexity of American cultural experience is oversimplified."[17] Ellison concludes that Christian's story is a call for a "closer study of roots and causes."[18]

My study brings these complex "roots and causes" to bear on an analysis of his style. This chapter will place the guitarist and his music in a changing American geography. More than just a bridge to bebop, Charlie Christian's playing connected past to present and old places to new ones. Throughout his short but dynamic recording career, Christian captured the energy of the era's migrations at the same time that he fashioned new musical places that bridged the fragmented geography of his life.

The Musical World of Oklahoma City and the "Territories"

Unfortunately we don't have any recordings from Christian's earliest experiences playing in Oklahoma City or with the many territory bands, such as Alphonso Trent's Orchestra, that he was associated with. But we can piece together a general sense of that diverse sound world. Situated as it is, almost in the middle of the United States, Oklahoma has historically been a crossroads for movement east to west and south to north. This created an unusual dynamic in the state between the major social groups of the region—blacks, whites, and Native Americans. Despite many key differences—the relatively short-lived experience of slavery, the long presence of a substantial free black community, the close relationship between free blacks and whites on the state's frontier—the racial policies of Oklahoma have always had a lot in common with those of its neighbors in the Deep South states of Mississippi, South Carolina, Alabama, Georgia, and Louisiana.[19] During the 1920s Oklahoma saw some of the worst outbreaks of racial violence in the country, including the devastating white attacks on the black residents of Tulsa in 1921. During the Great Depression, while thousands of white farmers lost or abandoned their farms owing to a combination of dust storms and economic collapse, some regions of the Southwest were insulated from the worst of the Depression because of the recent discovery of oil in East Texas. This in turn helped feed a vibrant nightlife throughout many parts of the region.[20] Positioned at a crossroads of transcontinental migration, Oklahoma became especially fertile soil for musical innovations and fusions. For historian William Savage, "The vigorous musical environment of Oklahoma was not an accidental thing. Some skeptics would say (and have said) that Oklahoma is the last place to look for meaningful cultural development; but any who know its history and understand something of the migrations of its people would say otherwise."[21]

Born in Bonham, Texas, on July 29, 1916, Christian spent most of his childhood and adolescence in Oklahoma City. The family left Texas after Charlie's father, Clarence, was blinded by an unknown illness. As Ralph Ellison and others have pointed out, the Oklahoma City school system offered very good "formal" music education—basic music theory, solfeggio, sight-reading skills, and instrument training. Peter Broadbent's biography of Christian devotes substantial coverage to Ms. Zelia N. Breaux, perhaps the primary force in the musical life of black children growing up in Oklahoma City. The black community in Oklahoma City, and statewide more generally, had managed to build a modest middle class of professionals to provide services to the community in spite of the intense racial segregation and discrimination. Christian didn't spend much time in school, but he did come under Breaux's guidance, and she even tried to get him to play the trumpet.[22] Although that didn't take, Christian's experience in the public schools laid the foundation for his future musical development.

The heart of Oklahoma City's African American economic and cultural life was North East Second Street, informally known as the "Deep Deuce" or "the Stem" (short for "Main Stem," the center of activity). When traveling bands passed through the area, they would play in the street's many clubs and dance halls. The bands of Bennie Moten, Andy Kirk, Terrence Holder, Thamon Hayes, Nat Towles, Alphonso Trent, Ernie Fields, George E. Lee, Clarence Love, and Tommy Douglas played the Deep Deuce several times a year. But because of its location, the city also hosted just about every major act on the dance band circuit, these groups often playing white venues in the other parts of town along with the black ones on Second Street: Louis Armstrong, Earl Hines, McKinney's Cotton Pickers, Cab Calloway, Duke Ellington, Don Redman, Fletcher Henderson, Claude Hopkins, Jimmie Lunceford, Mills Blue Rhythm Dance Band, and Chick Webb all played in the city and spent time in the Deep Deuce. Racial segregation meant that black musicians had to stay in the area's hotels like the Littlepage or with families in the neighborhood.[23]

The Deep Deuce saw a diverse mix of people pass through, including whites. Even with the city's segregation, discrimination, and bigotry, relations between whites and blacks were complex, even paradoxical. A documentary video on the guitarist notes how the local newspaper, the *Black Dispatch*, would frequently feature stories about lynching and other forms of racial hatred right next to advertisements for racially integrated gigs in venues all over town, including the Deep Deuce.[24] Racial boundaries, although tightly controlled by segregationist practices, were nonetheless porous. Besides the few adventurous whites who played at jam sessions in the Deep Deuce, many musicians could hear the music of black bands over local radio broadcasts. During his years in Oklahoma City, Charlie Christian could be heard with Leslie Sheffield's Rhythmaires on local radio station KXFR.[25] Interviews with those who grew up in the city during the late 1920s and 1930s and who knew Christian suggest a strong sense of community among musicians, despite the difficulties surrounding interracial socializing.

Although Oklahoma City was quite small relative to other American cities, the social and economic changes of the era would soon pull at the social fabric of the city, slowly unraveling the complex but tight-knit world. Like many traveling jazz musicians of the era, Christian glimpsed these changes before most of his family and friends. First venturing outside Oklahoma City in 1936, he would travel with territory bands all over the Plains states during the next several years.[26] Saxophonist Preston Love recounts hearing and playing with Christian in Omaha, and he tells of singer Anna Mae Winburn's heavy traveling schedule. Riding their "big bus," the band played "little towns, very provincial, in the Mid-West five or six nights a week."[27]

Oklahoma City was similar to other cities in the region, and writers have suggested a larger "southwestern musical culture" to characterize it. Historian Ross Russell, in his study of southwestern jazz, argues that Kansas City, because of its economic importance for commerce, was the "provincial capital" of a huge swath of the country that included the sparsely populated states west of the Mississippi River such as Oklahoma, Texas, Arizona, and New Mexico.[28] In *From Jazz to Swing*, historian Thomas Hennessey provides a more detailed account: "The Southwest combined the urban growth of the Midwest with the sizeable black population of the Southeast because the Great Migration movement of blacks from the farm to the city took place primarily within the Southwest itself." These cities drew their residents from the surrounding countryside. Many migrants moved to the big cities in Texas and Oklahoma, but those seeking something bigger headed for the regional metropolises of Kansas City or St. Louis. "The result," Hennessey writes, "was a stability of population that brought shared rural traditions to the shock of urbanization."[29]

Roughly speaking, for the purposes of musical culture, the Southwest spread out from several key cities, particularly Oklahoma City, Dallas, and Kansas City, into large parts of the surrounding areas including Plains states like Kansas and Nebraska.[30] During the mid-1920s through the 1930s this region was home to many interconnected styles. The sounds of the Southwest developed as adaptations and fusions of a variety of local and imported musical materials and practices. But Oklahoma City was also part of a larger, interconnected national musical life that played from much of the same sheet music and listened to many of the same records and radio shows. These media brought a diverse assortment of national sounds to Oklahoma City, especially from the world of the Tin Pan Alley popular song.

In addition to the music on radio or in film, Christian had access to an impressive local music scene, offering a variety of genres and styles: urban jazz, rural blues, hillbilly music, and other folk traditions (Mexican and Native American). He undoubtedly heard many regionally famous musicians such as the rural blues singer and guitar player Blind Lemon Jefferson and electric guitarist T-Bone Walker, one of Jefferson's great protégés.[31] Oral accounts suggest that the young Christian also played with a group of white musicians who were developing a regional, hillbilly-influenced version of 1930s jazz later called "western swing."[32] Haunting the clubs of the Deep Deuce, the young guitarist would also have heard lots of jazz, encountering some of the best black musicians and bands of the time: saxophonists Lester Young (a particular favorite) and Buster Smith, and the bands of Duke Ellington, Count Basie, and Louis Armstrong.[33] Not surprisingly, many important and innovative musicians emerged from this fecund environment, and the Texas-Oklahoma area spawned an unusually large number of musicians who went on to national fame: jazz pianist and bandleader Jay McShann, singer Jimmy Rushing, singing cowboy Gene Autry, folk singer Woody Guthrie, and blues guitarist T-Bone Walker.[34]

This complex musical milieu—a dynamic mixture of musical practices played by a multicultural, interconnected group of musicians— remained a part of Christian's musical language when he left the Southwest.[35] While certain phrases in Christian's playing with the Benny Goodman Sextet—a particular run of eighth notes here, a syncopated string bend there—can be sourced in the playing of his regional contemporaries, I am not interested in generating a typology of these common musical gestures. Rather, I want to explore how the sounds of this particular place (the "Southwest") traveled with Christian and shaped his developing improvisational style. As his playing developed over his brief career and he incorporated new melodic figures, harmonic structures, and rhythmic gestures, Christian built on what he already knew. The new did not displace the old—it was brought into alignment with it. In his recordings with Benny Goodman, as well as in the famous after-hours jam sessions at Minton's, we can hear the accretion of places in his music. We can hear what Lefebvre calls "representational spaces," symbolic cultural forms that register real physical and psychological spatial experiences.[36]

Leaving the Territory and "Flying Home"

One of the earliest recordings Charlie Christian made as a new member of Benny Goodman's organization was "Flying Home," recorded in New York on October 2, 1939, about six weeks after his first appearance with the bandleader. In the studio the guitarist recorded three numbers with the Goodman small group: "Rose Room," "Stardust" (a performance built around a rare Christian chordal solo), and "Flying Home."[37] It was this last tune that would become most closely associated with Christian, and I have located ten versions of it that span the guitarist's time with Benny Goodman. Table 4.1 lists the recordings of "Flying Home" along with the recording dates and personnel. Although the Goodman sextet recorded many tunes multiple times, this song stands out as among its most repeated. Clearly it had special

Table 4.1 Comparison of "Flying Home" recordings made from 1939 to 1941

	Recording Date	Live/Studio	Key	Group
1	August 19, 1939	Live: Los Angeles, Hollywood Bowl, "Camel Caravan" NBC radio network	E♭	Benny Goodman Sextet: Goodman (clarinet), Lionel Hampton (vibes), Fletcher Henderson (piano), Artie Bernstein (bass), Nick Fatool (drums)
2	September 9, 1939	Live: Radio City Studios, "Camel Caravan" NBC Radio network	E*	Benny Goodman Sextet: same as above
3	October 2, 1939, NYC	Studio	E♭	Benny Goodman Sextet: same as above
4	October 2, 1939	Studio-V-disc	E♭	Benny Goodman Sextet: same as above
5	October 6, 1939	Live: NYC, Carnegie Hall, ASCAP Twenty-fifth Anniversary Concert	E♭	Benny Goodman Sextet: same as above
6	October 16, 1939	Live: NYC, Empire Room, Waldorf Astoria Hotel, Mutual Radio Network	E♭	Benny Goodman Sextet: same as above
7	December 24, 1939	Sextet, Carnegie Hall, Spirituals to Swing Concert	E♭	Benny Goodman Sextet: same as above
8	February 10, 1941	Live: Benny Goodman Sextet and Guests, NYC "What's New," *Old Gold Radio Show*, NBC	E	Cootie Williams (trumpet), Goodman (clarinet) Auld (tenor sax), Red Norvo (vibes), Johnny Guarnieri (piano), Artie Bernstein (bass), Dave Tough (drums), Billy Butterfield, Irving Goodman (trumpets), Cutty Cutshall, Lou McGarity (trombones), Gus Bivona, Les Robinson (alto sax), Pete Mondello (tenor sax), Skip Martin (baritone sax), Mike Bryan (guitar)
9	March 10, 1941	Goodman Sextet, NYC "What's New," *Old Gold Radio Show*, NBC	E♭	Benny Goodman and His Sextet: Cootie Williams (trumpet), Benny Goodman (clarinet), Georgie Auld (tenor sax), Johnny Guarnieri (piano), Artie Bernstein (bass), Gene Krupa (drums)
10	May 5, 1941	Goodman Sextet and Guests, NYC Manhattan Center, "What's New?" *Old Gold Radio Show*, NBC	E♭	Benny Goodman Sextet and Guests: Cootie Williams (trumpet), Benny Goodman (clarinet), Teddy Wilson (piano), Artie Bernstein (bass), Jo Jones (drums); Billy Butterfield, Jimmy Maxwell, Irving Goodman (trumpets); Cutty Cutshall, Lou McGarity, (trombone); Les Robinson, Jimmy Horvath (alto saxes); Georgie Auld, Pete Mondello (tenor sax); Skip Martin (baritone sax); Mike Bryan (guitar)

Note: All these tracks are available on two comprehensive boxed sets: *Charlie Christian: Complete Live Recordings*, four compact discs. Definitive Records, Disconforme sl (DRCD 11177), 2001; *Charlie Christian: Complete Studio Recordings*, four compact discs. Definitive Records, Disconforme sl (DRCD 11176), 2001. A good, though incomplete, collection of cleanly remastered tunes is available on the four compact disc set *Charlie Christian: The Genius of the Electric Guitar*, four compact discs, Sony Music Entertainment (C4K 65564), 2002. The list does not include partial takes, false starts, or jam sessions. A recording made in the studio March 13, 1941, caught the Goodman Sextet jamming on what sounds like the changes to "Flying Home."

*The key of E in this recording and the one made on February 10, 1941, are likely the result of slower recording speeds and not conscious performing choices.

value for Goodman. "Flying Home" not only was one of the first three studio recordings made with Christian in the group, it was a song that was, by all reliable accounts, written by the guitarist himself (though Goodman and vibraphonist Lionel Hampton received the credit).[38] The song provided the introduction to a new Benny Goodman small group sound—bluesy, riff-based, and largely the result of Christian's influence. With so many surviving performances, live and in the studio, the song presents a comprehensive view of Christian's aesthetic. In "Flying Home" we can hear the particular qualities of movement so characteristic of the guitarist's music.

With his introduction to Goodman, Charlie Christian's life was dramatically split in two: there was his life as is it was in Oklahoma City and the "territory," and there was his new life as a member of perhaps the nation's most popular jazz band. Christian, as Wayne Goins and Craig McKinney write, "had come a long way in a very short time."[39] Eight months earlier, in February 1939, the guitarist was a relatively unknown member of Alphonso Trent's band playing a winter gig in Casper, Wyoming. Now he was on the Carnegie Hall stage with the preeminent swing band of the moment.[40] This dramatic change exposed Christian to a much larger world. Suddenly thousands, even millions, of listeners could hear him play as he toured the country and broadcast live on national radio programs. The venues the Goodman Orchestra (and his smaller sextet) played were much larger and more elegant than almost anything a smaller, black territory band in the Southwest would likely ever see. And of course Christian received a hefty pay raise, jumping from the range of $7 a week up to the $150 Benny Goodman paid him when he joined the band.[41] Needless to say, he could now afford better clothes, better accommodations, and better instruments. Yet despite crossing a major threshold and confronting an array of new experiences, much of what Christian experienced was a change in degree, not necessarily in kind. Constant travel remained—the venues were different and the transportation was more comfortable, but this basic aspect of dance band life never disappeared.

Playing with territory bands such as Alphonso Trent's Orchestra, Christian traveled great distances from his home base in Oklahoma City, reaching cities as far north as Deadwood, South Dakota.[42] With Goodman such long distances became more frequent, and buses, railroad coaches, and airplanes replaced cramped touring cars. Along with the travel came the inevitable racism and discrimination of mid-twentieth-century America. Many venues would not let Goodman's smaller interracial group play, only the larger all-white jazz orchestra.

Christian had more money now, but that still could not buy him accommodations and meals in many hotels and restaurants across the country. Despite the massive rupture in his life, many of the guitarist's experiences were intensifications of the same racism that had shaped his life in Oklahoma City. Still, the guitarist was separated from his home and family in dramatic new ways. The song "Flying Home," with its evocation of great distance and speed, also describes Christian's new life far from Oklahoma City.

We don't know who ultimately named the song, but "flying" was clearly the metaphor of choice when naming tunes most directly associated with the guitarist. After its first recording, "Flying Home" became a theme song for the Goodman Sextet, and it became closely associated with Christian himself. In April 1940 *Down Beat* magazine featured a guitar transcription of Christian's solo from the originally released studio recording. This was a public recognition that, although Goodman was still the leader, Christian was the sextet's star. When Goodman created another feature specifically for the guitarist—1941's landmark "Solo Flight"—flying again seemed the appropriate theme. Written specifically as a feature for Christian and the Goodman big band, and one of the guitarist's last studio recordings before his death, the tune was originally to be titled "Chonk, Charlie, Chonk." This clunky title was quickly abandoned for something more descriptive.[43] With unintentional poetry, Christian's professional career was framed by two "flying" songs.

"Flying Home" suggests not just the metaphorical creative flight of a soloist, but also the very real experience of airplane travel, a new but relatively small part of most Americans' lives. In the literature surrounding Christian there are anecdotes that connect the flying of the title to actual experiences with the newly emerging world of commercial airline travel, an expensive mode of transportation that involved patience, planning, and not a little courage. Saxophonist and clarinetist Jerry Jerome, a member of the Goodman Orchestra while Christian was with the group, recalled how scheduling difficulties forced the band to fly across the country:

We flew on a plane from coast to coast, from Burbank to Atlantic City. I believe it was the first time a band had flown that far. . . . TWA flew us over[.] They painted a plane with the name "TWA Swing King Special." . . . We would stop on our way over the country at different cities and we'd jam outside the plane and move on to the next place. We had to do short hops on the plane, we had all the instruments, the band, the wives. We had a cat and a dog called Tempo and Swing that belonged to Lionel and Gladys Hampton. There wasn't much room[,] it was only a DC3.

Everybody got used to it and said "Hey, this is fun." It was such a nice view up there that it sorta broke the ice. We had a very pleasant trip across and we made it well in time. We picked up a fleet of touring cars and got to the matinee at the Steel Pier. That was unique then, most of the time we traveled by Pullman, and a few one-nighters by bus.[44]

Like Jerome, Christian almost certainly had never traveled by plane before—he made his way to his first meeting with Benny Goodman by train. After the painful, cramped conditions of car and bus touring, what an extraordinary experience it must have been to be able to soar across the country to the next gig![45] As Ann Douglas and Gena Caponi-Tabery point out, the excitement (and fear) over the reality of airplane travel was part of a broader cultural preoccupation with flying and height, what writers of the time called "airmindedness."[46] The celebration of Charles Lindbergh's transatlantic flight in 1927 and the push to build taller and taller skyscrapers both suggest a widespread desire among Americans to seek out great height, to reach toward the sky. The future was experienced and symbolized through flight.[47]

Scholarship on Charlie Christian frequently mentions the intense feeling of forward motion in his solo lines, the profound sense of focused movement through musical space, although few writers have provided any sustained analysis of this. For theorists Clive Downs and Howard Spring the sense of motion and forward "drive" is the result of various strategies of metric displacement and the use of tension-building repetition that is released in long, linear phrases.[48] Undoubtedly both of these are contributing factors, but neither author reaches far enough. To adequately understand Christian's musical drive, we first need to outline how the guitarist moved in the musical spaces he occupied and helped construct. Then we need to connect these musical enactments of mobility to his lived experience of space—the places where he lived and worked. Musical techniques and practices—bent strings, linear melodies, formulas and patterns—have, in the context of Christian's life, strong associations with regionally specific musical practices. The formal manipulations of these musical materials suggest parallels to Christian's literal experiences of home and travel. Music and context combine to open a "hermeneutic window" onto the guitarist's spatial experience of America during the 1930s—an experience intimately shaped by the tension between the regional and the national: Christian takes elements of his southwestern musical milieu and reworks them into a representation of mobility that expresses a new, more expansive American identity.

Musical Motion

The sense of motion or movement in music is a complicated topic. For centuries writers have described music's ability to convey a sense of motion. Explanations of the origin and nature of this motion, though, have varied widely. From a strict empirical point of view, the only things actually moving are the sound waves passing through air and the vibrating receptors in our ears. And though this is certainly a component of the felt sense of movement, it is not what most writers mean when they identify musical motion. Most musical theoreticians locate the sense of movement and motion in music in the interaction of musical components. In this formalist understanding motion derives from the "articulation of motives, phrases, durational patterns, cadential progressions, and so on."[49] Musical *structure* is the central focus. Music theorist Robert Morgan labels this structural level "tonal space," a "part of a more generalized musical space that incorporates not only matters of texture but all the elements of compositional structure."[50] Most historical and theoretical analysis has focused almost exclusively on this type of musical space. In a jazz context, the analysis of musical structure or "tonal space" would include such elements as chord changes, rhythmic feel and syncopations, cross-rhythms, and the soloists' melodic lines. In the 1930s and '40s a jazz soloist worked "within" the changes, articulating important markers of the harmony as they unfolded in time. But a soloist also created tension by delaying or anticipating the move to other chords. Phrasing against the movement of the chords (or even against the beginnings and ends of choruses) created a sense of musical entities moving relative to one another. Similarly, playing with and against the implied or stated rhythmic pulse created a sense of motion among musical elements. In his guitar solos Christian skillfully does all these things.

But listeners and musicians understand and experience musical space and movement in other distinctive ways not found in the formal structures of the music. More than just notes, chords, or rhythms, we hear *musicians* interacting with each other. Musical sounds contain information about the nature of the physical movements that produced them. We hear musical performance as an expression of energy and force, and different instruments require and allow specific kinds of physical movement. How we decode this information—translate it back into physical experience—is determined by individual musical knowledge and experience.[51] As music theorists Patrick Shove and Bruno Repp write, "To hear [musical] attacks is to hear the performer move."[52] For example, guitarists (like other string players) can bend notes and slide in and out of notes. The sense of dynamic, forward motion in Christian's music works at both the level of structure *and* the level of performance. The following two sections analyze several recorded versions of "Flying Home." The first section focuses on formal structures and uses the conventional language of musical analysis to identify the relation between melodies, harmonies, and rhythms. The second part shifts to the performance level, examining how a sense of movement is generated through the physical actions of the musician. Here the language of traditional musical analysis is insufficient, and I offer some new ways to talk about this essential, and frequently overlooked, aspect of musical meaning.

"Flying Home": Motion in Tonal Space

As a vehicle for improvisation, "Flying Home" is relatively simple and straightforward, and it is constructed like many other popular songs of the era. It is thirty-two bars long and organized into the familiar AABA, Tin Pan Alley song form. The A sections are harmonically static: a descending chord sequence (I—I7—vi—sharp-V7—V7) repeats every two bars, and the bridge travels through a series of fifth-related dominant seventh chords (in the manner of Gershwin's "I Got Rhythm"). In terms of melodic content, the song is soaked in the blues. The harmonically straightforward melody—a classic "riff"—is repeated four times, the last with a cadential turn. The flat third "blue" note is key, and it is the pivot around which the riff moves, imparting the strong blues flavor. The bridge, with no predetermined melody, is an ad lib for a soloist. Example 4.1 is a lead sheet with the song's chords and melody. In contemporary jazz parlance, "Flying Home" is a "blowing tune" par excellence. With A sections firmly in E-flat, the soloist has a great deal of freedom, contending only with the brief modulations of the bridge. In fact, the blues scale works beautifully the entire way through the A sections, and it is something Christian will take great advantage of.

Example 4.1 Lead sheet for "Flying Home." In performance the bridge is often improvised. On the published sheet music, the bridge uses a melodic variation of Benny Goodman's playing on the original studio recording. Music licensed by Sunflower Entertainment Group.

The ten extant recordings of the song are generally very similar, matching each other closely in tempo, order of solos, comping styles, and supporting background lines. Christian's approach to improvising on the song is also similar across the recordings; in fact they exemplify his overall approach to solo improvisation. Over the A sections the guitarist manipulates short, riff-like melodies and blues gestures (string bends, slides, and blues notes). At the bridge, he largely abandons the riffs in favor of long lines that weave through the chords and often begin and end in surprising places. These melodies tend to be less blues-based and more chromatic, filled with passing and other non-harmonic tones. These two approaches—bluesy and motivic versus linear and chromatic—create very different experiences of musical space and motion. I have included solo transcriptions from three recordings of "Flying Home." Transcriptions have many limitations, but they are also very useful at conveying certain kinds of information. And while my discussion below will refer to these transcriptions in some detail, it is useful to study them in a more general way. Many of the musical techniques I discuss are very easy to see and don't require any formal knowledge of music theory. You can *see* the contour—the rising and falling—of the melodic lines and how they are spaced with respect to the lines that mark out the individual measures. Similarly, it is easy to see the striking contrast between the relatively sparse A sections and the much denser bridge sections where there are literally more notes in the same space.

In their analysis of another Goodman Sextet recording, "Seven Come Eleven," Al Avakian and Bob Prince summarize Christian's approach to improvisation and musical form:

The Sextet, as always, follows this pattern, opening with a riff by the ensemble against a bass figure. Then Charlie launches his solo with a repetitive single-note riff, develops a series of riffs through the first sixteen bars (tension); then, in the eight-bar release [the bridge], he contrasts this by playing melodic lines characteristically made up mainly of even eighth notes (relaxation), then returns to eight bars of riffs (tension), giving his solo contour and movement.[53]

Christian's "habit of attacking the midsection of an arrangement" has also been noted by fellow musicians.[54] According to bassist Red Callender, Christian would never "skate" through the bridge where chord and key changes became rapid: "he really dug the interrelated chords leading in and out of the bridge" and created a steady "flow" through the hard part of the tune. Listening to Christian play on songs like "Stompin' at the Savoy," saxophonist James Moody recalled how "as soon as he came to the difficult part, the bridge, he would tear it up, he would dive in."[55]

Avakian and Prince label the guitarist's distinctive style, with its rhythmic elasticity and intense drive, a new kind of "mobile swing."[56] Christian's bifurcated approach to soloing shows a consistent and pervasive tension between an urge for mobility and a desire for stability. His approach to musical form enacts a dialogue between place-rooted blues and the less specific place associations of his modernistic, chromatic melodic lines. This dialogue does not always manifest itself according to the formal structure of the tunes he plays. The tension we hear is woven throughout his solos—Christian will sometimes mix in longer chromatic lines during the A sections and play bluesy riffs in the bridge. But it is in these transitions between larger structural events, particularly the move from A section to bridge, that we can most clearly hear the place-stylistic tension in Christian's improvisations.

The opening to the August 19, 1939, recording, given in example 4.3, illustrates the guitarist's approach to the A sections of the form. There is movement here (in the structural sense), but it is contained within the region circumscribed by the descending chord progression. In other words, the guitarist, in developing his solo, only has to "inhabit" the tonal space of E-flat; there are no key changes and no formal divisions as obstacles. For such a highly skilled soloist of the era, this relatively static musical space favors specific improvisatory techniques and musical patterns.

First, it encourages a high degree of call-and-response. In the tonally active bridge, the imperative to "make the changes" eliminates the time and space needed to initiate a full call and an adequate response. In the A sections, Christian's phrases tend to be short, usually spanning just two or three measures, and based on the tonic triad (E-flat–G–B-flat). The guitarist manipulates these short phrases melodically and rhythmically, playing them off each other, as well as the background pattern (example 4.2) and the underlying pulse.[57] For example, in the first two A sections from the August 19, 1939, recording Christian works a lot with a very short melodic gesture—two eighth notes on the same pitch. This melodic fragment is woven throughout the section, appearing in measures 3, 9, 11, and 13. Significantly, it also sits on the downbeats, thus leaving space for the listener to hear the accompanying off-beat background line. In general, this type of soloing, where short, syncopated melodies are manipulated in unpredictable ways, leaves many opportunities for the rhythm section to rise to the musical foreground. Even when the rhythm section isn't responding with improvised figures, the fact that they are suddenly brought to the audible foreground— on par with the soloist—gives the A sections a distinctive dialogical feel where soloist and rhythm section are "talking" to each other.

For variety and drama, Christian also mixes in notes that are "outside" the E-flat key. These outside or chromatic notes appear most often as "blue" notes, technically the b3, b5, and b7 notes of the home key (in E-flat these are G-flat, B-double-flat, D-flat).[58] Importing these notes, Christian "colors" the triadic patterns he plays. For example, the opening cross-rhythmic figure of example 4.3 is a blues variation on the tonic triad (the phrase contains a D-flat—the flat-7 scale degree in E-flat major). Sometimes these blues notes function simultaneously as

Example 4.2 Rhythm of ensemble background figure to solos in "Flying Home." Transcribed by the author for use in this volume. Music licensed by Sunflower Entertainment Group.

passing dissonances—brief chromatic pitches that connect the consonant notes of the home key (see, for example, measure 4 in example 4.3). The most marked blues notes are the ones Christian creates by bending the guitar string, pushing up into the note. Blues string bends are part of the larger practice of blues guitar playing as it developed in the American South and Midwest. Because they are less tied to marking the changes, blues gestures enable one to play over several chords in a similar manner. The predictability of the A sections encourages these bluesy interpolations.

The feeling of movement in these A sections is multifaceted and depends on our auditory focus. Concentrating on the soloist, we hear Christian's short, syncopated melodies shifting against the underlying rhythmic and harmonic framework. His solo creates its own path, and we can follow it as it moves against the expected chords and rhythms played by the other musicians. But between the guitarist's phrases we hear the rhythm section's "voice." Our attention shifts to the ongoing back-and-forth between soloist and support, foreground and background. This alternating awareness of near and far is another kind of felt motion. The musical texture—foreground and background— appears to move as our attention refocuses itself.[59]

The movement we sense in these A sections is also paradoxical. The two-measure descending chord sequence that structures the music is highly directional, driving to the expected tonal closure, but also very open-ended—the tonal closure happens so often and so quickly that our attention shifts to the larger repeating unit itself, a unit that never changes. We hear and feel a sense of motion that is at one level forward-directed, but at a higher structural level static. Christian's solo melodies are similarly highly mobile and also static. The short, tonic-based, blues-inflected melodies are predictable in their length and basic tonal makeup, but unpredictable in their placement and variation.

When Christian reaches the bridge of "Flying Home," he abandons the short, bluesy riffs of the A sections for longer melodic lines that deftly explore the movement from chord to chord. The ensemble abandons the off-beat background lines for straight comping, giving the soloist a smoother foundation for his winding, chromatic, and rhythmically dense lines. Lou Donaldson's description of Benny Carter (a contemporary of Christian) is equally applicable to the guitarist: compared with other swing players, Donaldson says, Carter "was more like the guys who eventually ended up playing bebop. He flowed. He kept moving all the time."[60] With its changing chords and keys, the bridge necessitates specific moves through the tonal space, and Christian obliges with lines that "flow" over and through the harmonic obstacles. The guitarist often works against the chord changes, anticipating their arrivals and delaying their departures.

In each of the bridge sections of the recordings of "Flying Home" that I have transcribed (examples 4.3, 4.4, and 4.5), the guitarist positions his melodic lines off-center, starting and ending his phrases just out of alignment with the underlying rhythmic pulse. This creates, in the language of Avakian and Prince, "metric denials" of our expectations.[61] In example 4.3, Christian begins his first phrase of the bridge—a three-measure run of basically uninterrupted eighth notes—on the last off-beat of measure 16. He ends that phrase in the middle of measure 20. The entire line, then, is positioned so that it avoids accenting downbeats and the arrival of each new chord. Christian's second phrase of the bridge also begins on the off-beat of the measure before the chord change (to F7, measure 21). That line runs right through the change to B-flat7 and ends at the beginning of the last measure of the bridge. His improvised melodies on the other B sections of "Flying Home" are similarly placed, beginning and ending before or after the chord changes. Yet even as the solo lines are "off-center," they always clearly mark the chord changes as they go by. Christian almost always begins his lines on chord tones of the underlying seventh chord, and he carefully alters notes to anticipate or mark the change to a new harmony (for instance, in example 4.5 he changes Gs to G-flats on the change from E-flat7 to A-flat7 in measure 19).

This combination of long phrase length, rhythmic flexibility, and change marking generates solo lines that are strikingly different from the short, syncopated, rhythmically displaced bursts of the A sections. There is a cool-headedness and laid-back hipness in running changes this way: one sounds out of step but is in fact very much *in* step. But

Example 4.3 "Flying Home," Recorded August 19, 1939. Concert pitch. Transcribed by the author for use in this volume. Music licensed by Sunflower Entertainment Group.

Christian does more; he intensifies the tension of these lines by playing with the rhythmic density of his phrases and filling his lines with slippery chromaticisms and unusual, striking note choices. Example 4.5 has one of the most dramatic shifts in rhythmic profile: here Christian moves from a long run of eighth notes in the first half of the bridge to a brilliant run of eighth-note triplets in the second half. The effect is of increasing speed—suddenly more notes are flowing by in the same amount of space. Christian then fills these triplets with chromaticisms,

Example 4.4 "Flying Home," October 2, 1939. Concert pitch. Transcribed by the author for use in this volume. Music licensed by Sunflower Entertainment Group.

slipping in passing notes—primarily flat thirds and natural sevenths. Like his shorter, fragmented phrases from the A sections, Christian's linear melodies at the bridge have a similar melodic shape, often winding between a unison or an octave. This creates a feeling of having made a journey, even though we never exactly reach "home." Arriving on a tonic an octave away imparts a sense of return but with a significant affective difference.

To create even more drama and tension, Christian often features pungent chromatic alterations—in a sense, "wrong" notes—that were adventurous for the late 1930s and early 1940s. These are different

Example 4.5 "Flying Home," February 10, 1941. Concert pitch. Transcribed by the author for use in this volume. Music licensed by Sunflower Entertainment Group.

from the blues chromaticism we hear in the A sections. Again, "Flying Home" provides many specific examples of this general characteristic of his playing. In example 4.4 (the October 2, 1939, recording) we hear two striking examples, both in the bridge section. The first occurs in measure 18, where he plays a D-natural and E-natural against an E-flat7 chord. The second happens later in the bridge, when the guitarist strikes a prominent F-sharp against a B-flat7 chord.[62] From a music theory point of view, there are several explanations (cf. note 62), but the general purpose of both gestures is to amplify the dissonance and intensity of his playing. In both cases he intensifies the dominant chord—in tonal music the chord with the strongest directional pull (it wants to resolve to the tonic or home key). Christian is amplifying the already strong tonal drive of the bridge, with its sequence of dominant seventh chords. The increased tension drives the melody with greater force toward a resolution in the home key.

By dramatically marking off the bridge, Christian intensifies its character as a new space with new options for movement. All these characteristics—phrase length, rhythmic density, off-center phrase beginnings and endings, chromatic alterations—enhance the function of the bridge as a place of contrasting music, a break from the repetitions of the A sections. This feeling is confirmed when he returns to the final A sections, often playing bursts of short, accented blues phrases to mark the transition. These final eight measures often feature the most striking blues gestures, including staccato, dissonant double-stops, same-pitch alternations between strings, and dramatic slides to and away from notes. By returning to his bluesy, riff-based opening, Christian creates a satisfying symmetry to his solos and a sense of a return home, a journey completed. But we are also somewhere else—we might be back where we started, with the bluesy A sections, yet the journey itself has transformed our destination. Christian has explored the musical space and realized its potential for different types of movement.

It is tempting to interpret the bluesy A sections and modern, linear bridges homologically: the Southwest represented in the former, the new national experiences in the latter. From the smaller, more restricted life in a small midwestern city (A), Christian now had the expansiveness and movement of travel and the metropolis (B). In many ways this is compelling. If the riff playing on the A sections allows interlocking accompaniments with the rest of the group, the breathless lines on the bridge break from the integrated playing, striking out on an individual path that plays over and through the accompaniment. These two improvisational techniques suggest different models of social interaction and cooperation characteristic of two very different place experiences—the regional city and the cosmopolitan metropolis. The return to the final A is then a return "home" to the Southwest, a smaller place with its much more tight-knit community.

Such a specific and tightly fitted homology between musical structure and social experience, however, distorts the meanings of inherently multivalent musical practices. I want to emphasize a more flexible interpretation that understands Christian's improvisational style as a gestalt—a coherent set of concerns worked out through musical practice. These concerns are often most distinct at important structural points in the music. In the contrast between the A sections and the bridge, the melodies become, in the terminology of music theorist Eero Tarasti, "modalized"—earlier melodies impart a different mood and character to those that follow. The syntagmatic arrangement of musical materials (in this case, Christian's melodic improvisations) influences the character of each section. Compared with the relative stasis of the A sections, what Tarasti would call "being," we perceive the bridge, with its tonal drive and dissonant, off-center melodies, as "doing."[63] In his improvisations, exemplified by "Flying Home," the guitarist plays with this contrast between self-contained activity and directional, energetic flow across boundaries.

Christian is the instigator of these musical modes of being, but he is also part of a group, and his playing directly affects the playing of the musicians around him. By altering his approach, the guitarist brings about different interactive relationships among the musicians. Again, using the language of Tarasti's musical semiotics, the guitarist's playing modalizes their musical utterances. If the riff-based A sections leave space for the accompanying musicians to fill in, during the off-kilter bridges the band must hold itself together as the individual soloist spins outward, challenging the improvisational framework. While he seems just out of step, Christian's rhythmic confidence always carries him through and back to realignment. His fellow musicians must keep their places, confident that he will return and re-place himself into the tune's structure. Christian's approach to song structure—his stylistic alternations between A sections and bridge—is also an approach to "abstract" musical space. From this hermeneutic perspective, we hear not just a melodic, harmonic, or rhythmic statement, but an expression and an attitude toward movement in and through musical and—by extension—nonmusical space.

"Flying Home": Motion through Performance

The sense of motion in Christian's music, though, is the result of more than the formal, structural activities described above; it is also the result of the performer's physical movement encoded in sound. The bluesy double-stops, string bends, and slides so prevalent in "Flying Home" are more than blues gestures, they are strong references to place. They are sounds that evoke a world far from the bustle of New York City. These microscopic gestures evoke regional musical practices—especially the blues—of the Southwest and Christian's hometown of Oklahoma City.

In these particular notes and gestures a historically minded listener can hear Lonnie Johnson, Blind Lemon Jefferson, T-Bone Walker, western swing, and the jazz territory bands of Bennie Moten and Walter Page. Listening to the sonic quality of these moments is essential in understanding the distinctive split in Christian's life and musical style. As ethnomusicologist Vijay Iyer writes, "The story that an improviser tells does not unfold merely in the overall form of a 'coherent' solo, nor simply in antiphonal structures, but also in the microscopic musical details, as well as in the inherent structure of the performance itself. The story dwells not just in one solo at a time, but also in *a single note*, and equally in an entire lifetime of improvisations" (emphasis added). To hear these stories you must do more than find linear narratives such as my structural analysis above; you must capture the full "fractured, exploded" story: "the shifting, multiple, continually reconstructed subjectivities of the improvisers, encoded in a diverse variety of sonic symbols, occurring at different levels and subject to different stylistic controls."[64]

While many musical practices connect Christian to the world of the Southwest, *timbre* and *attack* are two of the most important. These are major, if often overlooked, components of Christian's characteristic "sound"—the assortment of specific physical actions that shaped and defined his playing for listeners.[65] These characteristics are inextricably connected to the electric guitar, an instrument he did much to promote and change.[66] Listening closely to the way he plucked, slid into, bent up, and otherwise manipulated his guitar strings takes us back in time and place to the sound world of Oklahoma City, where the potent mixture of blues, hillbilly, western swing, and jazz became the bedrock of his playing style.[67] The timbre and attack of Christian's electric guitar place him in a specific experience of American place.[68]

For Iyer, the improviser develops his music, in part, from a kinesthetic interaction between his body and the instrument. Thelonious Monk, for example, created many musical sounds that emerged from physical movements that come naturally to a pianist, such as pendular intervals of fourths, fifths, and sixths (melodic patterns that can be very challenging on other instruments such as horns or guitars). This kinesthetic relationship "can leave its trace on the music itself—that is, it can be communicated musically."[69] "Musical meaning," Iyer concludes, "is not conveyed only through motivic development, melodic contour, and other traditional musicological parameters; it is also embodied in improvisatory techniques." Musical gestures are "sonic symbols" with "traces of embodiment," and they point to nonmusical human activities. Music can suggest particular "way[s] of being embodied" in the world."[70]

When I first began listening intently to Christian, what particularly moved me was something in his rhythm and attack beyond the choices of notes, something connected to the particular way he handled his instrument. This aspect of Christian's guitar style was not really driven home until I tried to play some of his solos from transcriptions—they are deceptively fast, with each note articulated with brilliant punch. In the liner notes to a recently issued box set of Christian's recordings, the guitarist and inventor Les Paul remembers the guitarist's sound:

Charlie always was impressed with the fact that I was a technical player, a white technical player. But he was a *stomper*. "You only play one goddamn note," I'd tell him, "and you kill me!"

"What I'm doing was so much harder than what he's doing"—that's what I thought back then. But over time, through being with Charlie, I realized how tough it is to come down on that *one note* in the right place, and how much more of a drive he had. He had that ability, like Lionel Hampton, to take a note, to take one 'A' and just pound it into your head until it was the greatest note you'd ever heard.[71]

Bebop guitarist Barney Kessel echoes Paul's sentiments. To Kessel, another white player, "Christian was more aggressive, forceful and louder than I was. I said to him: 'You play loud'—not as a criticism or anything. He said, 'I like to hear myself!'"[72]

Both comments emphasize the forcefulness and rhythmic excitement of Christian's sound. They also subtly invoke a complicated racial discourse that equates powerful musical emotion with a black, less intellectualized, and more bodily approach to playing. Both Paul and Kessel are white, and their comments bear traces of the distortions of mid-twentieth-century American racial politics. Despite this, what they say is valuable. Among the many musicians quoted in the liner notes to this reissue (and elsewhere in other newspaper and magazine articles devoted to Christian's legacy), Paul and Kessel are unusually specific in their praise. Most musicians quoted fall back on less specific concepts of Christian's "genius" or progressive musical vision.

"I realized how tough it is to come down on that *one note* in the right place." The idea that one note struck the right way at precisely the right time can be the most powerful of all musical gestures seems almost mystical. After all, musicological analysis is predicated on the assumption that notes have meaning in conjunction with other notes, that musical meaning rests in the relation between pitches and rhythms. Yet many jazz musicians I have spoken to have repeatedly echoed this idea: that so-and-so could play one note and make it swing, that his playing was so simple yet so deep, that she blew one note and said more than anyone else. In his monumental ethnography of contemporary jazz practice, Paul Berliner reports that jazz reed and woodwind player "Ken McIntyre once commented that a great improviser could play an entire solo based on one pitch alone."[73] In another interview, a young drummer, after hearing a recording of flugelhornist Wilbur Hardin playing "a stream of single pitched rhythmic patterns at his solo's opening," exclaimed, "'Did you hear that? That's what our music's about. Listen to all that brother can say with one note!' "[74] In Western art music there is a strong, if marginalized, tradition that attributes enormous powers to particular notes or sonorities played at particular times. Scriabin based a grand, all-encompassing musical-social philosophy on this notion, and later experimenters such as composer La Monte Young would drone for days seeking similar transcendental states.[75]

Scholarly writing on Christian has emphasized his progressive melodic and harmonic sense, and these facets of his playing are still essential to understanding his approach to playing and his influence, but it is that "one note at the right time" that provides special insights into the guitarist's playing. Moments of timbral expression direct our attention to the *quality* of sound. This shifts our focus from the imperatives of tonal form and resolution to a different kind of musical motion. When our attention shifts to the "performance event," motion is conveyed through a complex and subtle mixture of factors: "the mode of production (bowing, tonguing), the style of articulation (staccato, legato), the physical 'shaping' of a sustained sound (vibrato, lip trill), the rate of movement (tempo and timing, or agogics), the pattern of movement (dynamics) and even the changes in pitch (musical space)." For musicologists Shove and Repp these characteristics "are represented kinematically in the acoustic array." Extracting this kinematic information from the sound waves "will shape the listener's perception of musical movement."[76]

Literary theorist Roland Barthes did something like this—extracting kinematic information—when he famously analyzed the "grain" of the voice in classical vocal lieder. In that essay Barthes was more concerned with how "music works on language," and he not surprisingly chose lieder and French art songs for analysis. The body he hears in the performance, the "grain," is a manner of signifying without pointing to a particular signified; it presents to the ear a process of meaning creation without burdening it with or limiting it to a particular meaning or network of meanings. For Barthes, the use of "grain" moves discourse on music away from the "adjective" with its necessary commodification. But Barthes's discussion is more than a little about defending particular recordings he cherishes, and there is a strong feeling throughout the brief essay that all the elaborate analytical apparatus is in the service of personal taste. Nevertheless, in his emphasis on hearing bodies, the materiality of performance, and the way these elements can signify, Barthes is useful for understanding Christian's embodied sound: "I hear without a doubt—the certitude here of the body, of the body's enjoyment—that Wanda Landowska's harpsichord comes from her inner body, and not from the minor digital knitting of so many harpsichordists. . . . I know immediately which part of the body it is that plays."[77] To hear the "grain" in Christian's voice is to hear the active body. Vijay Iyer nicely sums up the issues at stake: "The meaning of a vocal utterance is constituted not simply by its semantic content or its melodic logic, but also by its *sonorous* content."[78] This sonorous content is further shaped by specific cultural influences. In the case of Christian that dominating cultural influence was "Afrological." Coined by musician and scholar George Lewis, "Afrological" describes a system of musical beliefs and behaviors—a "logic"—emphasizing musical spontaneity grounded in historical awareness, musical freedom shaped through study and discipline, and personalized musical statements that tell particular and unique "stories."[79] "Sound," writes Iyer, "provides a kind of Afrological animation of the 'grain' in European performance."[80]

If we accept that "notions of personhood are transmitted via sounds," then it follows that Christian's sound—especially his timbre and attack—evokes a specific physical experience of place.[81] And in his case the place evoked was often the sound world of Oklahoma City and the musical "territory" of the Southwest. Christian's solos on "Flying Home" are musical experiences—told over and over again—of different types of movement. They are "representational spaces" in which we hear movement across a changing national geography.

Experimentation and Synthesis: "Stompin' at the Savoy" and "Solo Flight"

When Christian joined Benny Goodman in 1939, he moved to New York City, but this was only nominally his home—a relentless travel schedule kept him on the road most of the time. Even being in New York was hardly a break; the band was nearly always busy recording, broadcasting radio shows, and performing concerts. When in the city, Christian, like most black musicians, lived in a Harlem residential hotel. He spent most of his free time visiting friends and playing with other musicians.[82] For jazz historians and aficionados, his most productive free time was spent jamming at Minton's Playhouse, in the basement of Harlem's Cecil Hotel. In 1940 owner Henry Minton put former bandleader Teddy Hill in charge of the small nightclub's back room and its music. Hill recruited drummer Kenny Clarke, trumpeter Joe Guy, bassist Nick Fenton, and pianist Thelonious Monk as the house band. Monday nights were the most exciting as Hill invited the entire cast of the Apollo Theater to the club for "Celebrity Night" and a dinner buffet. A jam session inevitably followed the eating. These nights frequently drew the largest crowds and most expansive and fiery sessions.[83] White jazz fan Jerry Newman's amateur recordings made at this nightspot have become justly famous as some of the only audible evidence of what 1940s jazz jam sessions were like. For historians these recordings offer rare evidence of the development of swing into the style that would eventually be labeled "modern jazz" or "bebop."

In *The Birth of Bebop*, Scott DeVeaux briefly discusses one of these recordings, later titled "Swing to Bop." DeVeaux emphasizes Christian's "startlingly supple rhythms," the way his solo lines "dissolved the usual hierarchical distinctions between strong beats and weak beats . . . allowing him to shift effortlessly between sharply contrasting rhythmic grooves."[84] "Swing to Bop" exemplifies the rhythmic exploration characteristic of this new, underground style. DeVeaux gives over the discussions of harmonic innovations to other instrumentalists such as Dizzy Gillespie, Charlie Parker, and pianist Thelonious Monk.

Although Christian's Minton performances may not feature key bebop musical innovations such as tritone substitution (although they do feature something close to it), the performances highlight other harmonic and melodic techniques that would become associated with the style. The long, linear lines Christian favored over bridge sections became even longer during these after-hours jam sessions, the guitarist adding more passing tones, neighbor tones, appoggiaturas, and upper "color" chord tones (flat and natural ninths, natural and sharp elevenths, and flat and natural thirteenths). In addition, Christian would often anticipate chord changes, avoid chord roots in his melodies, and introduce harmonic substitutions, all practices that further obscured a sense of harmonic stability.[85] In his Goodman recordings he was already experimenting with diminished seventh chords and secondary dominants over the standard changes (especially when those changes involved V7 chords). In the Minton recordings these techniques appear much more frequently.[86] The advanced and dissonant sounds combined with those "supple" rhythms cited by DeVeaux set the Minton recordings apart from the more restrained Goodman Sextet performances.

Historians disagree on what was most revolutionary in the guitarist's playing, but they do agree that what Christian was doing was new and progressive. There is a strong argument for this. Yet hearing everything at Minton's as new and modern ignores just how much was old and familiar. Jonathan Finkelman writes, "While mature swing and mature bebop are easily distinguishable and the differences between them relatively easily described, a transitional figure like Christian tends to exemplify the commonality and continuity between the styles more than their radical differences (and both commonality and radical differences exist at the same time)."[87] This is better than viewing Christian solely as a bebop prophet, but Finkelman's conceptualization of the guitarist as "transitional" shorts his place in his immediate historical context. On these Minton recordings Christian demonstrates a complex relationship with his southwestern roots, a relationship that reveals strong connections as well as profound discontinuities. Amid all the "newness" of these jam sessions, we also hear many references to the musical culture of the Southwest, the milieu that shaped his musical development.

The Minton recordings also show how profoundly different Christian's life had become since traveling the South and Midwest with Alphonso Trent, Anna Mae Winburn, and other territory bands. Captured late at night in a Harlem nightclub in New York City, Christian inhabits a strikingly different social world. The relatively small, tight-knit community of the Deep Deuce has been replaced by the intense, radical urban experience of black Harlem. From regional metropolises such as Oklahoma City, Dallas, and St. Louis, Christian became a part of that "city-within-a-city," the "dream" world of Harlem.[88] In reminiscing about Christian many people mention his "country" or "rural" manner and appearance, and the difference between his country ways and the city.[89] Oklahoma City remained an important part of his identity, and he often traveled back to see his family and friends.[90]

One of the less written about and analyzed recordings from these Minton performances is a version of "Stompin' at the Savoy," a tune Christian must have played hundreds of times with Goodman (the song had become the Benny Goodman Orchestra's theme after 1935). Like "Swing to Bop," "Stompin'" features some of the best examples of the alternation of the new with the old—the mixing together of blues, riff-based playing with the more modern sounding runs of chromatically inflected eighth notes and polyrhythmic gestures. Over the six choruses he takes, Christian plays in a style recognizable from his recordings with the Goodman Sextet, although now greatly concentrated. The bluesy riffs we heard in "Flying Home" are fragmented even more: the eighth-note runs are longer and more disorienting, and the idiosyncratic guitar elements (string bends and slides) are even punchier and dirtier around the edges. The short blues riffs of "Flying Home" have been splintered into shards of melody. After listening to the A sections in his first solo, we hear how the eighth-note-heavy triadic phrases of "Flying Home" have become jagged, two- and three-note chromatic riffs. Single, syncopated eighth notes and bluesy double-stops come to dominate the few eighth-note runs. In fact—and historians and critics often pass over this—the accented double-stops are far more a part of rhythm and blues, and later rock 'n' roll, than they are signatures of the bop and post-bop guitar style of musicians such as Barney Kessel, Jimmy Raney, or even Wes Montgomery.

The bridge sections have also been dramatically intensified. The tune is fast, and Christian spins out some of his most impressive eighth-note melodies. Some of what we hear is undoubtedly new, especially the more adventurous chromaticisms, but most is an intensification of existing stylistic traits. This is not necessarily forward-looking—it is just as a much a statement of what is past as of what is to come. Even Gunther Schuller, perhaps the most formalistically inclined critic of Christian's playing, suggests the presence of western swing in the guitarist's long, even eighth-note lines during the remarkable bridge passages captured at Minton's.[91] And the blues are everywhere in "Stompin'," whether in actual blue notes and scales (flat thirds and fifths, minor pentatonics), or in stylistic markers such as call-and-response and timbral variation. In these Minton performances Christian creates some of the starkest alternations between his characteristic syncopated blues riffs and the long, uninterrupted flows of chromatically inflected eighth notes. Even when playing these "advanced" lines, Christian always uses an attack that is part of the musical language of the Southwest. Even through the poor-quality recording, Christian's physicality—the "grain" of his voice—is strong.

Most scholarly discussions position Christian's Minton recordings at the apex of his career. But there are other possible recordings that can stand for the guitarist's achievements, ones not tied to narratives of musical progress.[92] One example that seems to have gone out of fashion among recent critics and historians is "Solo Flight," a Goodman big band tune written specifically to feature the guitarist. Positioning "Solo Flight" in this way, as a different end point of Christian's story, changes the narrative shape of his life. With "Solo Flight" we hear a culminating synthesis of Christian's split geography. The recording is a fascinating integration of his southwestern blues-heavy style with the nationally popular big band sound. The Jimmy Mundy arrangement allows for a dynamic integration of Christian's riff-based and linear style. There are four surviving recordings of the work: two studio versions recorded on March 4, 1941 (only one was released), and two live versions, one recorded March 3, 1941, for the "What's New" segment on NBC's *Old Gold Radio Show*, the other recorded June 1941 for the Mutual Radio show *Monte Proser Dance Carnival*.[93] "Solo Flight" was released posthumously in December 1943, and it was an immediate commercial success, reaching number 1 on the *Billboard* Harlem Hit Parade and number 20 on the *Billboard* Hot 100.[94]

For a long time musicians and critics often did cite "Solo Flight" as a high point of Christian's recording career. Al Avakian and Bob Prince write that in "Solo Flight" "we have the culminating sophistication of Christian's art. With no strain, the voice of the jazz electric guitar fits into a showpiece provided by the big swing band. Christian does not compete with the volume and power of Benny's big band, but easily rides the crests of its waves. With a minimum of effort, he tells his quiet and complex story."[95] That assessment, though, has been superseded by a number of more recent, skeptical reviews. For Gunther Schuller the recordings, although important, were "over-all not a terribly successful affair" and not the best representative of Christian's true talent and voice. The "over-cluttered" arrangement "hardly leaves the soloist any room to play." The song is musically mechanical and calculated, and the band's "exaggeratedly clipped, cold staccato style" does not "relate in any way to Christian's linear, warmer idiom."[96] Loren Schoenberg is less harsh but still critical: "Jimmy Mundy fashioned an effective showcase of Christian's tune, though even a few bars of wide-open space would have been nice to offset the density of the writing. Part of the problem is that the band is too loud in the mix."[97]

These critical assessments gloss over the real cultural significance of the recording, a significance suggested years before by Avakian and Prince. Not only was "Solo Flight" a groundbreaking presentation of the electric guitar, it was also a unique integration of Goodman's small-group aesthetic with conventional big band arranging. And at the center of this achievement is Christian himself, the instigator and inspiration for the fusion of southwestern blues into Goodman's mainstream big band sound. "Solo Flight" is also a significant social and cultural event. The recordings present a new kind of "representational space" where region and nation are combined through interracial and inter-cultural musical performance.

All four available recordings of "Solo Flight" are very similar, and studied together they provide, like "Flying Home," another compendium of Christian's solo style: bluesy phrases, string slides, off-kilter melodic lines, and breathless, linear melodies that smoothly and clearly mark the changes. But in "Solo Flight" these characteristics are densely juxtaposed into a new synthesis. The tune is structured around sixteen-bar sections (AA) and a bridge, inserted after the third and fourth iterations; all together we hear five choruses and two bridge sections. The entire performance features Christian, with a single bridge reserved for Goodman's clarinet solo. The song and its arrangement cleverly provide Christian with material for both his blues riffs and his change-running eighth-notes. Syncopated ensemble background lines alternate with more sustained chords by the orchestra. The chorus structure alternates between a simple, relatively slow moving progression (C–C-sharp-dim–G7) and a much denser, faster-moving one (C–E7–Am7–G7–F6–Em7–Dm7–A-dim–G7) that fits well Christian's predilection for alternating blues-based licks with long, chromatically inflected melodies.

The most striking of these juxtapositions occur during the first bridge section of the performance after the third chorus (transcribed in example 4.6). In the original, studio-released version of "Solo Flight," Christian begins the bridge with a fast-moving triplet blues cliché that accentuates the natural/flat third tension. He punctuates that phrase with dramatic syncopated octaves followed by a bluesy double-stop. As the bridge continues, the harmonic motion increases with a descending series of chords (each moving by a whole step). Here Christian attacks the changes, elegantly marking them with arpeggiated figures that outline the chords. Again, as in "Flying Home," Christian twists through the changes in ways that run against our (tonal) expectations. Starting on the last beat of measure 9, Christian begins a three-measure run of eighth notes that cleverly places the tonic notes of the chords (E-flat, D-flat, and C) on unaccented beats or in unexpected places in the measure. We hear the E-flat of the E-flat13 chord on the last eighth note of the measure. Likewise we hear the root of the next two chords (D-flat and C) on beat three of their respective measures. In the post-bop era this would be par for the course—in fact, these sorts of dis-

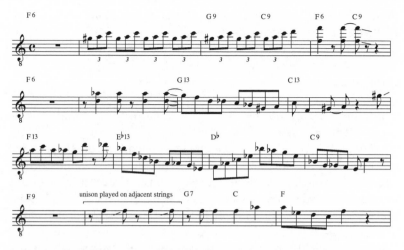

Example 4.6 First bridge section to "Solo Flight." Recorded March 4, 1941 (though not released by Columbia records until 1943). From Wolf Marshall, *The Best of Charlie Christian: A Step-by-Step Breakdown of the Styles and Techniques of the Father of Modern Jazz Guitar* (Milwaukee, WI: Hal Leonard, 2002), 50–51. Concert pitch. Music licensed by Hal Leonard Corporation.

placements are central to the bebop improvisational aesthetic. But in 1941 this was radically disorienting phrasing that, to a discerning ear, must have sounded as if the soloist were lost. Christian ends this melodic run with another blues gesture, a unison alternation between Fs on different strings that finishes with a jump up to the blue flat third (A-flat). Unlike in "Flying Home," the blues and the modern are dramatically compressed here; the distinctions between A and B sections are collapsed into a single bridge spanning sixteen measures.

This compression of Christian's style, though, is not limited to the bridge—each A section also features quick alternations between blues lines and eighth-note melodies. In fact, the arrangement was clearly tailored to highlight this dynamic tension in the guitarist's playing. "Solo Flight" integrates Christian's two primary ways of moving through musical space in a new (big band) context, and it is the guitarist's most elaborate statement of the larger desire for mobility that suffused American culture of the 1930s and '40s. Like the evocations of motion in films and industrial design described by Morris Dickstein (Fred Astaire and Ginger Rogers dancing in *Top Hat*, the new streamlined trains and cars), "Solo Flight" presents a musical landscape full of abrupt harmonic movement and rhythmic syncopation that is negotiated with ease, sophistication, and wit.

Confinement

In mid-June of 1941, during a midwestern tour with the Goodman Orchestra, Christian fell seriously ill. He left the band and immediately traveled back to New York City, where he entered Bellevue Hospital for treatment. His mobility was suddenly, radically short-circuited. After receiving treatment at Bellevue, he was transferred on July 11 to Sea View, a municipal tuberculosis sanitarium on Staten Island.[98] Before the wider availability of penicillin in 1946, the prognosis for tuberculosis was grim, and treatment primarily involved isolation from the general population. Christian chafed at the confinement. Anecdotal accounts suggest that he was not a totally compliant patient and "found his own way of dealing with the agony of immobility."[99] A cohort of Christian's friends allegedly sneaked the guitarist out of the hospital for nights of "combustible tea [marijuana] and chicks."[100] These brief excursions aside, Christian would never leave Sea View. After eight months of isolation, he died on March 2, 1942, at age thirty-two.[101]

Between the two fixed points of his life—his early life in Oklahoma City and his confinement at Sea View, Christian was in almost constant motion. The ability to travel so widely and often—Christian crisscrossed the country numerous times with Goodman—was rare in the African American community. For many blacks such large-scale travel was primarily associated with migration and the move from the rural South to the urban North and West. Economic collapse slowed this movement, but even during the worst years of the Great Depression, African Americans continued to leave the South in significant numbers. Scholars estimate that somewhere around 400,000 blacks moved to northern cities in the 1930s.[102] Migration was always difficult, but the devastating economic conditions made the journey that much more trying. Even after scraping together enough money for travel, there was no guarantee that work could be found. Many in the North—white and black—were hostile to the newcomers: among other things, they represented more competition for scarce jobs.[103] In sharp contrast to these experiences, Christian represented a very different kind mobility. He traveled for necessity (that went with the music business), but it was a mobility driven by his talent and not by racial hatred or dire economic necessity.

According to Gena Caponi-Tabery, many black cultural forms of the era—from the new jump shot in basketball to the dramatic aerial moves of the Lindy Hop—displayed an "obsession with height, flight, and speed" and a liberating experience of movement. This cultural energy would, in the coming decades, lead to a new "social, and eventually political, elevation."[104] At a very general level, American society seemed to be opening up to a more pluralistic understanding of itself, slowly recognizing the pervasive influence of African American life and culture. Caponi-Tabery writes, "At a time when international events made global heroes of Olympic athletes, Joe Louis, jazz musicians, and Lindy Hoppers, African Americans began to believe that if they counted for something in the eyes of the world—if, indeed, they stood for America—perhaps America itself might be ready to grant them full citizenship."[105]

The "migratory impulse" in Christian's music also resonated with much larger Depression-era tensions in American life between the experience of region and nation. Traditionally, scholars raise this topic when considering the American regionalist movement—a diffuse group of like-minded intellectuals and artists grappling with the profound changes caused by twentieth-century modernization. But regionalism, as an intellectual and artistic movement, was only one manifestation of a larger shift in American ideas about place and nation. Like the railroads of the nineteenth century, automobiles, parkways, and airplanes were further decreasing the time it took to cross the country, shrinking the continent's great distances. In a similar though more abstract way, radio and film were also connecting Americans to each other through the mediation of a growing, centralized culture industry. Along with these technological developments, the Roosevelt administration's New Deal and the nation's participation in the Second World War greatly enlarged the size, scope, and power of the federal government. These developments brought Washington, DC, directly into contact with its citizenry. Americans increasingly viewed the government as the federal one in Washington, not their city and state administrations.

These large social and geographic forces also reshaped jazz—the music was increasingly "nationalized." The local "territory" bands that serviced cities and towns all across the country were increasingly displaced by national big bands that were based largely in the giant metropolises of New York and Chicago. According to Thomas Hennessey, from 1890 to 1935, technological and other historical developments transformed jazz from a "primarily local music rooted in black folk traditions to the tightly managed product of a national industry."[106] Hennessey, though, overstates the triumph of a national sound; the regional persisted, and jazz musicians of the 1930s and '40s, with their nearly constant travel, directly experienced the new geographical configuration of an increasingly connected nation. This was a dramatic, transitional period in American life, and jazz registered these changes.[107]

Christian's synthesis of local and national was a solution to the larger cultural problem that obsessed regionalist intellectuals such as Donald Davidson, Howard Odum, and Lewis Mumford. For these writers, the region "was envisioned to be the utopian means for reconstructing the nationalizing, homogenizing urban-industrial complex, redirecting it toward an accommodation with local folkways and local environments."[108] In Christian's musical style, the regional is not the goal but only the jumping-off point. The "reconstruction" of American identity was happening through the fusion of local practices into a national mass-mediated industry. Moving dramatically between the regional and the national, Christian made music that not only registered this transition but created something new from it.

His stylistic synthesis was part of the era's yearning for movement. As discussed in the introduction, novels, films, photography, and industrial design all reveal a semantic and formal preoccupation with *movement*.[109] Popular culture concretized for Americans a desire for a liberated mobility that was very different from the mobility caused by economic necessity or financial ruin. The positive cultural representations of motion and freedom—Busby Berkeley's fluid, flying camera work, Fred Astaire and Ginger Rogers's graceful dance floor routines, the "loops and curves of . . . deco modernism"—were especially poignant and seductive.[110]

Charlie Christian's musical development was intertwined with a real physical journey from the Southwest to the nation—a new place made possible by the machine age and the New Deal. During his time with Goodman and in the after-hour nightclubs of Harlem, he constructed a musically hybrid place that represented and reconciled in sound larger social and geographic experiences. This new sonic place was racially integrated, intensely mobile, and national in scope.[111] From one point of view, Christian was a precursor to the next wave of the Great Migration initiated by mobilization for World War II. His synthetic and adventurous musical style captured an experience of transcontinental travel, which though unusual for black Americans of the time, would soon become common. World War II was a watershed in African American life, spurring a massive new wave of internal migration. It also provided a new spark of radicalism to the ongoing struggle for African

American civil rights. If the years of the New Deal laid the groundwork for the modern civil rights movement, then the war was its real beginning, reenergizing many segments of the black community. Christian's music was a portent of wartime mobility and migration. In the stasis of what historian Jani Scandura terms "depressive modernity," Christian moved in ways unavailable to most Americans, black or white.[112]

The comparison of Christian's improvisations to flying is not unique in the jazz lexicon. Hawk (Coleman Hawkins, 1904–69) and Bird (Charlie Parker, 1920–55) received nicknames that expressed their musical flights of virtuosity and lyricism.[113] They displayed freedom from clichés, habits, and the mundane realities of daily life. As Rudi Blesh writes, "The voice of his guitar, a whole third of a century later, is still modern. Musically, it still fulminates. But being a voice, it is also a message. Charlie Christian's message, like that of that other Southwest Charlie, 'the Bird,' [is] not yet wholly decoded. And yet they were both saying something so simple: freedom."[114] As he traveled, Christian incorporated new music and new spatial experiences—his approach to jazz improvisation embodied new and different qualities of motion, new ways of traversing American space. He developed a musical style that fused the fractured geography of his life into a new musical place that redefined both the American experience of region and nation and the limitations of a racially circumscribed geography. His music sutured together the places of his life and presented listeners with a new fluid, hybrid identity that was African American and Euro-American, regional and national. Christian's music looked both backward to the southwestern world he'd left behind and forward to the dynamic urban and cosmopolitan world he'd recently joined. Christian's immensely influential and emotionally gripping playing is the sound of traveling, of all Americans caught between the old and the new, the places we knew and the places we are moving toward.

Air Spaces

Taking Flight with Jimmie Lunceford and His Orchestra

Charlie Christian wasn't the only jazz musician taking flight in the early 1940s. In 1941 the Charlie Barnet Orchestra recorded "Wings over Manhattan," written by Barnet's trumpeter and primary arranger Billy May as a commission for the 1939 World's Fair in New York City. Originally titled "Aviation Suite," the work is unusual for the time: it is six and a half minutes long (both sides of a 78 rpm record) with multiple themes and tempo changes.[1] The variety of musical textures, the shifting spotlight on individual instrumentalists, and the important programmatic elements recall similar large-scale jazz compositions by Duke Ellington. The airplane—and transportation more generally—was one of the fair's primary themes, and although May's composition does not feature any obvious signifiers of planes (the buzzing of the low brass in the song's introduction does sound a bit like propellers revving up), the song's title, rapidly shifting textures, and adventurous arrangement reverberate with the sensations and experiences of flight. Moving from the driving rhythm of the first section with its rapid dialogue between reeds and brass to the languid half-time saxophone melody that follows, and then to an exuberant concluding section, the work offers a panorama of distinct musical landscapes. In addition, the changes in rhythmic feel and texture (dense brass fanfares to quiet solo electric guitar) suggest different ways of moving in and through this landscape. The theme of the work was tied to the fair, but Billy May and the rest of the Barnet band would have also found inspiration in the skies above them: a *New York Times* photo essay from August 6, 1939, shows a formation of U.S. Army planes soaring over Manhattan in a thirtieth anniversary celebration of the army's first airplane acquisition. Reporters estimated that between 30 million and 50 million people saw this display of military aviation strength—nearly 1,500 planes from across the country flew to Dayton, Ohio, for the celebration.[2]

In 1939 airplanes were a symbol for the nation's technofuture. "Wings over Manhattan" is one example of the many connections at the time between popular culture and the fascination with airplanes and air travel. As the automobile became thoroughly assimilated into American life, air travel presented a more radical experience of mobility. With the world again at the precipice of global war, the idea of flight was suffused with a heady mixture of American hopes and fears for the present and future. If the automobile had significantly altered America's spatial ordering, the airplane had the potential to reconfigure the spaces of the entire globe. As a mode of travel, air flight was largely out of reach of most Americans at the time, and it represented not only the current concerns with place and mobility discussed in previous chapters, but future ones too. A consideration of air flight points us toward the postwar American nation, toward new cultural formations that would replace those of the Depression and war years.

In the late 1930s and early 1940s flying was more of an idea than a reality for most, a distant and unlikely possibility, although its psychological effect was already profound.[3] Historian Ann Douglas characterizes the 1920s as an era smitten with the urge for height. Airspace was a new frontier and a new arena for colonization: "Netting the sky was part of the imperial ambition of the time, of the invisible but all-powerful American empire taking over the world via its machinery, its media, and its near-monopoly on modernization, means far more effective than the old-style method of territorial conquest." The massive skyscrapers constructed during the decade and the daredevil aviators of the time both testified to what writers called "airmindedness," a mood natural to the new "aerial age."[4]

Such excitement was not confined to the 1920s; it overflowed into the Depression and war years. Naturally, Hollywood of the 1930s played its part. In many films, airplanes were featured alongside movie stars. Howard Hawk's 1939 movie *Only Angels Have Wings* was one of the most popular and critically acclaimed dramatic films of the era. Cary Grant starred as a stoic pilot who flies a dangerous mail route over the Andes.

207

The ubiquitous musicals of the era were also "airminded." The end of the 1933 film *Flying Down to Rio* features a climactic musical number with chorus girls strapped to the wings of a plane.[5] The era's fascination with flight extended beyond its explicit representation in cinema to the design of commercial products, from automobiles and trains to household items such as light fixtures, teapots, and chairs. This new "streamlined" approach, pioneered and evangelized by designers such as Norman Bel Geddes, Raymond Loewy, and Walter Dorwin Teague, was rooted in contemporary aeronautic experimentation and theorizing. It emphasized smooth curves and teardrop shapes, making it seem that all these products were designed in a wind tunnel and capable of "cleaving the air or water" with great speed and efficiency.[6] The icons of this streamlined form were the DC airplanes manufactured by the Douglas company (the DC-1 and DC-2 of 1934 and the DC-3 of 1935–36). The new designs hid most of the plane's normally visible machine parts—propeller gears and landing wheels—under a riveted aluminum skin that "gave an overall impression of squares arranged in a streamlined pattern." Richard Guy Wilson writes that "in both image and performance the new Douglas planes captured the public imagination. Polished to a mirror-like finish from the projectile snout to the long, cigar-shaped body, tapered wings, and parabolic tail, the surfaces flowed into each other, creating a new standard of machine beauty."[7]

Actual travel in one of these Douglas planes was not possible for most Americans, but at the 1939 World's Fair—an event permeated with technological optimism—thousands of ordinary Americans were offered a taste of the power of flight in several exhibits, most famously in General Motors' Futurama. Bel Geddes, along with the other fair designers, constructed a ride that featured "low-flying airplane perspectives." "Because the airplane represented the most celebrated achievement of technology in the 1930s, the designers hit on the fortunate sales technique of providing fair patrons with a safe airplane perspective in several exhibits; they looked down on a vast landscape in miniature, the diorama, usually from a moving platform."[8] In the Futurama building, patrons sat in small cars that "flew" above a massive model of 1960s America filled with modern superhighways and futuristic skyscrapers. Transportation was one of the guiding themes of the fair's representation of "The World of Tomorrow," and the visitors could see lavish displays and watch performances celebrating the nation's advancement from horse-drawn carriages to automobiles (all funded, of course, by the transportation industry). The unifying exhibit of the fair's Transportation Zone was the Chrysler Building's history of American transportation. The show, using lighting effects, projected maps, sound, and film, culminated "with planes roaring through the sky, floating palaces gliding through the oceans and automobiles and trains speeding overland." This display was a prelude to the finale: the "launching" of a scaled-down rocket ship into space—a fitting culmination of America's historical search for greater distance, speed, and height.[9]

The "airmindedness" of these years was represented as "American" but was, in practice, experienced differently by African Americans (and other nonwhites) who, because of skin color, were excluded from full participation in American social, political, and economic life. A fascination with flight, with "airmindedness," is traceable in black life, but its cultural manifestations look very different from the films and public exhibitions described above. Legends of "flying" Africans are pervasive in the folklore of the African diaspora, and stories on the topic have been collected throughout the American South, Latin America, and the Caribbean.[10] Although there are many variants, the outline of the story is the same: enslaved Africans, after disembarking in the New World, turn around and fly home, defying their captors and their future of bondage. In some versions the Africans drown, in others they arrive home safely, but in all of them escape is through flight. One widely reported variant from the American South focuses on a shaman brought to the New World as a slave who teaches those around him the sacred and magical words that enable flight. These words are then passed on to other generations, often from mother to child. Here the power of flight is coded into language, and taking care of this knowledge preserves this ancient power for future generations.[11]

With the emergence of modern aviation, the Flying African legend took on new meaning, revitalized by the literal realization of mechanical human flight. Racial segregation and economic inequalities made it difficult for African Americans to find a place in the burgeoning aviation industry as inventors, engineers, mechanics, or pilots. But many blacks, as enamored of flight as their white counterparts, were drawn to this new technological frontier. The possibility of airplane flight combined naturally with notions of figurative uplift, and black aviators such as Bessie Coleman and Hubert Fauntleroy Julian became icons in the nation's black communities, representing a literal rising above discrimination and the limits imposed by white society.

The black celebration of flight, though, was tempered with suspicion, distrust, and even fear of the technology and how it would be used. The use of airplanes in Europe during the First World War (along with mechanized vehicles and poison gas) transformed warfare, making soldiers, and also civilians, vulnerable to attack in new and terrifying ways. With this in mind, black journalists in America were already expressing fears that this technology offered white racists new means of terrorizing blacks. What might have sounded farfetched to black readers in 1920 was disturbingly realized a year later when airplanes were used as part of the "Tulsa Race War"—a violent racial confrontation that caused the near total destruction of the "Little Africa" Greenwood neighborhood of Tulsa, Oklahoma, home to most of the city's black residents.[12]

The experience of flying continued to embody a mixture of fascination and fear. Airplanes offered the promise of transcending the cruelties of American racism, even as they suggested new risks and unforeseen dangers. In the short story "Flying Home," published in 1944, novelist Ralph Ellison uses the airplane and the idea of "flying" to illustrate the perilous conditions of African American existence at the time. His literary representation demonstrates the power of this trope to concentrate the hopes and fears embedded in the idea of flight.

Todd, Ellison's protagonist, can literally take to the air: he is a military pilot. He is also black and thus one of a handful of African Americans training to fly. Ellison's story begins not in the air but on the ground, with Todd lying near his crashed airplane, taken down by a wayward buzzard. In pain from the impact, Todd is helped by Jefferson, an old black sharecropper, and Ted, an African American adolescent. After sending Ted for help, the old man tries to calm Todd with conversation. Ellison's story becomes increasingly surrealistic and dreamlike as Todd, slipping in and out of consciousness, drifts between childhood memories and his talk with Jefferson. In the course of their conversation, Jefferson tells Todd a folk story—a "lie" he calls it—about the time he was in heaven and sprouted wings "just like them white angels had." But Negroes in heaven had to wear a special harness, and that meant you had to be extra strong to move around. Jefferson discards his harness and flies free—doing loop-the-loops like the birds, speeding through the sky. Saint Peter chastises him for disobeying the rules and banishes him to the middle of rural Alabama. Todd knows this story, but Jefferson's variation is new, and he is bothered and confused. Is the old man criticizing him for overreaching the limits of his skin color? Or is he being comforted? Todd's confusion turns to horror when "help" arrives in the form of Dabney Graves, the white landowner. Believing Todd is insane, Graves and two white attendants try to put him in a straitjacket. Jefferson intervenes, and the old man, with

Ted's help, carries the injured and dazed pilot off to the air base on a stretcher.

Ellison's story combines elements of the Flying African folktales with the myth of Icarus. In becoming a pilot, Todd stands as an emblem of success for the black community. But such an achievement comes with new risks—Todd feels the most anguish not about his injuries but about the likely response of his white superiors at the base. His achievements, it seems, have been permitted with the forbearance of white society. He has not transcended race; he has only discovered a new manifestation of its restrictive structures. In his surrealistic encounter with Jefferson, present and past collapse; he has crash-landed into a different "sense of time and space." Ellison's story is rich in symbolism: birds—specifically the buzzards that Ted calls "jimcrows"—circle through the text as harbingers of racist violence but also as emblems of a future where past and present, South and North are reconciled, providing a new foundation for African American identity. Ellison's story, for all its symbolism, is grounded in the technological present. The story references real airplane-related events such as the exploits of aviator Hubert Fauntleroy Julian, "the black eagle" of Harlem, and the August 1922 Ku Klux Klan airplane leafletting of Oklahoma City (the papers warned black residents away from the polls).[13] Flying is both a concrete reality—a striking example of present technological achievement and possibility—*and* a symbol of a mythic past and Flying Africans.

Given its centrality in African American culture, it is not surprising to find the trope in jazz. "Flying" has been (and continues to be) a prominent part of the jazz lexicon for both musicians and critics. In his 1969 book of music criticism, Henry Pleasants described the essence of jazz as swing and wrote, "Swinging is, after all, a kind of flying; and the essence of jazz is musical flight, sustained by rhythmic pulsations and by tensions resulting from controlled rhythmic deviation." Other musical styles that don't swing can seem, to the jazz musician, "comparatively earthbound."[14]

For some musicians of the era, flying was a real possibility. Although it was rare, some of the wealthiest musicians of the 1930s and '40s were able to fly themselves and their bands across the country. We already heard from Jerry Jerome (chapter 4) about flying with the Benny Goodman Orchestra. Newspapers covered Fletcher Henderson and his band when they flew to a gig in Cincinnati in January 1931.[15] Drummer Cliff Leeman, interviewed by Milt Hinton for the Smithsonian Institution Jazz Oral History Project, recalled traveling by plane when he was with the Tommy Dorsey Orchestra in the late 1930s: "We were the first band to fly in an airplane as a group. And they flew us to Toronto, Canada, here from Newark Airport, for the Canadian Exposition, 1939, Fall." The trip was exciting for Leeman but also anxiety-ridden:

When we arrived in Newark to leave, we were all a little bit nervous, nobody ever flew before, and of course it was a chartered plane, with a Rolls Royce engine and twin props. Flying today is so common with everybody, I don't think you can appreciate what this was like. It took us about two and a half to three hours to fly to Toronto from Newark, which is usually about a 40 minute trip today. And going over the mountains, they flew at pretty low altitudes then, into Buffalo and into Toronto, the air currents are pretty bad. However, it was quite an experience.[16]

Perhaps the most famous connection between planes and jazz was the death of Glenn Miller in a war-related crash, an ominous portent of the waning of the dance bands.

Like the shamans in the African American myth who pass along the secret of flying through their words, the best jazz players communicated the mysteries of flight through their music. The evocation of flying heard by many in the jazz music of the era had a physical manifestation in the dancing that accompanied it. The Lindy Hop, developed by the dancers in Harlem, was named for Charles Lindbergh, the most famous American pilot of the time. As it evolved, the dynamic horizontal energy of the Lindy—with all its intense footwork and exciting "breakaways"—went vertical with the introduction of "aerial" moves. The black dance troupes that invented and then perfected these moves, such as Whitey's Lindy Hoppers, literally took to the air.[17] African American dancer Frankie Manning (a member of Whitey's Lindy Hoppers) developed aerials in 1934 to accommodate the more even-flowing sound of the jazz dance bands. According to Manning, the music was changing "from a more up-and-down rhythm of the 20s to this real smooth type of swing. . . . Folks started to say, 'Man, you look like you're flying!' And I said to myself, 'Yeah, that's exactly the way I want to look. Like I'm flying!' "[18]

The life and music of African American bandleader Jimmie Lunceford provides another conjunction of jazz and flight. The bandleader was a lifelong aviation fanatic, and he closely followed the developments in airplane technology over the first decades of the twentieth century.[19] Between 1939 and 1940 Lunceford was making enough money from his band to take flying lessons. After earning his license, in 1941 he purchased a "sleek, fast three-seater, a Bellanca Model 19–9 Junior." The $20,000 plane had a "decidedly contemporary look," with "its additional fins on the tips of its tailplane." After crashing the plane several months later, Lunceford bought two new ones: a single-engine Fairchild Model 24 and a Cessna T-50.[20] Making flying more than a hobby, Lunceford often flew himself and a few close friends or family to gigs. While the rest of the band traveled by bus or car, a few musicians in the organization had the chance to fly with "Pops." Without a commercial license and a larger plane, Lunceford couldn't fly his entire operation around. After the war he finally earned that license, invested in a start-up coast-to-coast airline, and tried to buy a fully equipped, decommissioned wartime C-47. His plan was to fly his band "to Europe, by way of Canada, Greenland, and Iceland."

In 1934 the band released the tune "Stratosphere," a work that combines the leader's love of airplanes with the band's characteristic driving swing groove. According to Lunceford biographer Eddy Determeyer, the bandleader named the song after "the contemporary exploration of the atmosphere's envelope by Professor Auguste Piccard . . . a subject that must have appealed to Lunceford with his penchant for all aspects of aviation."[21] Like May's "Wings," the music, aside from its title, has few musical signifiers of air travel. However, as discussed earlier, titles are partly constitutive of musical meaning, and in conjunction with the multifaceted musical sign, they provide semantic "hooks" with which the listener can take hold of sound in a meaningful way. With the title in mind, "Stratosphere" evokes a sense of movement that is plausibly like flight. Receptive listeners could travel through a new kind of airspace.

The composition is an oddity by dance band standards, especially those of the early and mid-1930s. We experience a strange and unfamiliar musical space. For Gunther Schuller and Martin Williams, "Stratosphere" is "far out" and a preview of modernistic techniques employed by later experimental bands such as Boyd Raeburn's and Claude Thornhill's.[22] The song features no clear melody besides a repeated, off-beat single trumpet note that emerges after a brief forte ensemble introduction. And although the tune itself is in a conventional AABA form, Lunceford writes in several jarring interruptions to the form that feature dissonant tone clusters, raucous percussion, and intense chromaticism. The minor-key A sections have a dark, almost menacing quality reminiscent of Duke Ellington and his band's jungle music of the Cotton Club years. In contrast, the bridge is all long, winding melodies by the saxophone soloist, his virtuosic sixteenth notes clearly articulated even at the song's blazing tempo of nearly 240 beats per minute.

After the opening introductory blast, the music immediately takes off. The several interruptions are only minor obstacles for the urgent, driving rhythm—another example of the famous Lunceford "two-beat" groove. Over this propulsive beat we hear many textures form and reform. The song features two types of musical movement: the minimalist—the syncopated, dynamic swells of the trumpets' single-note theme—and the maximalist—the dense melodic runs of the saxophones (and, toward the end, the reeds). "Stratosphere" creates a space at the same time familiar (recognizable form and instrumentation) and strange (weird and dissonant melodies and harmonies). We are swept along by the fast, precise playing that moves us rapidly and abruptly through the contrasting A and B sections. Which came first—music or title—does not really matter. As a title, "Stratosphere" seems just right. (Rename it "Lazy River" and you get something completely different.) The breathless sixteenth-note runs in Lunceford's tune also evoke Ellington's "Daybreak Express" recorded a year earlier, another song about transportation, mobility, and speed.[23]

Contrary to the impression given by many writers, the big bands of the era did not adhere to any uniform notion of tempo across songs, and dancers and listeners were accustomed to a wide range of speeds (though rarely anything too fast to dance to). Songs such as "Stratosphere" are extreme—their superfast tempos make them challenging for dancer and listener alike (it is hard enough to keep track of the song form in such a dense, fast tune, let alone coordinate your body with the music). This was the dance era's way of representing an explicit and intense feeling of speed and transcendent motion. Significantly, the song title connects the actual speed of the musical performance to airplanes and air travel. In *Swinging the Machine*, historian Joel Dinerstein argues that big band music like this was one way Americans assimilated their bodies and their consciousness to the machine age's technological and social changes.[24]

The orchestra's sonic representation of movement is presented through the "two-beat," the band's distinctive approach to rhythm and ensemble groove. As I discussed earlier, swing era jazz represented and enacted many types of spaces and ways of moving in those spaces. Different rhythmic feels were linked to different dances and thus different ways of moving one's body—for example, the steady thump of Jan Garber's sweet orchestra lent itself to the restrained dancing desired by the referees in Catalina's Casino Ballroom. But these different ways of creating and sustaining rhythmic grooves offered listeners and dancers something more: they provided new aural ways of understanding and feeling movement in space. The Count Basie Orchestra, for example, developed an enormously influential relaxed but intensely driving swing that was greatly admired by musicians who heard it. During its heyday in the 1930s and early 1940s, the Jimmie Lunceford Orchestra was similarly celebrated for its particular version of swing, an infectious "two-beat" rhythmic groove. A casual listener today might not hear large differences, but during the 1930s and '40s dancers, fans, and attentive listeners often made fine discriminations between rhythmic styles. Rhythmic feel mattered a lot in the reception of bands and helped to define their character as much as did star soloists, singers, or arrangers.

What specifically was the Lunceford "two-beat"? How do we understand its meanings for listeners at the time? Jazz writer George Simon, who covered the dance bands during the era, described it as a "fantastically joyous swinging beat," projected by musicians "with uninhibited, completely infectious enthusiasm."[25] More precisely, the Lunceford "two-beat" refers to the band's emphasis on two beats in a 4/4 meter. As was discussed in chapter 1, this approach was different from the generally prevalent "smoothed" out, four equally strong beats to the bar, the sound of most hot swing bands. In fact, the Lunceford two-beat was sometimes heard as a little old-fashioned in the mid- to late 1930s. Longtime Lunceford drummer Jimmy Crawford often complained to arranger Sy Oliver that so many of the band's works featured the two-beat feel. As Crawford told George Simon, "I felt that if you were really going home in those last ride-out choruses, then you should really go home all the way, full steam and stay in four-four instead of going back into that two-four feel again."[26]

As a gross generalization, it is true that the Lunceford "two-beat" was a different, perhaps even archaic, rhythmic style for hot bands of the mid-1930s. But on a closer inspection, this description becomes more complicated. Although it is true that the Lunceford Orchestra's groove does appear to emphasize two beats in a four-beat unit (measure) of music, calling it a "two-beat" rhythm is not exactly correct. Not all the musicians, even in the rhythm section, are accenting or even playing just two beats. Listening across a variety of tunes, including "Stratosphere," we find that the band's characteristic groove features rhythm guitar strumming four beats to the measure, the bass player generally playing only beats one and three, and the drummer articulating all four beats of the meter but with a discernible accent on beats two and four, played on the hi-hat or snare drum. In addition, both the rhythm guitar and the drums vary their patterns, often interpolating eighth notes between the dominant quarter notes (as does the bass, though more infrequently). Their rhythmic figures sometimes reflect the basic jazz "swing" rhythm, other times variations of it. All the rhythm players can improvise a little while still maintaining the overall character of the groove.

Of course, the rhythm section is not the sole generator of the groove—the phrasing of the horn and reeds is also key. The Lunceford band members rehearsed not simply to perfect their arrangements but also to make sure they worked with the underlying rhythm. They had to groove too. Their phrasing—the way melodies were attacked, timed, and shaped—had to create the right kind of fit and contrast with the rhythm section's articulation of the pulse. In his focus on rehearsals, Lunceford wanted to make sure that the various musical elements of his orchestra—reed melodies, horn riffs, rhythm section—created the correct balance. Phrasing and rhythm had to fit together in the right ways to create the desired groove.

Also essential to creating their groove were the spaces left between the articulations of the pulse. Unlike Jan Garber's "Avalon" or Charlie Barnet's "Pompton Turnpike," the Lunceford band clips the ending of the notes, intensifying the tension between sound and silence. The "holes" in the rhythmic texture draw our attention to the relation between what Anne Danielsen calls the "virtual" reality of the rhythm—the nonsounding "structures of reference" that undergird the music—and its realization in sound, "the figure."[27] What is fascinating is that, even with all this variation, we hear a groove with a definite shape and content. We *hear* a "two-beat" rhythm, even though the musicians are actually playing a variety of individually inflected rhythmic figures. The Lunceford two-beat groove exists not in the bass player's rhythm but in the ensemble gestalt, the complex interaction of each musician with the others.

The Lunceford two-beat, evident in so many of the band's records, performs a style of mobility that takes on special meaning in the context of the leader's obsession with flight. Lunceford was in a sense a literal manifestation of the "Flying African." But rather than traveling back to Africa, he found a different home on the road and in the thousands of dance halls and concert halls he played in. In his confidence, business savvy, musical discipline and polish, Lunceford was very different from Todd, the anguished pilot of Ellison's "Flying Home." Like Fletcher Henderson and Duke Ellington, Lunceford embodied many of the values of his middle-class upbringing and college education. The lift of his groove was a musical concretization of "racial uplift," a popular social ideal for many middle-class blacks that emphasized education, industry, and appearance. It was a philosophy that would have suffused his education at Fisk University.[28] The band reflected the leader—the Lunceford Orchestra was confident, polished, buoyant, and joyous. This mixture of discipline and freedom is embodied in the band's most famous creation—its distinctive collective groove, the Lunceford "two-beat," heard to dramatic effect in "Stratosphere." Tight but just loose enough, the Lunceford Orchestra could launch listener and dancer into the stratosphere, momentarily outstripping the anxieties of flight embodied by Ellison's pilot Todd. The band offered a trial run through a new kind of space, high above the nation's roads and highways.

———

As one of central forms of popular culture of the era, jazz presented its listeners with a variety of ways of locating themselves in some kind of American community. Because music is an activity and not a thing, we can understand it as a process that organizes not just sound waves but also people in time and space. Musical sounds can literally fill space, changing our perception of that space. They can transform a sterile public building into a place temporarily rich in beauty and significance. Even listening to music on the radio can make wherever you are feel different or special, perhaps even turning your bedroom into a "Make Believe Ballroom." In this sense music infuses the spaces of our lives with new meanings; it creates and sustains new places. This situation is made more complex because music itself has meaning. It has a content generated through the formal materials and practices of composers and musicians—melody, form, harmony, timbre, and rhythm. Music creates meaning through the arrangement of its materials into recognizable patterns that can echo nonmusical behavior or signify through association. These musical meanings interact with the real spaces (and places) we occupy. Thus music is a way of making sense of lived geography. Big band jazz of the 1930s and '40s helped shape Americans' perception of the spaces of their lives and created locales infused with particular meanings. The jazz of the era provided listeners and musicians with new maps of their reality.[29]

The musicians analyzed in the previous chapters participated in a larger national discourse on the nature of America's spaces and places. This discourse was most vigorous among the diffuse group of academics, writers, and intellectuals of the era's regionalist movement.[30] These writers sought a new foundation for modern American life in the culture of the "folk" and ordinary people. Although the regionalists rarely wrote about it, the commercial dance band music of Jan Garber, Charlie Barnet, Duke Ellington and Charlie Christian provided a vernacular, concrete and unidealized example of the regionalist's abstract concerns with the changed relationship between the local and national in American life.

The stories of these jazz and dance band musicians also demonstrate how the concern with the regional was as much about race as it was about geography. Remaking American life to focus on the local would mean rethinking the basic racialized geography of the nation, especially the pervasive de jure and de facto segregation and discrimination that affected all of American society to varying degrees. In this sense jazz musicians are similar to Antonio Gramsci's "organic intellectuals" who through their daily life and musical creations, sought to make sense of the geographic and demographic changes they experienced.[31] Their music offered responses to the question posed by intellectuals of the time: What was or should be the relationship between region and nation?

Essential to all these case studies is the dialectical relation between the literal experience of place—migration, urbanization, transportation—and its representation in sound and lyrics. As Grace Elizabeth Hale argues, space in America was racialized—specific locations were designated for different peoples.[32] Jazz, with its hybrid mixture of styles, was also understood through a pervasive racial discourse. Swing-style jazz of the era—in all its various forms and colors, from small groups to vocal pop to large, hot orchestras—registered a tension between place and mobility and white and black. Musicians, more so than most Americans, lived day to day in what Ralph Ellison, in the early 1950s, called our "hot world of fluidity."[33] These musicians understood both the possibility and the pain of the many social changes going on around them and attempted to channel and shape these forces into a music that would provide a stable platform from which to comfortably navigate this terrain. They might not all have been successful, but they certainly tried. Jazz of the era provided a dynamic and accessible way of locating oneself on the literal and figurative map of the nation.

Over the course the book, I hope I have shown how music itself is a text and practice that can provide new historical information. As literary critic and theorist Raymond Williams argues, society's cultural products—its books, films, art, and music—are not just "artistic formation[s]," they are also "social location[s]."[34] Studying the formal properties of artistic expression—color and line in painting, plot and language in a novel, shots and cuts in film, melody, rhythm, harmony, and timbre in music—in their historical contexts reveals social values and social relations. Recorded music has properties that make it a unique window into the past. Music is more than the abstract assemblage of controlled vibrating air; it is a deeply meaningful activity reflecting social values. Through its formal and tonal properties, music can communicate a wide variety of emotions and ideas, from the very general to the surprisingly specific. As a "system of communication involving structured sounds," music can, in the words of Charles Seeger, "functionalize, for the members of a society, the values of continuity and variance of the culture and of its potentialities for elaboration and extension."[35] Christopher Small has stated this point in less abstract language: making, listening, dancing to music—in fact all the activities associated with music, what he calls "musicking"—are explorations of social relationships and identity.[36] We ignore the sounds at our peril—it is, after all, the sensuous sounding experience that draws us to music. The sounds of the dance band era may seem dated to us today, but at the time they were part of a broader cultural belief in the "now" and the possibilities of a machine age America.

The era of the dance bands, very roughly 1930 through 1946, remains a vital topic in contemporary American life. The swing dance revival of the 1990s and the continuing production of Hollywood films about World War II show that Americans are still fascinated by the era and its culture—it was a time that has been consistently represented as more nationalistic and unified in the face of crisis, something that speaks to American life in the aftermath of the terrorist attacks of September 11, 2001. Dance band jazz, later dubbed "swing," was not the only popular music of the era, but it reached across class, race, and ethnic lines in ways strikingly different from the fractured musical-cultural landscape of today. What, besides geographic contiguity, unites us as Americans? Can music bring us together, literally in space and more abstractly in feeling? Understanding what this widely popular musical culture was all about is part of a larger, and continuing, project of understanding the nature of identity and place in American history.

Notes

1. On Acuff, Autry, and other popular country and western performers of the era, see Bill C. Malone, *Country Music, U.S.A.*, rev. ed. (1968; Austin: University of Texas Press, 2002), 93–197. For general information on the Mills Brothers, see "Mills Brothers," in *Encyclopedia of Popular Music*, 4th ed., ed. Colin Larkin, Oxford Music Online, http://www.oxfordmusiconline.com. For the Ink Spots, see Marv Goldberg, *More Than Words Can Say: The Ink Spots and Their Music* (Lanham, MD: Scarecrow Press, 1998), and Deek Watson and Lee Stephenson, *The Story of the Ink Spots* (New York: Vantage, 1967).

2. David Stowe, *Swing Changes: Big-Band Jazz in New Deal America* (Cambridge, MA: Harvard University Press, 1994); Lewis A. Erenberg, *Swinging the Dream: Big Band Jazz and the Rebirth of American Culture* (Chicago: University of Chicago Press, 1996); Joel Dinerstein, *Swinging the Machine: Modernity, Technology, and African American Culture between the World Wars* (Amherst: University of Massachusetts Press, 2003); Kenneth Bindas, *Swing, That Modern Sound* (Jackson: University Press of Mississippi, 2001).

3. For Erenberg, "swing was more racially and ethnically mixed than any other arena of American life" and helped democratize social life (Erenberg, *Swinging the Dream*, 250). Dinerstein echoes Erenberg but focuses on how swing combined a stylizing of machine age mechanization with a New Deal cultural pluralism: "Through contact with Euro-American musicians and cultural elites, as well as with black workers and the urban soundscape, African American artists integrated the speed, drive, precision, and rhythmic

flow of factory work and modern cities into a nationally (and internationally) unifying cultural form" (Dinerstein, *Swinging the Machine*, 5). Stowe, though acknowledging the music's "utopian impulse" and "latent sense of racial experimentation," presents a more balanced assessment. Swing "was a cultural form whose meanings were overdetermined, 'up for grabs,' open to a variety of interpretations by an audience that brought strikingly different assumptions and expectations to the music. Swing music could be held up as a proletarian protest music, a cultural expression of oppressed Americans that carried an implicit political message. It could just as easily be hailed as a product of the American way of life, the flowering of those qualities of individual liberty, social equality, and illustrious ethnic pluralism thought to be unique to the United States. Thirties jazz could be hailed as an authentic folk music, the end product of a lineage that began with work songs and spirituals. But it could also be reviled as trite commercialism: music debased by the need to win the widest possible segment of a new audience constituted by the new media of recordings, radio, and movies" (Stowe, *Swing Changes*, 93, 100).

4. Here I refer to "swing" as a noun. Later in the book I will discuss the verb form—a way jazz musicians, critics, and fans describe the rhythmic feel characteristic of the genre.

5. The origin of the swing craze is usually traced to Benny Goodman's July 1935 concert at the Palomar Ballroom in Los Angeles, a concert that convinced Goodman that hot dance band music was commercially viable. This story is part of the mythology of the swing era, and, as Stowe points out, the craze was more likely sparked by the enormous success of a 1935 recording, "The Music Goes 'Round and Round," by the Riley-Farley Orchestra. Stowe, *Swing Changes*, 7.

6. Josh Kun, *Audiotopia: Music, Race, and America* (Berkeley: University of California Press, 2005), 2–3, 23.

7. "The Lonesome Road," music by Nathaniel Shilkret and lyrics by Gene Austin, published 1927; "Street of Dreams," music by Victor Young, lyrics by Sam Lewis, published 1932.

8. Robert Lynd and Helen Merrell Lynd, *Middletown in Transition: A Study in Cultural Conflicts* (1937; New York: Harcourt Brace Jovanovich, 1982), 264.

9. An excellent introduction to this literature is Tim Cresswell, *Place: A Short Introduction* (Malden, MA: Blackwell, 2004). Other useful surveys include David Harvey, *Justice, Nature and the Geography of Difference* (Cambridge, MA: Blackwell, 1996), 207–326; David Harvey, "Space as a Key Word," in his *Spaces of Global Capitalism* (New York: Verso, 2006), 119–48; Edward W. Soja, *Thirdspace: Journeys to Los Angeles and Other Real-and-Imagined Places* (Cambridge, MA: Blackwell, 1996); Phil Hubbard et al., *Thinking Geographically: Space, Theory and Contemporary Human Geography* (New York: Continuum, 2002); and Edward S. Casey, "How to Get from Space to Place in a Fairly Short Stretch of Time: Phenomenological Prolegomena,"

in *Senses of Place*, ed. Steven Feld and Keith Basso (Santa Fe, NM: School of American Research Press, 1996), 13–52.

10. As David Harvey writes, "There is no such thing as space or time outside of the processes that define them. Processes do not occur *in* space but define their own spatial frame." Harvey, "Space as a Keyword," 123.

11. Harvey, *Justice, Nature and the Geography of Difference*, 261.

12. Cresswell, *Place*, 12.

13. In their provocative essay on rural places and "rusticity," Barbara Ching and Gerald Creed outline a very useful "grounded concept/metaphor" of place. They believe this formulation occupies "a theoretical middle ground in which 'place' can be metaphoric yet still refer to a particular physical environment and its associated socio-cultural qualities." Gerald W. Creed and Barbara Ching, "Recognizing Rusticity: Identity and the Power of Place," in *Knowing Your Place: Rural Identity and Cultural Hierarchy*, ed. Gerald Creed and Barbara Ching (New York: Routledge, 1997), 7, 9.

14. As an academic discipline, geography has grown over the years to encompass many theoretical and methodological approaches. There is, in fact, not a single, unified field but multiple ones all calling themselves "geography." Hubbard et al., *Thinking Geographically*, 10–21, 56.

15. Cresswell, *Place*, 11–12.

16. Graham Lock, *Blutopia: Visions of the Future and Revisions of the Past in the Work of Sun Ra, Duke Ellington, and Anthony Braxton* (Durham, NC: Duke University Press, 1999), 40.

17. Steve Waksman, *Instruments of Desire: The Electric Guitar and the Shaping of Musical Experience* (Cambridge, MA: Harvard University Press, 1999), 23.

18. This is precisely how jazz historian Leroy Ostransky organizes his *Jazz City: The Impact of Our Cities on the Development of Jazz* (Englewood Cliffs, NJ: Prentice-Hall, 1978).

19. Ray Pratt, *Rhythm and Resistance: Explorations in the Political Uses of Popular Music* (New York: Praeger, 1990), 26–27.

20. See, for example, Max Roach's highly critical discussion of the traditional jazz nightclub, "Beyond Categories," in *Keeping Time: Readings in Jazz History*, ed. Robert Walser (New York: Oxford University Press, 1999), 305–9.

21. Otis Ferguson, "The Spirit of Jazz," *New Republic*, December 30, 1935.

22. Geoffrey C. Ward and Ken Burns, *Jazz: A History of America's Music* (New York: Alfred A. Knopf, 2000), xxi.

23. For example, see Charles Garrett's discussion of Louis Armstrong and the Great Migration. Charles Hiroshi Garrett, *Struggling to Define a Nation: American Music in the Twentieth Century* (Berkeley: University of California Press, 2008), 83–120. In *Blues People*, LeRoi Jones (Amiri Baraka) makes a similar argument, though focusing on the migration of the blues from the South to the industrial cities of the North. LeRoi Jones, *Blues People: Negro Music in White America* (New York: William Morrow, 1963), 101–3.

24. Hillbilly music grew substantially in popularity during the 1930s and especially the 1940s. A style once largely identified with the South spread across the nation as migrants moved north and west in search of work. During the Depression hillbilly recordings sold much smaller numbers than big band records—a former executive with Decca Records' country music division "estimated that a 'hillbilly hit' during the Depression was one which sold a total of ten thousand copies." By the war years, however, hillbilly began making significant inroads into the more general popular music market. Artists such as Roy Acuff, Bob Wills, and Ernest Tubb had major nationwide hits, and the music of many other artists could be heard on jukeboxes from Detroit to Los Angeles. Malone, *Country Music, U.S.A.,* 95, 177–97.

25. Kun, *Audiotopia*, 23.

26. John Connell and Chris Gibson, *Sound Tracks: Popular Music, Identity and Place* (New York: Routledge, 2003), 9, 18, 46.

27. David Peeler, *Hope among Us Yet: Social Criticism and Social Solace in Depression America* (Athens: University of Georgia Press, 1987), 14–55.

28. Michael Steiner, "Regionalism in the Great Depression," *Geographical Review* 73, no. 4 (October 1983): 436.

29. David Jacobson, *Place and Belonging in America* (Baltimore: Johns Hopkins University Press, 2002), 22.

30. David Harvey, *The Condition of Postmodernity* (1990; Cambridge, MA: Blackwell, 2004), 211.

31. I am borrowing here from David Harvey: "The process of place formation is a process of carving out 'permanences' from the flow of processes creating spaces. But the permanences—no matter how solid they may seem— are not eternal: they are always subject to time as 'perpetual perishing.' They are contingent on the processes that create, sustain, and dissolve them." Harvey, *Justice, Nature, and the Geography of Difference*, 242–47.

32. In an important assessment of the current state of American life, government researchers in 1933 reflected on the social impact of new transportation and communication technologies. For these writers, the automobile was especially important, instigating profound, even radical, social change: "The new mobility is illustrated by the shortest mail (land) time from San Francisco to Washington, which in 1870 was 161 hours and 15 minutes, in 1900 was 109 hours and 15 minutes and in 1930 was 79 hours and 55 minutes. In 1798 the mail time from Philadelphia to Lexington, Kentucky, was 19 to 30 days, depending on the state of the weather. To all this the telephone, the radio and the automobile have contributed even more, and the automobile especially has operated with devastating effect upon local boundary lines. Important readjustments were begun in every field of government—rural, urban, state, even national. New rural units, reorganized counties, regional groupings, interstate agreements, municipal home rule and city states, even interna-

tional rearrangements are the signs of the new movement." United States, President's Research Committee on Social Trends, *Report of the President's Research Committee on Social Trends: Recent Social Trends*, foreword by President Herbert Hoover (New York: McGraw-Hill, 1933), 1491.

33. Warren I. Susman, *Culture as History: The Transformation of American Society in the Twentieth Century* (1973; New York: Pantheon Books, 1984), 191.

34. Steiner, "Regionalism in the Great Depression," 430–31.

35. For an excellent discussion of this debate among 1930s writers, politicians, and academics, see Terry A. Cooney, *Balancing Acts: American Thought and Culture in the 1930s* (New York: Twayne, 1995), 105–28, 191–218.

36. For a comprehensive study of regionalist thought, see Robert L. Dorman, *Revolt of the Provinces: The Regionalist Movement in America, 1920–1945* (Chapel Hill: University of North Carolina Press, 1993). On the New Dealers and their ideas about American culture and community, see Alan Lawson, "The Cultural Legacy of the New Deal," in *Fifty Years Later: The New Deal Evaluated*, ed. Harvard Sitkoff (Philadelphia: Temple University Press, 1985), 155–86. The notion of a "cultural front" is Michael Denning's term for the informal alliance, begun in the 1930s, between industrial unions, left-wing popular front activism, and artists. See Michael Denning, *The Cultural Front: The Laboring of American Culture in the Twentieth Century* (New York: Verso, 1996).

37. One key example is Margaret Mitchell's 1936 novel *Gone with the Wind*, the best-selling book of the decade (and three years later an Academy Award–winning film). The novel traces Scarlett O'Hara's stubborn attempt to revive the family plantation, Tara, trying to recapture the idyllic life it represented in the years before the Civil War. Steiner, *Regionalism in the Great Depression*, 431, 435.

38. Susman, *Culture as History*, 193.

39. John W. Jeffries, *Wartime America: The World War II Home Front* (Chicago: Ivan R. Dee, 1996), 69.

40. In his discussion of wartime migrations, Jeffries provides some telling statistics: "By one estimate twelve million people—nearly one of every ten— moved permanently to another state during the war. The farm population declined dramatically, by roughly one-fifth, as more than six million rural people left for the armed forces and for centers of defense production. Metropolitan areas, by contrast, expanded rapidly during the war, their populations growing by some 21 percent from 1940 to 1950, three times the rate of nonmetropolitan areas. Suburbs grew especially dramatically— by some 35 percent, while central cities grew by 13 percent—for suburbs had space available for new manufacturing plants, and space too for the new housing needed by war workers." Jeffries, *Wartime America*, 71.

41. A brief account of these newly heterogeneous cities is in Jeffries, *Wartime America*, 75. See also George Lipsitz, *Rainbow at Midnight: Labor and Culture in the 1940s* (Urbana: University of Illinois Press, 1994).

42. Denning, *Cultural Front*, 34.

43. Zora Neale Hurston, *Mules and Men* (1935; New York: Harper Perennial Library, 1990).

44. Claude McKay, *Harlem: Negro Metropolis* (New York: E. P. Dutton, 1940); Roi Ottley, *"New World a-Coming": Inside Black America* (Cleveland, OH: World, 1943); St. Clair Drake and Horace R. Cayton, *Black Metropolis: A Study of Negro Life in a Northern City* (New York: Harcourt, Brace, 1945).

45. The Harper Perennial Edition of *Black Boy* includes *American Hunger*. Richard Wright, *Black Boy (American Hunger): A Record of Childhood and Youth* (New York: Harper Perennial, 1993).

46. Several of Gwendolyn Brooks's books of poetry and prose, including *A Street in Bronzeville*, are collected in Gwendolyn Brooks, *The World of Gwendolyn Brooks* (New York: Harper and Row, 1971). Ann Petry, *The Street* (1946; Boston: Beacon Press, 1984).

47. Philip Gleason, "Americans All: World War II and the Shaping of American Identity," *Review of Politics* 43, no. 4 (October 1981): 483–518; Nelson Lichenstein, "The Making of the Postwar Working Class: Cultural Pluralism and Social Structure in World War II," *Historian* 51, no. 1 (November 1988): 42–63. For another account of this transformation see Eric Foner, *The Story of American Freedom* (New York: W. W. Norton, 1998), 219–47.

48. Denning, *Cultural Front*, 34.

49. Daniel Belgrad, *The Culture of Spontaneity: Improvisation and the Arts in Postwar America* (Chicago: University of Chicago Press, 1998), 249–60.

50. Georgina Born, *Rationalizing Culture: IRCAM, Boulez, and the Institutionalization of the Avant-Garde* (Berkeley: University of California Press, 1995), 53.

51. Susman, *Culture as History*, 159.

52. Susan J. Douglas, *Listening In: Radio and the American Imagination, from Amos 'n' Andy and Edward R. Murrow to Wolfman Jack and Howard Stern* (New York: Times Books/Random House, 1999), 100–123.

53. Steiner, "Regionalism in the Great Depression," 439.

54. Morris Dickstein, "Depression Culture: The Dream of Mobility," in *Radical Revisions: Rereading 1930s Culture*, ed. Bill Mullen and Sherry Lee Linkon (Urbana: University of Illinois Press, 1996), 239. Dickstein provides a more extended discussion of this idea in his new book on Depression-era culture, *Dancing in the Dark: A Cultural History of the Great Depression* (New York: W. W. Norton, 2009).

55. Frank Capra's screwball comedy *It Happened One Night* is one of the era's best examples. The film is all movement and restlessness: Claudette Colbert and Clark Gable spend most of the movie literally traveling the nation's roads. Film scholar Bennet Schaber writes that "the film includes a visual account of nearly every possible means of transportation: from walking to boats, buses, cars, motorcycles, planes, autogyros, and

trains, even swimming." This list could be expanded to include all the "transport[s] of communication: phone, telegraph, mail, newspaper, newsreel, radio, intercom, all points bulletin." Bennet Schaber, "Hitler Can't Keep 'em That Long," in *The Road Movie Book*, ed. Steven Cohan and Ina Rae Hark (New York: Routledge, 1997), 22.

56. Not all this movement was successful. The 1930s saw an overall decrease in domestic migration; for most Americans mobility was, in fact, just a dream. Along with the fantasies of travel and movement, much literature and film of the decade captured its antipode, a sense of stagnation, of movement without end or destination. Migration and homelessness loomed over the era. Jan Scandura terms this "depressive modernity," suggesting that the 1930s were a time when life appeared stalled and real social and geographical movement was unrealistic and futile. As Morris Dickstein writes, novels such as *The Grapes of Wrath* and films such *I Am a Fugitive from a Chain Gang* and *Wild Boys of the Road* were "about ordinary people uprooted from a stable life and forced to wander in search of something better, only to find more hellish conditions among other displaced, unwanted, or viciously mistreated people." Steiner, "Regionalism in the Great Depression," 442; Jani Scandura, *Down in the Dumps: Place, Modernity, American Depression* (Durham, NC: Duke University Press, 2008), 4–5; Dickstein, "Depression Culture," 234.

57. Grace Elizabeth Hale, *Making Whiteness: The Culture of Segregation in the South, 1890–1940* (New York: Vintage, 1998), 6.

58. Ibid., 7.

59. In *Lying Up a Nation*, ethnomusicologist Ronald Radano traces the origins of this association to colonial reactions to African and New World musical practices. Ronald Radano, *Lying Up a Nation: Race and Black Music* (Chicago: University of Chicago Press, 2003).

60. Patrick Burke provides a nuanced analysis of the racial understandings of jazz of this era in his study of New York City's Fifty-Second Street. Patrick Lawrence Burke, *Come In and Hear the Truth: Jazz and Race on 52nd Street* (Chicago: University of Chicago Press, 2008). Although covering a later period of music, Brian Ward's *Just My Soul Responding: Rhythm and Blues, Black Consciousness, and Race Relations* (Berkeley: University of California Press, 1998) is founded on a similar premise: "The third key proposition in this book is that in America there exists a conventionally recognized spectrum of musical techniques and devices which ranges from nominally 'black' to nominally 'white' poles." As Ward recognizes, the objective truth of this assertion has its problems, but "the idea of a black-white musical spectrum remains a useful conceptual framework simply because both black and white audiences have cognitively accepted its existence" (6).

In the growing literature on "whiteness," scholars frequently speak about white racial identity as "unmarked" or the silent other of racial discourse. But as the Casa Loma's recordings "White Jazz" and "Black Jazz" show, the situation was often more explicit. Audiences had a category of both "whiteness" and "blackness" available, though the exact content of these categories was fluid and variable. For a comprehensive critical survey of the literature on whiteness, see Peter Kolchin, "Whiteness Studies: The New History of Race in America," *Journal of American History* 89, no. 1 (June 2002): 154–73. Recent musicological studies of whiteness include Richard Mook, "White Masculinity in Barbershop Quartet Singing," *Journal of the Society for American Music* 1, no. 4 (November 2007): 453–83, and Theo Cateforis, "Performing the Avant-Garde Groove: Devo and the Whiteness of the New Wave," *American Music* 22, no. 4 (Winter 2004): 564–88.

61. Barry Shank, "From Rice to Ice: The Face of Race in Rock and Pop," in *The Cambridge Companion to Pop and Rock*, ed. Simon Frith, Will Straw, and John Street (Cambridge: Cambridge University Press, 2001), 257, 262.

62. In *Popular Music in Theory*, author Keith Negus offers the notion of "articulation" as a more productive way to analyze the relation between music and identity. The use of the concept avoids the reifications of essentialist positions. Keith Negus, *Popular Music in Theory: An Introduction* (Hanover, NH: Wesleyan University Press, 1997), 134–35.

63. In the introduction to their edited collection *Music and the Racial Imagination*, Ronald Radano and Philip Bohlman trace this mutually constitutive relationship in the history of academic musicology and ethnomusicology in Europe and America. "The imagination of race," they argue, "not only informs perceptions of musical practice but is at once constituted within and projected into the social through sound." Ronald Radano and Philip V. Bohlman, "Introduction: Music and Race, Their Past, Their Presence," in *Music and the Racial Imagination*, ed. Ronald Radano and Philip V. Bohlman (Chicago: University of Chicago Press, 2000), 5.

64. Gunther Schuller doesn't believe the joke would have worked on the predominantly white college students who were the Casa Loma Orchestra's primary audience in the early 1930s. They would not, he argues, have been exposed to enough "authentic" jazz. Perhaps, but this is a narrow reading that greatly underestimates the widespread notions of racial identity and music. Gunther Schuller, *The Swing Era, 1930–1945* (New York: Oxford University Press, 1989), 635.

65. In Gifford's arrangements Schuller hears the influence of John Nesbitt, who wrote for the black dance band McKinney's Cotton Pickers. Schuller, *Swing Era*, 632–45.

66. Shank, "From Ice to Rice," 257.

67. For Barry Shank this is key in understanding a notion such as "black music" in a way that is musically specific but not essentialist. Shank, "From Ice to Rice," 261–63.

68. Christopher Small, *Musicking: The Meaning of Performance and Listening* (Hanover, NH: University Press of New England/Wesleyan University Press, 1998), 142.

69. Burke, *Come In and Hear the Truth*, 6.

70. Ibid., 259.

71. Olly Wilson, "Black Music as an Art Form," in *The Jazz Cadence of American Culture*, ed. Robert G. O'Meally (New York: Columbia University Press, 1998), 82–101.

72. Samuel A. Floyd, *The Power of Black Music: Interpreting Its History from Africa to the United States* (New York: Oxford University Press, 1995), 6–7.

73. Radano, *Lying Up a Nation*, 3–4.

74. For instance, the sound of the banjo in today's country music is strongly associated with whites, and specifically with rural, poor Appalachian whites (think of the famous "dueling banjo" scene in the 1972 film *Deliverance*). Historically, the banjo traveled to the Americas from Africa, but discursively the instrument developed a racial association with "whiteness." Jay Scott Odell and Robert B. Winans, "Banjo," in *Grove Music Online*, http://www.oxfordmusiconline.com (accessed July 15, 2010). Guthrie P. Ramsey, *Race Music: Black Cultures from Bebop to Hip-Hop* (Berkeley: University of California Press, 2003), 36.

75. Shank, "From Ice to Rice," 263.

76. For a thoughtful recent assessment of these continuing debates, see anthropologist Kenneth Bilby's review essay on Richard Price's *Travels with Tooy: History, Memory, and the African American Imagination* (Chicago: University of Chicago Press, 2006). Kenneth Bilby, "African American Memory at the Crossroads: Grounding the Miraculous with Tooy," *Small Axe* 29 (July 2009): 185–99.

77. Krin Gabbard, *Jammin' at the Margins: Jazz and the American Cinema* (Chicago: University of Chicago Press, 1996), 8.

78. Gena Caponi-Tabery, *Jump for Joy: Jazz, Basketball and Black Culture in 1930s America* (Amherst: University of Massachusetts Press, 2008), 139.

79. By the middle to late 1940s this list would also include "modern" jazz or "bebop," though it wasn't until after the Second World War that the music began to definitively displace the dominant, mainstream swing styles. Characteristics of bebop playing, though, insinuated themselves into the swing style during the late 1930s and early 1940s. A detailed history of the development and emergence of bebop and its overlap with swing is Scott DeVeaux's *The Birth of Bebop: A Social and Musical History* (Berkeley: University of California Press, 1997).

80. George T. Simon, *The Big Bands* (New York: Macmillan, 1969), 4.

81. Stanley Dance, *The World of Swing: An Oral History of Big Band Jazz* (New York: Da Capo Press, 2001).

82. Recent biographies and important studies (since 2000) of these figures include John Fass Morton, *Backstory in Blue: Ellington at Newport '56*

(Piscataway, NJ: Rutgers University Press, 2008); John Howland, *Ellington Uptown: Duke Ellington, James P. Johnson, and the Birth of Concert Jazz* (Ann Arbor: University of Michigan Press, 2009); A. H. Lawrence, *Duke Ellington and His World: A Biography* (New York: Routledge, 2001); Jeffrey Magee, *The Uncrowned King of Swing: Fletcher Henderson and Big Band Jazz* (New York: Oxford University Press, 2005); Lewis Porter, *Lester Young*, rev. ed. (Ann Arbor: University of Michigan Press, 2005); Douglas Henry Daniels, *Lester Leaps In: The Life and Times of Lester "Pres" Young* (Boston: Beacon Press, 2003); Dave Gelly, *Being Prez: The Life and Music of Lester Young* (New York: Oxford University Press, 2007); Donald Clarke, *Billie Holiday: Wishing on the Moon* (New York: Da Capo Press, 2002); Robert O'Meally, *Lady Day: The Many Faces of Billie Holiday* (New York: Da Capo Press, 2000); Farah Jasmine Griffin, *If You Can't Be Free, Be a Mystery: In Search of Billie Holiday* (New York: One World/Ballantine, 2002); Frank Büchmann-Møller, *Someone to Watch over Me: The Life and Music of Ben Webster* (Ann Arbor: University of Michigan Press, 2008); Jeroen De Valk, *Ben Webster: His Life and Music* (Berkeley, CA: Berkeley Hills Books, 2000).

83. Sherrie Tucker, *Swing Shift: "All-Girl" Bands of the 1940s* (Durham, NC: Duke University Press, 2000). Other important recent books include Frank Driggs and Chuck Haddix, *Kansas City Jazz: From Ragtime to Bebop—a History* (New York: Oxford University Press, 2005), and Pete Townsend, *Pearl Harbor Jazz: Change in Popular Music in the Early 1940s* (Jackson: University Press of Mississippi, 2007).

84. Burke, *Come In and Hear the Truth*; Schuller, *Swing Era*. Other general histories include Simon, *Big Bands* (1967); Albert J. McCarthy, *The Dance Band Era, the Dancing Decades from Ragtime to Swing: 1910–1950* (London: Spring Books, 1974); Dave Oliphant, *The Early Swing Era, 1930 to 1941* (Westport, CT: Greenwood Press, 2002); Lawrence McClellan, *The Later Swing Era, 1942 to 1955* (Westport, CT Greenwood Press, 2004); Richard M. Sudhalter, *Lost Chords: White Musicians and Their Contribution to Jazz, 1915–1945* (New York: Oxford University Press, 1999); Gene Fernett, *Swing Out: Great Negro Dance Bands* (Midland, MI: Pendell, 1970); Thomas Hennessey, *From Jazz to Swing: African American Jazz Musicians and Their Music, 1890–1935* (Detroit: Wayne State University Press, 1994); Leo Walker, *The Wonderful Era of the Dance Bands* (1964; New York: Da Capo Press, 1990); and Bruce Crowther, Mike Pinfold, and Franklin S. Driggs, *The Big Band Years* (New York: Facts on File, 1988).

85. Susanne K. Langer provides a classic statement of this view in *Feeling and Form: A Theory of Art* (New York: Charles Scribner's Sons, 1953), 120–32. For another broad survey of the historical discourse on music as a temporal art, see Raymond Monelle, *The Sense of Music: Semiotic Essays* (Princeton, NJ: Princeton University Press, 2000), 81–114.

86. Harvey, *Justice, Nature and the Geography of Difference*, 207.

87. Patrick Shove and Bruno H. Repp, "Musical Motion and Performance: Theoretical and Empirical Perspectives," in *The Practice of Performance: Studies in Musical Interpretation*, ed. John Rink (Cambridge: Cambridge University Press, 1995), 55–83.

88. Eric F. Clarke, *Ways of Listening: An Ecological Approach to the Perception of Musical Meaning* (New York: Oxford University Press, 2005), 63.

89. Arnold Schoenberg, *Style and Idea: Selected Writings of Arnold Schoenberg* (Berkeley: University of California Press, 1984), 214–45. In his writings, twentieth-century American composer George Rochberg provides a lengthy and useful analysis of Schoenberg's spatial conception of his twelve-tone method. George Rochberg, *The Aesthetics of Survival: A Composer's View of Twentieth-Century Music* (Ann Arbor: University of Michigan Press, 1984), 78–86.

90. Lawrence M. Zbikowski, *Conceptualizing Music: Cognitive Structure, Theory, and Analysis* (New York: Oxford University Press, 2002), 67–68. Recent experiments by music psychologists confirm that listeners have strong spatial associations with music, but they also show that our cognitive mappings of music onto space and motion are more complicated than usually thought. For example, pitch frequency also has lateral associations (left and right) as well as vertical ones. Zohar Eitan and Roni Y. Granot, "How Music Moves: Musical Parameters and Listeners' Images of Motion," *Music Perception* 23, no. 3 (2006): 221–47.

91. Hugh Masekela and D. Michael Cheers, *Still Grazing: The Musical Journey of Hugh Masekela* (New York: Crown, 2004); Joshua M. Greene, *Here Comes the Sun: The Spiritual and Musical Journey of George Harrison* (Hoboken, NJ: Wiley, 2006); Horace Tapscott and Steven Isoardi, *Songs of the Unsung: The Musical and Social Journey of Horace Tapscott* (Durham, NC: Duke University Press, 2001).

92. Examples are easy to find. In a concert review of a recent Massachusetts performance by rock band Pearl Jam, author Jay Miller describes how lead singer Eddie Vedder's "passion [was] perfectly in sync with the music's transporting power." In another recent article from the *San Francisco Chronicle*, critic David Wiegand, watching a PBS documentary on the life of Duke Ellington collaborator Billy Strayhorn, was reminded of the power of the great song "Lush Life": "Even today, as we are transported by the truth of its longing and regret, it's astounding to think that the song was written by a teenager." Jay N. Miller, "Why Go See Pearl Jam? Because Their Music Comes Alive," *Patriot Ledger* (Quincy, MA), July 1, 2008; David Wiegand, "Billy Strayhorn, the Prodigy behind Duke Ellington's Music," *San Francisco Chronicle*, February 3, 2007.

93. Sara Cohen, "The Sensuous Production of Place," in *The Place of Music*, ed. Andrew Leyshon, David Matless, and George Revill (New York: Guilford Press, 1998), 279.

94. Pratt, *Rhythm and Resistance*, 22.

95. Ibid. Pratt is quoting from the influential essay "Auditory Space" by Edmund Carpenter and Marshall McLuhan, in *Explorations in Communication: An Anthology*, ed. Edmund Carpenter and Marshall McLuhan (London: Jonathan Cape, 1970), 67.

96. For the former, see Robert Morgan, "Musical Time/Musical Space," *Critical Inquiry* 6, no. 3 (Spring 1980): 527–38; and Robert Cogan and Pozzi Escot, *Sonic Design: The Nature of Sound and Music* (Englewood Cliffs, NJ: Prentice-Hall, 1976). Semioticians have similarly discussed musical space as metaphorical and the product of formal musical materials such as pitch, rhythm, and harmony. See Eero Tarasti, *A Theory of Musical Semiotics* (Bloomington: Indiana University Press, 1994).

    In contrast to these narrowly formal projects, many recent studies have been published that explore the relation between music and place as largely discursive and, to varying degrees, independent of specific musical sounds. See Sheila Whiteley, Andy Bennett, and Stan Hawkins, eds., *Music, Space, and Place: Popular Music and Cultural Identity* (Aldershot, UK: Ashgate Press, 2004); Andrew Leyshon, David Matless, and George Revill, eds., *The Place of Music* (New York: Guilford Press, 1998); Martin Stokes, ed., *Ethnicity, Identity, and Music: The Musical Construction of Place* (Providence, RI: Berg, 1994); Murray Forman, *The 'Hood Comes First: Race, Space, and Place in Rap and Hip-Hop* (Middletown, CT: Wesleyan University Press, 2002); Gill Valentine, "Creating Transgressive Space: The Music of kd lang," *Transactions of the Institute of British Geographers* 20, no. 4 (1995): 474–85; Thomas Solomon, "Dueling Landscapes: Singing Places and Identities in Highland Bolivia," *Ethnomusicology* 44, no. 2 (Spring/Summer 2000): 257–80; Louise Wrazen, "Relocating the Tatras: Place and Music in Gorale Identity and Imagination," *Ethnomusicology* 51, no. 2 (Spring/Summer 2007): 185–204; and Connell and Gibson, *Sound Tracks*.

97. There is another strand of writing on music and space/place that focuses on how musicians and composers employ spatial effects in performance through, for instance, the choice of venue, the positioning of musicians in a particular musical space, or the new capabilities of electronic and computer music. A few useful surveys of this type of spatial music are Barry Blesser and Linda-Ruth Salter, *Spaces Speak, Are You Listening?* (Cambridge, MA: MIT Press, 2007), 167–83; Richard Zvonar, "An Extremely Brief History of Spatial Music in the 20th Century," http://cec.concordia.ca/econtact/ Multichannel/spatial_music.html; and Maria Ann Harley, "An American in Space: Henry Brant's 'Spatial Music,'" *American Music* 15, no. 1 (Spring 1997): 70–92.

98. Susan McClary, "This Is Not My Story to Tell: Musical Time and Space according to Laurie Anderson," in her *Feminine Endings: Music, Gender, and Sexuality* (Minneapolis: University of Minnesota Press, 1991), 132–47; Steven Feld, "Waterfalls of Sound: An Acoustemology of Place Resounding in Bosavi, Papua New Guinea," in *Senses of Place*, ed. Steven Feld and Keith

H. Basso (Santa Fe, NM: School of American Research Press, 1996), 91–135; Garrett, "Louis Armstrong and the Great Migration," in his *Struggling to Define a Nation*, 83–120; Vijay Iyer, "Exploding the Narrative in Jazz Improvisation," in *Uptown Conversation: The New Jazz Studies*, ed. Robert G. O'Meally, Brent Hayes Edwards, and Farah Jasmin Griffin (New York: Columbia University Press, 2004), 393–403.

99. There are only a handful of full-length treatments of musical space and time from a phenomenological perspective. See Clifton Hood, *Music as Heard: A Study in Applied Phenomenology* (New Haven, CT: Yale University Press, 1983), and Judith Lochhead, "The Temporal Structure of Recent Music: A Phenomenological Investigation" (PhD diss., State University of New York, Stony Brook, 1982). Also helpful is Lochhead's review and critique of Hood in *Journal of Musicology* 4, no. 3 (Summer 1985–Summer 1986): 355–64. Recent literature in musicology and music theory that draws on developments in cognitive science and neurobiology includes Clarke, *Ways of Listening*; Charles O. Nussbaum, *The Musical Representation: Meaning, Ontology, and Emotion* (Cambridge, MA: MIT Press, 2007); Shove and Repp, "Musical Motion and Performance"; and Zbikowski, *Conceptualizing Music*.

100. Don Ihde, *Listening and Voice: A Phenomenology of Sound* (Athens: Ohio University Press, 1976), 77.

101. Sociologist Ray Pratt makes a related argument in his *Rhythm and Resistance*. In the course of arguing about the political dimensions and uses of popular music, Pratt develops a notion of musical space that connects social experience of the places of daily life with the virtual spaces created by musical sound. For Pratt, "Sound is dynamic and symptomatic of energy. It does not occur in the absence of activity." We are programmed to respond immediately to it, and sound easily "takes over" any physical space in which it is heard. In this way, music creates "sound space[s]." With recorded music "people are free to create spaces in which they program their environment. . . . The free space created through sound is identifiable with a basic psychological sense of freedom," even though it may last only a moment. "One measure of any music is 'its "presence," its ability to "stop" time, to make us feel we are living within a moment, with no memory or anxiety about what has come before, what will come after.'" Pratt, *Rhythm and Resistance*, 22.

102. The term "sensuous production of place" is from Sara Cohen, "Sounding Out the City: Music and the Sensuous Production of Place," in *The Place of Music*, ed. Andrew Leyshon, David Matless, and George Revill (New York: Guilford Press, 1998). Also see her full-length monograph, *Decline, Renewal and the City in Popular Music Culture: Beyond the Beatles* (Hampshire, UK: Ashgate Press, 2007).

103. For a discussion of the negative implications of music delocalization, see Jody Berland, "Locating Listening: Technological Space, Popular Music,

and Canadian Mediations," in *The Place of Music*, ed. Andrew Leyshon, David Matless, and George Revill (New York: Guilford Press, 1998), 129–50.

104. George Lipsitz, *Dangerous Crossroads: Popular Music, Postmodernism, and the Poetics of Place* (New York: Verso, 1994), 3–21.

105. Henri Lefebvre, *The Production of Space*, trans. Donald Nicholson-Smith (1974; Oxford: Blackwell, 1991), 39.

106. Discussing the Chavin of the Peruvian Andes, Lefebvre specifically includes artworks as examples of representational spaces: "There have been societies—the Chavin of the Peruvian Andes are a case in point—whose representation of space is attested to by the plans of their temples and palaces, while their representational spaces appear in their art works, writing-systems, fabrics, and so on." Lefebvre, *Production of Space*, 43.

107. Lefebvre's few mentions of music are provocative and tantalizingly short. After a discussion of the Renaissance town, Lefebvre specifically includes music (along with "sounds, evocations, architectural constructions") in its "spatial code." Later, he confirms the role of music and other "non-verbal signifying sets" in his theoretical project in a passage attacking the limitations of critical theories overly reliant on the analysis of language and "discourse." Lefebvre's most detailed discussion of music comes significantly later in his book, in a digression from his larger topic of absolute versus abstract space, and concerns the triumph of a visual spatial order over earlier spatial orders. According to Lefebvre, during the eighteenth century "music was in command. It was the pilot of the arts." As a nonverbal spatial system, music, particularly the concept of harmony, challenged an encroaching, dominating "visual-geometric character" spatial order. Lefebvre, *Production of Space*, 46, 61–62, 284–85.

108. Rob Shields, *Lefebvre, Love and Struggle: Spatial Dialectics* (London: Routledge, 1999), 165.

109. In his writing on music and space, philosopher Victor Zuckerkandl echoes Shields's ideas. Music, Zuckerkandl asserts, can offer us new ways to understand the human experience of space: "Far from being unable to testify in matters of space, music makes us understand that we do not learn all that is to be said about space from eye and hand, from geometry, geography, astronomy, physics. The full concept of space must include the experience of the ear, the testimony of the music." Victor Zuckerkandl, *Sound and Symbol: Music and the External World*, trans. Willard R. Trask, Bollingen Series 44 (New York: Pantheon Books, 1956), 292.

110. Arguing for an understanding of music as a *practice* rather than a *thing*, musicologist Christopher Small adopts the gerund "musicking" to help undo ingrained patterns of thinking. Understood in this way, music becomes less a sonic artifact than a network of social relationships that allow listeners, at least for the duration of a performance, to *be* in different ways: "To affirm and celebrate our relationships through musicking, especially in company with like-feeling people, is to explore and celebrate

our sense of who we are, to make us feel more fully ourselves." Small, *Musicking*, 142.

111. The felicitous phrase "momentary acoustic community" is from Dave Hickey's essay on jazz trumpeter Chet Baker in his *Air Guitar: Essays on Art and Democracy* (Los Angeles: Art Issues Press, 1997), 81.

112. Kun, *Audiotopia*, 2–3.

113. There is one element of spatial experience that I don't talk about; the acoustical experience of music in a particular place and time—for instance, what a band sounded like to its listeners in a particular venue. Because I focus on recordings, this element is difficult to recapture. Hearing the Ellington band in a specific venue at a specific time certainly shaped the meanings created for musicians and listeners. For instance, hearing the band playing a big, noisy ballroom was undoubtedly a very different sonic experience from hearing it in a quiet concert hall. The sense of the space the band's music literally filled would play a part in the experience of place felt by musicians and listeners. This is an elusive topic for a historian, and though it will enter the discussion when relevant, I do not address it in depth.

114. Ann Douglas, *Terrible Honesty: Mongrel Manhattan in the 1920s* (New York: Noonday Press/Farrar, Straus and Giroux, 1995), 434–61.

115. Lawrence Kramer, *Musical Meaning: Toward a Critical History* (Berkeley: University of California Press, 2001), 27–28.

116. Peter J. Levinson, *Tommy Dorsey: Livin' in a Great Big Way* (New York: Da Capo Press, 2005), 103–5.

117. Edwin M. Bradley, *The First Hollywood Musicals: A Critical Filmography of 171 Features, 1927 through 1932* (Jefferson, NC: McFarland, 1996), 166–68; Scott Allen Nollen, *Paul Robeson, Film Pioneer* (Jefferson, NC: McFarland, 2010), 57; Thomas Hischak, *The Rogers and Hammerstein Encyclopedia* (Westport, CT: Greenwood Press, 2007), 246.

118. Raymond Williams, *The Politics of Modernism: Against the New Conformists*, ed. and intro. Tony Pinkney (New York: Verso, 1989), 174–75. Williams is writing not specifically about jazz, but about cultural artifacts more generally.

CHAPTER ONE

1. Discussions of the Casino Ballroom invariably show up in almost any writing on Catalina, and the most significant books on the island have been published by individuals close to the Santa Catalina Island Company, the Wrigley family, or the Santa Catalina Island Museum. Patricia Ann Moore's *The Casino: Catalina Island's "Two Million Dollar Palace of Pleasure,"* rev. ed. (Avalon, CA: Catalina Island Museum Society, 1979) comprehensively details the creation and history of the ballroom. See also William Sanford White and Steven Kern Tice, *Santa Catalina Island: Its*

Magic, People, and History, rev. ed. (Glendora, CA: White Limited Editions, 1997), 131–42; Jeannine L. Pedersen, *Catalina Island*, Images of America Series (Charleston, SC: Arcadia, 2004), 84–87; Alma Overholt, *The Catalina Story* (Avalon, CA: Catalina Island Museum, 1962), 71–72; and Gayle Baker, *Catalina Island: A Harbor Town History* (Santa Barbara, CA: Harbor Town Histories, 2003), 62.

2. For example, Albert McCarthy's *Big Band Jazz*, George Simon's *The Big Bands*, and Gunther Schuller's comprehensive *The Swing Era do not* discuss the ballroom at all, nor do recent accounts of the era by cultural historians Lewis Erenberg, David Stowe, Kenneth Bindas, Thomas Hennessey, and Joel Dinerstein. Leo Walker's *The Wonderful Era of the Great Dance Bands* and Bruce Crowther, Mike Pinfold, and Franklin Driggs's *The Big Band Years* briefly mention the venue and feature a few photographs of the ballroom. Occasionally the Casino Ballroom appears in biographical and autobiographical accounts of specific musicians, including Benny Goodman, who played there in 1940, and jazz writers such as Floyd Levin, who lived in Southern California during the 1930s and '40s. See Albert J. McCarthy, *Big Band Jazz* (1974; London: Peerage Books, 1983); George T. Simon, *The Big Bands* (1967; New York: Macmillan, 1969); Gunther Schuller, *The Swing Era: The Development of Jazz, 1930–1945* (New York: Oxford University Press, 1989); Lewis Erenberg, *Swingin' the Dream: Big Band Jazz and the Rebirth of American Culture* (Chicago: University of Chicago Press, 1998); David W. Stowe, *Swing Changes: Big-Band Jazz in New Deal America* (Cambridge, MA: Harvard University Press, 1994); Kenneth Bindas, *Swing, That Modern Sound* (Jackson: University Press of Mississippi, 2001); Thomas Hennessey, *From Jazz to Swing: African American Jazz Musicians and Their Music, 1890–1935* (Detroit: Wayne State University Press, 1994); Joel Dinerstein, *Swinging the Machine: Modernity, Technology, and African American Culture between the World Wars* (Amherst: University of Massachusetts Press, 2003); Leo Walker, *The Wonderful Era of the Dance Bands* (1964; New York: Da Capo Press, 1990); Bruce Crowther, Mike Pinfold, and Franklin S. Driggs, *The Big Band Years* (New York: Facts on File, 1988); Ross Firestone, *Swing, Swing, Swing: The Life and Times of Benny Goodman* (New York: W. W. Norton, 1993), 280–81; and Floyd Levin, *Classic Jazz: A Personal View of the Music and the Musicians* (Berkeley: University of California Press, 2000), 232.

3. I have located only a few partial radio broadcasts from the ballroom. A website run by the family of the popular dance bandleader Dick Jurgens featured several brief clips of the orchestra at the ballroom during the 1930s, but the site is no longer available. The Santa Catalina Island Research Center has a few brief recordings of Benny Goodman and Kay Kyser from the summer of 1940.

4. The recording I located of the Jurgens Orchestra (see note 3) features the band playing "Avalon" as the introduction to a remote radio broadcast.

5. Moore, *Casino*, 88–89; see also Lew Oesterle, "Jan Garber Returns," *Catalina Islander*, July 1, 1937.

6. Michael Kammen, *Mystic Chords of Memory: The Transformation of Tradition in American Culture* (New York: Alfred A. Knopf, 1991), 300.

7. Bindas, *Swing, That Modern Sound*, xiii–xiv.

8. Lawrence Levine, *The Unpredictable Past: Explorations in American Cultural History* (New York: Oxford University Press, 1993), 205.

9. Recent scholarly works with important discussions of jazz in Los Angeles, California, and the West include Clora Bryant et al., eds., *Central Avenue Sounds: Jazz in Los Angeles* (Berkeley: University of California Press, 1998); Jacqueline Cogdell DjeDje and Eddie S. Meadows, eds., *California Soul: Music of African Americans in the West* (Berkeley: University of California Press, 1998); Ted Gioia, *West Coast Jazz: Modern Jazz in California, 1945–1960* (1992; Berkeley: University of California Press, 1998); Steven Louis Isoardi, *The Dark Tree: Jazz and the Community Arts in Los Angeles* (Berkeley: University of California Press, 2006); Philip Pastras, *Dead Man Blues: Jelly Roll Morton Way Out West* (Berkeley: University of California Press, 2001); and Horace Tapscott and Steven Louis Isoardi, *Songs of the Unsung: The Musical and Social Journey of Horace Tapscott* (Durham, NC: Duke University Press, 2001).

10. Baker, *Catalina Island*, 34–35. Also Overholt, *Catalina Story*, 25–26.

11. Avalon is the mythical paradise where King Arthur withdraws to heal his wounds and die peacefully, away from the troubles of the mortal world. Baker, *Catalina Island*, 34–35.

12. The pre-twentieth-century Anglo history of the island is covered in several sources: Baker, *Catalina Island*, 23–50; Overholt, *Catalina Story*, 20–35; Pedersen, *Catalina Island*, 9–60; and White and Tice, *Santa Catalina Island*, 21–42.

13. White and Tice, *Santa Catalina Island*, 42, 51–52; see also Overholt, *Catalina Story*, 26.

14. White and Tice, *Santa Catalina Island*, 52; see also Baker, *Catalina Island*, 60.

15. Since many of the working class that patronized Coney Island were also white "ethnics"—Jews, Italians, and Irish—Wrigley's comments contain a whiff of contempt for these recent European and East European immigrants and their offspring. Thanks to Ben Piekut for drawing my attention to this dimension of Wrigley's statement. For a discussion of the character and development of Coney Island during the twentieth century, see Gary S. Cross and John K. Walton, *The Playful Crowd: Pleasure Places in the Twentieth Century* (New York: Columbia University Press, 2005), 131–40.

16. White and Tice, *Santa Catalina Island*, 57.

17. Baker, *Catalina Island*, 60–66.

18. Some of these attempts at re-creating an "early" California ambience are detailed in "Flag Presentation at Casino on Saturday," *Catalina Islander*,

July 18, 1940. Photographs also bear witness to Philip K. Wrigley's project. See the images in Pedersen, *Catalina Island*, 97–128. For other discussions of Philip K.'s transformation of Avalon, see Moore, *Casino*, 124–26, and White and Tice, *Santa Catalina Island*, 66.

19. Paul M. Angle, *Philip K. Wrigley: A Memoir of a Modest Man* (Chicago: Rand McNally, 1975), 55.

20. For the film industry on Catalina, see White and Tice, *Santa Catalina Island*, 109–22, and *Hollywood's Magical Island: Catalina*, dir. Greg Reitman, Blue Water Entertainment/Hollywood Isle, 2003. William Sanford White and Steven Kern Tice, *Santa Catalina Island Goes to War: World War II, 1941–1945* (Glendora, CA: White Limited Editions, 1997), covers Catalina during wartime.

21. The post-1975 struggles of Catalina's tourist economy are detailed in Marty Cohen, "No Tourists, No Money: Avalon's Problem, How to End Off-Season Stagnation," *Los Angeles Times*, September 26, 1971; and Bonnie Harris, "Catalina Weighs Growth Options as Tourism Ebbs," *Los Angeles Times*, July 4, 2001. The websites of the Conservancy and SCIC offer brief histories of their organizations: Catalina Island Conservancy, "About Us," http://www.catalinaconservancy.org/about/history/index.htm; and Santa Catalina Island Company, "About Us," http://www.visitcatalinais land.com.

22. Detailed information on the architectural dimensions of the building are available in a press release by the Publicity Bureau of the William Wrigley Jr. Interests, "Salient Facts about the New Catalina Casino, Briefed for Convenient Reference," Santa Catalina Island Museum Research Center. See also Moore, *Casino*, 17–22.

23. "Salient Facts about the New Catalina Casino"; see also Moore, *Casino*, 77. Remodeled in 1994, the impressive theater was largely devoted to showing movies, though other theatrical events were also held in the room during the 1930s and '40s. Bandleader Kay Kyser held his popular radio show, *Kay Kyser's College of Musical Knowledge*, in the theater (the band also played the ballroom above). See Moore, *Casino*, 110.

24. Moore, *Casino*, 75.

25. "Salient Facts about the New Catalina Casino."

26. Moore, *Casino*, 39–45.

27. "Salient Facts about the New Catalina Casino."

28. Moore, *Casino*, 45–54.

29. Salient Facts about the New Catalina Casino"; see also Moore, *Casino*, 27.

30. Guy Stafford, "Catalina Casino Opened, Island Fashion Revue Intrigues Eyes," *Los Angeles Times*, May 30, 1929.

31. In her history of the building, Moore reproduces a similar photo, taken at the same event, that shows the arrival, in yet another chest, of "Miss Catalina," a costumed young girl. The two black adolescents are also present but are turned to face the scene behind them; see Moore, *Casino*, 31.

32. Ibid.

33. The island did have a small Chicano community: the *Catalina Islander* documents a Cinco de Mayo celebration by the "Mexican residents of Avalon." Photos of mariachi bands in front of buildings modeled on old Mexican ranches of California before annexation suggest that, at least by the 1930s, Philip K. Wrigley found the presence of a Mexican community useful in imparting a more authentic sense of early California to his island experience. While the ballroom was almost certainly segregated in terms of white and black, the position of Chicanos in Avalon is less clear— the local newspaper's photos of graduating high school seniors show that a small number of these students were integrated into the tiny public school system on the island; see *Catalina Islander*, June 23, 1938.

34. Occasionally newspapers record the rare appearance of a prominent African American on the island. A *Los Angeles Times* article from 1935 announces a boxing match between the white Wally Hally and the "clever Negro" Archie Grant to be held at the Avalon Athletic Club on August 9; see "Training No Drudgery for Wally Hally," *Los Angeles Times*, August 9, 1935. White writes of an incident about 1950 where angry residents confronted Malcolm Renton regarding a rumor about the sale of a home to "Negroes." Renton reported the situation to Philip K. Wrigley, who then allegedly dismissed the complaint, arguing that those who were upset should read the United States Constitution. Regardless of the accuracy of this account, it certainly provides additional circumstantial evidence of the absence of any significant African American presence on the island. William Sanford White and Kim Lianne Stotts, *The Wrigley Family: A Legacy of Leadership in Santa Catalina Island* (Glendora, CA: White Limited Editions and White Family Trust, 2005), 65.

35. There were occasionally black performers, however, at the neighboring Hotel St. Catherine, another venue for musicians visiting the island. When Benny Goodman's band was hired to play the Casino Ballroom in 1940, he apparently used an all-white version of his band, despite the presence in the group of several prominent African American musicians such as vibraphonist Lionel Hampton and guitarist Charlie Christian. Photos of the Goodman Orchestra from Catalina show the band without Hampton or Christian (Moore, *Casino*, 91). Live recordings, though, have survived of Goodman leading his smaller sextet with Hampton and Christian at the Hotel St. Catherine. Another photo, available at Leo Valdes's website, allegedly shows Christian on the ferry to (or from) Catalina Island in 1940, http://home.elp.rr.com/valdes/photos.htm. The live broadcasts from the Hotel St. Catherine are available on disc 3 of *Charlie Christian: Complete Live Recordings* (four CDs), Definitive Records/Disconform sl DRCD11177, 2000.

36. Burton W. Peretti, *The Creation of Jazz: Music, Race, and Culture in Urban America* (Urbana: University of Illinois Press, 1992), 177–210. See also

Erenberg, *Swingin' the Dream*, 49–50. Although many cities in the West implemented segregation policies, Los Angeles had an especially bitter history of racial discrimination and violence. Real estate "covenants" restricted the overwhelming majority of blacks to the south central part of the city, and many city leaders were vocal in support of such segregation. Although nightclub policies regarding the booking of nonwhite bands varied and many venues did not hire black bands, there were many places where whites could hear African American bands. For a detailed exploration of African American musical life in Los Angeles during the 1930s and '40s, see Ralph Eastman, "Pitchin' Up a Boogie," in *California Soul: Music of African Americans in the West*, ed. Jacqueline Cogdell DjeDje and Eddie S. Meadows (Berkeley: University of California Press, 1998), 79–103; and Levin, *Classic Jazz*. For a survey of black life in Los Angeles in the years before World War II, see Douglas Flamming, *Bound for Freedom: Black Los Angeles in Jim Crow America* (Berkeley: University of California Press, 2005).

37. These photographs are available in a series of poster-sized displays in the Catalina Island Museum.

38. The first African American band to be displayed is Fletcher Henderson's "ghost" band of 1961 (Henderson died in 1952). A "ghost band" is the informal name for dance bands that continued playing, touring, and recording after the death of their leaders. "Ghost Band," *Grove Music Online*, ed. L. Macy, http://www.grovemusic.com (accessed March 9, 2008).

39. As George Yoshida has documented, during these years Los Angeles boasted many Japanese American dance bands that played mostly for local community events; see George Yoshida, *Reminiscing in Swingtime: Japanese Americans in American Popular Music: 1925–1960* (San Francisco: National Japanese American Historical Society, 1997).

40. Moore, *Casino*, 85.

41. Ibid., 86.

42. Erenberg, *Swingin' the Dream*, 13–24.

43. Ibid., 53.

44. For instance, listen to the Barnet Orchestra's recording of "I Hear a Rhapsody" (1940) and the Dorsey's band's string-laden version of "Street of Dreams" (1942), a song discussed in the introduction.

45. Bindas, *Swing, That Modern Sound*, 13–19. For an excellent history of this debate on the definition of swing versus jazz styles and the relation of both of these to bebop, see Bernard Gendron, " 'Moldy Figs' and Modernists: Jazz at War (1942–1946)," in *Jazz among the Discourses*, ed. Krin Gabbard (Durham, NC: Duke University Press, 1995), 31–56. John Gennari provides a detailed history of jazz critics and their ideological battles in *Blowin' Hot and Cool: Jazz and Its Critics* (Chicago: University of Chicago Press, 2006).

46. Even defining swing as a distinct style of jazz was not at all clear to writers, fans, and musicians of the time. During the late 1930s, Duke Ellington defined swing as a "distinct class of music," and something he helped develop, while also asserting that the jazz that emerged in New Orleans was "something pretty close to swing." Drummer Zutty Singleton believed swing was "just a modern term to denote jazz," while Jimmy Dorsey asserted that jazz was "that old stuff," and swing was "modern" and organized. The historiography of jazz, especially from the 1950s on, resolved these complexities in favor of a single, straightforward narrative. Swing was "a stage in the development of jazz characterized by written arrangements and performed by big bands—or small ensembles culled from those bands—during the 1930s and 40s." Stowe, *Swing Changes*, 5. Scott DeVeaux presents an incisive critique of this historiographical consensus in his essay "Constructing the Jazz Tradition: Jazz Historiography," *Black American Literature Forum* 25, no. 3 (Autumn 1991): 525–60. Period designations vary, but most historians situate this musical style between the late 1920s and just after World War II, ending sometime between 1946 and 1948. Kenneth Bindas, for example, dates the genre he is analyzing as 1935–47 (Bindas, *Swing, That Modern Sound*, 18–19). Lewis Erenberg suggests roughly the same years, 1935–48 (Erenberg, *Swingin' the Dream*, xi). David Stowe offers 1935–45 (Stowe, *Swing Changes*, 1). Gunther Schuller offers the broadest conception, tracing the emergence of the big bands to the early 1930s and lasting until 1945, the last great year before many of the most famous groups disbanded. (Schuller, *Swing Era*).

47. An early and influential attempt to objectively define "hotness" as a specifically African-derived approach to rhythm is Richard A. Waterman's "'Hot' Rhythm in Negro Music," *Journal of the American Musicological Society* 1, no. 1 (Spring 1948): 24–37. In his pioneering study *Jazz: Hot and Hybrid* (1938; New York: Da Capo Press, 1975), Winthrop Sargeant provides a surprisingly complex analysis of hot and sweet music, asserting that both are in fact jazz. In most jazz histories, hot and sweet are separated more distinctly, with clear linkages claimed between "hot" and African or African American culture; see Louis Harap, "The Case for Hot Jazz," *Musical Quarterly* 27, no. 1 (January 1941): 47–61, and Frank Tirro, *Jazz: A History*, 2nd ed. (New York: W. W. Norton, 1993), 173.

48. In his biography of Fletcher Henderson, Jeffrey Magee provides a useful discussion of stock arrangements and the publishing practices of music firms during the 1920s and '30s. Jeffrey Magee, *The Uncrowned King of Swing: Fletcher Henderson and Big Band Jazz* (New York: Oxford University Press, 2005), 39–71.

49. Paul Eduard Miller, "Blind Critics Add Confusion to Jazz. . . . Symphonic, Sweet, and Hot Jazz Need Real Standards of Comparison," *Down Beat*, September 1936, 2.

50. Many scholars have examined jazz critics of the era and their diverse and often competing sets of aesthetic and political commitments. See Stowe, *Swing Changes*, 50–93; Erenberg, *Swingin' the Dream*, 120–49; and Gennari, *Blowin' Hot and Cool*, 19–163.

51. The idea that swing was a commercial music, cynically devised, marketed, and sold to Americans to make a quick buck is an idea that still percolates through scholarship on the music. Discussing the influence of recordings—the products of an increasingly centralized, national music industry—historian Kenneth Bindas writes that "many of the musicians learned how to play jazz or swing from records." These musicians "were inspired less from the improvisational nature of the music and were drawn more to the formula performance exposed to them through the radio or phonograph." This assessment is clearly a legacy of the earlier critique of swing as a vapid invention of the money-driven culture industry. Bindas is correct in that there may have been less unfettered improvisation in the larger bands of the late 1930s and 1940s, but there was still plenty of solo space. More important, musicians learned about timbre and rhythm, attributes just as important. Bindas's assessment also eliminates the arranger in the reception of swing—interesting, compelling arrangements were inspirational to musicians who heard them and tried to incorporate into their playing the harmonic or melodic concepts they heard. Bindas, *Swing, That Modern Sound*, 36–37.

52. Trumpeter Mario Bauza called swing a "big promotion. . . . a gimmick" meant to sell the American people something that had been played for years. Bindas, *Swing, That Modern Sound*, 17–19.

53. In some cases, sweet and hot were considered real but not necessarily pejorative divisions. Polls in magazines like *Down Beat* let readers pick their favorite groups in each category, showing the results right next to each other. Furthermore, many of the hot bands showed up in the sweet polls, too. See "Have You Voted for Your Favorite Swing Musician Yet?" *Down Beat*, May 1936; "Contest Results," *Down Beat*, January 1, 1940; "Final Poll Results," *Down Beat*, January 1, 1941, 12.

54. *Benny Goodman at the Madhattan Room*, lp, Sunbeam Records (SB-118), 1972.

55. "Hepper Musicians Choose Leading Band," *Metronome*, June 1940.

56. "Contest Results," *Down Beat*, January 1, 1940; "Final Poll Results," *Down Beat*, January 1, 1941.

57. Andy Kirk, *Twenty Years on Wheels*, as told to Amy Lee, discography compiled by Howard Rye (Ann Arbor: University of Michigan Press, 1989), 1, 57, 71, 73–74, 87. Also, Erenberg, *Swingin' the Dream*, 173.

58. An exception to these standard discussions of hot and sweet jazz is Krin Gabbard's analysis of bandleader Kay Kyser's film appearances. See Krin Gabbard, *Jammin' at the Margins: Jazz and the American Cinema* (Chicago: University of Chicago Press, 1996), 19–33.

59. Christopher Wilkinson, *Jazz on the Road: Don Albert's Musical Life* (Berkeley: University of California Press, 2001), 83–84.

60. Elijah Wald, "Louis Armstrong Loves Guy Lombardo!" *Jazz Research Journal* 1, no. 1 (2007): 135. See also Magee, *Uncrowned King of Swing*, 138.

61. Wald, "Louis Armstrong Loves Guy Lombardo!" 144. See also Gennari, *Blowin' Hot and Cool*, 99–100.

62. Radano, *Lying Up a Nation*, 230–77.

63. Ibid., 4.

64. Concerned mainly with discursive issues, Radano sidesteps musical analysis. For a discussion of the relation between musical sounds and notions of black music, see David Brackett, *Interpreting Popular Music* (1995; Berkeley: University of California Press, 2000), 108–56.

65. Erenberg, *Swingin' the Dream*, 49–50.

66. Stowe, *Swing Changes*, 42–44.

67. David M. Renton to J. C. Houck, July 5, 1932, Santa Catalina Island Museum Research Center.

68. Alas, Renton's prediction of bigger and better things for the Houck Orchestra proved untrue. The band is not listed or discussed in either George Simon's *Big Bands* or Leo Walker's *Big Band Almanac*, two comprehensive, if dated, listings of bands. I have not found any recordings commercially available, and Internet searches have turned up nothing.

69. For example, Samuel A. Floyd Jr., *The Power of Black Music: Interpreting Its History from Africa to the United States* (New York: Oxford University Press, 1995), 96, and Gunther Schuller, *Early Jazz: Its Roots and Musical Development* (1968; New York: Oxford University Press, 1986), 54–57.

70. Paul Whiteman's famous concert at Carnegie Hall was labeled an "experiment," and the bandleader himself organized the program to demonstrate the evolution of jazz. In his own writing Whiteman reports being worried when audience members, and later critics, appeared to love the opening small combo jazz number, designed as an explicit parody of such unpolished groups as the Original Dixieland Jazz Band. For Whiteman, the ODJB's "Livery Stable Blues" was a "million miles" from the sophisticated symphonic jazz of Gershwin's "Rhapsody in Blue," and the concert was intended to show the progress jazz had undergone in such a short time. See Paul Whiteman and Mary Margaret McBride, *Jazz* (1926; New York: Arno Press, 1974), 94, 99, 104.

71. "Salient Facts about the New Catalina Casino."

72. Moore, *Casino*, 108–9. Philip K. Wrigley tells the story of raising the Casino's profile through radio broadcasts of name bands in a rare 1972 interview for the *Los Angeles Times*; see Digby Diehl, "Q & A: Philip K. Wrigley," *Los Angeles Times*, June 10, 1972. This new booking policy is also evident in the articles on bands featured in the *Catalina Islander*. Reporting on the imminent arrival of Little Jack Little, the unnamed reporter writes,

"His engagement for Santa Catalina Island brings to the coast another nationally famed orchestra which is heard daily over the coast-to-coast network. The vision of Philip K. Wrigley in bringing to the island the biggest orchestras the country affords means much to the cultural progress of the coast and places Santa Catalina Island on a par with the fashionable watering resorts of the Atlantic seaboard." "Casino to Open," *Catalina Islander*, May 14, 1936.

73. Diehl, "Q & A," *Los Angeles Times*, June 10, 1972.

74. Though far from an infallible tool, *Down Beat*'s annual readers' polls provide a helpful index of which bands were generally considered "hot" versus "sweet." Significantly, many bands fall into both categories: the bands of Duke Ellington, Glenn Miller, Tommy Dorsey, and Paul Whiteman are ranked in both "hot" and "sweet" categories. Interestingly, in the overwhelming majority of cases the reverse is not true: bands like those of Dick Jurgens, Jan Garber, and Kay Kyser do not appear in the hot columns.

75. From 1935 through the beginning of World War II, the Frank Sortino Orchestra and the Capolungo Orchestra played at yearly benefits sponsored by President Roosevelt for the fight against infantile paralysis. See Moore, *Casino*, 92.

76. Ibid., 79–84. According to Ann Wagner, traditional religious opponents of close couple dancing were not too concerned with the various types of partner dancing created for big band dance music, like the Lindy Hop or the jitterbug. These were athletic dances, and partners stayed farther apart than in the more troubling movements of the tango or the waltz. See Ann Wagner, *Adversaries of Dance: From the Puritans to the Present* (Urbana: University of Illinois Press, 1997), 320–59. Stowe echoes this point in his summary of the various reactions to the swing fad of post-1935. See Stowe, *Swing Changes*, 23–30. The managers of the Casino Ballroom were expressing anachronistic concerns about partner dancing, out of step with the rest of the nation.

77. Lewis Erenberg writes, "Whatever the setting, white jitterbugs crossed racial barriers by doing black dances. Not only did whites and blacks perform similar dances, whites acknowledged that the steps originated in black culture and that the best dancers were black" (Erenberg, *Swingin' the Dream*, 49–50).

78. Milton Coffin, "Avalon Varieties," *Catalina Islander*, June 3, 1937.

79. Lew C. Oesterle, "Doings at the Casino," *Catalina Islander*, June 24, 1937. Apparently not all dance halls were so well ordered. In an article from the following year, columnist Milton Coffin expresses dismay at the informality of young dancers he saw during a visit to Santa Monica, on the mainland; there were very few requests of "May I have the next dance?" But at the Casino ballroom "one will see a lot of swing dancing (in moderation)," but there was waltzing too. See Milton L. Coffin, "Avalon Varieties," *Catalina Islander*, June 9, 1938.

80. "Doings at the Casino," *Catalina Islander*, August 13, 1936.
81. "Avalon," in Thomas S. Hischak, *The Tin Pan Alley Song Encyclopedia* (Westport, CT: Greenwood Press, 2002), 25; Roger Lax and Frederick Smith, eds., *The Great Song Thesaurus* (New York: Oxford University Press, 1989), 43, 191.
82. Hal Holley, *Tempo*'s "Hollywood Reporter," featured column with no title, *Tempo*, December 1936, 6.
83. Ibid. This story is unverifiable, however satisfying it might be to think that the Wrigleys actually paid Jolson for the free advertising of their revitalized resort town.
84. For information on approximate record sales, see Edward Foote Gardner, *Popular Songs of the Twentieth Century: A Charted History*, vol. 1, *1900–1949* (St. Paul, MN: Paragon House, 2000), 249–50, 332.
85. Since the mid-1940s the song has been recorded by a wide range of artists in jazz, pop, and even country. Bob Crosby, Chet Atkins, Al Hirt, Nat King Cole with the Count Basie Orchestra, Charlie Ventura, Erroll Garner, Art Farmer and the Jazztet, Elmo Hope, Red Holloway, Natalie Cole, and Harry Connick Jr. have all recorded the tune; see Hischak, *Tin Pan Alley*, 25.
86. In the 1940s, Bob Crosby's New Orleans–revival big band recorded a version of "Avalon" that is a superb example of this tension between modern, Tin Pan Alley–based dance band music and earlier polyphonic New Orleans small combo jazz. See *Those Swingin' Days of the Big Bands!* Showcase Records, Pickwick Intl., SH-3301, n.d.
87. Dave Hickey, *Air Guitar: Essays on Art and Democracy* (Los Angeles: Art Issues Press, 1997), 81.
88. Simon, *Big Bands*, 328–29. See Eddy Determeyer's *Rhythm Is Our Business: Jimmie Lunceford and the Harlem Express* (Ann Arbor: University of Michigan Press, 2006) for a full historical treatment of this underappreciated band.
89. Gunther Schuller and Martin Williams, liner notes, *Big Band Jazz: From the Beginnings to the Fifties* (Washington, DC: Smithsonian Collection of Recordings, 1983), 21–22.
90. Simon, *Big Bands*, 333.
91. Lunceford died while on the road with his band, just before a concert in Seaside, Oregon. The local coroner put down heart attack as the official cause of death, but almost immediately rumors began that something else killed the bandleader: a cerebral hemorrhage, unusual eating habits (too many sweet peppers), an airplane crash, a gangland murder. In his recent biography of Lunceford, Eddy Determeyer suggests food poisoning, possibly intentional. Earlier, on their way to Seaside, the band stopped in a Portland diner for supper. After being refused service, Lunceford lost his temper. The restaurant finally relented, and Determeyer believes the tainted food might have been served in retaliation against Lunceford's public display of anger. Determeyer, *Rhythm Is Our Business*, 230–42.

92. The performance discussed here, arranged by Eddie Durham and recorded in 1935, is very well known and has even appeared as part of Jazz at Lincoln Center's educational *Essential Jazz Editions* series, a collection of big band charts transcribed from famous recordings and designed for study and performance. Information on the published series is at http://www .jazzatlincolncenter.org/prod/elli/editions.html.

93. Simon, *Big Bands*, 330.

94. Floyd, *Power of Black Music*, 96.

95. Simon, *Big Bands*, 117; see also Schuller, *Swing Era*, 632–45.

96. Schuller, *Swing Era*, 633.

97. Simon, *Big Bands*, 120.

98. Ibid., 122.

99. Erenberg, *Swingin' the Dream*, 82.

100. Schuller, *Swing Era*, 635.

101. Simon, *Big Bands*, 492.

102. Ibid. Along with Simon, background on Jan Garber, his band, and their music comes from several other sources: Leo Walker, liner notes, *The Uncollected Jan Garber and His Orchestra*, 1939–1941, Hindsight Records (HSR-130), 1978; Paul F. Roth, liner notes, Jan Garber, "The Idol of the Air Lanes," and His Orchestra, *A Melody from the Sky*, Living Era (CD AJA 5326), 2004; Con Good, "At 75, the 'Idol' Rolls Along," *Dancing USA*, June/July 2000, 27. Occasional articles in jazz periodicals are also helpful, for example: "Jan Garber Returns to Trianon after Catalina Trip," *Down Beat*, September 1934. A website maintained by musician Howard Schneider also has materials on Garber and the legacy of his band. http://www .jangarber.com.

103. Roth, liner notes, *Melody from the Sky*, 2004.

104. Ibid.

105. Leo Walker, liner notes, *Uncollected Jan Garber and His Orchestra*.

106. In his recent history of jazz, Alyn Shipton sums up this consensus understanding of swing band rhythm. During the early 1930s, Shipton writes, "There was a general fashion for rhythm sections to abandon the two-four of 1920s jazz, following the trend begun by [Luis] Russell and Ellington to add guitars and double basses in place of banjos and tubas, and moving towards an even four-four pulse, generated as much by smooth interaction between guitar and bass, as by drums and piano." Alyn Shipton, *A New History of Jazz* (New York: Continuum, 2001), 283. In their jazz history textbook, Henry Martin and Keith Waters make virtually the same statement—the replacement of the tuba by the string bass, the change from banjo to guitar, and the drummers' shift to the hi-hats and bass drum (from the snare drum) created a new "hard-driving swing" different from the two-beat heavy sound of earlier jazz and ragtime. Henry Martin and Keith Waters, *Jazz: The First 100 Years*, 2nd ed. (Belmont, CA: Thomson-Schirmer, 2006), 127.

107. In his massive ethnography of jazz practice, *Thinking in Jazz*, Paul Berliner documents a variety of ways musicians understand swing feel. Relevant quotations are scattered throughout the book, but for a concise discussion, see Paul Berliner, *Thinking in Jazz: The Infinite Art of Improvisation* (Chicago: University of Chicago Press, 1994), 244—47. Some researchers have sought more empirical ways to document this essential—and seemingly elusive— rhythmic feeling. The journal *Music Perception* dedicated the entire Spring 2002 issue (19, no. 3) to exploring this. Using a mixture of traditional music analysis, lab experiments, and statistical analysis, contributors offer a variety of perspectives on the microtiming involved in producing a jazz sense of swing.

108. For example, Gunther Schuller argues that the Casa Loma Orchestra, a white band that was instrumental in bringing the new big band style of jazz to the greater public, often did not swing. The players knew about it, and the "difference between jazz and dance music," but they did not fully understand the "syncopation and the true essence of black rhythm." The Casa Lomans sometimes played jazz, but because of their rhythmic limitations, they often played imitations of the real thing—illusions of jazz that captured the "spirit" of the music if not its authentic nature. Schuller, *Swing Era*, 637–40.

109. Charles Keil, "Motion and Feeling through Music," in *Music Grooves*, ed. Charles Keil and Steven Feld (Chicago: University of Chicago Press, 1994), 59.

110. Steven Feld, "Aesthetics as Iconicity of Style" (uptown title), or (downtown title) "Lift-up-over Sounding," in *Music Grooves*, ed. Charles Keil and Steven Feld (Chicago: University of Chicago Press, 1994), 109–11.

111. In her recent book *Presence and Pleasure: The Funk Grooves of James Brown and Parliament*, Anne Danielsen offers a comprehensive rethinking of what grooves are and how they work. Her work draws on Keil and Feld's *Music Grooves* but offers a significant expansion and development of their ideas of "participatory discrepancies," "vital drive," "style as process," and "feelingful participation." For the quotation above, see Anne Danielsen, *Presence and Pleasure: The Funk Groove of James Brown and Parliament* (Middletown, CT: Wesleyan University Press, 2006), 189.

112. Ibid., 163.

113. Ibid., 159, 164.

114. Robert Gold's useful *Jazz Lexicon* (1964) offers entries on "groove," "in the groove," and "groovy." He dates the second term earliest, citing sources from as early as 1936. Gold offers this definition of "in the groove": "Excellent, esp. applied to music . . . also, by extension, excellent or sophisticated." Robert S. Gold, *A Jazz Lexicon* (New York: Alfred A. Knopf, 1964), 130–31. See also Clarence Major, ed., *Juba to Jive: A Dictionary of African-American Slang* (New York: Viking, 1994), 215. Major's primary source is Gold's *Lexicon*.

115. Doron K. Antrim, *Secrets of Dance Band Success* (New York: Famous Stars, 1936), 37.

116. Keil, "Motion and Feeling through Music," 53–76. Keil's overarching concept of "participatory discrepancies" (PDs) remains a controversial hypothesis. A recent empirical study by music psychologist Matthew Butterfield challenges the perceptual reality and importance of PDs in music cognition. Critique of the idea, though, has not been limited to music psychology. A forum in a special Winter 1995 issue of *Ethnomusicology* (39, no. 1) offers a lively debate about the concept from social science and humanities scholars as well as scientists.

117. Svetlana Boym, *The Future of Nostalgia* (New York: Basic Books, 2001), xv.

118. Ibid.

119. Ibid., xvi.

120. For a helpful clarification of the term "modernization" and its close cousins "modernity" and "modernism," see Boym, *Future of Nostalgia*, 22; see also Matei Calinescu, *Five Faces of Modernity: Modernism, Avant-Garde, Decadence, Kitsch, Postmodernism* (1977; Durham, NC: Duke University Press, 1987), 13–92.

121. For a discussion of this idea, see Richard Guy Wilson, Dianne H. Pilgrim, and Dickran Tashjian, *The Machine Age in America: 1918–1941* (New York: Harry N. Abrams, 1986).

122. Levine, *Unpredictable Past*, 191.

123. Ibid., 204.

124. Susman, *Culture as History*, 154, 189–90.

125. For discussions of swing as modern, see Erenberg, *Swingin' the Dream*; Stowe, *Swing Changes*; and Bindas, *Swing, That Modern Sound*.

126. See David Goldberg, *Discontented America: The United States in the 1920s* (Baltimore: Johns Hopkins University Press, 1999), for an excellent survey of the conservative—at times reactionary—political and social movements of the 1920s.

127. Susman, *Culture as History*, 185, 196–97.

128. Max Horkheimer and Theodor W. Adorno, "The Culture Industry: Enlightenment as Mass Deception," in their 1944 *Dialectic of Enlightenment*, trans. John Cumming (New York: Continuum, 1998). For a brief but excellent discussion of Garber's approach to the business of big band music, see Walker, liner notes, *Uncollected Jan Garber and His Orchestra*.

129. Stowe, *Swing Changes*, 132.

130. Charlie Barnet with Stanley Dance, *Those Swinging Years: The Autobiography of Charlie Barnet* (1984; New York: Da Capo Press, 1992), 160–61.

131. The classic statement defining place as a location imbued with personal or social meaning is Edward C. Relph, *Place and Placelessness* (London: Pion, 1976), 42–43.

132. Radano, *Lying Up a Nation*, 236.

CHAPTER TWO

1. Liner notes by Ian Crosbie, *Charlie Barnet and His Orchestra: The Transcription Performances 1941*, compact disc, Metronome Series HEP CD53, England, 1997.
2. Ibid.
3. Charlie Barnet with Stanley Dance, *Those Swinging Years: The Autobiography of Charlie Barnet* (1984; New York: Da Capo Press, 1992), 13.
4. Ibid., 114.
5. Ibid., 18.
6. Lewis A. Erenberg, *Swingin' the Dream: Big Band Jazz and the Rebirth of American Culture* (Chicago: University of Chicago Press, 1998), 66.
7. Ibid., 65–71.
8. David Stowe, *Swing Changes: Big Band Jazz in New Deal America* (Cambridge, MA: Harvard University Press, 1994), 100.
9. Barnet, *Those Swinging Years*, 27. Also, Dan Mather, *Charlie Barnet: An Illustrated Biography and Discography* (Jefferson, NC: McFarland, 2002), 2.
10. Barnet, *Those Swinging Years*, 13.
11. Gunther Schuller, *The Swing Era: The Development of Jazz, 1930–1945* (New York: Oxford University Press, 1989), 715, 715–23.
12. Barnet, *Those Swinging Years*, 70.
13. Mather, *Charlie Barnet*, 11–12.
14. Barnet, *Those Swinging Years*, 58.
15. I have not been able to verify if the Barnet band was truly the first white jazz band to play the Apollo Theater. Barnet claims this in his autobiography, *Those Swinging Years*, 61. In his bio-discography, Dan Mather suggests he *may* have been the first. Mather, *Charlie Barnet*, 14.
16. Morris Dickstein, "Depression Culture: The Dream of Mobility," in *Radical Revisions: Rereading 1930s Culture*, ed. Bill Mullen and Sherry Lee Linkon (Urbana: University of Illinois Press, 1996), 225–41.
17. Josh Kun, *Audiotopia: Music, Race, and America* (Berkeley: University of California Press, 2005), 2.
18. Andy Razaf and Paul Denniker, "Make Believe Ballroom," 1936.
19. For a discussion of Block, his show, and its important ramifications in the music business of the time, see Russell Sanjek and David Sanjek, *Pennies from Heaven: The American Popular Music Business in the Twentieth Century* (New York: Da Capo Press, 1996), 128–30; also, Erik Barnouw, *The Golden Web, 1933–1953*, vol. 2 of *A History of Broadcasting in the United States* (New York: Oxford University Press, 1968), 217–19.
20. Barnet, *Those Swinging Years*, 71.
21. Susan J. Douglas, *Listening In: Radio and the American Imagination, from Amos 'n' Andy and Edward R. Murrow to Wolfman Jack and Howard Stern* (New York: Times Books/Random House, 1999), 83.

22. Stowe, *Swing Changes*, 132.

23. Georg Simmel, "Bridge and Door," in *Rethinking Architecture*, ed. Neil Leach (New York: Routledge, 1997), 66.

24. "Pompton Turnpike," words and music by Will Osborne and Dick Rodgers, recorded by Charlie Barnet and His Orchestra, New York, July 19, 1940.

25. *Original Performances of Big Band Themes on The Air, 1932–1946*, First Time Records, Portland, OR (FTR-2501), n.d.

26. Marshall Berman, *All That Is Solid Melts into Air: The Experience of Modernity* (1982; New York: Penguin Books, 1988), 295.

27. Bennet Schaber, "Hitler Can't Keep 'em That Long," in *The Road Movie Book*, ed. Steven Cohan and Ina Rae Hark (New York: Routledge, 1997), 30.

28. Kathleen Moran and Michael Rogin, "'What's the Matter with Capra?': Sullivan's Travels and the Popular Front," *Representations* 71 (Summer 2000), 106–34.

29. Ilya Ilf and Eugene Petrov, *Little Golden America: Two Famous Soviet Humorists Survey These United States*, trans. Charles Malamuth, Foreign Travelers in America, 1810–1935 (1937; New York: Arno Press, 1976), 76, 81.

30. For illustrations and descriptions of the Futurama exhibit see Larry Zim, Mel Lerner, and Herbert Rolfes, *The World of Tomorrow: The 1939 New York World's Fair* (New York: Harper and Row, 1988), 108–15. Norman Bel Geddes offers more illustrations along with explanations for his designs of the exhibit in *Magic Motorways* (New York: Random House, 1940).

31. John Brinckerhoff Jackson, *A Sense of Time, a Sense of Place* (New Haven, CT: Yale University Press, 1994), 6.

32. John B. Rae, *The Road and the Car in American Life* (Cambridge, MA: MIT Press, 1971), 51; John C. Spychalski, "Transportation," in *The Columbia History of the 20th Century*, ed. Richard W. Bulliet (New York: Columbia University Press, 1998), 403–36.

33. Rae, *Road and the Car in American Life*, 49.

34. Mark H. Rose, *Interstate: Express Highway Politics, 1941–1956* (Lawrence: Regents Press of Kansas, 1979), ix.

35. Rae, *Road and the Car in American Life*, 49–50.

36. Rose, *Interstate*, 3.

37. Robert Lynd and Helen Merrell Lynd, *Middletown in Transition: A Study in Cultural Conflicts* (1937; New York: Harcourt Brace Jovanovich, 1982), 265.

38. Stephen B. Goddard, *Getting There: The Epic Struggle between Road and Rail in the American Century* (Chicago: University of Chicago Press, 1994), 157.

39. Rose, *Interstate*, 4.

40. Joseph Interrante, "The Road to Autopia: The Automobile and the Spatial Transformation of American Culture," *Michigan Quarterly Review*, 15–16 (Fall 1980–Winter 1981): 508.

41. Bruce Crowther and Mike Pinfold, *The Big Band Years* (New York: Facts on File, 1988), 54.

42. Goddard, *Getting There*, 162.

43. Tom Lewis, *Divided Highways: Building the Interstate Highways, Transforming American Life* (New York: Penguin Books, 1997), 47.

44. Dan McNichol, *The Roads That Built America: The Incredible Story of the U.S. Interstate Highway System* (New York: Barnes and Noble, 2003), 82–83.

45. Goddard, *Getting There*, 162; for a detailed account of the construction of the Pennsylvania Turnpike, see Lewis, *Divided Highways*, 47–70.

46. Lewis, *Divided Highways*, 68–69.

47. Rose, *Interstate*, x.

48. Interrante, "Road to Autopia," 504–8, 517.

49. Jackson, *Sense of Time, a Sense of Place*, 6.

50. According to the online *Oxford English Dictionary*, the word "turnpike" is found in sources as early as 1420 to describe a kind of "spike barrier in or across a road or passage" as protection against intruders. Over time the word lost its military connotations, becoming a more general term for any kind of barrier across a road to control access. Since the mid-eighteenth century, the word has become shorthand for "Turnpike Road" and refers to any road that collects tolls for its use. "Turnpike," *Oxford English Dictionary Online*, Oxford University Press, 2005, http://www.oed.com, accessed April 23, 2005.

51. Andy Newman, "Bloomfield Avenue's Twists and Turns," *New York Times*, December 13, 1998; see also Steven Anderson, http://www.nycroads.com/roads/NJ-23/, accessed April 23, 2005.

52. Lon A. Gault, *Ballroom Echoes* (n.p.: Andrew Corbet Press, 1989), 46–49. Gault writes that Cab Calloway was the first black band to play the venue in 1940. This is not true: the Count Basie Orchestra played there in 1937, as did Fats Waller's band. See Chris Sheridan, ed., *Count Basie: A Bio-Discography* (New York: Greenwood Press, 1986), 109.

53. Irving Kolodin, "The Dance Band Business: A Study in Black and White," *Harper's*, June 1941.

54. Timothy D. May, "Back in the Swing—Church Converting Music Hall Where Sinatra Sang for a Quarter," *Record* (New Jersey), December 16, 1999.

55. This story is in Phillip Edward Jaeger, *Cedar Grove (New Jersey)*, Images of America (Mount Pleasant, SC: Arcadia, 2000), 51.

56. Barry Kernfeld, ed., "Nightclubs and Other Venues: America/Cedar Grove, New Jersey/Meadowbrook Inn," *Grove Dictionary of Jazz* (1988; New York: St. Martin's Press, 1994), 863; Jaeger, *Cedar Grove*, 48–53.

57. Kathleen O'Brien, "Childhood Memories of the '40s: Edwin Burke," *Newark Star-Ledger*, February 29, 2008.

58. Kolodin, "Dance Band Business."

59. May, "Back in the Swing"; e-mail communication, Chris Werndly, president, Cedar Grove Historical Society, October 20, 2006.

60. Michael Melody, "Ramblin' along Tin Pan Alley," *Down Beat*, June 15, 1940.

61. "Our next stop after the Playland Casino was Frank Dailey's Meadowbrook on the Pompton Turnpike in New Jersey, just outside Newark. It was a famous spot for bands, but for the summer Dailey had an outdoor setting surrounded by big trees. The dance floor had tables all around from either side of the bandstand, and altogether it made a picturesque scene." Barnet, *Those Swinging Years*, 85.

62. Reebee Garofalo, *Rockin' Out: Popular Music in the USA* (Boston: Allyn and Bacon, 1997), 124–25. Garofalo has a useful chart featuring the many "car" (and "bird") named Doo Wop groups from the 1950s and early 1960s. Not only does Chuck Berry's music represent the most paradigmatic fusion of the musical characteristics constituting rock 'n' roll, but his lyrics deal extensively with America's automobile culture, part of the country's post–World War II economic expansion and consumer culture. See Paul Gilroy's discussion of the two Berry songs "Maybelline" and "No Particular Place to Go" in *Darker Than Blue: On the Moral Economies of Black Atlantic Culture* (Cambridge, MA: Harvard University Press, 2010), 28–30.

63. The concept of a virtual, unheard rhythmic structure is borrowed from Anne Danielsen's study of funk music. Anne Danielsen, *Presence and Pleasure: The Funk Grooves of James Brown and Parliament* (Middletown, CT: Wesleyan University Press, 2006), 46–48.

64. "Virtual room of sound" is from Danielsen's rhythmic analysis of 1960s and '70s funk. Danielsen, *Presence and Pleasure*, 52.

65. Billy May was so good that Glenn Miller, then leader of arguably the most successful white swing band, hired him away from Barnet in 1940. Jack Mirtle, ed., *The Music of Billy May: A Discography* (Westport, CT: Greenwood Press, 1998), 6–7.

66. In his influential study of swing-era jazz, David Stowe correlates this balance between individual and collective expression in the music with the larger social developments of the New Deal. He writes that the "turn away from the loose, open-ended, and non-hierarchical playing of the 1920s jazz toward the more regimented modes of swing registered the move toward larger, more bureaucratic, and more rationalized units of organization characteristic of American society during the 1930s. It was analogous to the arrangements worked out among business, unions, and the government under the New Deal, for example. Swing's much noted quality of enabling the individual voice to contribute to the collective whole also accords well with the notion of a cooperative commonwealth central to Franklin Roosevelt's vision of America." David Stowe, *Swing Changes: Big-Band Jazz in New Deal America* (Cambridge, MA: Harvard University Press, 1994), 10–11.

67. Schuller, *Swing Era*, 717.

68. The basic discussion of the concept of "Signifyin(g)" is in Henry Louis Gates Jr., *The Signifying Monkey: A Theory of African-American Literary*

Criticism (New York: Oxford University Press, 1988). For applications to music see Robert Walser, "Out of Notes: Signification, Interpretation, and the Problem of Miles Davis," *Musical Quarterly* 77, no. 2 (Summer 1993): 343–65; Gary Tomlinson, "Cultural Dialogics and Jazz: A White Historian Signifies," *Black Music Research Journal* 22 (2002): 71–105; and Ingrid Monson, *Saying Something: Jazz Improvisation and Interaction* (Chicago: University Chicago Press, 1996), 103–6.

69. Crowther and Pinfold, *Big Band Years*, 57–58.
70. Ibid., 54–55.
71. Peter Townsend, *Pearl Harbor Jazz: Change in Popular Music in the Early 1940s* (Jackson: University Press of Mississippi, 2007), 101–6.
72. Ibid., 54.
73. Andy Kirk, Amy Lee, and Howard Rye, *Twenty Years on Wheels* (Ann Arbor: University of Michigan Press, 1989), 88–89.
74. George T. Simon, *The Big Bands* (1967; New York: Macmillan, 1969), 333.
75. Crowther and Pinfold, *Big Band Years*, 54.
76. Kirk, *Twenty Years on Wheels*, 115.
77. Clyde McCoy, "A Thousand and One-Night Stands," *Down Beat*, January 1, 1935.
78. Kirk, *Twenty Years on Wheels*, 52.
79. "400 Mile Limit on One-Nighters," *Down Beat*, July 1, 1941.
80. Crowther and Pinfold, *Big Band Years*, 55.
81. Kirk, *Twenty Years on Wheels*, 52.
82. Townsend, *Pearl Harbor Jazz*, 107–10.
83. Crowther and Pinfold, *Big Band Years*, 54.
84. "Skinnay Ennis Band Accident One of Worst," *Down Beat*, July 15, 1941.
85. "Six Musicians Killed in Crash on One Nighter," *Down Beat*, November 1, 1941.
86. Crowther and Pinfold, *Big Band Years*, 55.
87. Bill Crow, *Jazz Anecdotes* (New York: Oxford University Press, 1990), 70–71, 75.
88. Scott DeVeaux, *The Birth of Bebop: A Social and Musical History* (Berkeley: University of California Press, 1997), 240.
89. Ibid., 251–53.
90. Ibid., 243.
91. Ibid.
92. Barnet, *Those Swinging Years*, 114–15.
93. Kirk, *Twenty Years on Wheels*, 88–89.
94. Crow, *Jazz Anecdotes*, 78.
95. Ibid.
96. Gilroy, *Darker Than Blue*, 35.
97. Erenberg, *Swingin' the Dream*, 174–78, provides a concise account of the specific problems black bands faced while on the road.
98. Kirk, *Twenty Years on Wheels*, 77.

99. Ibid., 114. According to Kirk, "Billy Butler, the head of Travelguide, could confidently proclaim, 'Vacation, recreation, without humiliation.'"

100. The companion book for Ken Burns's television series *Jazz* contains some photographs and insightful reminiscences about the difficulties faced by black traveling bands. Geoffrey C. Ward and Ken Burns, *Jazz: A History of America's Music* (New York: Alfred A. Knopf, 2000), 250–51.

101. Barnet, *Those Swinging Years*, 95.

102. Kirk, *Twenty Years on Wheels*, 88.

103. Ibid., 92.

104. Simon, *Big Bands*, 335.

105. Crowther and Pinfold, *Big Band Years*, 55.

106. See chapter 3.

107. A discussion of the difficulties of securing steady hotel work is in Kirk, *Twenty Years on Wheels*, 94.

108. Ibid., 89.

109. Ibid., 75.

110. Crowther and Pinfold, *Big Band Years*, 54.

111. Though, with few exceptions, it was an overwhelmingly male community, and wives and girlfriends were rarely allowed to tour with most groups. The few women who did travel with bands faced a set of complex issues ranging from the relatively benign (personal privacy) to the very serious (sexual harassment, even violence). Sherrie Tucker, *Swing Shift: "All-Girl" Bands of the 1940s* (Durham, NC: Duke University Press, 2000), 63–69; Crowther and Pinfold, *Big Band Years*, 59–60.

112. Crowther and Pinfold, *Big Band Years*, 62.

113. Crow, *Jazz Anecdotes*, 75; another version of the story is on a detailed website on trumpeter Ron Simmonds. The site features information on Simmonds, his relationships with other jazz musicians over the years, and many oral histories of jazz musicians. http://www.jazzprofessional.com/interviews/terry%20gibbs_2.html, accessed April 23, 2005.

114. Oral History, Charlie Barnet interviewed by Patricia Willard, Smithsonian Institution Jazz Oral History Project, reel 4, 33.

115. "White Bands Big in Harlem: Barnet Kills Sepians in Debut at Apollo; Miller Big at Savoy; Feeling Reciprocal," *Metronome*, January 1940.

116. Oral History, Charlie Barnet, reel 4, 31–39.

117. Ibid., 33.

118. Barnet, *Those Swinging Years*, 144–45.

119. Loren Schoenberg, liner notes, Charlie Barnet and His Orchestra, *Drop Me Off in Harlem*, Decca Jazz/GRP (GRD-612), 1992, 7.

120. Barnet, *Those Swinging Years*, 64–65.

121. Schoenberg, liner notes, 7–8.

122. Erenberg, *Swingin' the Dream*, 206.

123. Stowe, *Swing Changes*, 130.

124. Erenberg, *Swingin' the Dream*, 203.
125. Anita O'Day with George Eells, *High Times, Hard Times* (1981; New York: Limelight Editions, 2007), 105.
126. Ibid.
127. Gilroy, *Darker Than Blue*, 34.
128. Barry Shank, "From Rice to Ice: The Face of Race in Rock and Pop," in *The Cambridge Companion to Pop and Rock*, ed. Simon Frith, Will Straw, and John Street (Cambridge: Cambridge University Press, 2001), 262.
129. Ibid., 182.
130. Barnet, *Those Swinging Years*, 69.
131. DeVeaux, *Birth of Bebop*, 256–57.
132. Barnet, *Those Swinging Years*, 101.
133. Ibid., 116–17.
134. Before Gibson, Barnet had also briefly paid Benny Carter to write arrangements for his band. Barnet, *Those Swinging Years*, 60–61, 78.
135. Ibid., 62.
136. Ronald Radano and Philip V. Bohlman, "Introduction: Music and Race, Their Past, Their Presence," in *Music and the Racial Imagination*, ed. Ronald Radano and Philip V. Bohlman (Chicago: University of Chicago Press, 2000), 8.
137. Lawrence Kramer, *Music as Cultural Practice, 1800–1900* (Berkeley: University of California Press, 1990), 1–20.
138. Albert Murray, *The Omni-Americans* (New York: Avon, 1970), 39.
139. Shank, "From Rice to Ice," 260.
140. In 1939 Barnet and his band recorded a parody of sweet jazz titled "The Wrong Idea." Unlike the Casa Loma Orchestra's more serious (though still playful) recording "White Jazz," the Barnet performance is pure silliness with its whimpering, out-of-tune trumpets, crazy "Hawaiian" guitar effects, and ridiculous vocal performances.
141. George Simon, "Barnet's—Blackest White Band of All," *Metronome*, August 1939.
142. Stowe, *Swing Changes*, 76.
143. Ibid., 76, 130.
144. Radano and Bohlman, "Introduction," 8.
145. Barnet, *Those Swinging Years*, 71–72.
146. Dickstein, "Depression Culture," 240.
147. On the development of rural and suburban roads and cross-country "trunk" highways as a solution to urban congestion and decay, see Rose, *Interstate*, 2, 15–28, 55–67, and Rae, *Road and the Car in American Life*, 214–22. Kenneth T. Jackson traces the rise of the suburbs and the decline of urban centers in *Crabgrass Frontier: The Suburbanization of the United States* (New York: Oxford University Press, 1985).
148. I am indebted to Robert Fink for pointing out this historical irony.
149. Dickstein, "Depression Culture," 240.

150. See Robert Putnam's influential sociological study on the decline of community in an atomized society, *Bowling Alone: The Collapse and Revival of American Community* (New York: Simon and Schuster, 2000). On the specific condition of rootlessness, see William Leach, *Country of Exiles: The Destruction of Place in American Life* (New York: Pantheon Books, 1999), and E. C. Relph, *Place and Placelessness* (London: Pion, 1976).

151. Dickstein, "Depression Culture," 240.

152. Gilroy, *Darker Than Blue*, 11.

153. Ibid., 22.

154. Dan Neil, "Song of the Open Road," *Chicago Tribune* (via *Los Angeles Times*) June 23, 2004. http://www.chicagotribune.com/travel/chi-040621road music.story, accessed April 23, 2005.

155. Gilroy, *Darker Than Blue*, 24–25.

156. Stowe, *Swing Changes*, 245.

CHAPTER THREE

1. Some caution is necessary with titles. According to the files of the Victor record company, Ellington's "Harlem Air Shaft" (1940) was slated to be named "Rumpus in Richmond." Still, it was Ellington who in all likelihood changed the name. Titles can neither be ignored for the music "itself" nor used unthinkingly for analysis. They are a necessary part of a work's meaning, at whatever point they are appended to the music. Titles, in other words, are partially constitutive of musical meaning. But words for Ellington were never in a separate category from his music. In his article "The Literary Ellington," Brent Hayes Edwards discusses at length the importance of titles to Ellington's broader aesthetic project of musical-literary fusion. Gunther Schuller has also discussed Ellington's predilection for programmatic works, signaled primarily by song titles. See also Brian Priestley and Alan Cohen, " 'Black, Brown and Beige,' " in *The Duke Ellington Reader*, ed. Mark Tucker (New York: Oxford University Press, 1993), 187; Brent Hayes Edwards, "The Literary Ellington," in *Uptown Conversations: The New Jazz Studies*, ed. Robert G. O'Meally, Brent Hayes Edwards, and Farah Jasmine Griffin (New York: Columbia University Press, 2004), 338; Gunther Schuller, *The Swing Era: The Development of Jazz, 1930–1945* (New York: Oxford University Press, 1989), 151–52. Dates next to song titles refer to date of first recording. W. E. Timner, ed., *Ellingtonia: The Recorded Music of Duke Ellington and His Sidemen*, 4th ed., Studies in Jazz 7 (Lanham, MD: Scarecrow Press, 1996).

2. Duke [Edward Kennedy] Ellington, *Music Is My Mistress* (1973; New York: Da Capo Press, n.d.), x–xi.

3. Duke Ellington with Stanley Dance, " 'The Art Is in the Cooking' (1962)," in *The Duke Ellington Reader*, ed. Mark Tucker, 332–38 (New York: Oxford University Press, 1993).

4. John Edward Hasse, *Beyond Category: The Life and Genius of Ellington* (New York: Da Capo Press, 1993), 354–55.

5. David Hajdu, *Lush Life: A Biography of Billy Strayhorn* (New York: Farrar Straus Giroux, 1996), 55–56.

6. Dave Hickey, *Air Guitar: Essays on Art and Democracy* (Los Angeles: Art Issues Press, 1997), 81.

7. Terry A. Cooney, *Balancing Acts: American Thought and Culture in the 1930s* (New York: Twayne, 1995), 117–28.

8. In fact, the decade begins with two important civil rights achievements. First, A. Philip Randolph, after threatening a massive protest march in Washington, DC, in 1941, successfully pressured President Roosevelt to issue Executive Order 8802 making antidiscrimination in the defense industries government policy. A year later, in 1942, black activists created the Congress of Racial Equality (CORE), a group that introduced many of the direct action tactics adopted by later activists in the 1950s.

9. For discussions of black life on the homefront during the Second World War, see George Lipsitz, *Rainbow at Midnight: Labor and Culture in the 1940s* (Urbana: University of Illinois Press, 1994); Neil A. Wynn, *The Afro-American and the Second World War*, rev. ed. (New York: Holmes and Meier, 1993); Maureen Honey, ed., *Bitter Fruit: African American Women in World War II* (Columbia: University of Missouri Press, 1999); Lewis A. Erenberg and Susan Hirsch, eds., *The War in American Culture: Society and Consciousness during World War II* (Chicago: University of Chicago Press, 1996).

10. Farah Jasmine Griffin, *"Who Set You Flowin'?" The African-American Migration Narrative* (New York: Oxford University Press, 1995), 3.

11. Many of Lawrence's "Migration Series" paintings are available online at the Phillips Collection website, http://www.phillipscollection.org/migration_series/index.cfm. More images are available through Artstor (www.artstor.org). For a general background on Lawrence and his work, see Jacqueline Francis, "The Make of the Modern," review of *Jacob Lawrence: The "Migration" Series*, ed. Elizabeth Hutton Turner, 1993, *Callaloo* 17, no. 4 (Autumn 1994): 1269–72; Richard J. Powell, "Jacob Lawrence: Keep on Movin'" *American Art* 15, no. 1 (Spring 2001): 90–93; "Jacob Lawrence," *Bulletin of the Museum of Modern Art* 12, no. 2 (November 1944): 11; Ellen Harkins Wheat, "Jacob Lawrence and the Legacy of Harlem," *Archives of American Art Journal* 26, no. 1 (1986): 18–25; Jutta Lorensen, "Between Image and Word, Color and Time: Jacob Lawrence's 'The Migration Series,'" *African American Review* 40, no. 3 (Fall 2006): 571–86.

12. M. M. Bakhtin, *The Dialogic Imagination: Four Essays*, ed. Michael Holquist, trans. Caryl Emerson and Michael Holquist (Austin: University of Texas Press, 1981), 259–422. For other uses of Bakhtin in a jazz context see Ingrid Monson, *Saying Something: Jazz Improvisation and Interaction* (Chicago: University Chicago Press, 1996), 81, 98–100, 125.

13. Bakhtin, *Dialogic Imagination*, 426–27, 428.

14. The overwhelming majority of the Gottlieb photos span the years 1945 through 1948, with many photos from the Ellington Orchestra's four-week gig at New York's Aquarium nightclub in the fall of 1946. The caption for this particular image on the Smithsonian website is tentative and inaccurate. It reads: "Portrait of Duke Ellington, Ray Nance, Tricky Sam Nanton (?), Johnny Hodges (?), Ben Webster (?), Otto Toby Hardwick(e), Harry Carney, Rex William Stewart, Juan Tizol, Lawrence Brown, Fred Guy (?), and Sonny Greer, Howard Theater, Washington, D.C., early 1940." Because two bassists are visible, Oscar Pettiford (with Ellington from November 1945 until March 1948) and either bassist Lloyd Trotman or Al Lucas, the image must be from right around November 1945, a period when Ellington had two bass players in the group. The photo is also most likely from a New York nightclub—according to author Ken Vail, the band didn't travel to Washington, DC, during November and December of 1945. Ken Vail, *Duke's Diary: The Life of Duke Ellington, 1927–1950* (Lanham, MD: Scarecrow Press, 2002), 284–309. Accounting for everyone in the photo has been difficult, and I have made some of the identifications using circumstantial evidence (for example, rosters of the band from 1945–46). More information on the band's personnel from this time is available in A. H. Lawrence, *Duke Ellington and His World: A Biography* (New York: Routledge, 2001), 307–8, and Hasse, *Beyond Category*, 279.

15. For a contrast, consider Benny Goodman, whose approach to band management was more ruthless and authoritarian. Goodman demanded far more unity in his group in both personality and playing style. See Ross Firestone, *Swing, Swing, Swing: The Life and Times of Benny Goodman* (New York: W. W. Norton, 1993), and James Lincoln Collier, *Benny Goodman and the Swing Era* (New York: Oxford University Press, 1989).

16. Schuller, *Swing Era*, 156–57.

17. Martin Williams, "Form Beyond Form," in *The Duke Ellington Reader*, ed. Mark Tucker (New York: Oxford University Press, 1993), 401.

18. Billy Strayhorn, "The Ellington Effect," in *The Duke Ellington Reader*, ed. Mark Tucker (New York: Oxford University Press, 1993), 269–70.

19. Duke Ellington, "Ellington Explains Swing," in *Keeping Time: Readings in Jazz History*, ed. Robert Walser (New York: Oxford University Press, 1999), 106–10. In his editorial introduction, Walser briefly discusses oral interviews with Lawrence Brown and Barney Bigard on the topic of composition, invention, and the crediting of authorship.

20. In a 1944 interview for *Metronome*, new Ellington tenor saxophonist Al Sears told George Simon, "In another band you just sit down and read the parts. Here you can sit down and read the parts and suddenly you find you're playing something entirely different from what the rest of the band's playing. . . . You start at letter 'A' and go to 'B' and then suddenly, for no reason at all, when you go to 'C' the rest of the band's playing

something else which you find out later isn't what's written at 'C' but what's written at 'J' instead. And then on the next number, instead of starting at the top, the entire band starts at 'H'—that is, everybody except me. See, I'm the newest man in the band and I just haven't caught on to the system yet." "Reactions of a Newcomer: Al Sears Interviewed by George T. Simon," in *The Duke Ellington Reader*, ed. Tucker, 460–61.

21. John Chilton, *Who's Who of Jazz: Storyville to Swing Street*, 4th ed. (New York: Da Capo Press, 1985), 142.

22. For example, Indiana-born trombonist Wilbur de Paris performed in his teens and early twenties with his father's circus band on the TOBA circuit. In the mid-1920s he moved to Philadelphia to lead his own group. Frequently visiting New York City to perform, de Paris toured Europe in the 1930s with bandleader Teddy Hill. While in New York City, he joined the Ellington band in 1945, spending two years with the group before moving on to play with bands led by Ella Fitzgerald and Roy Eldridge. William H. Kenney, "De Paris, Wilbur," in *The New Grove Dictionary of Jazz*, 2nd ed., ed. Barry Kernfeld. Grove Music Online, http://www.grovemusic.com.

23. Those who weren't migrants from the South, that is, were not direct participants, were nonetheless still in many cases a part of communities that were dealing with the influx of newcomers. In *Coming of Age: Urban America, 1915–1945*, historian William H. Wilson provides a survey of the impact of southern migrants on northern, midwestern, and western cities (New York: John Wiley, 1974), 7–28. One of the best primary sources for data on and descriptions of black rural to urban migration is St. Clair Drake and Horace R. Cayton's *Black Metropolis: A Study of Life in a Northern City* (New York: Harcourt, Brace, 1945).

24. "Migration/Population," in *Encyclopedia of African-American Culture and History*, vol. 4, ed. Jack Salzman, David Lionel Smith, and Cornel West (New York: Simon and Schuster Macmillan, 1996), 1779–85.

25. David Harvey, *Justice, Nature and the Geography of Difference* (Cambridge, MA: Blackwell, 1996), 261.

26. Lawrence, *Duke Ellington and His World*, 223.

27. Stuart Nicholson, *Reminiscing in Tempo: A Portrait of Duke Ellington* (Boston: Northeastern University Press, 1999), 259–60.

28. Eric Foner, *The Story of American Freedom* (New York: W. W. Norton, 1998), 219.

29. George Simon, *The Big Bands* (1967; New York: Macmillan, 1969), 32.

30. Lewis Erenberg, *Swingin' the Dream: Big Band Jazz and the Rebirth of American Culture* (Chicago: University of Chicago Press, 1998), 213.

31. Hasse, *Beyond Category*, 234.

32. Lawrence, *Duke Ellington and His World*, 310.

33. Stanley Dance, liner notes, *The World of Duke Ellington*, two LPs, CBS Records G32564, 1974. For a history of this "battle of the speeds" see Russell Sanjek and David Sanjek, *Pennies from Heaven: The American Popular Music*

Business in the Twentieth Century (New York: Da Capo Press, 1996), 231–38; also Andre Millard, *America on Record: A History of Recorded Sound*, 2nd ed. (Cambridge: Cambridge University Press, 2005), 201–22.

34. Vail, *Duke's Diary*, 288–309; Klaus Stratemann, *Duke Ellington: Day by Day and Film by Film* (Copenhagen: JazzMedia, 1992), 264–84.

35. Hasse, *Beyond Category*, 270–98.

36. Michael Denning, *The Cultural Front: The Laboring of American Culture in the Twentieth Century* (New York: Verso, 1996), 135.

37. Paul Lopes, *The Rise of a Jazz Art World* (Cambridge: Cambridge University Press, 2002), 157–216.

38. Norman Pellegrini, *150 Years of Opera in Chicago* (DeKalb: Northern Illinois University Press, 2006), 104–6.

39. Karyl Lynn Zietz, *The National Trust Guide to Great Opera Houses in America* (New York: Preservation Press/John Wiley, 1996), 95–98.

40. Claudia Cassidy, "On the Aisle: Brilliant Soloists Step Out of the 'Duke's' Orchestra to Make Concert Bow," *Chicago Daily Tribune*, November 11, 1946; "Duke Ellington Again Demonstrates His Superiority in Field Of Jazz," *Chicago Defender*, November 23, 1946.

41. Timner, *Ellingtonia*, 99. Also Vail, *Duke's Diary*, 305.

42. For a discussion of Reinhardt's performance that night in Chicago, see Andrew Berish, "Negotiating a Blues Riff: Listening for Django Reinhardt's Place in American Jazz," *Jazz Perspectives* 3, no. 3 (2009): 233–64.

43. Walter Van de Leur, *Something to Live For: The Music of Billy Strayhorn* (New York: Oxford University Press, 2002), 198.

44. Barry Ulanov, *Duke Ellington* (1947; New York: Da Capo Press, 1972), 241–46. Ulanov's story of "Air-Conditioned Jungle" is also discussed in John Franceschina, *Duke Ellington's Music for the Theatre* (Jefferson, NC: McFarland, 2001), 170; and Lock, *Blutopia*, 84.

45. Graham Lock hears echoes of this original story in Ellington's unpublished comic opera *Queenie Pie: An Opera Buffa in Seven Scenes*, one the bandleader's last musical projects before his death in 1974. Lock, *Blutopia*, 245n28.

46. For a discussion of Ellington's and Strayhorn's predilection for puns and other rhetorical figures in their titles, see Edwards, "Literary Ellington," 338.

47. Ibid., 339.

48. "Urban jungle," *Oxford English Dictionary Online*, ed. John Simpson, http://www.oed.com.

49. Lock, *Blutopia*, 80.

50. Ibid., 77–88.

51. In this system, first elaborated by nineteenth-century logician and polymath Charles Peirce, iconic signs resemble their signifieds (a portrait photo to its model), and indexes signify "by virtue of contiguity or causality" (smoke indexes fire). Peirce had a third category, the symbol, which

signifies through "learned cultural codes." (The language here is from Raymond Monelle's useful discussion in his collection of essays *The Sense of Music: Semiotic Essays*.) Applying the terminology, however, is complicated, and it is often difficult to fix a discrete category of sign onto a particular musical event. The imitation of a cock's crow would signify a bird iconically, but also the coming of morning indexically. Raymond Monelle, *The Sense of Music: Semiotic Essays* (Princeton, NJ: Princeton University Press, 2000), 14–19.

52. There are several other extant recordings of "Air-Conditioned Jungle": *Duke Ellington V-Disc*, Collector's Choice Music, 1997; *The World of Duke Ellington*, Columbia (G32564), 1974 [rec. 1947]; and *Duke Ellington Carnegie Hall Concerts, January 4, 1946*, Prestige (2407), 1977. These versions of the song are taken at similarly blazing tempos.

53. For sources on the concept of "Signifyin(g)" see chapter 2, note 68.

54. Stanley Dance, *The World of Duke Ellington* (New York: Charles Scribner's Sons, 1970), 142–43.

55. Monson, *Saying Something*, 189.

56. Georg Simmel, "The Metropolis and Mental Life," in *On Individuality and Social Forms: Selected Writings*, ed. Donald N. Levine (Chicago: University of Chicago Press, 1971), 325–26.

57. Robert Park, "Human Migration and the Marginal Man," in *Classic Essays on the Culture of Cities*, ed. Richard Sennett (Englewood Cliffs, NJ: Prentice-Hall, 1969), 142.

58. Lyn Lofland, *A World of Strangers: Order and Action in the Urban Public Space* (New York: Basic Books, 1973).

59. Kevin Lynch, *The Image of the City* (Cambridge, MA: MIT Press, 1960), 1–13.

60. Frederic Jameson, *Postmodernism, or The Cultural Logic of Late Capitalism* (Durham, NC: Duke University Press, 1991), 38–45, 51–52.

61. Griffin provides an impressive survey and synthesis of this literature in *"Who Set You Flowin'?"* 48–141.

62. Ralph Ellison, *Invisible Man* (1947; New York: Vintage Books, 1995), 499.

63. Bakhtin, *Dialogic Imagination*, 259–422, 428.

64. Griffin, *"Who Set You Flowin'?"* 49.

65. Barry Brummett, *Rhetorical Homologies: Form, Culture, Experience* (Tuscaloosa: University of Alabama Press, 2004), 1.

66. Patrick Shove and Bruno H. Repp, "Musical Motion and Performance: Theoretical and Empirical Perspectives," in *The Practice of Performance: Studies in Musical Interpretation*, ed. John Rink (Cambridge: Cambridge University Press, 1995), 78.

67. Griffin, *"Who Set You Flowin'?"* 54.

68. Werner Sollors, *Ethnic Modernism* (Cambridge, MA: Harvard University Press, 2008), 15.

69. Hasse, *Beyond Category*, 285–87.

70. A recording of this version, meticulously transcribed by David Berger, a musician and adviser to Jazz at Lincoln Center, was recorded by the orchestra at a concert in Marciac, France, in 1993 and broadcast most recently on the *Jazz at Lincoln Center Radio* program in 2004, a show carried by many public radio stations nationwide. The show is available as an online streaming broadcast at Jazz at Lincoln Center Radio, http://www .jalc.org/jazzcast/archive.asp.

71. Ellington, *Music Is My Mistress*, 183. Also Lock, *Blutopia*, 113.

72. *The Duke Ellington Reader* contains a reprint of the program for the 1943 Carnegie Hall concert featuring *Black, Brown, and Beige*. "Program for the First Carnegie Hall Concert (23 January 1943)," 160–65. Even with the extensive accompanying texts, the specific politics of *Jump for Joy* and *Black, Brown, and Beige* were not necessarily all that clear. Debate about *Black, Brown, and Beige*, in particular, has been intense and ongoing. See Mark Tucker, *The Duke Ellington Reader* (New York: Oxford University Press, 1993), 153–204. For its part, *Jump for Joy* did not express any explicit single or coherent "message." The show, like other African American musicals of the era, was an assortment of skits, vignettes, and songs. Some of the show's ballads and blues songs had no explicit political stance. For a recent analysis of the production, see Denning, *Cultural Front*, 309–19. Also Tucker, *Duke Ellington Reader*, 148–51, and Hasse, *Beyond Category*, 246–48.

73. Ellington, *Music Is My Mistress*, 185.

74. Denning, *Cultural Front*, 314. Also Hasse, *Beyond Category*, 247–48.

75. On Washington, DC, as a "border" city see Mark Tucker, *Ellington: The Early Years* (Urbana: University of Illinois Press, 1991), 3–15. Also Gunnar Myrdal, *An American Dilemma: The Negro Problem and Modern Democracy* (1944; New York: Harper and Row, 1962), 631–32, 1127–28.

76. Mercer Ellington with Stanley Dance, *Duke Ellington in Person: An Intimate Memoir* (1978; New York: Da Capo Press, 1979), 182–83.

77. Lock, *Blutopia*, 100–101.

78. Ibid., 97.

79. Transcribed from an October 14, 2004, National Public Radio broadcast of *Jazz at Lincoln Center*, "Duke Ellington—In the Spirit of Place," recorded Marciac, France, 1994.

80. Two undated, full ensemble scores are available in the Duke Ellington Collection at the National Museum of American History in Washington, DC. The first score is in Ellington's hand and is filled with the bandleader's notes and markings. The second is cleaner and most likely by Tom Whaley, Ellington's longtime copyist. Neither version has any musical notation or marginal writing that provides instructions to play "Dixie" or "Old Folks at Home." At the beginning of the two primary instrumental solos (the first is just marked "solo," the second specifically for Brown), Ellington provides the same eight-bar melody. On the available recordings Brown begins his solo with a slight variation of this written melody, but

everything after that is entirely his own creation. Except for these initial first eight bars, the rest of Brown's solo is marked on both scores, "Brown ad lib." The Ellington original handwritten score is in the Duke Ellington Collection, #301, series 1A, box 95, National Museum of American History, Washington, DC. The cleaner score is available in the Ruth Ellington Collection, #415, subseries 2A, box 7, also at the National Museum of American History.

81. James Lincoln Collier believes the main melody in the first movement is a variation on "Ole Miss," the University of Mississippi's football song. James Lincoln Collier, *Duke Ellington* (New York: Oxford University Press, 1987), 281.

82. Where Collier hears this fondness is unclear because of some confusion over exactly what he is listening to. He claims that he hears "a charming picture of the South" in the first half of "Magnolias Just Dripping with Molasses," a section dominated by Lawrence Brown on trombone. However, the music Collier describes is on neither the V-disc nor the Chicago Civic Opera House concert. "Magnolias" does indeed have a trombone solo, but only in the solo section after the statement of the main theme. Furthermore, it is not clear what Collier means by the piece's two sections—there is a very brief introduction, but the tune proper is clearly of a single piece. Collier, *Duke Ellington*, 280–82.

83. Krin Gabbard, "Paris Blues," in *Uptown Conversations: The New Jazz Studies*, ed. Robert G. O'Meally, Brent Hayes Edwards, and Farah Jasmine Griffin (New York: Columbia University Press, 2004), 297–311.

84. Brian Priestly and Alan Cohen discuss this issue in their detailed analysis of *Black, Brown, and Beige*: "One may start wondering at which point exactly in 'Come Sunday' do 'the workers have a church of their own,' and whether the aggressive bit before the alto solo is another work-song to suggest the building of the church." Priestley and Cohen, "'Black, Brown and Beige,'" in *Duke Ellington Reader*, 187.

85. Edwards, "Literary Ellington," 339, 350–51.

86. Monson, *Saying Something*, 124.

87. Ibid.

88. Griffin, *"Who Set You Flowin'?"* 142–83.

89. Schuller, *Swing Era*, 150.

90. Dance, *World of Duke Ellington*, 26; Nicholson, *Reminiscing in Tempo*, 322.

91. Joel Dinerstein, *Swinging the Machine: Modernity, Technology, and African American Culture between the World Wars* (Amherst: University of Massachusetts Press, 2003), 97.

92. Ibid., 99.

93. Ibid., 63.

94. Ibid., 64.

95. Ibid., 72. The original discussion by Albert Murray is in *Stomping the Blues* (1976; New York: Da Capo Press, 2000), 117–26.

96. Ellington, *Music Is My Mistress*, 441.

97. Marshall Berman, *All That Is Solid Melts into Air: The Experience of Modernity* (1982; New York: Penguin Books, 1988).

98. Edward S. Casey, "How to Get from Space to Place in a Fairly Short Stretch of Time: Phenomenological Prolegomena," in *Senses of Place*, ed. Steven Feld and Keith H. Basso (Santa Fe, NM: School of American Research Press, 1996), 24-25.

99. Josh Kun, *Audiotopia: Music, Race, and America* (Berkeley: University of California Press, 2005), 2-3, 16-17.

CHAPTER FOUR

1. Patrick Lawrence Burke, *Come In and Hear the Truth: Jazz and Race on 52nd Street* (Chicago: University of Chicago Press, 2008).

2. Gunther Schuller, *The Swing Era: The Development of Jazz 1930-1945* (New York: Oxford University Press, 1989), 563.

3. Wayne E. Goins and Craig R. McKinney, *A Biography of Charlie Christian, Jazz Guitar's King of Swing*, Studies in the History and Interpretation of Music 118 (Lewiston, NY: Edwin Mellen Press, 2005), 65.

4. Steve Waksman, *Instruments of Desire: The Electric Guitar and the Shaping of Musical Experience* (Cambridge, MA: Harvard University Press, 1999), 14-35.

5. For instance, in his history of jazz, Ted Gioia describes Christian as one of Goodman's most "forward-looking" musicians who "would prove to be a leader and instigator of the defining modern style: namely, bebop." The guitarist's playing was "not a modernism resonant of Bartok and Hindemith, but one driven by hard-swinging, monophonic lines, drenched in chromaticism and executed with lightning speed." Christian was a "harbinger of jazz to come." In the *Birth of Bebop*, Scott DeVeaux covers Christian's role in the development of the new style, particularly through his participation in the after-hours jam sessions at Minton's Playhouse in Harlem. Gunther Schuller makes a very similar assessment in *The Swing Era*. While he may not have instigated the harmonic developments of be-boppers like Dizzy Gillespie, Christian's solos were "modern, streamlined . . . almost completely linear . . . filled out with more chromatic passing tones." Schuller concludes that "there can be little doubt that at the time of his death in 1942 Christian was on the threshold of becoming a major voice, perhaps, had he lived, *the* major voice in shaping the new language of jazz." Other writers on the guitarist, such as Bill Simon, also focus heavily on his progressive style and innovations that contributed to the bebop language: "Easily the most important, revealing work of Christian on records is the material gleaned from Jerry Newman's well-worn ac-etates." These acetates captured Christian at Minton's Playhouse jamming with other jazz modernists like Thelonious Monk and Kenny Clarke. Ted

Gioia, *The History of Jazz* (New York: Oxford University Press, 1997), 154; Scott DeVeaux, *The Birth of Bebop: A Social and Musical History* (Berkeley: University of California Press, 1997), 220–21; Gunther Schuller, *The Swing Era: The Development of Jazz, 1930–1945* (New York: Oxford University Press, 1989), 577–78; Bill Simon, "Charlie Christian," in *The Guitar in Jazz: An Anthology*, ed. James Sallis (Lincoln: University of Nebraska Press, 1996), 68.

6. Raymond Williams, *The Politics of Modernism: Against the New Conformists*, ed. and intro. Tony Pinkney (New York: Verso, 1989), 175.

7. Goins and McKinney, *Biography of Charlie Christian*, 155.

8. Waksman, *Instruments of Desire*, 15.

9. Christian was not the only jazz musician who made this type of journey from the regional to the national. Two of the central figures in the development of the music, Louis Armstrong and Charlie Parker, both similarly emerged from small, regional urban centers (New Orleans and Kansas City, respectively) to become nationally known musicians. Parker himself once claimed that his music combined "the midwestern beat and the fast New York tempos." Eric Lott, "Double V, Double-Time: Bebop's Politics of Style," in *The Jazz Cadence of American Culture*, ed. Robert G. O'Meally (New York: Columbia University Press, 1998), 459–60.

10. Rudi Blesh, "Flying Home," in *Reading Jazz: A Gathering of Autobiography, Reportage, and Criticism from 1919 to Now*, ed. Robert Gottlieb (New York: Vintage Books, 1996), 516–36.

11. Schuller, *Swing Era*, 563.

12. Ibid., 563–64.

13. Ralph Ellison, *Living with Music: Ralph Ellison's Jazz Writings*, ed. Robert G. O'Meally (New York: Modern Library, 2002), 34–42.

14. Ibid., 40.

15. Ibid., 36.

16. Ibid., 38–39.

17. Ibid., 39.

18. Ibid., 35.

19. Jimmie Lewis Franklin, *Journey toward Hope: A History of Blacks in Oklahoma* (Norman: University of Oklahoma Press, 1982), xi.

20. Bill C. Malone, *Country Music, U.S.A.*, rev. ed. (1968; Austin: University of Texas Press, 2002), 137–38.

21. William W. Savage Jr., *Singing Cowboys and All That Jazz: A Short History of Popular Music in Oklahoma* (Norman: University of Oklahoma Press, 1983), 8–9.

22. Goins and McKinney, *Biography of Charlie Christian*, 12.

23. Peter Broadbent, *Charlie Christian: Solo Flight; The Seminal Electric Guitarist*, 2nd ed. (Blaydon on Tyne, UK: Ashley Mark, 2003), 30–40.

24. *Solo Flight: The Genius of Charlie Christian*, V.I.E.W. Video Jazz Series, New York, 1996, 31 min. Gary Don Rhodes, filmmaker.

25. Broadbent, *Charlie Christian*, 50.

26. Ibid., 52–53.

27. Ibid., 56.

28. Ross Russell, *Jazz Style in Kansas City and the Southwest* (Berkeley: University of California Press, 1973), 2–5.

29. Thomas J. Hennessey, *From Jazz to Swing: African-American Jazz Musicians and Their Music, 1890–1935* (Detroit: Wayne State University Press, 1994), 116.

30. In his essay on the music of the Southwest for Greenwood Press's series of regional American encyclopedias, author Richard Holland acknowledges that "the defined region for this reference book [Nevada, New Mexico, Arizona, and Texas] is problematical when it comes to music." While various Mexican American and Native American musics allow Holland to safely limit his geographical scope to the book's boundaries, his discussion of blues, jazz, and rock 'n' roll necessarily falls outside these parameters and encompasses Russell's and Hennessey's conceptions of the Southwest. Richard Holland, "Music," in *The Southwest: The Greenwood Encyclopedia of American Regional Cultures*, ed. Mark Busby (Westport, CT: Greenwood Press, 2004), 315.

31. David Evans, "Musical Innovation in the Blues of Blind Lemon Jefferson," *Black Music Research Journal* 20, no. 1 (Spring 2000): 103, 105; Goins and McKinney, *Biography of Charlie Christian*, 21–23, 380–81.

32. Interestingly, T-Bone Walker and several western swing guitar players such as Zeke Campbell and Bob Dunn were also early tinkerers and experimenters with the electric guitar. Although experiments with guitar amplification were happening simultaneously in many parts of the country, Oklahoma City contained an unusually high number of early guitarists, perhaps the result of a long tradition of guitar playing mixing with the vibrant live music. On early electric guitarists playing western swing, see Jerome S. Shipman, "In Search of the Electric Guitar: A Platonic Dialogue with Music," *Annual Review of Jazz Studies* 7 (1994–95): 201–16. There are many books chronicling the invention of the electric guitar, but for a concise and critical synopsis see, Waksman, *Instruments of Desire*, 1–74.

33. Goins and McKinney, *Biography of Charlie Christian*, 62; Broadbent, *Charlie Christian*, 30–31.

34. For a history of Oklahoma City and its twentieth-century musical legacy, see Savage, *Singing Cowboys and All That Jazz*.

35. Christian played with white musicians, including western swing guitarist Noel Boggs and pianist Clarence Clagle. Broadbent, *Charlie Christian*, 45–46.

36. Henri Lefebvre, *The Production of Space*, trans. Donald Nicholson-Smith (Oxford: Blackwell, 1991), 38–39.

37. Loren Schoenberg, liner notes, *Charlie Christian: The Genius of the Electric Guitar*, four compact discs, Sony Music Entertainment (C4K 65564), 2002, 45–47.

38. In the late 1930s "Flying Home" was very popular with audiences, but it became much more so after a 1942 recording made by Lionel Hampton's band, just a few years after the vibraphonist left the Goodman Sextet. Hampton's recording of "Flying Home," featuring the fiery Illinois Jacquet on tenor saxophone, became a massive hit, the band's anthem, and—in hindsight—a significant moment in the birth of rhythm and blues and rock 'n' roll. John McDonough, "Flying Home: A Tribute to Lionel Hampton, 1908–2002," *Down Beat* 69, no. 11 (November 2002): 26–29; John McDonough, "The Beat—Illinois Jacquet: 1922–2004," *Down Beat* 71, no. 10 (October 2004): 24; Gary Giddins, "Lionel Hampton, 1908–2002," *Village Voice* 47, no. 39 (2002): 71.

39. Goins and McKinney, *Biography of Charlie Christian*, 191.

40. Ibid.

41. Ibid., 176.

42. Broadbent, *Charlie Christian*, 53.

43. Goins and McKinney, *Biography of Charlie Christian*, 304.

44. Ibid., 80.

45. Another story connects the origin of the song to an earlier flight where Goodman heard Lionel Hampton whistling a tune to calm his nerves. "'What is that?' Benny asked. 'I don't know,' Lionel told him. Benny suggested he work on it; Lionel did, and the resulting composition became his theme tune, 'Flyin' Home.'" According to Peter Broadbent this story is almost certainly spurious, as is the attribution of "Flying Home" to vibraphonist Lionel Hampton. Broadbent (as well as biographers Wayne Goins and Craig McKinney) believes that Christian brought the melody with him from Oklahoma City, a tune that in fact may have been created by territory bandleader and pianist Leslie Sheffield, in whose band Christian played for many years while in Oklahoma City. Despite this, the anecdote does draw attention again to the discursive connection between the song and the real and very new experience of airplane travel. See Bruce Crowther, Mike Pinfold, and Franklin S. Driggs, *The Big Band Years* (New York: Facts on File, 1988), 61; Broadbent, *Charlie Christian*, 75–76; Goins and McKinney, *Biography of Charlie Christian*, 53, 179–80.

46. Ann Douglas, *Terrible Honesty: Mongrel Manhattan in the 1920s* (New York: Noonday Press/Farrar, Straus and Giroux, 1995), 434–61; Gena Caponi-Tabery, *Jump for Joy: Jazz, Basketball, and Black Culture in 1930s America* (Amherst: University of Massachusetts Press, 2008), xi–xx.

47. For an overview of Bel Geddes and the Futurama exhibit, see Tom Lewis, *Divided Highways: Building the Interstate Highways, Transforming American Life* (New York: Penguin Books, 1997), 43–44.

48. Clive Downs, "Metric Displacement in the Improvisation of Charlie Christian," *Annual Review of Jazz Studies* 11 (2000–2001): 39–68; Howard Allen Spring, "The Improvisational Style of Charlie Christian," (Master's thesis, York University, 1980).

49. In their synopsis of the scholarship on this topic, Patrick Shove and Bruno Repp identify three modes of "musical awareness" that we attend to when listening to music (depending in part on our musical knowledge and background): the *structural event*, the *performance event*, and the *expressive event*. The varied explanations of musical movement are in part attributable to whatever mode of awareness a particular writer focuses on. Attending to the *performance event*, we focus on "the musician playing an instrument or singing." The *structural event*, in contrast, corresponds to hearing the "articulation of motives, phrases, durational patterns, cadential progressions, and so on." Different from either of these, the *expressive event* conveys "patterns of movement whose general characteristics are similar to bodily movements symptomatic of human emotions, moods, or feelings." Patrick Shove and Bruno H. Repp, "Musical Motion and Performance: Theoretical and Empirical Perspectives," in *The Practice of Performance: Studies in Musical Interpretation*, ed. John Rink (Cambridge: Cambridge University Press, 1995), 59–60.

50. Robert P. Morgan, "Musical Time/Musical Space," *Critical Inquiry* 6, no. 3 (Spring 1980): 529.

51. Shove and Repp, "Musical Motion," 60.

52. Ibid.

53. Al Avakian and Bob Prince, "Charlie Christian," in *The Art of Jazz: Ragtime to Bebop*, ed. Martin Williams (New York: Da Capo Press, 1959), 184.

54. Goins and McKinney, *Biography of Charlie Christian*, 245.

55. Ibid.

56. Avakian and Prince, "Charlie Christian," 184.

57. Like many improvising jazz players, past and present, Christian has a set of stock patterns he draws from—in musicians' lingo, his "bag of tricks." Their appearances and reappearances, though, are almost always varied, with the guitarist manipulating their rhythmic profile and placement. Many of his melodic phrases outline tonic triads (E-flat—G—B-flat), and often begin and end on the "home" note of E-flat. One very common pattern Christian employs in many of these recordings, flat-3—3—5—1, strongly affirms the A sections E-flat tonality while also evoking the blues through the flat-3—natural-3 alternation. According to Howard Spring and Jonathan Finkelman, this phrase is one of the core patterns of the guitarist's style. For a complete discussion of patterns in the guitarist's playing, see Spring, "Improvisational Style of Charlie Christian"; Howard Spring, "The Use of Formulas in the Improvisations of Charlie Christian," *Jazzforschung/Jazz Research* 22 (1990): 24; and Jonathan Finkelman, "Charlie Christian and the Role of Formulas in Jazz Improvisation," *Jazzforschung/Jazz Research*, 29 (1997): 165–66. For other important discussions of the role of formulas in jazz improvisation, see Thomas Owens, "Charlie Parker: Techniques of Improvisation" (PhD diss., University of California at Los Angeles, 1974); Lawrence Gushee, "Lester Young's 'Shoeshine

Boy,'" *IMSCR XII: Berkeley 1977*, 151–69; Henry Martin, *Charlie Parker and Thematic Improvisation* (Metuchen, NJ: Scarecrow Press, 1996); Gregory Eugene Smith, "Homer, Gregory, and Bill Evans? The Theory of Formulaic Composition in the Context of Jazz Piano Improvisations" (PhD diss., Harvard University, 1983); Carl Woideck, *Charlie Parker: His Music and Life* (Ann Arbor: University of Michigan Press, 1996); Andrew Scott, "I See the Fretboard in Diagrams: An Examination of the Improvisatory Style of Herbert Lawrence 'Sonny' Greenwich," *Canadian University Music Society Review* 23, no. 1 (2003): 62–78; and Benjamin M. Givan, "Django Reinhardt's Style and Improvisational Process" (PhD diss., Yale University, 2003).

58. Blues notes are often discussed as part of a blues scale—a complex topic that has generated a great deal of scholarly literature. Specific identification of the "blues scale" varies widely in the scholarly literature: in jazz pedagogical literature, the minor pentatonic is closely related to the "blues scale." For these writers and musicians, the blues scale differs by one note, a "passing note" between scale degrees four and five. However, because of the small difference—an optional chromatic interpolation—the two scales are often discussed together. For an example of an author who distinguishes between the six-note "blues scale" and the minor pentatonic while still emphasizing their very close relationship, see Mark Levine, *The Jazz Theory Book* (Petaluma, CA: Sher Music Company, 1995), 230–36. In the scholarly literature the blues scale has been discussed in a variety of ways since the 1930s. For a sample of viewpoints and positions, see Samuel Charters, *The Bluesmen: The Story and the Music of the Men Who Made the Blues* (New York: Oak, 1967), 29–30; Winthrop Sargeant, *Jazz: Hot and Hybrid* (1938; New York: Da Capo Press, 1975), 160; Gunther Schuller, *Early Jazz: Its Roots and Musical Development* (1968; New York: Oxford University Press, 1986), 43–54; Gerhard Kubik, *Africa and the Blues* (Jackson: University of Mississippi Press, 1999), 118–45; and Jeff Todd Titon, *Early Downhome Blues: A Musical and Cultural Analysis* (Urbana: University of Illinois Press, 1977), 154–65.

59. Philosopher Don Ihde discusses auditory foreground and background—what he calls "focus" and "field"—in his study of the phenomenology of sound. Don Ihde, *Listening and Voice: A Phenomenology of Sound* (Athens: Ohio University Press, 1976), 38–41, 72–83.

60. Paul F. Berliner, *Thinking in Jazz: The Infinite Art of Improvisation* (Chicago: University of Chicago Press, 1994), 128.

61. Avakian and Prince, "Charlie Christian," 184.

62. In measure 18, Christian plays a partial arpeggio that contains both a D-natural and an E-natural, two notes not part of the E-flat7 chord (or the underlying A-flat key). It is sometimes difficult to extrapolate the logic behind a particular note choice. In this case it appears that the guitarist is implying, and then altering, a B-flat7 chord, the dominant of E-flat. The

notes Christian plays in the first half of the measure, D—F—C—B-flat, are the third, fifth, ninth, and root of a B-flat7. In this context, the E-natural in the second half of the measure would be an augmented fifth (and the D-flat, a flat third). This reading makes sense, in part, because the F-sharp heard later in measure 23 is also an augmented fifth. The alteration is part of Christian's improvisational trick bag. In his transcription book of Christian solos, Stan Ayeroff describes this particular gesture as a iv6 substitution over the V chord. Either way, these kinds of substitutions are an early example of the kind of harmonic-melodic procedures the beboppers would develop more fully with tritone substitutions and other kinds of harmonic interpolations. Finally, it is worth pointing out that the augmented fifth also creates a partial whole-tone scale, the strange-sounding symmetry of that scale enhancing the bridge's off-kilter feel. The intimations of whole-tone scales suggest the possible influence of Django Reinhardt, who frequently used this sound in his own playing. Stan Ayeroff, *Swing to Bop: The Music of Charlie Christian, Pioneer of the Electric Guitar* (Pacific, MO: Mel Bay, 2005), 38.

63. Eero Tarasti, *A Theory of Musical Semiotics* (Bloomington: Indiana University Press, 1994), 38–43, 304.

64. Vijay Iyer, "Exploding the Narrative in Jazz Improvisation," in *Uptown Conversation: The New Jazz Studies*, ed. Robert G. O'Meally, Brent Hayes Edwards, and Farah Jasmin Griffin (New York: Columbia University Press, 2004), 395.

65. Iyer has made a similar point in regard to John Coltrane: "Many have tried to establish 'motific development' in Coltrane's individual improvisations as that which creates structure and hence meaning. But it seems to me that such structure is merely a consequence of a greater formation—Coltrane's 'sound,' his holistic approach to music, which yields these elements." Iyer, "Exploding the Narrative," 400.

66. For a discussion of Christian and his explorations of the potentialities of the newly electrified instrument, see Waksman, *Instruments of Desire*, 14–35.

67. At a conference I attended in 2004, I heard Travis Jackson develop a similar analysis of the power of timbre and its evocation of place. Travis Jackson, "'Honking on One Note': The Texas Tenor Sound and Its Challenge to Jazz Discourse," paper presented at the Joint meeting of the Society for American Music and the Association for Recorded Sound Collections, Cleveland, OH, March 10–14, 2004.

68. This notion—that these less notable, but very tactile and powerful musical attributes deeply shape musical identity—is widely held by musicians themselves. In *Thinking in Jazz*, Paul Berliner discusses the "constellation of traits" that make up a soloist's style: timbre or tone quality, "articulation of pitches with various qualities of hardness and softness," "pitch inflections like scoops and more extensive, embellishing microtonal

shapes," evocation of mood, treatment of common stock formulas or phrases, "symmetrical or asymmetrical divisions of the beats" and other rhythmic articulations, patterns of "accentuation" in melodic phrasing, "characteristic phrase length," vertical or horizontal harmonic approach or predilection. The heart of Berliner's discussion comes in chapter 5, "Seeing Out a Bit: Expanding upon Early Influences," 124–38. Specifically, see Berliner, *Thinking in Jazz*, 125, 126, 127, 128, 130, 135, 147.

69. Iyer, "Exploding the Narrative," 398.
70. Ibid., 401–2.
71. "To Charlie," liner notes, *Charlie Christian: The Genius of the Electric Guitar*, four compact discs, Sony Music Entertainment (C4K 65564), 2002, 5, 8.
72. Schoenberg, liner notes, *Charlie Christian: The Genius of the Electric Guitar*, 11.
73. Berliner, *Thinking Jazz*, 147.
74. Ibid. Musicologist Lewis Porter terms this "one-noting," in reference to saxophonist Lester Young's habit of doing this in his solos. Ibid., 147n1.
75. For Scriabin see Richard Taruskin, "Scriabin and the Superhuman: A Millennial Essay," in *Defining Russia Musically: Historical and Hermeneutical Essays* (Princeton, NJ: Princeton University Press, 1997), 308–59. In an interview from 2002, La Monte Young explained to Gabrielle Zuckerman, "Harmony comes from harmonicity, which relates to periodicity, which relates to sustained tones, which relates to the idea of cosmic sound, which relates to the idea of universal structure, which relates to the idea that we have bodies that allow us to understand vibrational structure through studying sound. Through this we are beginning to understand about universal structure and the study of vibrations on a higher spiritual level." "An Interview with La Monte Young and Marian Zazeela by Gabrielle Zuckerman, American Public Media, July 2002," American Mavericks Website, a project of American Public Media http://musicmavericks.public radio.org/features/interview_young.html.
76. Shove and Repp, "Musical Motion," 64.
77. Roland Barthes, *The Responsibility of Forms: Critical Essays on Music, Art, and Representation*, trans. Richard Howard (1982; Berkeley: University of California Press, 1991), 267–77.
78. Iyer, "Exploding Narrative," 399.
79. George E. Lewis, "Improvised Music after 1950: Afrological and Eurological Perspectives," in *The Other Side of Nowhere: Jazz, Improvisation, and Communities in Dialogue*, ed. Daniel Fischlin and Ajay Heble (Middletown, CT: Wesleyan University Press, 2004), 131–62.
80. Iyer, "Exploding Narrative," 400.
81. Ibid. The quotation appeared originally in Lewis, "Improvised Music after 1950," 156.

82. Peter Broadbent asserts that when he was free, Christian often played with Mary Lou Williams in the basement of the Dewey Square Hotel. Broadbent, *Charlie Christian*, 108–9.
83. DeVeaux, *Birth of Bebop*, 219.
84. Ibid., 220–22.
85. Jonathan Finkelman, "Charlie Christian, Bebop, and the Recordings at Minton's," *Annual Review of Jazz Studies* 6 (1993): 193.
86. Ibid., 191–201.
87. Ibid., 189.
88. This description of Harlem is from Ralph Ellison's *Invisible Man* (1947; New York: Vintage Books, 1995), 158–59.
89. Broadbent, *Charlie Christian*, 74.
90. Goins and McKinney, *Biography of Charlie Christian*, 211–13; Broadbent, *Charlie Christian*, 89, 97–103.
91. Schuller, *Swing Era*, 577.
92. For a discussion of the progress narrative in jazz historiography, see Scott DeVeaux, "Constructing the Jazz Tradition: Jazz Historiography," *Black American Literature Forum* 25, no. 3 (Autumn 1991): 525–60.
93. Discographic information available in Schoenberg, liner notes; Broadbent, *Charlie Christian*; and liner notes for *Charlie Christian: Complete Live Recordings Disconforme*.
94. Peter Broadbent, "His Life," liner notes to *Charlie Christian: The Genius of the Electric Guitar* 2002, Sony Music, four compact discs, C4K 655564, 30.
95. Avakian and Prince, "Charlie Christian," 186.
96. Schuller, *Swing Era*, 576.
97. Schoenberg prefers an unreleased alternative take that "finds Christian in a more voluble mood. Drummer Dave Tough's constant counterpoint is totally original and in keeping with his ascetic approach of the Sextet session recorded just 9 days later." Loren Schoenberg, "His Music," liner notes to *Charlie Christian: The Genius of the Electric Guitar* 2002, 68.
98. Goins and McKinney, *Biography of Charlie Christian*, 313.
99. Ibid., 322.
100. Ibid.
101. Ibid., 329.
102. Scholarly discussion of northward migration, though, often does not take into account the movement of southern African Americans into the growing *southern* cities. The collapse of agriculture hurt all farmers in the South but was especially brutal for the black farmers, whether they were wage earners, sharecroppers, tenants, or landowners. Because so much "traditional" African American work dried up in the 1930s (such as jobs for domestic servants and street cleaners), blacks who did manage to move to the cities faced hostility and competition from whites seeking these once disdained jobs. See Gunnar Myrdal, *An American Dilemma: The Negro Problem and Modern Democracy* (1944; New York: Harper and Row, 1962),

182–201; Harvard Sitkoff, *A New Deal for Blacks: The Emergence of Civil Rights as a National Issue; The Depression Decade* (New York: Oxford University Press, 1978), 34–40.

103. Myrdal, *American Dilemma*, 196–201, 293–303. For a discussion of black migration of the 1930s and '40s in a particular city, see Josh Sides, *L.A. City Limits: African American Los Angeles from the Great Depression to the Present* (Berkeley: University of California Press, 2003), 36–56.

104. Caponi-Tabery, *Jump for Joy*, xv.

105. Ibid.

106. Hennessey, *From Jazz to Swing*, 156.

107. A thorough history of regionalist thought in American interwar history is Robert L. Dorman, *Revolt of the Provinces: The Regionalist Movement in America, 1920–1945* (Chapel Hill: University of North Carolina Press, 1993). Also useful is Michael C. Steiner, "Regionalism in the Great Depression," *Geographical Review* 73, no. 4 (October 1983): 430–46.

108. Dorman, *Revolt of the Provinces*, xii–xiii.

109. Morris Dickstein, "Depression Culture: The Dream of Mobility," in *Radical Revisions: Rereading 1930s Culture*, ed. Bill Mullen and Sherry Lee Linkon (Urbana: University of Illinois Press, 1996), 227–40.

110. Not all these cultural representations were so uplifting or magical. In the film *I Am a Fugitive from a Chain Gang*, the unjustly imprisoned James Allen escapes the chain gang a second time only to end up on a permanent "flight to nowhere." In John Steinbeck's novel *The Grapes of Wrath*, and John Ford's film adaptation, the Joad family must keep moving to survive. Both film and book end with no final destination in sight. For Dickstein this was "not travel but desperation, a way of standing still or running in place." Dickstein, "Depression Culture," 237.

111. Although resonating with many Americans, the experiences of Christian, Armstrong, and Parker were decidedly male: the specific geographical trajectory of Christian's life, while rare in the black community, was still far more available to African American men than women. We should not lose sight of the gendered specificities of Christian's experience when tracing the larger cultural import of his music. For useful discussions of the experiences of African American women in the jazz world of the 1920s, '30s, and '40s, see Hazel Carby, "It Jus Be's Dat Way Sometime: The Sexual Politics of Women's Blues," in *The Jazz Cadence of American Culture*, ed. Robert G. O'Meally (New York: Columbia University Press, 1998), 469–82; Billie Holiday's intermittently reliable autobiography *Lady Sings the Blues* (New York: Doubleday, 1956); and Sherrie Tucker, *Swing Shift: "All-Girl" Bands of the 1940s* (Durham, NC: Duke University Press, 2000).

112. Jani Scandura, *Down in the Dumps: Place, Modernity, American Depression* (Durham, NC: Duke University Press, 2008), 4.

113. Coleman Hawkins was also nicknamed "Bean," a reference to his intelligence. The origin of Parker's nickname is obscure but appears to predate

its figurative usage as a descriptor of the saxophonist's virtuosity. Anecdotes by fellow musicians attribute the name either to an incident involving a dead "yardbird" Parker insisted on retrieving from the road or his love of chicken. DeVeaux, *Birth of Bebop*, 65; Carl Woideck, *Charlie Parker*, 20–21.

114. Blesh, "Flying Home," 527.

CONCLUSION

1. Jack Mirtle, ed., *The Music of Billy May: A Discography* (Westport, CT: Greenwood Press, 1998), 6.

2. Hanson W. Baldwin, "Army Corps Sends 1,500 Planes in the Air," *New York Times*, August 3, 1939.

3. In 1930 the United States had thirty-eight domestic airlines that covered 30,293 route miles and carried 374,935 paying passengers—four years earlier the country could count just 5,782 paying passengers. Over the next two decades growth would be exponential, with passenger volume increasing fivefold between 1930 and 1939. For transportation historian John Spychalski, 1936 to 1941 were "watershed" years for commercial air transportation technology. Despite the interruption of World War II, the development in the mid- to late 1930s of "pressurized, long-range, four engine aircraft" would fuel the rapid postwar growth of the industry. Growth was even faster after the introduction in 1952 of jet engines: "By the late 1950s . . . air transport had largely supplanted rail and water carriage for long distance overland and transoceanic business travel, and had captured sizeable footholds in personal travel among upper-income groups." However, even as late as 1960, "only 10 percent of people over 18 years of age had ever used scheduled air service." By 1998 this number would rise to nearly 70 percent. John C. Spychalski, "Transportation," in *The Columbia History of the 20th Century*, ed. Richard W. Bulliet (New York: Columbia University Press, 1998), 407, 410–11.

4. Ann Douglas, *Terrible Honesty: Mongrel Manhattan in the 1920s* (New York: Noonday Press/Farrar, Straus and Giroux, 1995), 434.

5. For a concise history of Hollywood's representation of air flight, see Dominick A. Pisano, "The Greatest Show Not on Earth: The Confrontation between Utility and Entertainment in Aviation," in *The Airplane in American Culture*, ed. Dominick A. Pisano (Ann Arbor: University of Michigan Press, 2003), 39–74.

6. Richard Guy Wilson, Dianne H. Pilgrim, and Dickran Tashjian, eds., *The Machine Age in America: 1918–1941* (New York: Harry N. Abrams, 1986), 125–47, 303–37.

7. Ibid., 129.

8. James R. McGovern, *And a Time for Hope: America in the Great Depression* (Westport, CT: Praeger, 2000), 168; Larry Zim, Mel Lerner, and Herbert

Rolfes, *The World of Tomorrow: The 1939 New York World's Fair* (New York: Harper and Row, 1988), 97–121.

9. "Rocket as Plane Is Demonstrated," *New York Times*, May 14, 1939; Zim, Lerner, and Rolfes, *World of Tomorrow*, 107.

10. Gay Wilentz, "If You Surrender to the Air: Folk Legends of Flight and Resistance in African American Literature," *MELUS: Folklore and Orature* 16, no. 1 (Spring 1989–Spring 1990): 21–32.

11. Ibid., 23.

12. Jill D. Snider, "Great Shadow in the Sky: The Airplane in the Tulsa Race Riot of 1921 and the Development of African American Aviation, 1921–1926," in *The Airplane in American Culture*, ed. Dominick A. Pisano (Ann Arbor: University of Michigan Press, 2003), 105–46.

13. Ibid., 137.

14. Henry Pleasants, *Serious Music, and All That Jazz: An Adventure in Music Criticism* (New York: Simon and Schuster, 1969), 65.

15. Thomas J. Hennessey, *From Jazz to Swing: African-American Jazz Musicians and Their Music, 1890–1935* (Detroit: Wayne State University Press, 1994), 146.

16. Cliff Leeman interviewed by Milt Hinton for the Smithsonian Institution Jazz Oral History Project, reel 1, transcription, 23–24 (1979). Flying, as Leeman points out, was not like it is today. Planes were smaller and could not travel as far without refueling. What might be an hour's flight today was, in the early years of commercial aviation, significantly longer. A *New York Times* article from November 26, 1939, reports the opening of the New York Municipal Airport-LaGuardia Field, the first airport to operate "within the city limits." The article has an accompanying map showing how the airport will speed travelers across the country. Patrons leaving North Beach airport could be in Los Angeles in eighteen hours, Dallas in nine, Seattle in eighteen, and Boston in an hour and a half. "Men will fly on Saturday to breakfast in Chicago, dine in California, to land in Hawaii 16 hours later, Hong Kong in less than a week." New York will now be linked to the "'sun spots' of America in Texas, Florida, and the West Coast—just a question of eighteen hours or thereabouts." David Anderson, "New York's Great Airport Awaits the Starting Signal," *New York Times*, November 29, 1939.

17. Gena Caponi-Tabery, *Jazz, Basketball and Black Culture in 1930s America* (Amherst: University of Massachusetts Press, 2008), 51–67. See also the chapters on the Lindy Hop from Marshall Stearn and Jean Stearn's *Jazz Dance: The Story of American Vernacular Dance* (1968; New York: Da Capo Press, 1994), 315–36. For a firsthand account from one of the innovators of the Lindy and "air steps," see Frankie Manning and Cynthia R. Millman, *Ambassador of Lindy Hop* (Philadelphia: Temple University Press, 2007), 101–3.

18. Manning and Millman, *Ambassador of Lindy Hop*, 80–81.

19. Lunceford's love affair with airplanes was part of a larger "passion for all things technical." He was one of the first bandleaders to incorporate into his band the new musical technology of electrically amplified bass and guitar. Eddy Determeyer, *Rhythm Is Our Business: Jimmie Lunceford and the Harlem Express* (Ann Arbor: University of Michigan Press, 2006), 185.

20. Ibid., 183–84.

21. Ibid., 78.

22. Liner notes, *Big Band Jazz: From the Beginning to the Fifties*, selected and annotated by Gunther Schuller and Martin Williams (Washington, DC: Smithsonian Collection of Recordings, 1983), 21.

23. See Gunther Schuller's detailed analysis of "Daybreak Express" in *The Swing Era: The Development of Jazz, 1930–1945* (New York: Oxford University Press, 1989), 61–65.

24. Joel Dinerstein, *Swinging the Machine: Modernity, Technology, and African-American Culture between the Wars* (Amherst: University of Massachusetts Press, 2003), 4.

25. Simon, *Big Bands*, 329.

26. Ibid., 332.

27. "Rhythm happens, so to speak, in the midst of actual sound and non-sounding virtual structures of reference (which, moreover, might have to do with the perceptual processes generated in the listener), and the sounding event may play both with and against the virtual structure." Anne Danielsen, *Presence and Pleasure: The Funk Grooves of James Brown and Parliament* (Middletown, CT: Wesleyan University Press, 2006), 46–47, 56.

28. The philosophy of "racial uplift" was an idea with roots in both folk and elite black culture, and its manifestations in middle-class black life in the first half of the twentieth century were various and sometimes contradictory. See Kevin K. Gaines, *Uplifting the Race: Black Leadership, Politics, and Culture in the Twentieth Century* (Chapel Hill: University of North Carolina Press, 1996).

29. The idea of music generating "new maps" for listeners is from Josh Kun, *Audiotopia: Music, Race, and America* (Berkeley: University of California Press, 2005), 22–23.

30. Michael C. Steiner, "Regionalism in the Great Depression," *Geographical Review* 73, no. 4 (October 1983): 432.

31. Antonio Gramsci, *The Modern Prince and Other Writings* (New York: International Publishers, 1972), 118–25. For an influential discussion of this idea in the context of American popular music, see George Lipsitz, *Time Passages: Collective Memory and American Popular Culture* (1990; Minneapolis: University of Minnesota Press, 2007), 152.

32. Grace Elizabeth Hale, *Making Whiteness: The Culture of Segregation in the South, 1890–1940* (New York: Vintage, 1998), 8.

33. Ralph Ellison, *Invisible Man* (1947; New York: Vintage Books, 1995), 498.

34. Raymond Williams, *The Politics of Modernism: Against the New Conformists*, ed. and intro. Tony Pinkney (New York: Verso, 1989), 175.
35. Quoted in Anthony Seeger, "Ethnography of Music," in *Ethnomusicology: An Introduction*, ed. Helen Myers, Norton/Grove Handbooks in Music (New York: W. W. Norton, 1992), 93.
36. For an excellent synopsis of Christopher Small's ideas see the introduction to *Musicking: The Meaning of Performance and Listening* (Hanover, NH: University Press of New England/Wesleyan University Press, 1998), 1–18.

Bibliography

Adams, Paul C., Steven Hoelscher, and Karen E. Till. *Textures of Place: Exploring Humanist Geographies*. Minneapolis: University of Minnesota Press, 2001.

Ake, David. *Jazz Cultures*. Berkeley: University of California Press, 2001.

——. *Sound Matters: Sound, Place and Time since Bebop*. Berkeley: University of California Press, 2010.

Angle, Paul M. *Philip K. Wrigley: A Memoir of a Modest Man*. Chicago: Rand McNally, 1975.

Antrim, Doron K. *Secrets of Dance Band Success*. New York: Famous Stars, 1936.

Austerlitz, Paul. *Jazz Consciousness: Music, Race, and Humanity*. Middletown, CT: Wesleyan University Press, 2005.

Avakian, Al, and Bob Prince. "Charlie Christian." In *The Art of Jazz: Ragtime to Bebop*, edited by Martin Williams, 181–86. 1959. Reprint, New York: Da Capo Press, 1980.

Ayeroff, Stan. *Charlie Christian*. Jazz Masters Series. New York: Amsco, 1979.

——. *Swing to Bop: The Music of Charlie Christian, Pioneer of the Electric Guitar*. Pacific, MO: Mel Bay, 2005.

Baker, Gayle. *Catalina Island: A Harbor Town History*. Santa Barbara, CA: Harbor Town Histories, 2003.

Bakhtin, M. M. *The Dialogic Imagination: Four Essays*. Edited by Michael Holquist. Translated by Caryl Emerson and Michael Holquist. Austin: University of Texas Press, 1981.

Balachandran, Chandra S., and Surinder M. Bhardwaj. "Geography as Melody in Muttusvami Dikshita's Indian Musical Works." *Geographical Review* 91, no. 4 (October 2001): 690–701.

Barnet, Charlie, with Stanley Dance. *Those Swinging Years: The Autobiography of Charlie Barnet*. 1984. Reprint, New York: Da Capo Press, 1992.

Barnouw, Erik. *The Golden Web, 1933—1953.* Vol. 2. of *A History of Broadcasting in the United States.* New York: Oxford University Press, 1968.

————. *A Tower in Babel: To 1933.* Vol. 1 of *A History of Broadcasting in the United States.* New York: Oxford University Press, 1966.

Barthes, Roland. *The Responsibility of Forms: Critical Essays on Music, Art, and Representation.* 1982. Translated by Richard Howard. Berkeley: University of California Press, 1991.

Basie, Count, and Albert Murray. *Good Morning Blues: The Autobiography of Count Basie.* New York: Random House, 1985.

Bechet, Sidney. *Treat It Gentle.* 1960. Reprint, New York: Da Capo Press, 2002.

Bel Geddes, Norman. *Magic Motorways.* New York: Random House, 1940.

Belgrad, Daniel. *The Culture of Spontaneity: Improvisation and the Arts in Postwar America.* Chicago: University of Chicago Press, 1998.

Berendt, Joachim E. *The Jazz Book: From Ragtime to Fusion and Beyond.* Chicago: Lawrence Hill Books, 1992.

Berish, Andrew. "Negotiating a Blues Riff: Listening for Django Reinhardt's Place in American Jazz." *Jazz Perspectives* 3, no. 3 (2009): 233–64.

Berland, Jody. "Locating Listening: Technological Space, Popular Music, and Canadian Mediations." In *The Place of Music*, edited by Andrew Leyshon, David Matless, and George Revill, 129–50. New York: Guilford Press, 1998.

Berliner, Paul F. *Thinking in Jazz: The Infinite Art of Improvisation.* Chicago: University of Chicago Press, 1994.

Berman, Marshall. *All That Is Solid Melts into Air: The Experience of Modernity.* 1982. Reprint, New York: Penguin Books, 1988.

Bilby, Kenneth. "African American Memory at the Crossroads: Grounding the Miraculous with Tooy." *Small Axe* 29 (July 2009): 185–99.

Bindas, Kenneth. *Swing, That Modern Sound.* Jackson: University Press of Mississippi, 2001.

Blesh, Rudi. "Flying Home." In *Reading Jazz: A Gathering of Autobiography, Reportage, and Criticism from 1919 to Now*, edited by Robert Gottlieb, 516–36. New York: Vintage Books, 1996.

Blesser, Barry, and Linda-Ruth Salter. *Spaces Speak, Are You Listening?* Cambridge, MA: MIT Press, 2007.

Blum, John Morton. *V Was for Victory: Politics and American Culture during World War II.* New York: Harcourt Brace Jovanovich, 1976.

Bontemps Arna, and Jack Conroy. *Anyplace but Here.* Originally published as *They Seek a City*, 1966. Reprint, Columbia: University of Missouri Press, 1997.

Born, Georgina. *Rationalizing Culture: IRCAM, Boulez, and the Institutionalization of the Avant-Garde.* Berkeley: University of California Press, 1995.

Boyd, Jean A. *The Jazz of the Southwest: An Oral History of Western Swing.* Austin: University of Texas Press, 1998.

Boym, Svetlana. *The Future of Nostalgia.* New York: Basic Books, 2001.

Brackett, David. *Interpreting Popular Music*. 1995. Reprint, Berkeley: University of California Press, 2000.

Bradley, Edwin M. *The First Hollywood Musicals: A Critical Filmography of 171 Features, 1927 through 1932*. Jefferson, NC: McFarland, 1996.

Broadbent, Peter. *Charlie Christian: Solo Flight; The Seminal Electric Guitarist*. 2nd ed. Blaydon on Tyne, UK: Ashley Mark, 2003.

Brooks, Gwendolyn. *The World of Gwendolyn Brooks*. New York: Harper and Row, 1971.

Bryant, Clora, et al., eds. *Central Avenue Sounds: Jazz in Los Angeles*. Berkeley: University of California Press, 1998.

Büchmann-Møller, Frank. *Someone to Watch over Me: The Life and Music of Ben Webster*. Ann Arbor: University of Michigan Press, 2008.

Bulliet, Richard W., ed. *The Columbia History of the 20th Century*. New York: Columbia University Press, 1998.

Burke, Patrick Lawrence. *Come In and Hear the Truth: Jazz and Race on 52nd Street*. Chicago: University of Chicago Press, 2008.

Busby, Mark, ed. *The Southwest: The Greenwood Encyclopedia of American Regional Cultures*. Westport, CT: Greenwood Press, 2004.

Calinescu, Matei. *Five Faces of Modernity*. 1987. Durham, NC: Duke University Press, 2003.

Caponi-Tabery, Gena. *Jazz, Basketball and Black Culture in 1930s America*. Amherst: University of Massachusetts Press, 2008.

Carby, Hazel, "It Jus Be's Dat Way Sometime: The Sexual Politics of Women's Blues." In *The Jazz Cadence of American Culture*, edited by Robert G. O'Meally, 469–82. New York: Columbia University Press, 1998.

Carpenter, Edmund, and Marshall McLuhan, eds. *Explorations in Communication: An Anthology*. London: Jonathan Cape, 1970.

Casey, Edward S. *The Fate of Place: A Philosophical History*. Berkeley: University of California Press, 1997.

———. *Getting Back into Place: A Renewed Understanding of the Place-World*. Bloomington: Indiana University Press, 1993.

———. "How to Get from Space to Place in a Fairly Short Stretch of Time: Phenomenological Prolegomena." In *Senses of Place*, edited by Steven Feld and Keith H. Basso. Santa Fe, NM: School of American Research Press, 1996.

Cateforis, Theo. "Performing the Avant-Garde Groove: Devo and the Whiteness of the New Wave." *American Music* 22, no. 4 (Winter 2004): 564–88.

Charters, Samuel. *The Bluesmen: The Story and the Music of the Men Who Made the Blues*. New York: Oak, 1967.

Chernoff, John Miller. *African Rhythm and African Sensibility: Aesthetics and Social Action in African Musical Idioms*. Chicago: University of Chicago Press, 1979.

Chilton, John. *Who's Who of Jazz: Storyville to Swing Street*. 4th ed. New York: Da Capo Press, 1985.

Clarke, Donald. *Billie Holiday: Wishing on the Moon*. New York: Da Capo Press, 2002.

Clarke, Eric F. *Ways of Listening: An Ecological Approach to the Perception of Musical Meaning*. New York: Oxford University Press, 2005.

Clifford, James. *Routes: Travel and Translation in the Late Twentieth Century*. Cambridge, MA: Harvard University Press, 1997.

Cogan, Robert, and Pozzi Escot. *Sonic Design: The Nature of Sound and Music*. Englewood Cliffs, NJ: Prentice-Hall, 1976.

Cohan, Steven, and Ina Rae Hark, eds. *The Road Movie Book*. New York: Routledge, 1997.

Cohen, Barbara, Seymour Chwast, and Steven Heller. *Trylon and Perisphere: The 1939 New York World's Fair*. New York: Abrams, 1989.

Cohen, Sara. *Decline, Renewal and the City in Popular Music Culture: Beyond the Beatles*. Hampshire, UK: Ashgate Press, 2007.

———. "Sounding Out the City: Music and the Sensuous Production of Place." In *The Place of Music*, edited by Andrew Leyshon, David Matless, and George Revill. New York: Guilford Press, 1998.

Coker, Jerry. *Improvising Jazz*. 1964. Reprint, New York: Fireside Books/Simon and Schuster, 1987.

Collette, Buddy, and Steven Louis Isoardi. *Jazz Generations: A Life in American Music and Society*. New York: Continuum, 2000.

Collier, Geoffrey L., and James Lincoln Collier, "Microrhythms in Jazz: A Review of Papers." *Annual Review of Jazz Studies* 8 (1996): 117–39.

Collier, James Lincoln. *Benny Goodman and the Swing Era*. New York: Oxford University Press, 1989.

———. *Duke Ellington*. New York: Oxford University Press, 1987.

———. *The Making of Jazz: A Comprehensive History*. New York: Dell, 1978.

Connell John, and Chris Gibson. *Sound Tracks: Popular Music, Identity and Place*. New York: Routledge, 2003.

Cooke, Mervyn, and David Horn, eds. *The Cambridge Companion to Jazz*. Cambridge: Cambridge University Press, 2002.

Cooney, Terry A. *Balancing Acts: American Thought and Culture in the 1930s*. New York: Twayne, 1995.

Creed, Gerald W., and Barbara Ching, eds. *Knowing Your Place: Rural Identity and Cultural Hierarchy*. New York: Routledge, 1997.

Cresswell, Tim. *Place: A Short Introduction*. Malden, MA: Blackwell, 2004.

Cross, Gary S., and John K. Walton. *The Playful Crowd: Pleasure Places in the Twentieth Century*. New York: Columbia University Press, 2005.

Crow, Bill. *Jazz Anecdotes*. New York: Oxford University Press, 1990.

Crowther, Bruce and Mike Pinfold. *The Big Band Years*. New York: Facts on File, 1988.

Dance, Stanley. Liner notes, *The World of Duke Ellington*, Two LPs, CBS Records G32564, 1974.

———. *The World of Duke Ellington*. New York: Charles Scribner's Sons, 1970.

——. *The World of Swing: An Oral History of Big Band Jazz.* New York: Da Capo Press, 2001.

Daniels, Douglas Henry. *Lester Leaps In: The Life and Times of Lester "Pres" Young.* Boston: Beacon Press, 2003.

Danielsen, Anne. *Presence and Pleasure: The Funk Grooves of James Brown and Parliament.* Middletown, CT: Wesleyan University Press, 2006.

DeLong, Thomas, A. *The Mighty Music Box: The Golden Age of Musical Radio.* Los Angeles: Amber Crest Books, 1980.

Denning, Michael. *The Cultural Front: The Laboring of American Culture in the Twentieth Century.* New York: Verso, 1996.

Determeyer, Eddy. *Rhythm Is Our Business: Jimmie Lunceford and the Harlem Express.* Ann Arbor: University of Michigan Press, 2006.

De Valk, Jeroen. *Ben Webster: His Life and Music.* Berkeley, CA: Berkeley Hills Books, 2000.

DeVeaux, Scott. *The Birth of Bebop: A Social and Musical History.* Berkeley: University of California Press, 1997.

——. "Constructing the Jazz Tradition: Jazz Historiography." *Black American Literature Forum* 25, no. 3 (Autumn 1991): 525–60.

Dickstein, Morris. "Depression Culture: The Dream of Mobility." In *Radical Revisions: Rereading 1930s Culture*, edited by Bill Mullen and Sherry Lee Linkon, 225–41. Urbana: University of Illinois Press, 1996.

——. *Dancing in the Dark: A Cultural History of the Great Depression.* New York: W. W. Norton, 2009.

Dinerstein, Joel. *Swinging the Machine: Modernity, Technology, and African American Culture between the World Wars.* Amherst: University of Massachusetts Press, 2003.

DjeDje, Jacqueline Cogdell, and Eddie S. Meadows, eds. *California Soul: Music of African Americans in the West.* Berkeley: University of California Press, 1998.

Dorman, Robert L. *Revolt of the Provinces: The Regionalist Movement in America, 1920–1945.* Chapel Hill: University of North Carolina Press, 1993.

Douglas, Ann. *Terrible Honesty: Mongrel Manhattan in the 1920s.* New York: Noonday Press/Farrar, Straus and Giroux, 1995.

Douglas, Susan J. *Listening In: Radio and the American Imagination, from Amos 'n' Andy and Edward R. Murrow to Wolfman Jack and Howard Stern.* New York: Times Books/Random House, 1999.

Downs, Clive G. "An Annotated Bibliography of Notated Charlie Christian Solos." *Annual Review of Jazz Studies* 6 (1993): 153–67.

——. "Metric Displacement in the Improvisation of Charlie Christian." *Annual Review of Jazz Studies* 11 (2000–2001): 39–68.

Drake, St. Clair, and Horace R. Cayton. *Black Metropolis: A Study of Negro Life in a Northern City.* New York: Harcourt, Brace, 1945.

Driggs, Frank, and Chuck Haddix. *Kansas City Jazz: From Ragtime to Bebop—a History.* New York: Oxford University Press, 2005.

Eastman, Ralph. "Pitchin' Up a Boogie." In *California Soul: Music of African Americans in the West,* edited by Jacqueline Cogdell DjeDje and Eddie S. Meadows, 79–103. Berkeley: University of California Press, 1998.

Edwards, Brent Hayes. "The Literary Ellington." In *Uptown Conversations: The New Jazz Studies,* edited by Robert G. O'Meally, Brent Hayes Edwards, and Farah Jasmine Griffin, 326–56. New York: Columbia University Press, 2004.

Eitan, Zohar, and Roni Y. Granot. "How Music Moves: Musical Parameters and Listeners' Images of Motion." *Music Perception* 23, no. 3 (2006): 221–47.

Ellington, Duke [Edward Kennedy]. *Daybreak Express.* 1933. Transcribed and edited by Gunther Schuller. Jazz Masterworks Editions, no. 1. Washington, DC: Smithsonian Institution, 1993.

———. "Ellington Explains Swing." In *Keeping Time: Readings in Jazz History,* edited by Robert Walser, 106–10. New York: Oxford University Press, 1999.

———. *Music Is My Mistress.* New York: Doubleday, 1973. Reprint, New York: Da Capo Press, n.d.

Ellington, Mercer, with Stanley Dance. *Duke Ellington in Person.* 1978. Reprint, New York: Da Capo Press, 1979.

Ellison, Ralph. *Invisible Man.* 1947. Reprint, New York: Vintage Books, 1995.

———. *Living with Music: Ralph Ellison's Jazz Writings.* Edited by Robert G. O'Meally. New York: Modern Library, 2002.

Erenberg, Lewis A. *Swingin' the Dream: Big Band Jazz and the Rebirth of American Culture.* Chicago: University of Chicago Press, 1998.

Erenberg, Lewis A., and Susan Hirsch, eds. *The War in American Culture: Society and Consciousness during World War II.* Chicago: University of Chicago Press, 1996.

Evans, David. "Musical Innovation in the Blues of Blind Lemon Jefferson." *Black Music Research Journal* 20, no. 1 (Spring 2000): 83–116.

Feld, Steven. "Waterfalls of Sound: An Acoustemology of Place Resounding in Bosavi, Papua New Guinea." In *Senses of Place,* edited by Steven Feld and Keith H. Basso, 91–135. Santa Fe, NM: School of American Research Press, 1996.

Feld, Steven, and Keith H. Basso, eds. *Senses of Place.* Santa Fe, NM: School of American Research Press, 1996.

Ferguson, Otis. "The Spirit of Jazz." *New Republic,* December 30, 1935.

Fernett, Gene. *Swing Out: Great Negro Dance Bands.* Midland, MI: Pendell, 1970.

Finkelman, Jonathan. "Charlie Christian and the Role of Formulas in Jazz Improvisation." *Jazzforschung/Jazz Research* 29 (1997): 159–88.

———. "Charlie Christian, Bebop, and the Recordings at Minton's." *Annual Review of Jazz Studies* 6 (1993): 187–203.

Firestone, Ross. *Swing, Swing, Swing: The Life and Times of Benny Goodman.* New York: W. W. Norton, 1993.

Fischlin, Daniel, and Ajay Heble, eds. *The Other Side of Nowhere: Jazz, Improvisation, and Communities in Dialogue*. Middletown, CT: Wesleyan University Press, 2004.

Flamming, Douglas. *Bound for Freedom: Black Los Angeles in Jim Crow America*. Berkeley: University of California Press, 2005.

Flinn, Carol. *Strains of Utopia: Gender, Nostalgia, and Hollywood Film Music*. Princeton, NJ: Princeton University Press, 1992.

Floyd, Samuel A. *The Power of Black Music: Interpreting Its History from Africa to the United States*. New York: Oxford University Press, 1995.

Foner, Eric. *The Story of American Freedom*. New York: W. W. Norton, 1998.

Forman, Murray. *The 'Hood Comes First: Race, Space, and Place in Rap and Hip-Hop*. Middletown, CT: Wesleyan University Press, 2002.

Fox, Dan, ed. *Charlie Christian: The Art of Jazz Guitar*. 1964. Reprint, New York: Goodman Group/Hal Leonard, 1988.

Franceschina, John. *Duke Ellington's Music for the Theatre*. Jefferson, NC: McFarland, 2001.

Francis, Jacqueline. "The Make of the Modern." Review of *Jacob Lawrence: The "Migration" Series*, edited by Elizabeth Hutton Turner. *Callaloo* 17, no. 4 (Autumn 1994): 1269–72.

Franklin, Jimmie Lewis. *Journey toward Hope: A History of Blacks in Oklahoma*. Norman: University of Oklahoma Press, 1982.

Frith, Simon, Will Straw, and John Street, eds. *The Cambridge Companion to Pop and Rock*. Cambridge: Cambridge University Press, 2001.

Gabbard, Krin. *Jammin' at the Margins: Jazz and the American Cinema*. Chicago: University of Chicago Press, 1996.

———, ed. *Jazz among the Discourses*. Durham, NC: Duke University Press, 1995.

———. "Paris Blues." In *Uptown Conversations: The New Jazz Studies*, edited by Robert G. O'Meally, Brent Hayes Edwards, and Farah Jasmine Griffin, 297–311. New York: Columbia University Press, 2004.

———, ed. *Representing Jazz*. Durham, NC: Duke University Press, 1995.

Gaines, Kevin K. *Uplifting the Race: Black Leadership, Politics, and Culture in the Twentieth Century*. Chapel Hill: University of North Carolina Press, 1996.

Gardner, Edward Foote. *Popular Songs of the Twentieth Century: A Charted History*. Vol. 1, *1900–1949*. St. Paul, MN: Paragon House, 2000.

Garofalo, Reebee. *Rockin' Out: Popular Music in the USA* Boston: Allyn and Bacon, 1997.

Garofalo, Reebee, ed. *Rockin' the Boat: Mass Music and Mass Movements*. Boston: South End Press, 1992.

———. *Rockin' Out: Popular Music in the USA*. Boston: Allyn and Bacon, 1997.

Garrett, Charles Hiroshi. *Struggling to Define a Nation: American Music in the Twentieth Century*. Berkeley: University of California Press, 2005.

Gates, Henry Louis, Jr. *The Signifying Monkey: A Theory of African-American Literary Criticism*. New York: Oxford University Press, 1988.

Gault, Lon A. *Ballroom Echoes*. N.p.: Andrew Corbet Press, 1989.

Gebhardt, Nicholas. *Going for Jazz: Musical Practices and American Ideology*. Chicago: University of Chicago Press, 2001.

Gelly, Dave. *Being Prez: The Life and Music of Lester Young*. New York: Oxford University Press, 2007.

Gendron, Bernard. " 'Moldy Figs' and Modernists: Jazz at War (1942–1946)." In *Jazz among the Discourses*, edited by Krin Gabbard, 31–56. Durham, NC: Duke University Press, 1995.

Gennari, John. *Blowin' Hot and Cool: Jazz and Its Critics*. Chicago: University of Chicago Press, 2006.

Giddins, Gary. *Celebrating Bird: The Triumph of Charlie Parker*. New York: Beech Tree Books, 1987.

Gilroy, Paul. *Darker Than Blue: On the Moral Economies of Black Atlantic Culture*. Cambridge, MA: Harvard University Press, 2010.

Gioia, Ted. *The History of Jazz*. New York: Oxford University Press, 1997.

———. *West Coast Jazz: Modern Jazz in California, 1945–1960*. 1992. Reprint, Berkeley: University of California Press, 1998.

Gitler, Ira. *Swing to Bop: An Oral History of the Transition of Jazz in the 1940s*. New York: Oxford University Press, 1985.

Givan, Benjamin M. "Django Reinhardt's Style and Improvisational Process." PhD diss., Yale University, 2003.

Gleason, Philip, "Americans All: World War II and the Shaping of American Identity." *Review of Politics* 43, no. 4 (October 1981): 483–518.

Goddard, Stephen B. *Getting There: The Epic Struggle between Road and Rail in the American Century*. Chicago: University of Chicago Press, 1994.

Goins, Wayne E., and Craig R. McKinney. *A Biography of Charlie Christian, Jazz Guitar's King of Swing*. Studies in the History and Interpretation of Music 118. Lewiston, NY: Edwin Mellen Press, 2005.

Gold, Robert S. *A Jazz Lexicon*. New York: Alfred A. Knopf, 1964.

Goldberg, David. *Discontented America: The United States in the 1920s*. Baltimore: Johns Hopkins University Press, 1999.

Goldberg, Marv. *More Than Words Can Say: The Ink Spots and Their Music*. Lanham, MD: Scarecrow Press, 1998.

Goodman, Benny, and Irving Kolodin. *The Kingdom of Swing*. New York: Stackpole Sons, 1939.

Gottlieb, Robert, ed. *Reading Jazz: A Gathering of Autobiography, Reportage, and Criticism from 1919 to Now*. New York: Vintage, 1999.

Greene, Joshua M. *Here Comes the Sun: The Spiritual and Musical Journey of George Harrison*. Hoboken, NJ: Wiley, 2006.

Gridley, Mark. *Jazz Styles: History and Analysis*. 8th ed. Englewood Cliffs, NJ: Prentice-Hall, 2002.

Griffin, Farah Jasmine. *If You Can't Be Free, Be a Mystery: In Search of Billie Holiday*. New York: One World/Ballantine, 2002.

———. *"Who Set You Flowin'?" The African-American Migration Narrative.* New York: Oxford University Press, 1995.

Gushee, Lawrence. "Lester Young's 'Shoeshine Boy.'" *IMSCR XII: Berkeley 1977*, 151–69.

Habermas, Jürgen. *The Philosophical Discourse of Modernity: Twelve Lectures.* Translated by Frederick Lawrence. Cambridge, MA: MIT Press, 1987.

Hajdu, David. *Lush Life: A Biography of Billy Strayhorn.* New York: Farrar, Straus, and Giroux, 1996.

Hale, Grace Elizabeth. *Making Whiteness: The Culture of Segregation in the South, 1890–1940.* New York: Vintage, 1998.

Hammond, John, and Irving Townshend. *John Hammond on Record: An Autobiography.* New York: Summit, 1977.

Harap, Louis. "The Case for Hot Jazz." *Musical Quarterly* 27, no. 1 (January 1941): 47–61.

Harley, Maria Ann. "An American in Space: Henry Brant's 'Spatial Music.'" *American Music* 15, no. 1 (Spring 1997): 70–92.

Harvey, David. *The Condition of Postmodernity.* 1990. Reprint, Cambridge, MA: Blackwell, 2004.

———. *Justice, Nature and the Geography of Difference.* Cambridge, MA: Blackwell, 1996.

———. *Spaces of Global Capitalism.* New York: Verso, 2006.

Hasse, John Edward. *Beyond Category: The Life and Genius of Ellington.* New York: Da Capo Press, 1993.

Hayden, Dolores. *The Power of Place: Urban Landscapes as Public History.* Cambridge, MA: MIT Press, 1995.

Heartz, Daniel. *Music in the European Capitals: The Galant Style, 1720–1780.* New York: W. W. Norton, 2003.

Hennessey, Thomas J. *From Jazz to Swing: African-American Jazz Musicians and Their Music, 1890–1935.* Detroit: Wayne State University Press, 1994.

Hersch, Charles. *Subversive Sounds: Race and the Birth of Jazz in New Orleans.* Chicago: University of Chicago Press, 2007.

Hickey, Dave. *Air Guitar: Essays on Art and Democracy.* Los Angeles: Art Issues Press, 1997.

Hischak, Thomas S. *The Rogers and Hammerstein Encyclopedia.* Westport, CT: Greenwood Press, 2007.

———, ed. *The Tin Pan Alley Song Encyclopedia.* Westport, CT: Greenwood Press, 2002.

Hodeir, André. *Jazz: Its Evolution and Essence.* New York: Grove Press, 1956.

Hodson, Robert. *Interaction, Improvisation, and Interplay in Jazz.* New York: Routledge, 2007.

Holiday, Billie, and William Dufty. *Lady Sings the Blues.* New York: Doubleday, 1956.

Holland, Richard. "Music." In *The Southwest: The Greenwood Encyclopedia of American Regional Cultures*, edited by Mark Busby, 315–50. Westport, CT: Greenwood Press, 2004.

Honey, Maureen, ed. *Bitter Fruit: African American Women in World War II*. Columbia: University of Missouri Press, 1999.

Hood, Clifton. *Music as Heard: A Study in Applied Phenomenology*. New Haven, CT: Yale University Press, 1983.

Horkheimer, Max, and Theodor W. Adorno. *Dialectic of Enlightenment*. Translated by John Cumming. New York: Continuum, 1998.

Howland, John. *Ellington Uptown: Duke Ellington, James P. Johnson, and the Birth of Concert Jazz*. Ann Arbor: University of Michigan Press, 2009.

Hubbard, Phil, Rob Kitchen, Brendan Bartley, and Duncan Fuller. *Thinking Geographically: Space, Theory and Contemporary Human Geography*. New York: Continuum, 2002.

Hurston, Zora Neale. *Mules and Men*. 1935. Reprint, New York: Harper Perennial Library, 1990.

Ihde, Don. *Listening and Voice: A Phenomenology of Sound*. Athens: Ohio University Press, 1976.

Ilf, Ilya, and Eugene Petrov. *Little Golden America: Two Famous Soviet Humorists Survey These United States*. Translated by Charles Malamuth. Foreign Travelers in America, 1810–1935, edited by Arthur M. Schlesinger Jr. and Eugene P. Moehring. New York: Farrar, Rinehart, 1937. Reprint, New York: Arno Press, 1974.

Interrante, Joseph. "The Road to Autopia: The Automobile and the Spatial Transformation of American Culture." *Michigan Quarterly Review* 15–16 (Fall 1980–Winter 1981): 502–17.

Isoardi, Steven Louis. *The Dark Tree: Jazz and the Community Arts in Los Angeles*. Berkeley: University of California Press, 2006.

Iyer, Vijay. "Exploding the Narrative in Jazz Improvisation." In *Uptown Conversation: The New Jazz Studies*, edited by Robert G. O'Meally, Brent Hayes Edwards, and Farah Jasmin Griffin, 393–403. New York: Columbia University Press, 2004.

Jackson, John Brinckerhoff. *A Sense of Time, a Sense of Place*. New Haven, CT: Yale University Press, 1994.

Jackson, Kenneth T. *Crabgrass Frontier: The Suburbanization of the United States*. New York: Oxford University Press, 1985.

"Jacob Lawrence." *Bulletin of the Museum of Modern Art* 12, no. 2 (November 1944): 11.

Jacobson, David. *Place and Belonging in America*. Baltimore: Johns Hopkins University Press, 2002.

Jaeger, Phillip Edward. *Cedar Grove (New Jersey)*. Images of America. Mount Pleasant, SC: Arcadia, 2000.

Jameson, Frederic. *Postmodernism, or The Cultural Logic of Late Capitalism*. Durham, NC: Duke University Press, 1991.

Jeffries, John W. *Wartime America: The World War II Home Front.* Chicago: Ivan R. Dee, 1996.

Johansson, Ola, and Thomas L. Bell, eds. *Sound, Society and the Geography of Popular Music.* Farnham, UK: Ashgate Press, 2009.

Johnson, Mark L., and Steve Larson. "'Something in the Way She Moves'— Metaphors of Musical Motion." *Metaphor and Symbol* 18, no. 2 (2003): 63–84.

Jones, LeRoi [Amiri Baraka]. *Black Music.* New York: William Morrow, 1967.

———. *Blues People: Negro Music in White America.* New York: Morrow Quill Paperbacks, 1963.

Kammen, Michael. *Mystic Chords of Memory: The Transformation of Tradition in American Culture.* New York: Alfred A. Knopf, 1991.

Keil, Charles. "Motion and Feeling through Music." In *Music Grooves,* edited by Charles Keil and Steven Feld, 53–76. Chicago: University of Chicago Press, 1994.

Keil, Charles, and Steven Feld. *Music Grooves: Essays and Dialogues.* Chicago: University of Chicago Press, 1994.

Kelley, Robin D. G. *Race Rebels: Culture, Politics, and the Black Working Class.* New York: Free Press, 1994.

Kennedy, David. *Freedom from Fear: The American People in Depression and War, 1929–1945.* New York: Oxford University Press, 2001.

Kenney, William Howland. *Chicago Jazz: A Cultural History, 1904–1930.* New York: Oxford University Press, 1993.

———. *Jazz on the River.* Chicago: University of Chicago Press, 2005.

———. *The Phonograph and Recorded Music in American Life, 1870–1945.* New York: Oxford University Press, 1999.

Kirchner, Bill, ed. *The Oxford Companion to Jazz.* New York: Oxford University Press, 2000.

Kirk, Andy, with Amy Lee and Howard Rye. *Twenty Years on Wheels.* Ann Arbor: University of Michigan Press, 1989.

Kolchin, Peter. "Whiteness Studies: The New History of Race in America." *Journal of American History* 89, no. 1 (June 2002): 154–73.

Kramer, Lawrence. *Music as Cultural Practice, 1800–1900.* Berkeley: University of California Press, 1990.

———. *Musical Meaning: Toward a Critical History.* Berkeley: University of California Press, 2001.

Kubik, Gerhard. *Africa and the Blues.* Jackson: University of Mississippi Press, 1999.

Kun, Josh. *Audiotopia: Music, Race, and America.* Berkeley: University of California Press, 2005.

Langer Susanne K. *Feeling and Form: A Theory of Art.* New York: Charles Scribner's Sons, 1953.

Lawrence, A. H. *Duke Ellington and His World: A Biography.* New York: Routledge, 2001.

Lawson, Alan. "The Cultural Legacy of the New Deal." In *Fifty Years Later: The New Deal Evaluated*, edited by Harvard Sitkoff, 155–86. Philadelphia: Temple University Press, 1985.

Lax, Roger, and Frederick Smith, eds. *The Great Song Thesaurus*. New York: Oxford University Press, 1989.

Leach, Neil, ed. *Rethinking Architecture*. New York: Routledge, 1997.

Leach, William. *Country of Exiles: The Destruction of Place in American Life*. New York: Pantheon Books, 1999.

Lefebvre, Henri. *The Production of Space*. Translated by Donald Nicholson-Smith. Oxford: Blackwell, 1991.

Lenthall, Bruce. *Radio's America: The Great Depression and the Rise of Modern Mass Culture*. Chicago: University of Chicago Press, 2007.

Leuchtenburg, William E. *Franklin D. Roosevelt and the New Deal, 1932–1940*. New York: Harper and Row, 1963.

Levin, Floyd. *Classic Jazz: A Personal View of the Music and the Musicians*. Berkeley: University of California Press, 2000.

Levine, Lawrence. *Black Culture and Black Consciousness: Afro-American Folk Thought from Slavery to Freedom*. 1977. Reprint, New York: Oxford University Press, 1981.

———. *The Unpredictable Past: Explorations in American Cultural History*. New York: Oxford University Press, 1993.

Levine, Mark. *The Jazz Theory Book*. Petaluma, CA: Sher Music Company, 1995.

Levinson, Peter J. *Tommy Dorsey: Livin' in a Great Big Way*. New York: Da Capo Press, 2005.

Lewis, George E. "Improvised Music after 1950: Afrological and Eurological Perspectives." In *The Other Side of Nowhere: Jazz, Improvisation, and Communities in Dialogue*, edited by Daniel Fischlin and Ajay Heble, 131–62. Middletown, CT: Wesleyan University Press, 2004.

Lewis, Tom. *Divided Highways: Building the Interstate Highways, Transforming American Life*. New York: Penguin Books, 1997.

Leyshon, Andrew, David Matless, and George Revill, eds. *The Place of Music*. New York: Guilford Press, 1998.

Lichtenstein, Nelson. "The Making of the Postwar Working Class: Cultural Pluralism and Social Structure in World War II." *Historian* 51 (November 1988): 42–63.

Light, Andrew, and Jonathan M. Smith, eds. *Philosophies of Place*. Philosophy and Geography 3. New York: Rowman and Littlefield, 1998.

Lippard, Lucy. *The Lure of the Local: A Sense of Place in a Multi-centered Society*. New York: New Press, 1997.

Lippman, Edward. *The Philosophy and Aesthetics of Music*. Lincoln: University of Nebraska Press, 1999.

Lipsitz, George. *Dangerous Crossroads: Popular Music, Postmodernism, and the Poetics of Place*. New York: Verso, 1994.

―――. *Rainbow at Midnight: Labor and Culture in the 1940s.* Urbana: University of Illinois Press, 1994.

―――. *Time Passages: Collective Memory and American Popular Culture.* 1990. Minneapolis: University of Minnesota Press, 2007.

Lochhead, Judith. "The Metaphor of Musical Motion: Is There an Alternative?" *Theory and Practice* 14–15 (1989–90): 83–103.

―――. "The Temporal Structure of Recent Music: A Phenomenological Investigation." PhD diss., State University of New York, Stony Brook, 1982.

―――. Review of *Music as Heard: A Study in Applied Phenomenology,* by Clifton Hood. *Journal of Musicology* 4, no. 3 (Summer 1985–Summer 1986): 355–64.

Lock, Graham. *Blutopia: Visions of the Future and Revisions of the Past in the Work of Sun Ra, Duke Ellington, and Anthony Braxton.* Durham, NC: Duke University Press, 1999.

Lofland, Lyn H. *A World of Strangers: Order and Action in Urban Public Space.* New York: Basic Books, 1973.

Lomax, Alan. *Mister Jelly Roll: The Fortunes of Jelly Roll Morton, New Orleans Creole and "Inventor of Jazz."* New York: Pantheon, 1993.

Lopes, Paul. *The Rise of a Jazz Art World.* Cambridge: Cambridge University Press, 2002.

Lorensen, Jutta. "Between Image and Word, Color and Time: Jacob Lawrence's 'The Migration Series.'" *African American Review* 40, no. 3 (Fall 2006): 571–86.

Lott, Eric. "Double V, Double-Time: Bebop's Politics of Style." In *The Jazz Cadence of American Culture,* edited by Robert G. O'Meally, 457–68. New York: Columbia University Press, 1998.

―――. *Love and Theft: Blackface Minstrelsy and the American Working Class.* New York: Oxford University Press, 1993.

Lynch, Kevin. *The Image of the City.* Cambridge, MA: MIT Press, 1960.

Lynd, Robert S., and Helen Merrell Lynd. *Middletown in Transition: A Study in Cultural Conflicts.* 1937. Reprint, New York: Harcourt Brace Jovanovich, 1982.

Magee, Jeffrey. *The Uncrowned King of Swing: Fletcher Henderson and Big Band Jazz.* New York: Oxford University Press, 2005.

Major, Clarence, ed. *Juba to Jive: A Dictionary of African-American Slang.* New York: Viking, 1994.

Malone, Bill C. *Country Music, U.S.A.* 1968. Rev. ed., Austin: University of Texas Press, 2002.

Manning, Frankie, and Cynthia R. Millman, *Ambassador of Lindy Hop.* Philadelphia: Temple University Press, 2007.

Marling, Karal Ann. *Wall-to-Wall America: A Cultural History of Post-Office Murals in the Great Depression.* Minneapolis: University of Minnesota Press, 1982.

Marshall, Wolf. *The Best of Charlie Christian: A Step-by-Step Breakdown of the Styles and Techniques of the Father of Modern Jazz Guitar.* Milwaukee, WI: Hal Leonard, 2002.

Martin, Henry. *Charlie Parker and Thematic Improvisation.* Metuchen, NJ: Scarecrow Press, 1996.

Martin, Henry, and Keith Waters. *Jazz: The First 100 Years,* 2nd ed. Belmont, CA: Thomson-Schirmer, 2006.

Masekela, Hugh, and D. Michael Cheers. *Still Grazing: The Musical Journey of Hugh Masekela.* New York: Crown, 2004.

Mather, Dan. *Charlie Barnet: An Illustrated Biography and Discography.* Jefferson, NC: McFarland, 2002.

McCarthy, Albert J. *Big Band Jazz.* 1974. Reprint, London: Peerage Books, 1983.

———. *The Dance Band Era, the Dancing Decades from Ragtime to Swing: 1910–1950.* London: Spring Books, 1974.

McClary, Susan. *Feminine Endings: Music, Gender, and Sexuality.* Minneapolis: University of Minnesota Press, 1991.

McClellan, Lawrence. *The Later Swing Era, 1942 to 1955.* Westport, CT: Greenwood Press, 2004.

McElvaine, Robert S., ed. *Down and Out in the Great Depression: Letters from the "Forgotten Man."* Chapel Hill: University of North Carolina Press, 1983.

———. *The Great Depression: America, 1929–1941.* New York: Times Books, 1994.

McGovern, James R. *And a Time for Hope: America in the Great Depression.* Westport, CT: Praeger, 2000.

McKay, Claude. *Harlem: Negro Metropolis.* New York: E. P. Dutton, 1940.

McNichol, Dan. *The Roads That Built America: The Incredible Story of the U.S. Interstate Highway System.* New York: Barnes and Noble, 2003.

Melnick, Jeffrey. *A Right to Sing the Blues: African-Americans, Jews, and Popular Song.* Cambridge, MA: Harvard University Press, 1999.

Mezzrow, Milton "Mezz," and Bernard Wolfe. *Really the Blues.* 1946. Reprint, New York: Citadel Press/Carol, 1990.

Middleton, Richard, ed. *Reading Pop: Approaches to Textual Analysis in Popular Music.* Oxford: Oxford University Press, 2000.

Millard, Andre. *America on Record: A History of Recorded Sound,* 2nd ed. Cambridge: Cambridge University Press, 2005.

Mirtle, Jack, ed. *The Music of Billy May: A Discography.* Westport, CT: Greenwood Press, 1998.

Monelle, Raymond. *The Sense of Music: Semiotic Essays.* Princeton, NJ: Princeton University Press, 2000.

Monson, Ingrid T. *Freedom Sounds: Civil Rights Call Out to Jazz and Africa.* Oxford: Oxford University Press, 2007.

———. *Saying Something: Jazz Improvisation and Interaction.* Chicago: University Chicago Press, 1996.

Mook, Richard. "White Masculinity in Barbershop Quartet Singing." *Journal of the Society for American Music* 1, no. 4 (November 2007): 453–83.

Moore, Patricia Anne. *The Casino: Catalina's "Two Million Dollar Palace of Pleasure."* Rev. ed. Avalon, CA: Catalina Island Museum Society, 1979.

Morgan, Robert. "Musical Time/Musical Space." *Critical Inquiry* 6, no. 3 (Spring 1980): 527–38.

Morton, John Fass. *Backstory in Blue: Ellington at Newport '56.* Piscataway, NJ: Rutgers University Press, 2008.

Mowry, George E. *The Urban Nation, 1920–1960.* New York: Hill and Wang, 1965.

Mullen, Bill, and Sherry Lee Linkon, eds. *Radical Revisions: Rereading 1930s Culture.* Urbana: University of Illinois Press, 1996.

Murray, Albert. *The Hero and the Blues.* Columbia: University of Missouri Press, 1973.

———. *The Omni-Americans.* New York: Avon, 1970.

———. *Stomping the Blues.* 1976. New York: Da Capo Press, 2000.

Myers, Helen, ed. *Ethnomusicology: An Introduction.* Norton/Grove Handbooks in Music. New York: W. W. Norton, 1992.

Myrdal, Gunnar. *An American Dilemma: The Negro Problem and Modern Democracy.* 1944. Reprint, New York: Harper and Row, 1962.

Negus, Keith *Popular Music in Theory: An Introduction.* Hanover, NH: Wesleyan University Press, 1997.

Nicholls, David, ed. *Cambridge History of American Music.* Cambridge: Cambridge University Press, 1998.

Nicholson, Stuart. *Reminiscing in Tempo: A Portrait of Duke Ellington.* Boston: Northeastern University Press, 1999.

Nollen, Scott Allen. *Paul Robeson, Film Pioneer.* Jefferson, NC: McFarland, 2010.

Nussbaum, Charles O. *The Musical Representation: Meaning, Ontology, and Emotion.* Cambridge, MA: MIT Press, 2007.

O'Brien, Kenneth Paul, and Lynn H. Parsons. *The Home-Front War: World War II and American Society.* Westport, CT: Greenwood Press, 1995.

O'Day, Anita, with George Eells. *High Times, Hard Times.* 1981. Reprint, New York: Limelight Editions, 2007.

O'Donnell, Shaugn. "Space, Motion, and Other Musical Metaphors." In *Perspectives on the Grateful Dead: Critical Writings,* edited by Robert G. Weiner, 127–35. Westport, CT: Greenwood Press, 1999.

Oliphant, Dave. *The Early Swing Era, 1930 to 1941.* Westport, CT: Greenwood Press, 2002.

———. "Eddie Durham and the Texas Contribution to Jazz History." *Southwest History Quarterly* 96 (April 1993): 490–525.

———. *Texan Jazz.* Austin: University of Texas Press, 1996.

Olson, James Stuart, ed. *Historical Dictionary of the Great Depression, 1929–1940.* Westport, CT: Greenwood Press, 2001.

O'Meally, Robert G., ed. *The Jazz Cadence of American Culture.* New York: Columbia University Press, 1998.

———. *Lady Day: The Many Faces of Billie Holiday*. New York: Da Capo Press, 2000.

O'Meally, Robert G., Brent Hayes Edwards, and Farah Jasmin Griffin, eds. *Uptown Conversation: The New Jazz Studies*. New York: Columbia University Press, 2004.

Ostransky, Leroy. *Jazz City: The Impact of Our Cities on the Development of Jazz*. Englewood Cliffs, NJ: Prentice-Hall, 1978.

Ottley, Roi. *"New World a-Coming": Inside Black America*. Cleveland, OH: World, 1943.

Overholt, Alma S. *The Catalina Story*. Avalon, CA: Island Press, 1962.

Owens, Thomas. "Charlie Parker: Techniques of Improvisation." PhD diss., University of California at Los Angeles, 1974.

Panassié, Hugues. *Hot Jazz: The Guide to Swing Music*. Translated by Lyle Downing and Eleanor Dowling from *Le jazz hot*. Revised by the author for the English edition. Westport, CT: Negro Universities Press, 1970.

Pastras, Philip. *Dead Man Blues: Jelly Roll Morton Way Out West*. Berkeley: University of California Press, 2001.

Pearson, Nathan W. *Goin' to Kansas City: Music in American Life*. Urbana: University of Illinois Press, 1994.

Pedersen, Jeannine L. *Catalina Island*. Images of America Series. Charleston, SC: Arcadia, 2004.

Peeler, David. *Hope among Us Yet: Social Criticism and Social Solace in Depression America*. Athens: University of Georgia Press, 1987.

Pellegrini, Norman. *150 Years of Opera in Chicago*. DeKalb: Northern Illinois University Press, 2006.

Pells, Richard. *Radical Visions and American Dreams: Culture and Social Thought in the Depression Years*. New York: Harper and Row, 1973.

Peretti, Burton W. *The Creation of Jazz: Music, Race, and Culture in Urban America*. Urbana: University of Illinois Press, 1992.

———. *Jazz in American Culture*. Chicago: Ivan R. Dee, 1997.

Petry, Ann. *The Street*. 1946. Reprint, Boston: Beacon Press, 1984.

Pike, Lionel. "Towards a Study of Musical Motion: Robert Simpson's Variations and Finale on a Theme of Haydn (1948)." *Music Review* 54, no. 2 (May 1, 1993): 137.

Pisano, Dominick A., ed. *The Airplane in American Culture*. Ann Arbor: University of Michigan Press, 2003.

Pleasants, Henry. *Serious Music, and All That Jazz: An Adventure in Music Criticism*. New York: Simon and Schuster, 1969.

Polenberg, Richard. *War and Society: The United States, 1941–1945*. Philadelphia: J. B. Lippincott, 1972.

Porter, Eric. *What Is This Thing Called Jazz? African American Musicians as Artists, Critics, and Activists*. Berkeley: University of California Press, 2002.

Porter, Lewis. *Lester Young*. Rev. ed. Ann Arbor: University of Michigan Press, 2005.

Powell, Richard J. "Jacob Lawrence: Keep on Movin'." *American Art* 15, no. 1 (Spring 2001): 90–93.

Pratt, Ray. *Rhythm and Resistance: Explorations in the Political Uses of Popular Music*. New York: Praeger, 1990.

Putnam, Robert D. *Bowling Alone: The Collapse and Revival of American Community*. New York: Simon and Schuster, 2000.

Pyron, Darden Asbury, ed. *Recasting "Gone with the Wind" in American Culture*. Miami: University Presses of Florida, 1983.

Radano, Ronald. *Lying Up a Nation: Race and Black Music*. Chicago: University of Chicago Press, 2003.

Radano, Ronald, and Philip V. Bohlman. "Introduction: Music and Race, Their Past, Their Presence." In *Music and the Racial Imagination*, edited by Ronald Radano and Philip V. Bohlmann, 1–53. Chicago: University of Chicago Press, 2000.

———, eds. *Music and the Racial Imagination*. Chicago: University of Chicago Press, 2000.

Rae, John B. *The Road and Car in American Life*. Cambridge, MA: MIT Press, 1971.

Ramsey, Guthrie P. *Race Music: Black Cultures from Bebop to Hip-Hop*. Berkeley: University of California Press, 2003.

Rattenbury, Ken. *Duke Ellington: Jazz Composer*. New Haven, CT: Yale University Press, 1990.

Relph, Edward C. *Place and Placelessness*. London: Pion, 1976.

Rhodes, Don. *Solo Flight: The Genius of Charlie Christian*. VIEW Video Jazz Series. New York: VIEW, 1996. Videocassette.

Rink, John, ed. *The Practice of Performance: Studies in Musical Interpretation*. Cambridge: Cambridge University Press, 1995.

Roach, Max. "Beyond Categories." In *Keeping Time: Readings in Jazz History*, edited by Robert Walser, 305–9. New York: Oxford University Press, 1999.

Rochberg, George. *The Aesthetics of Survival: A Composer's View of Twentieth-Century Music*. Ann Arbor: University of Michigan Press, 1984.

Rose, Mark H. *Interstate: Express Highway Politics, 1941–1956*. Lawrence: Regents Press of Kansas, 1979.

Rukeyser, Muriel. *Theory of Flight*. New Haven, CT: Yale University Press, 1935.

Russell, Ross. *Jazz Style in Kansas City and the Southwest*. Berkeley: University of California Press, 1973.

Rustin, Nichole T., and Sherrie Tucker, eds. *Big Ears: Listening for Gender in Jazz Studies*. Durham, NC: Duke University Press, 2008.

Sallis, James, ed. *The Guitar in Jazz: An Anthology*. Lincoln: University of Nebraska Press, 1996.

———. *The Guitar Players: One Instrument and Its Masters in American Music*. Lincoln: University of Nebraska Press, 1982.

Salzman, Jack, ed. *Encyclopedia of African-American Culture and History*. Vol. 4. New York: Simon and Schuster/Macmillan, 1996.

Sanjek, Russell, and David Sanjek. *Pennies from Heaven: The American Popular Music Business in the Twentieth Century.* New York: Da Capo Press, 1996.

Sargeant, Winthrop. *Jazz: Hot and Hybrid.* 1938. Reprint, New York: Da Capo Press, 1975.

Savage, William W., Jr. *Singing Cowboys and All That Jazz: A Short History of Popular Music in Oklahoma.* Norman: University of Oklahoma Press, 1983.

Scandura, Jani. *Down in the Dumps: Place, Modernity, American Depression.* Durham, NC: Duke University Press, 2008.

Schaber, Bennet. "Hitler Can't Keep 'em That Long." In *The Road Movie Book,* edited by Steven Cohan and Ina Rae Hark, 17–44. New York: Routledge, 1997.

Schoenberg, Arnold. *Style and Idea: Selected Writings of Arnold Schoenberg.* Berkeley: University of California Press, 1984.

Schoenberg, Loren. Liner notes. *Charlie Christian: The Genius of the Electric Guitar.* Four compact discs. Legacy Recordings, Columbia, Sony Music Entertainment (C4K 65564), 2002.

Schuller, Gunther. *Early Jazz: Its Roots and Musical Development.* 1968. Reprint, New York: Oxford University Press, 1986.

———. *The Swing Era: The Development of Jazz, 1930–1945.* New York: Oxford University Press, 1989.

Schuller, Gunther, and Martin Williams. Liner notes. *Big Band Jazz: From the Beginnings to the Fifties.* Washington, DC: Smithsonian Collection of Recordings, 1983.

Schwarz, David, Anahid Kassabian, and Lawrence Siegel, eds. *Keeping Score: Music, Disciplinarity, Culture.* Charlottesville: University Press of Virginia, 1997.

Scott, Andrew. "I See the Fretboard in Diagrams: An Examination of the Improvisatory Style of Herbert Lawrence 'Sonny' Greenwich." *Canadian University Music Society Review* 23, no. 1 (2003): 62–78.

Seeger, Anthony. "Ethnography of Music." In *Ethnomusicology: An Introduction,* edited by Helen Myers, 88–109. Norton/Grove Handbooks in Music. New York: W. W. Norton, 1992.

Shank, Barry. "From Rice to Ice: The Face of Race in Rock and Pop." In *The Cambridge Companion to Pop and Rock,* edited by Simon Frith, Will Straw, and John Street, 256–71. Cambridge: Cambridge University Press, 2001.

Shapiro, Nat, and Nat Hentoff. *Hear Me Talkin' to Ya: The Story of Jazz as Told by the Men Who Made It.* New York: Dover, 1955.

Sheridan, Chris, ed. *Count Basie: A Bio-discography.* New York: Greenwood Press, 1986.

Shields, Rob. *Lefebvre, Love and Struggle: Spatial Dialectics.* London: Routledge, 1999.

Shipman, Jerome S. "In Search of the Electric Guitar: A Platonic Dialogue with Music." *Annual Review of Jazz Studies* 7 (1994–95): 201–16.

Shipton, Alyn. *A New History of Jazz.* New York: Continuum, 2001.

Shove, Patrick, and Bruno H. Repp. "Musical Motion and Performance: Theoretical and Empirical Perspectives." In *The Practice of Performance: Studies in Musical Interpretation*, edited by John Rink, 55–83. Cambridge: Cambridge University Press, 1995.

Sickels, Robert. *The 1940s: American Popular Culture through History.* Westport, CT: Greenwood Press, 2004.

Sides, Josh. *L.A. City Limits: African American Los Angeles from the Great Depression to the Present.* Berkeley: University of California Press, 2003.

Sidran, Ben. *Black Talk.* 1971. New York: Da Capo Press, 1981.

Simmel, Georg. "Bridge and Door." In *Rethinking Architecture*, edited by Neil Leach, 66–69. New York: Routledge, 1997.

———. "The Metropolis and Mental Life." In *On Individuality and Social Forms: Selected Writings*, edited by Donald N. Levine, 324–39. Chicago: University of Chicago Press, 1971.

———. *On Individuality and Social Forms: Selected Writings.* Edited by Donald N. Levine. Chicago: University of Chicago Press, 1971.

Simon, Bill. "Charlie Christian." In *The Guitar in Jazz: An Anthology*, edited by James Sallis. Lincoln: University of Nebraska Press, 1996.

Simon, George T. *The Big Bands.* 1967. Reprint, New York: Macmillan, 1969.

Sitkoff, Harvard, ed. *Fifty Years Later: The New Deal Evaluated.* Philadelphia: Temple University Press, 1985.

———. *A New Deal for Blacks: The Emergence of Civil Rights as a National Issue; The Depression Decade.* New York: Oxford University Press, 1978.

Small, Christopher. *Music of the Common Tongue: Survival and Celebration in African-American Music.* 1987. Hanover, NH: Wesleyan University Press, 1998.

———. *Musicking: The Meaning of Performance and Listening.* Hanover, NH: University Press of New England/Wesleyan University Press, 1998.

Smiley, Gene. *Rethinking the Great Depression.* Chicago: Ivan R. Dee, 2002.

Smith, Gregory Eugene. "Homer, Gregory, and Bill Evans? The Theory of Formulaic Composition in the Context of Jazz Piano Improvisations." PhD diss., Harvard University, 1983.

Snider, Jill D. "Great Shadow in the Sky: The Airplane in the Tulsa Race Riot of 1921 and the Development of African American Aviation, 1921–1926." In *The Airplane in American Culture*, edited by Dominick A. Pisano, 105–46. Ann Arbor: University of Michigan Press, 2003.

Soja, Edward W. *Postmodern Geographies: The Reassertion of Space in Critical Social Theory.* New York: Verso, 1989.

———. *Thirdspace: Journeys to Los Angeles and Other Real-and-Imagined Places.* Cambridge, MA: Blackwell, 1996.

Sollors, Werner. *Ethnic Modernism.* Cambridge, MA: Harvard University Press, 2008.

Solomon, Thomas. "Dueling Landscapes: Singing Places and Identities in Highland Bolivia." *Ethnomusicology* 44, no. 2 (Spring/Summer 2000): 257–80.

Solomon, William. *Literature, Amusement and Technology in the Great Depression.* New York: Cambridge University Press, 2002.

Spring, Howard Allen. "The Improvisational Style of Charlie Christian." Master's thesis, York University, 1980.

———. "The Use of Formulas in the Improvisations of Charlie Christian." *Jazzforschung/Jazz Research* 22 (1990): 11–51.

Spychalski, John C. "Transportation." In *The Columbia History of the 20th Century*, edited by Richard W. Bulliet, 403–36. New York: Columbia University Press, 1998.

Stearns, Marshall. *The Story of Jazz.* 1956. Reprint, New York: Oxford University Press, 1970.

Stearns, Marshall, and Jean Stearns. *Jazz Dance: The Story of American Vernacular Dance.* 1968. Reprint, New York: Da Capo Press, 1994.

Steinbeck, John. *The Grapes of Wrath.* 1939. Reprint, New York: Penguin Books, 1992.

Steiner, Michael C. "Regionalism in the Great Depression." *Geographical Review* 73, no. 4 (October 1983): 430–46.

Stewart, Rex. *Boy Meets Horn.* Ann Arbor: University of Michigan Press, 1991.

———. *Jazz Masters of the Thirties.* 1972. Reprint New York: Da Capo Press, 1986.

Stokes, Martin, ed. *Ethnicity, Identity, and Music: The Musical Construction of Place.* Providence, RI: Berg, 1994.

Stowe, David. *Swing Changes: Big-Band Jazz in New Deal America.* Cambridge, MA: Harvard University Press, 1994.

Stratemann, Klaus, *Duke Ellington: Day by Day and Film by Film.* Copenhagen: JazzMedia, 1992.

Sudhalter, Richard M. *Lost Chords: White Musicians and Their Contribution to Jazz, 1915–1945.* New York: Oxford University Press, 1999.

Susman, Warren I. *Culture as History: The Transformation of American Society in the Twentieth Century.* 1973. Reprint, New York: Pantheon Books, 1984.

Szostak, Rick. *Technological Innovation and the Great Depression.* Boulder, CO: Westview Press, 1995.

Tanner, Paul O. W., David W. Megill, and Maurice Gerow. *Jazz.* 9th ed. Boston: McGraw-Hill, 2001.

Tapscott, Horace, and Steven Louis Isoardi. *Songs of the Unsung: The Musical and Social Journey of Horace Tapscott.* Durham, NC: Duke University Press, 2001.

Tarasti, Eero. *A Theory of Musical Semiotics.* Bloomington: Indiana University Press, 1994.

Taruskin, Richard. *Defining Russia Musically: Historical and Hermeneutical Essays.* Princeton, NJ: Princeton University Press, 1997.

Terkel, Studs. *Hard Times: An Oral History of the Great Depression.* 1970. Reprint, New York: Pantheon Books, 1986.

Timner, W. E., ed. *Ellingtonia: The Recorded Music of Duke Ellington and His Sidemen,* 4th ed. Studies in Jazz 7. Lanham, MD: Scarecrow Press, 1996.

Tirro, Frank. *Jazz: A History,* 2nd ed. New York: W. W. Norton, 1993.

Titon, Jeff Todd. *Early Downhome Blues: A Musical and Cultural Analysis*. Urbana: University of Illinois Press, 1977.

Todd, Neil P. McAngus. "Motion in Music: A Neurobiological Perspective." *Music Perception: An Interdisciplinary Journal* 17, no. 1 (Fall 1999): 115.

Tomlinson, Gary. "Cultural Dialogics and Jazz: A White Historian Signifies." *Black Music Research Journal* 22 (2002): 71–105.

Townsend, Peter. *Pearl Harbor Jazz: Change in Popular Music in the Early 1940s*. Jackson: University Press of Mississippi, 2007.

Tuan, Yi-Fu. *Space and Place: The Perspective of Experience*. Minneapolis: University of Minnesota Press, 1977.

Tucker, Mark, ed. *The Duke Ellington Reader*. New York: Oxford University Press, 1993.

———. *Ellington: The Early Years*. Urbana: University of Illinois Press, 1991.

Tucker, Sherrie. *Swing Shift: "All-Girl" Bands of the 1940s*. Durham, NC: Duke University Press, 2000.

Ulanov, Barry. *Duke Ellington*. 1947. Reprint, New York: Da Capo Press, 1972.

———. *History of Jazz in America*. New York: Viking Press, 1952.

United States, President's Research Committee on Social Trends. *Report of the President's Research Committee on Social Trends: Recent Social Trends*. Foreword by President Herbert Hoover. New York: McGraw-Hill, 1933.

Vail, Ken. *Duke's Diary: The Life of Duke Ellington, 1927–1950*. Lanham, MD: Scarecrow Press, 2002.

Valentine, Gill. "Creating Transgressive Space: The Music of kd lang." *Transactions of the Institute of British Geographers* 20, no. 4 (1995): 474–85.

Van de Leur, Walter. *Something to Live For: The Music of Billy Strayhorn*. New York: Oxford University Press, 2002.

Von Glahn, Denise. *The Sounds of Place: Music and the American Cultural Landscape*. Boston: Northeastern University Press, 2003.

Wagner, Ann. *Adversaries of Dance: From the Puritans to the Present*. Urbana: University of Illinois Press, 1997.

Waksman, Steve. *Instruments of Desire: The Electric Guitar and the Shaping of Musical Experience*. Cambridge, MA: Harvard University Press, 1999.

Wald, Elijah. "Louis Armstrong Loves Guy Lombardo!" *Jazz Research Journal* 1, no. 1 (2007): 135.

Walker, Leo. *The Big Band Almanac*. 1978. Reprint, New York: Da Capo Press, 1989.

———. *The Wonderful Era of the Dance Bands*. 1964. Reprint, New York: Da Capo Press, 1990.

Walser, Robert. "Deep Jazz: Notes on Interiority, Race, and Criticism." In *Inventing the Psychological: Toward a Cultural History of Emotional Life in America*, edited by Joel Pfister and Nancy Schnog, 271–96. New Haven, CT: Yale University Press, 1997.

———, ed. *Keeping Time: Readings in Jazz History*. New York: Oxford University Press, 1999.

———. "Out of Notes: Signification, Interpretation, and the Problem of Miles Davis." *Musical Quarterly* 77, no. 2 (Summer 1993): 343–65.

———. "Valuing Jazz." In *The Cambridge Companion to Jazz*, edited by Mervyn Cooke and David Horn, 301–20. Cambridge: Cambridge University Press, 2002.

Ward, Brian. *Just My Soul Responding: Rhythm and Blues, Black Consciousness, and Race Relations*. Berkeley: University of California Press, 1998.

Ward, Geoffrey C., and Ken Burns. *Jazz: A History of America's Music*. New York: Alfred A. Knopf, 2000.

Waterman, Richard A. "'Hot' Rhythm in Negro Music." *Journal of the American Musicological Society* 1, no. 1 (Spring 1948): 24–37.

Watson, Deek, and Lee Stephenson. *The Story of the Ink Spots*. New York: Vantage, 1967.

Wells, Dicky, and Stanley Dance. *The Night People: The Jazz Life of Dicky Wells*. Washington, DC: Smithsonian Institution Press, 1991.

Wheat, Ellen Harkins. "Jacob Lawrence and the Legacy of Harlem." *Archives of American Art Journal* 26, no. 1 (1986): 18–25.

White, William Sanford. *Santa Catalina Island: Its Magic, People, and History*. Glendora, CA: White Limited Editions, 1997.

White, William Sanford, and Kim Lianne Stotts. *The Wrigley Family: A Legacy of Leadership in Santa Catalina Island*. Glendora, CA: White Limited Editions and White Family Trust, 2005.

White, William Sanford, and Steven Kern Tice. *Santa Catalina Island: Its Magic, People, and History*. Rev. ed. Glendora, CA: White Limited Editions, 1997.

———. *Santa Catalina Island Goes to War: World War II, 1941–1945*. Glendora, CA: White Limited Editions, 1997.

Whiteley, Sheila, Andy Bennett, and Stan Hawkins, eds. *Music, Space, and Place: Popular Music and Cultural Identity*. Aldershot, UK: Ashgate Press, 2004.

Whiteman Paul, and Mary Margaret McBride. *Jazz*. 1926. Reprint, New York: Arno Press, 1974.

Wilentz, Gay. "If You Surrender to the Air: Folk Legends of Flight and Resistance in African American Literature." *MELUS: Folklore and Orature* 16, no. 1 (Spring 1989–Spring 1990): 21–32.

Wilkinson, Christopher. *Jazz on the Road: Don Albert's Musical Life*. Berkeley: University of California Press, 2001.

Williams, Martin, ed. *The Jazz Tradition*. New York: Oxford University Press, 1970.

Williams, Raymond. *The Country and the City*. New York: Oxford University Press, 1973.

———. *Marxism and Literature*. New York: Oxford University Press, 1977.

———. *The Politics of Modernism: Against the New Conformists*. Edited and introduced by Tony Pinkney. New York: Verso, 1989.

Wilson, Olly. "Black Music as an Art Form." In *The Jazz Cadence of American Culture*, edited by Robert G. O'Meally, 82–101. New York: Columbia University Press, 1998.

Wilson, Richard Guy, Dianne H. Pilgrim, and Dickran Tashjian, eds. *The Machine Age in America: 1918–1941*. New York: Harry N. Abrams, 1986.

Wilson, William H. *Coming of Age: Urban America, 1915–1945*. New York: John Wiley, 1974.

Windle, Ernest. *Windle's History of Santa Catalina Island (and Guide)*. Avalon, CA: Catalina Islander, 1931.

Woideck, Carl. *Charlie Parker: His Music and Life*. Ann Arbor: University of Michigan Press, 1996.

Wrazen, Louise. "Relocating the Tatras: Place and Music in Gorale Identity and Imagination." *Ethnomusicology* 51, no. 2 (Spring/Summer 2007): 185–204.

Wright, Richard. *Black Boy (American Hunger): A Record of Childhood and Youth*. New York: Harper Perennial, 1993.

———. *Twelve Million Black Voices: A Folk History of the Negro in the United States*. 1941. Reprint, New York: Arno Press/New York Times, 1969.

Wynn, Neil A. *The Afro-American and the Second World War*. Rev ed. New York: Holmes and Meier, 1993.

Yoshida, George. *Reminiscing in Swingtime: Japanese Americans in American Popular Music, 1925–1960*. San Francisco: National Japanese American Historical Society, 1997.

Young, William H., and Nancy K. Young. *Music of the Great Depression*. Westport, CT: Greenwood Press, 2005.

Zbikowski, Lawrence M. *Conceptualizing Music: Cognitive Structure, Theory, and Analysis*. New York: Oxford University Press, 2002.

Zietz, Karyl Lynn. *The National Trust Guide to Great Opera Houses in America*. New York: Preservation Press/John Wiley, 1996.

Zim, Larry, Mel Lerner, and Herbert Rolfes. *The World of Tomorrow: The 1939 New York World's Fair*. New York: Harper and Row, 1988.

Zuckerkandl, Victor. *Sound and Symbol: Music and the External World*. Translated by Willard R. Trask. Bollingen Series 44. New York: Pantheon Books, 1956.

Zvonar, Richard. "An Extremely Brief History of Spatial Music in the 20th Century." http://cec.concordia.ca/econtact/Multichannel/spatial_music .html.

Selected Recordings

Big Band Jazz: From the Beginnings to the Fifties. Six LPs. Washington, DC: Smithsonian Collection of Recordings (DMM 6–0610), 1983.

Charlie Barnet. *Charlie Barnet and His Orchestra, 1936–1937*. Chronological Series. Compact disc. France: Classic Records (Classics 1159), 2000.

———. *Cherokee*. Compact disc. Living Era (CD AJA 5288), 1999.

Charlie Barnet. *Drop Me Off in Harlem*. Compact disc. Original Decca Recordings. Decca, GRP (GRD-612), 1992.

Charlie Christian. *Charlie Christian: Complete Live Recordings.* Four compact discs. Definitive Records, Disconforme sl (DRCD 11177), 2001.

———. *Charlie Christian: Complete Studio Recordings.* Four compact discs. Definitive Records, Disconforme sl (DRCD 11176), 2001.

Duke Ellington and His Orchestra. *The Blanton-Webster Band.* Three compact discs. RCA, Bluebird (5659–2-RB), 1986.

———. *Complete Musicraft Recordings.* Definitive Records, Disconforme sl (DRCD 11215), 2001.

———. *Duke Ellington Carnegie Hall Concerts, January 4, 1946.* Two compact discs. Prestige (2407), 1977.

———. *Duke Ellington V-Disc.* Two compact discs. Collector's Choice Music, 1997.

———. *Unreleased Masters, the Travelog Edition: The Great Chicago Concert.* Two compact discs. Music Masters Jazz (01612–65110-2), 1994.

———. *The World of Duke Ellington.* LP. Columbia (G32564), 1974.

Glen Gray and the Casa Loma Orchestra. *Best of the Brunswick Years, 1932–1934.* Compact disc. Collectables, Sony Music Entertainment (COL-CD-7574), 2004.

Jan Garber "the Idol of the Air Lanes" and His Orchestra. *A Melody from the Sky.* Compact disc. Living Era (CD AJA 5326), 2004.

———. *The Uncollected Jan Garber and His Orchestra, 1939–1941.* LP. Hindsight Records (HSR-130), 1978.

Hittin' on All Six: A History of the Jazz Guitar. Four compact discs. Proper Records (Properbox 9), 2000.

Jimmie Lunceford. *Life Is Fine.* Quadromania Jazz Edition. Four compact discs. Membrane Music (222456–444), 2005.

The Original Decca Recordings: An Anthology of Big Band Swing, 1930–1955. Two compact discs. Decca, GRP (GRD-2–629), 1993.

Original Performances of Big Band Themes on the Air, 1932–1946. LP. Portland, OR, First Time Records (FTR-2501) n.d.

Singers and Soloists of the Swing Bands. Six LPs. Washington, DC: Smithsonian Collection of Recordings, 1987.

Index

Page numbers in italics refer to examples, figures, and tables.